Arming the Free World

Chester J. Pach, Jr.

Arming the FREE WORLD

The Origins of the United States Military Assistance Program, 1945–1950

The University of North Carolina Press

Chapel Hill and London

The paper in this book meets the guidelines for permanence and
durability of the Committee of Production Guidelines for
Book Longevity of the Council on Library Resources.

95 94 93 92 91   5 4 3 2 1

Library of Congress Cataloging-in-Publication Data

Pach, Chester J.
    Arming the free world : the origins of the United States military
assistance program, 1945–1950 / by Chester J. Pach, Jr.
        p. cm.
    Includes bibliographical references and index.
    ISBN 0-8078-1943-3 (cloth : alk. paper)
    1. United States—Foreign relations—1945–1953.   2. Military assistance,
American—History.   I. Title.
D990.E87   1991
355'.032'097309044—dc20   90-41120
                                                                              CIP

60 035 8046 8

Portions of chapter 2 appeared earlier in somewhat different form in
Chester J. Pach, Jr., "The Containment of Military Aid to Latin America,
1944–49," *Diplomatic History* 6 (Summer 1982): 225–43, and are reprinted
here by permission of Scholarly Resources, Inc.

Portions of chapter 7 appeared earlier in somewhat different form in
Chester J. Pach, Jr., "Military Assistance and American Foreign Policy: The
Role of Congress," in *Congress and United States Foreign Policy: Controlling
the Use of Force in the Nuclear Age,* ed. Michael Barnhart (Albany: State
University of New York Press, 1987), and are reprinted here by permission
of the State University of New York Press.

For my grandmother
and the memory
of my grandfather

Contents

Acknowledgments

Writing this book was a personal, but never a solitary, enterprise. At every stage of the work, I benefited from the advice, encouragement, and support of many others. It is a pleasure to acknowledge these debts, and I hope that those who assisted are pleased with the results.

Generous financial aid from the U.S. Army Center of Military History, Texas Tech University, and, on two occasions, the Harry S. Truman Library Institute helped defray the expenses of research. I am grateful to the staffs of the Bentley Historical Library, the Center of Military History, the Seeley G. Mudd Library, the Naval History Division, and the Washington National Records Center. Special thanks go to Dennis E. Bilger, Harry Clark, Erwin J. Mueller, C. Warren Ohrvall, and Elizabeth Safly of the Truman Library. At the Diplomatic Branch of the National Archives, Milton O. Gustafson and Kathie Nicastro were especially helpful. I am particularly indebted to the staff of the Modern Military Branch of the National Archives for such informed and friendly assistance. William H. Cunliffe shared with me his unique knowledge of military records, and Marilla B. Guptil processed innumerable requests for documents. LeRoy Jackson, Edward J. Reese, and Charles Shaugnessy also made my work easier. At the Spencer Research Library in Lawrence, Kansas, Dan Barkley and Ingeburg Starr helped me locate many government documents. I also wish to acknowledge the estate of James V. Forrestal for allowing me to examine the papers of the former secretary of defense.

Among my greatest debts are those to teachers and colleagues who helped shape my work. I began this book while I was a student of Richard W. Leopold, who was an inspiring instructor and an exacting critic. Michael S. Sherry helped me to refine my arguments and clarify my prose. Burton I. Kaufman and William Stueck read the entire manuscript and provided many thoughtful suggestions for improving it. Also valuable was the assistance of T. H. Breen, George Q. Flynn, and Garry Wills.

Vicky Pachall, Paula Malone, and Pam LeRow typed the manuscript, and Linda Pickett copyedited it. Lewis Bateman, Ron Maner, and the staff at the University of North Carolina Press skillfully guided the manuscript through the steps of publication.

Portions of this book previously appeared in *Diplomatic History* 6 (Summer 1982) and *Congress and United States Foreign Policy: Controlling the Use of Force in the Nuclear Age,* edited by Michael Barnhart. I am grateful to Scholarly Resources, Inc. and the State University of New York Press for kindly granting me permission to use that material.

Several friends contributed in essential ways to the completion of this work. Donald R. McCoy and Theodore A. Wilson were constant sources of encouragement. Mary Lou Locke was a wonderful colleague and an even better friend. Beth Bailey I can never thank enough for so many things.

My greatest debt is to Mary Jane Kelley, who never let me forget the unsurpassed pleasures of the present, even when I was preoccupied with the past.

This book is dedicated to the best teachers I ever had, my grandparents, Frank and Janie Kaminski. By living their lives with simplicity, integrity, and dignity, they taught me what is truly important.

Arming the Free World

At the outset, it should be firmly fixed in mind that the mere giving of assistance to other countries will not necessarily enhance the national security of the United States.

—The Joint Chiefs of Staff, 12 May 1947

Introduction

I think the concern I have run into is this, is this the beginning of the United States taking on an obligation to supply military assistance to every country in the world? . . . If we once take on the obligation, establish the precedent, where do we wind up?
—Paul G. Hoffman, Economic Cooperation Administrator, 20 April 1949

In his annual report of 1988, Secretary of Defense Frank C. Carlucci warned Congress against cutting President Ronald Reagan's request for military assistance to foreign nations. During the previous three years, Carlucci complained, Congress had slashed the Reagan administration's requests for military assistance by as much as 25 percent. He insisted that the results had been disastrous. These reductions had eroded "the security and well-being of friendly countries." But their greatest effect, Carlucci asserted, had been "on the perceptions of friends and allies who fear that the United States cannot honor its commitments nor exert strong and effective leadership." In addition, "adversaries are gaining confidence that they can challenge our interests with impunity." He concluded that, should Congress once again cut the administration's proposed annual military aid budget, American security would suffer "serious damage."[1]

Carlucci's warnings recall those issued by the Pentagon four decades earlier when the administration of Harry S. Truman considered reducing spending on military aid. In this instance the cuts were proposed not by Congress but by the Bureau of the Budget, which maintained that after allocating $1.314 billion to arms aid in 1949, the United States could not afford a similar expenditure in 1950. The Joint Chiefs of Staff strenuously objected. Much like Carlucci, they argued that a drastic cut would undermine the security of the members of the North Atlantic Treaty Organization, who were the recipients of the bulk of American military assistance at that time. Even worse, the service leaders predicted, it would raise doubts not only about American resolve, but also about the credibility of President Truman, who, in his inaugural address of 1949, had promised arms aid to the members of the North Atlantic alliance. They concluded that a sharp reduction in military assistance would "give renewed impetus to Communist strength in Western Europe."[2]

In the four decades since the comments of the Joint Chiefs, military assistance has been a major instrument of American national security policy. The Joint Chiefs made their remarks just before the passage of the Mutual Defense Assistance Act of 1949, the first in a long series of global arms aid bills. During the next decade the Military Assistance Program expanded rapidly in size and scope, and the president secured broad powers to transfer armaments. In the late 1960s sales began to replace grants as the principal means of providing military equipment to foreign nations. At the same time, partly because of opposition to the Vietnam War, Congress curtailed the Military Assistance Program and began to regulate more closely the flow of American armaments abroad, both by grants and sales. Nonetheless, arms assistance remained an important component of the foreign aid program during the 1980s, amounting to between $3 billion and $4 billion annually during the last years of the Reagan administration. In the forty years since 1949 the United States has provided grants amounting to more than $90 billion in military equipment and training to some 120 countries.[3]

These expenditures have been extraordinarily controversial. Important national security officials have long considered military aid essential to the attainment of vital objectives. They have justified arms aid as a means of deterring aggression, containing Communist expansion, protecting overseas interests short of the dispatch of combat troops, and securing foreign cooperation with American military, economic, and political policies. Critics, however, have stood these arguments on their heads. They have charged that American arms have exacerbated local and regional hostilities, assisted more often in the suppression of legitimate opposition than in the repulsion of external aggression, and burdened the United States with new obligations to defend foreign countries. They have also maintained that the Military Assistance Program is extravagant and wasteful even to the point of absurdity, as when President Mobutu Sese Seku of Zaire tried to use arms aid funds to secure $60,000 worth of Coca-Cola for troops engaged in suppressing an invasion.[4]

Many of these issues were first broached during the late 1940s, when military assistance emerged as a major tool of national security policy. During that time the Truman administration launched a series of country and regional programs, principally in Western Europe but also in the Near East, Latin America, and East Asia. These first efforts resulted from piecemeal planning and reflected a variety of purposes, such as preparing for a possible war, securing customers for American armaments industries, checking the spread of Soviet influence, and cultivating foreign goodwill. The Truman administration, however, soon replaced this diverse collection of programs with a coordinated, worldwide effort, whose principal goal was the containment of Communist expansion. This transformation culminated in the passage of the Mutual Defense Assistance Act of 1949, the progenitor of the annual military aid bills that have become a fixture in American national security policy. The time, then, between the end of World War II and the beginning of the Korean War constituted the formative period of the Military Assistance Program. This book explores the history of those critical years.

In writing that history I have emphasized three themes. The first is that the main impetus for the startling growth of military aid during the late 1940s was the belief that it would provide critical political and psychological reassurance to friendly nations. Whatever the ultimate military objectives of these programs, their most important and immediate goals were raising foreign morale, solidifying the will to resist Communist expansion, and demonstrating American resolve and reliability. Other justifications were important, but not important enough to bring about the consolidation and expansion of the Military Assistance Program.

The second theme is that sharp bureaucratic disputes took place over military assistance. The first programs for postwar arms aid divided the War and Navy departments from the State Department. Both sides saw military assistance as a vehicle for enlarging their influence over national security policy; both at times fought bitterly to secure control over specific programs. Although service authorities were the strongest supporters of arms aid immediately after World War II, State Department officials became the leading advocates by the late 1940s, once they were convinced of the political and psychological utility of military aid. Bureaucratic alignments actually changed so dramatically that, during the planning for the Mutual Defense Assistance Act, some intramural conflicts focused on Pentagon fears that military aid would drain resources from domestic rearmament programs or lead to commitments that the United States could not sustain.

The final theme is that confusion and uncertainty marked the Truman administration's attitude toward the future of the Military Assistance Program. Policymakers described the role of military assistance in raising the morale of recipients and the amount of aid needed to maintain that confidence only in general, even imprecise, terms. Several committees tried, but none was able, to design an acceptable long-range program of foreign military aid before the outbreak of the Korean War. Secretary of State Dean Acheson later recalled that despite extensive planning "there was absolutely no organized, careful thought about what it was that we were trying to do."[5]

This lack of clarity was one of the principal legacies of early military assistance policy. Alarmed by what it perceived as a global Communist challenge, the Truman administration rapidly expanded arms aid programs during the Korean War, often with little thought about their ultimate goals. Without clear objectives some programs, driven mainly by bureaucratic momentum, parochial interests, or vague anticommunism, continued even after they ceased serving useful purposes, if indeed they had ever done so. The momentum imparted to the Military Assistance Program during the Truman years may have slowed, but still remains strong, as demonstrated by Secretary of Defense Carlucci's remarks. In the intervening forty years that momentum has contributed to America's arming of almost the entire "free world."

1 | The Emergence of Military Assistance Programs

US military assistance to foreign nations since Lend-Lease does not appear to have sprung from any well-coordinated program.
—Report by the National Security Council, 1 July 1948

Less than a year after the end of the Second World War, American officials had made ambitious plans to provide military assistance to several foreign nations. In the spring of 1946 President Harry S. Truman asked Congress to approve long-term arms aid to the Philippines, China, and Latin America. He also requested authority to send military advisers to any foreign country whenever he thought that such help would advance the national interest. While the administration's plans were not so extensive as to constitute a program of "peacetime lend-lease," as they were characterized by one awestruck observer, they were nonetheless remarkable.[1] Never before, except in time of war, had the United States used military assistance as a major, continuing instrument of national policy.

Before World War II the U.S. government seldom sent arms or military advisers beyond the Western Hemisphere. Although private manufacturers exported large quantities of munitions to non-American nations, the government participated in this commerce only in unusual circumstances, such as when it disposed of surplus military supplies in Europe after the First World War. Indeed, for almost two decades after these exceptional sales, Washington officials tried to limit government transfers of armaments. In 1923 President Warren G. Harding urged the secretaries of war and navy to avoid selling munitions abroad for fear of encouraging warfare, and as late as 1938 the War Department still felt bound by this directive.[2] Even rarer than government arms sales was the stationing of American military advisers overseas. In 1869 a group of former American army officers began training the Egyptian army, but they did so as private individuals rather than as representatives of the U.S. government. The only official missions established outside the Americas before World War II were in Korea in 1888 and the Philippines in 1935.[3]

Military aid was far more important as a tool of policy in Latin America. State Department officials did not let Harding's instructions hinder their efforts to help friendly Latin American governments suppress internal uprisings. During the 1920s the administrations of Calvin Coolidge and Herbert C. Hoover sent surplus armaments to several countries—Mexico, Cuba, Honduras, and Nicaragua—in which the government was beset by revolutionary forces. At the same time that the United States armed beleaguered Latin American regimes, it also imposed embargoes on the sale of munitions to groups that opposed them. Further assistance came from army and marine advisers, who organized and trained military and police forces in Cuba, Haiti, the Dominican Republic, Nicaragua, and Panama—countries in which the United States maintained protectorates by force of arms. In addition, military and naval missions went to Peru, Guatemala, and Brazil under statutes enacted during the 1920s that allowed the dispatch of such advisory groups throughout the Americas.[4] The overriding purpose of these measures of military assistance was to preserve political stability in an area in which the United States had important economic and strategic interests.[5]

Following the outbreak of war in Europe in 1939, the administration of Franklin D. Roosevelt relied far more extensively on arms aid to protect American security. Roosevelt used military assistance not only to help unite the Western Hemisphere against the Axis but also to sustain Great Britain—America's first line of defense—in the war against Nazi Germany. As early as June 1940 Roosevelt offered "the material resources of this nation" to "opponents of force."[6] Yet this dramatic promise greatly exceeded American capabilities. Hamstrung by neutrality legislation, isolationist sentiment, and his own cautiousness in leading public opinion, FDR had to resort to complex maneuvering to transfer armaments overseas. He sidestepped legal barriers by selling government munitions to Britain through private intermediaries and exchanging American destroyers for British bases. Such legal stratagems, however, could not solve critical supply problems arising from the competing demands of domestic rearmament and foreign aid programs. Only by declaring as "surplus" the military and naval equipment that might have been used to meet their own pressing needs, could the War and Navy departments furnish materiel to Britain. Even then, much of the available equipment was obsolescent, such as World War I rifles and over-age destroyers. Clearly the Roosevelt administration needed broader authority to meet the armament needs of Hitler's foes.[7]

A small but important step toward obtaining the needed powers came on 15 June 1940 with the enactment of the Pittman Resolution, which allowed government sales of some surplus military equipment to Latin America.[8] The administration had introduced this measure more than a year earlier in the hope of supplying armaments to reduce German and Italian influence in Latin American military circles and to strengthen hemispheric defense. The legislation, however, languished in Congress until the spring of 1940, when the German blitzkrieg that overwhelmed France created a new sense of urgency. As amended by Congress, the Pittman Resolution was narrower than the administration desired; it allowed only the sale of antiaircraft and coastal defense materiel to the other American nations. The resolution did not have much practical effect since the army and navy had little equipment to spare and no credits to offer Latin American purchasers, but it was significant as an indication of congressional acceptance of the principle of supplying arms to nations considered important to the defense of the United States.[9]

This principle gave rise to a far more ambitious innovation, lend-lease. By the end of 1940 some new form of assistance was imperative if Britain was to obtain the American tanks, guns, and planes it needed to carry on the war against Germany. Ingenious expedients, useful in circumventing legal obstacles, could not stanch the drain of Britain's dollar holdings, which threatened to halt purchases of essential military equipment. Months of discussion culminated in Roosevelt's announcement in December 1940 that he wanted "to eliminate the dollar sign" from American arms transfers to Great Britain. FDR appealed to Congress to make the United States "the great arsenal of democracy," an extension of the policy he had been following since the beginning of the war. After first considering the legislation as an amendment to the Pittman Resolution, Congress passed on 11 March 1941 a separate Lend-Lease Act, which granted the president extraordinary powers to sell, lend, lease, exchange, or otherwise transfer virtually any item to any country whose defense he deemed vital to the security of the United States.[10] Conceived as a device for helping Britain before American belligerency, lend-lease became a powerful instrument of coalition warfare after Pearl Harbor and was a foreign aid program of unprecedented scope and magnitude. Before the end of World War II the United States furnished lend-lease supplies valued at $49.1 billion to thirty-eight nations.[11]

Lend-lease was a "weapon for victory," an emergency measure whose primary purpose was winning the war.[12] In most cases, military requirements governed the allocation of war supplies, especially during the first two years of the program, when production of many items fell far short of needs. The Joint Chiefs of Staff, the president's principal military advisers, generally opposed the use of lend-lease to build up armed forces solely for postwar purposes.[13] They approved, for example, the arming of eight French divisions in December 1944, only to cancel the program the following spring when it became clear that those troops were not needed in the European war. Service authorities similarly reduced planned allocations to China as the war progressed. Although more than three dozen nations received lend-lease munitions, the great bulk—some 86 percent—went to America's two principal wartime partners, Great Britain and the Soviet Union.[14]

Despite the emphasis on military necessity, political considerations inevitably influenced lend-lease decisions. The United States and Great Britain, for example, both seeking, in the words of an official historian, "substantial good will of post war value," clashed over the assignment of lend-lease munitions to the Middle East.[15] This rivalry was keenest in regard to Saudi Arabia, whose oil resources rapidly gained importance to Washington officials after American entry into the war. According to government and industry experts, the combination of a dramatic increase in demand for petroleum brought on by the war and the slackening in discoveries of proven reserves threatened the oil self-sufficiency of the United States, long the world's leading producer. Although Saudi production was modest—it ranked seventeenth among all nations in 1941—the country's enormous reserves seemed a critical asset, especially since they were being exploited by the California Arabian Standard Oil Company (CASOC). Newly suspicious of Britain's long-standing involvement in Saudi affairs and prodded by CASOC officials, the State Department was determined to protect American oil concessions from any intrusions. Eager to win King Ibn Saud's favor, diplomatic officials took the lead in arranging for lend-lease aid in February 1943 and in establishing a year later an American mission to train the king's army. An Anglo-American compromise provided that each country would furnish approximately half of the Saudis' modest internal security needs. Yet such agreements by no means calmed fears of British wartime and postwar designs on Saudi oil. As the war came to an end, State Department officials arranged for the continuation of lend-lease and the construction of an air base at Dhahran. They explained that the national interest, not military necessity, justified these measures of assistance.[16]

Military officials also used lend-lease to pursue postwar objectives, especially in Latin America, a region they considered vital to the security of the Unites States. Even after any major military danger to the hemisphere had passed, the Joint Chiefs of Staff endorsed the continuation of arms aid to Latin America, albeit in modest amounts intended primarily to maintain the goodwill of local military and political leaders. The Joint Chiefs hoped that lend-lease would lead to the standardization of hemispheric military establishments and the consequent exclusion of European arms and missions, thus insuring the orientation of Latin America toward the United States. During the last two years of the war military and naval officers used lend-lease to lay the foundation for a permanent system of inter-American military cooperation.[17]

Drastic restrictions at the end of hostilities, however, all but eliminated lend-lease as a means of strengthening foreign armed forces. Truman severely cut back lend-lease aid after V-E Day and practically halted it after the Japanese surrender. With the exception of the Nationalist government in China, which continued to receive American military assistance in extending its authority over Japanese-occupied territory, and Saudi Arabia, which obtained modest amounts of internal security equipment, the flow of lend-lease armaments to foreign governments abruptly stopped.[18]

To a great extent congressional pressures were responsible for the administration's stringent policies. Domestic support for large-scale foreign aid waned as Allied forces drove to victory in Europe and the Pacific. In renewing lend-lease during the spring of 1945, Congress demanded the termination of the program as soon as the fighting ceased and specifically prohibited the use of lend-lease for postwar reconstruction. These restrictions were imposed at the insistence of Republicans and conservative Democrats who were suspicious of Roosevelt's secret diplomacy, weary of high taxes, fearful of a raging postwar inflation fueled by extravagant overseas spending, and convinced that American dollars could not purchase foreign goodwill. By early 1945 Roosevelt's critics were joined by other members of Congress who had grown tired of deferring to executive leadership in international affairs during the war. As senator and vice president, Truman was keenly aware of the deterioration of executive-congressional relations during the last months of FDR's presidency. As president, Truman was eager to conciliate Congress over lend-lease, lest he stir a latent "isolationist spirit" that might easily "break out into the open" and jeopardize ratification of the United Nations Charter or American participation in the International Monetary Fund and World Bank. Bowing to congressional pressure, Truman drastically curtailed lend-lease at war's end. These sudden and severe limitations, which dashed British expectations and Soviet hopes of generous postwar aid, elicited angry but futile protests from London and Moscow. Churchill considered the cuts "rough and harsh," and Stalin denounced them as "brutal." Yet Truman preferred rankling America's wartime partners to challenging a Congress eager to reclaim its influence over foreign policy and determined to liquidate lend-lease at the close of the war.[19]

The effects of lend-lease, however, lasted beyond the formal termination of the program. The widespread distribution of American arms as a result of lend-lease created pressures for continued military aid. Many nations that had received American armaments desired spare parts and additional equipment, but lacked the foreign exchange to purchase these munitions on the open market. Officials in the War and Navy departments were eager to satisfy these demands in order to prevent European suppliers from reestablishing their prewar control of the arms trade. Even more important, wartime experience persuaded officials in the State, War, and Navy departments that arms aid, in certain circumstances, could help advance American interests in the postwar world. The State-War-Navy Coordinating Committee (SWNCC), for example, advised Roosevelt in December 1944 that military assistance could provide "a lever to exercise a certain measure of influence on French policy for a number of years." The same body also concluded that military aid to Latin America would help preserve the security of the Western Hemisphere. After lend-lease, military aid, for many Washington officials, was no longer an unfamiliar or unusual device but a tested instrument for securing American objectives overseas.[20]

Lend-lease had no sequel. Indeed wartime planners did not even try to formulate a comprehensive program of military aid to follow lend-lease. Although the Truman administration continued to furnish arms and advisers to several nations, these first postwar programs were piecemeal, rather than concerted, efforts. Despite some important similarities, postwar programs arose from separate decisions and reflected the disparate and often conflicting interests of their various sponsors in the State, War, and Navy departments. Looking back on these early postwar efforts, the National Security Council rightly concluded that "US military assistance since Lend-Lease does not appear to have sprung from any well-coordinated program."[21]

A major reason for the failure to plan such a postwar arms program was the military's preoccupation with the immediate requirements of winning the war. This concentration on short-term needs shaped the reaction of the Joint Chiefs of Staff to a British proposal in August 1944 to rebuild the armed forces of the liberated nations of Western Europe, an obligation that promised to last for several years after the defeat of Germany. The British maintained that these rearmed forces would help preserve postwar stability and reduce the occupation responsibilities of British and American troops. They also stressed that the proposed arms aid would advance a vital strategic interest by forging lasting ties between Western European military establishments and those of the United States and Great Britain. The Joint Chiefs' response, however, was cool. They preferred a more limited assistance to small military units that could maintain internal security in Western Europe and assume minor roles in combat. They also worried about raising Soviet fears of an Anglo-American effort to forge a "Western European bloc."[22]

The demands of the European war ultimately settled this debate over the arming of liberated nations. When the Allied drive across France stalled in late 1944, General Dwight D. Eisenhower, the supreme Allied commander, urgently called for additional troops to deliver the final blows against Germany. Accordingly, the Joint Chiefs approved extensive military assistance to liberated nations, and the United States began furnishing lend-lease supplies for eight new French divisions. The State Department heartily endorsed such action for political reasons, since it provided "proof of our desire to see her [France] as a strong nation," yet wartime needs once again determined the extent of American military assistance to France. Even though the eight divisions were only partly equipped, the Joint Chiefs halted lend-lease to the French army as Germany collapsed in the spring of 1945. Preoccupied with the exigencies of wartime logistics, the Joint Chiefs deferred any comprehensive planning for postwar military aid until after victory was secure.[23]

The rush to demobilize, however, created new obstacles to the development of postwar arms aid policy.[24] At the close of hostilities, officials in the State, War, and Navy departments concentrated on implementing Truman's directive halting lend-lease rather than on devising a program to succeed it. Members of Congress called not only for the liquidation of wartime assistance but also for the restriction of sales of surplus American equipment to countries carrying out occupation responsibilities or contributing to the peacekeeping efforts of the United Nations. These pressures precluded the enactment of any postwar lend-lease program.[25] Instead political and military officials concentrated on planning arms assistance of more limited scope—country and regional programs that could be implemented without new appropriations from Congress.

Institutional arrangements also helped to account for the absence of broad military aid planning. For most of the war no agency or committee was responsible for arms aid policy. Postwar planners in the War and Navy departments occasionally considered this subject but concentrated on more important and traditional tasks—preparing blueprints of the peacetime armed forces, defining roles and missions, formulating a strategic concept for a future war.[26] Their counterparts in the State Department focused on the occupation of the defeated Axis powers, the creation of the United Nations, and possible arrangements for the international regulation of armaments. A reluctance to hazard detailed estimates of the requirements of postwar security only reinforced the tendency of the State Department not to devote much attention to future arms assistance policy. A reluctance to become involved in political matters—which their informal chairman, Admiral William D. Leahy, considered beyond their purview—only confirmed the tendency of the Joint Chiefs to concentrate on wartime imperatives and postpone questions of postwar military aid. Not until the establishment in December 1944 of the SWNCC, composed of assistant secretaries from the three departments, was there an organization for the discussion of political-military matters such as postwar arms aid;

and not until the creation six months later of the Rearmament Subcommittee of the SWNCC was there an agency specifically charged with formulating policy on military assistance. With limited authority and even less prestige, the Rearmament Subcommittee could by no means exert strong leadership in dealing with an issue that had major implications for foreign and defense policy. Because of this lack of central direction, military aid policy emerged in piecemeal fashion, the product of the special concerns and bureaucratic rivalries of military and political agencies.[27]

The War Department was the foremost advocate of postwar military aid. Plans for the largest of the early postwar programs, those for Latin America and China, originated within that agency. War Department officials were determined not to lose to such rival powers as Great Britain and the Soviet Union favored positions in Latin America and China, areas in which they sought bases, access to strategic raw materials, dependable customers for American armaments industries, and—most of all—cooperative military establishments. Nor were they willing to rely on State Department officials, whom they considered unsympathetic if not downright hostile, to secure by diplomatic means the foreign concessions that they desired. Military aid, advisory groups, and foreign training programs were powerful instruments not only for building American influence abroad but also for providing defense officials with a major voice in postwar foreign policy. War Department authorities thus urged programs of military assistance to advance their own interests both abroad and at home.[28]

Organizational interests also accounted in large measure for the enthusiastic support of the army air forces (AAF) for military assistance programs. One of the AAF's principal objectives was the establishment of a strong postwar aviation industry that could rapidly manufacture combat planes in the event of a national emergency. This goal was linked to a new concept of national preparedness. In a future war, AAF planners predicted, the United States could no longer count on ocean barriers or strong allies to allow a protracted mobilization of human and industrial resources, but would have to build up to full combat strength within a year. Such rapid mobilization required a high degree of wartime readiness in peacetime, including the maintenance of a large productive capacity in critical defense industries. AAF planners recalled, however, that partly because of an enormous surplus of equipment after World War I, 90 percent of the aircraft industry melted away in the first year of peace. Determined to avoid a similar situation, General Henry H. Arnold, the commanding general of the AAF, urged the disposal of surplus American aircraft to foreign nations. Arnold pointed out that such action would not only reduce the glut of planes left over from the war but also provide the domestic aircraft industry with a head start in the competition for foreign markets.[29]

AAF officials quite explicitly linked their support of several military assistance programs to their concern for the domestic aircraft industry. In the fall of 1944 Arnold proposed the disposal of thousands of surplus planes to standardize the Latin American air forces on U.S. equipment and thereby preempt competition from European suppliers. Eager to corner another overseas market, the AAF in early 1945 advanced a grandiose plan to build a forty-and-one-half-group postwar Chinese air force.[30] When the British suggested a joint Anglo-American effort to equip the French air force in December 1944, War Department spokesmen urged caution. Robert A. Lovett, assistant secretary for air, told Assistant Secretary John J. McCloy that the fundamental consideration should be "the importance of supporting our aircraft plants during the post-war years." McCloy agreed, as did one of his subordinates on the SWNCC, who argued, "We should make every effort to reserve for our well developed aircraft industry any postwar market that may appear. If the British introduce a few planes and the French grow to like them . . . the business will be lost to us."[31] Lovett and McCloy both undoubtedly hoped that such foreign business would contribute to the health of the postwar economy. But any economic benefit was distinctly secondary in their minds to the strategic advantage of maintaining American preparedness.

Special concerns also shaped the navy's attitude toward military assistance programs. The navy strongly backed the provision of armaments to the Philippines and China. Naval officers were eager to retain bases in the Philippines since postwar plans were intended to achieve American naval predominance in the Pacific. They also wanted to dispose of surplus ships, whose maintenance was a drain on the service's manpower and budget. Reflecting the navy's Pacific orientation as well as his own grave misgivings about Soviet ambitions, Secretary of the Navy James V. Forrestal repeatedly urged military support of Chiang Kai-shek's Nationalist regime in China. Naval leaders were far less enthusiastic, however, about inter-American military cooperation. They expressed long-standing doubts about the capacity of the Latin American navies to contribute to hemispheric defense. In the autumn of 1945, for example, Admiral Ernest J. King, the chief of naval operations, asserted that the arming of Latin America would only nourish domestic strife and local quarrels. Yet by early 1946 the navy withdrew these objections in the face of foreign competition for naval influence and shipbuilding orders in Latin America.[32]

If particular interests conditioned the services' attitudes toward the extension of military assistance to foreign countries, so did a common concern about the nation's future security. This outlook sprang from the traumatic events of the previous decade—the collapse of international order and the experience of global war—rather than the rise of any prospective enemy. Long before they worried about the hostile designs of the Soviet Union, military planners recognized that Pearl Harbor and the revolutionary changes in weaponry that occurred during the Second World War had overturned traditional concepts of national security. "In the future," the Joint Chiefs of Staff predicted, "neither geography nor allies will render a nation immune from sudden and paralyzing attack should an aggressor arise to plague the peace of the world." Convinced that weakness had encouraged Axis expansion, military authorities maintained that only overwhelming force, constantly in readiness, could deter or subdue future aggressors. Indeed, in a world where war had become frighteningly dangerous, the Joint Chiefs advocated nothing less than "the absolute military security of the United States."[33]

Statements of postwar military policy approved by the Joint Chiefs in September and October 1945 reflected this ambitious goal. Because they expected the next conflict to exact "a terrible cost in blood and treasure," the Joint Chiefs recommended the maintenance of sufficient military power "to make it unwise for any major aggressor nation to initiate a major war against the opposition of the United States." Should deterrence fail, the service chieftains suggested the extreme alternative of preemptive war. "When it becomes evident that forces of aggression are being arrayed against us by a potential enemy," they argued, "we cannot afford, through any misguided and perilous idea of avoiding an aggressive attitude to permit the first blow to be struck against us. Our government, under such conditions, should press the issue to a prompt political decision, while making all preparations to strike the first blow if necessary." Whether through deterrence or preemption, unilateral action was essential to protect the nation's security, since the United Nations could not resolve "a major conflict of interest among the great powers."[34]

Such a conflict seemed possible by the autumn of 1945 because of the "undefined character of Russian aspirations, the background of mutual suspicion between the Soviet Union and the rest of the world, and the lack of a common basis of information and understanding with Russia." The Joint Chiefs had come slowly and somewhat reluctantly to this conclusion. In mid-1944 they expected that Britain and Russia would become competitors for European power and influence but predicted that the United States could use its influence to mitigate this postwar rivalry. During the last months of the war, a majority of the service chiefs resisted the pessimistic conclusions of Leahy, who considered Stalin "a liar and a crook" and of Forrestal, who compared Soviet leaders to oriental despots and condemned any concessions to their postwar aspirations as tantamount to appeasement. By the autumn of 1945, however, the Soviets' domination of Eastern Europe and their peremptory rejection of American proposals for diplomatic solutions to a host of postwar problems convinced the Joint Chiefs that Russia was a hostile, aggressive power and the only conceivable enemy in a future war. As early as November 1945 the Joint Intelligence Committee began conducting preliminary studies of targets for an atomic offensive against Russia. There seemed to be little immediate danger of war—at least one launched by Soviet design—because of Russia's need to repair the enormous devastation caused by World War II. Yet American demobilization and the maintenance of large Soviet conventional forces raised fears that if war did occur through accident or miscalculation, the Soviets would easily overrun most of the European continent. Thus even if their ultimate intentions were unclear, the Soviets, in the eyes of the Joint Chiefs, posed a danger to world peace and American security.[35]

To counter these threats, the Joint Chiefs urged an unprecedented program of national preparedness. They advocated the development of the world's best-trained armed forces, equipped with "superior materiel," deployed for use "at the source of enemy military power," and supported by "an adequate system of bases and machinery for the rapid mobilization of our national resources." These measures, the services hoped, would lead to "the maintenance of world peace, under conditions which insure the security, well-being and advancement of our country."[36]

The Joint Chiefs assigned programs of military assistance a limited, though not insignificant, role in postwar strategy. Although they endorsed arms aid to countries that strengthened the security of the United States or the Western Hemisphere, they specifically recommended such help only for Latin America, Canada, and the Philippines. If the selection of recipients suggested a return to traditional, prewar policies on arms aid, the reason for providing assistance was novel and ambitious. By aiding Latin America, Canada, and the Philippines, the Joint Chiefs hoped to build "security in depth," a strategic necessity in an age of long-range aircraft and atomic weapons. The Joint Chiefs aimed at "keeping a prospective enemy at the maximum possible distance, and . . . projecting our advanced bases into areas well removed from the United States . . . [and] nearer the enemy."[37] Military aid to the other American nations would help orient their military establishments toward the United States and shield the hemisphere from hostile military influences. Arms assistance to the Philippines would strengthen "a primary base area" by facilitating the establishment of a "trained naval organization capable of assisting the United States in a future war."[38] Not merely a device for maintaining stability in areas of long-standing American interest, arms aid to the other American nations and the Philippines would contribute to an unprecedented program of "active—as contrasted to our traditional policy of passive—defense."[39]

The State Department expressed strong reservations about these ambitious plans for postwar preparedness. In formal comments completed on 16 November 1945 the Staff Committee of Secretary of State James F. Byrnes castigated the Joint Chiefs for placing too much emphasis on the possibility of a breakdown in relations among the United States, Great Britain, and the Soviet Union and too little on American obligations under the Charter of the United Nations. The Staff Committee, which consisted of senior officials from the major offices within the department, also worried about the Joint Chiefs' concentration on unilateral efforts to protect national security. It seemed to these top diplomatic officials that the assistance of allies rather than preemptive action would assure American success in the next war. The differences between the State Department and the Joint Chiefs were so great that the SWNCC during the first year of peace failed in its efforts to produce a comprehensive statement of American defense policy.[40]

The State Department also worried about the political implications of the services' proposals for postwar arms assistance. Career diplomats in the Office of American Republic Affairs maintained that an extensive program of inter-American military cooperation would strengthen authoritarian regimes and thereby undermine their policy of promoting democracy in Latin America. The department's China hands insisted that long-term arms aid to the Nationalist regime was at odds with their efforts to discourage Chiang Kai-shek from seeking a military solution to China's internal problems. Experts on U.N. affairs warned that unilateral action to build up foreign military establishments might harm collective efforts to regulate the international arms traffic and keep the peace. In addition to these particular objections, State Department officials expressed a common fear that the War and Navy departments were encroaching on their authority over foreign policy. This was a particularly sensitive subject since they had long resented Roosevelt's preference for personalized diplomacy and the military's wartime influence over foreign policy. They believed that, in peacetime, political considerations rather than strictly military requirements should govern the transfer of armaments to foreign nations. At the end of the war the State Department's vigorous assertion of this principle caused bitter disputes with the services over arms aid, especially to Latin America and China.

State Department officials became advocates rather than critics when arms aid accorded with their political goals. They asserted, for example, that limited military assistance to Saudi Arabia would protect American oil interests. They also urged more extensive aid to help turn France into a bulwark against Soviet expansion. A strong and stable France, argued Ambassador Jefferson Caffery, could resist internal Communist challenges and also prevent the resurgence of German power. So important were these objectives that Secretary of State Edward R. Stettinius, Jr., informed Truman on the first full day of his presidency that "the best interests of the United States require that every effort be made by this Government to assist France . . . to regain her strength and her influence." Following the termination of lend-lease, the State Department responded with alacrity to a French request for continued military aid. During the next two years the Foreign Liquidation Commission sold to France some $116 million in surplus military and naval equipment for less than 10 percent of the procurement cost.[41]

While concerns about Soviet expansion influenced some early plans for arms aid, there was no consensus in the State Department in the first months of peace about how to deal with the Russians. Most Soviet experts, such as Eldridge Durbrow, George F. Kennan, and Loy W. Henderson, advocated firm opposition to Russian violations of the Yalta accords in Eastern Europe. Yet other foreign service officers, including Soviet specialist Charles E. Bohlen, maintained that the United States ought to recognize legitimate Soviet security interests in neighboring countries and pursue opportunities for cooperation with the Russians in shaping the peace. In a report submitted in December 1945 Bohlen suggested initiatives, such as the sharing of atomic information, aimed at "long-term stabilization of American-Russian relations." But Senior department officials such as Benjamin Cohen, the counselor, and Leo Pasvolsky and Alger Hiss, both responsible for U.N. affairs, urged accommodation with the Soviets and emphasized the resolution of great-power disputes through the United Nations. Dean Acheson, the under secretary, condemned Soviet police-state tactics in Eastern Europe; at the same time he recognized the need for the existence of governments friendly to the Russians in bordering countries and hoped for Soviet-American cooperation in the international control of atomic energy. Secretary Byrnes, committed more to working out postwar agreements than to any particular view of the Soviets, oscillated between truculent intimidation and ingratiating conciliation. Thus, for the first six months after the war, State Department thinking was divided, uncertain, and fluid. As historian Robert L. Messer has aptly written, there was "no single mainstream of thought regarding Soviet policy" but instead "a series of rivulets meandering over a broad expanse of opinion from unilateral gestures of conciliation . . . to hard-line atomic diplomatic saber-rattling."[42]

These many currents of thought produced divergent reactions within the State Department to plans for arms aid to check the increase of Soviet power. Byrnes's Staff Committee, strongly influenced by Cohen, Hiss, and Pasvolsky, opposed the Joint Chiefs' plans for unilateral peacekeeping. Yet the department's senior specialists in Western European affairs, such as James C. Dunn, H. Freeman Matthews, and John D. Hickerson, secured approval of the sale of surplus American armaments to build up France as a counterweight to the Soviet Union.

Aid to China divided the department. Some career officials, such as John Carter Vincent, the director of the Office of Far Eastern Affairs, preferred using political and economic instruments rather than military aid to encourage settlement of the civil war between the Nationalist and Communist Chinese. Byrnes, however, feared the entrenchment of Soviet power in Manchuria should the Nationalist government not receive American military assistance in extending its authority into that Soviet-occupied province.[43]

Thus the first plans for postwar military assistance produced fragmentation rather than consensus within the Roosevelt and Truman administrations. Wartime experience and postwar ambition imparted momentum to several programs of arms aid. Yet policymakers tended to think of these projects as discrete efforts instead of parts of a comprehensive design. The separateness of these early programs also reflected the divisions among political and military planners over arms assistance. Indeed about the only thing on which these planners agreed was that military aid could be an important element in postwar national security policy.

Requests for military supplies from France, China, the Philippines, and several other nations convinced service officials during the fall of 1945 that the Truman administration should establish a comprehensive policy governing postwar military aid. General George A. Lincoln, the army's chief strategic planner, told his colleagues on the Joint Staff that at stake were "major strategic and military factors, including standardization [of armaments] and strengthening of nations whose aims were compatible with U.S. interests."[44] A related subject, the settlement of lend-lease obligations, reinforced the services' desire to clarify military aid policy. Before requesting the return of lend-lease items, the War and Navy departments sought political guidance about the desirability of supporting the postwar military establishments of foreign nations with American resources. They also wanted to know whether the State Department would use lend-lease as a bargaining lever to acquire bases and other overseas military rights. In October 1945, at the request of the services, the SWNCC began to study these questions.[45]

During its deliberations, the SWNCC received a report from the Joint War Plans Committee, which recommended a set of principles and priorities to guide decisions on furnishing military assistance. The service planners thought that the United States should aid only those nations whose interests coincided with American objectives and should refrain from helping countries build up armed forces that they did not need or could not support. The committee assigned high priority to those nations that required military help to maintain internal security or to complete the unfinished tasks of World War II, such as disarming and repatriating Japanese soldiers. The planners also urged prompt aid to prospective allies in a future conflict in order to encourage standardization on American equipment. Although they did not explicitly advocate the use of military aid to check the spread of communism, their rankings of potential recipients reflected that view. The committee recommended that among countries with current requirements China, Korea, and the Philippines, in that order, receive immediate help; although their needs were less urgent, France and Latin America should also receive American arms. Because of changing world conditions, the Joint War Plans Committee noted that any list of potential recipients or priorities should be reviewed periodically and any request for assistance should be examined carefully.[46]

The draft report that the SWNCC completed on 24 January 1946 was a more extensive, but disjointed, analysis of the role of military assistance in postwar national security policy. The report considered both the settlement of lend-lease obligations and the provision of additional arms to foreign nations. The SWNCC advised the War and Navy departments not to request the return of lend-lease items for fear of weakening the military establishments of friendly nations. The committee, however, urged the State Department to try to extract the concessions the services desired—base and air-transit rights—in return for such largess.[47] The SWNCC declared eligible for additional arms aid almost every independent nation except Germany and Japan, the Eastern European countries in which Soviet influence was predominant, and neutral Switzerland. Yet the planners failed to integrate such a potentially large program of arms aid into any comprehensive policy for protecting American security. Instead the committee compiled a long list of local and regional objectives—strengthening hemispheric defense, protecting American oil concessions in the Middle East, securing base rights in the Azores from Portugal, and maintaining America's special relationship with Liberia. Despite its global sweep, the SWNCC report contained no broad strategic, political, or economic justification for arming foreign nations.[48]

Nor did it provide specific advice about the allocation of American military aid among a host of potential recipients. While the report established maximum limits on armaments assistance to foreign nations, it stopped short of recommending such lavish help. It also failed to designate the countries the United States should aid first because of either the urgency of their needs or their value to American security. The document did conclude that whatever aid the United States sent abroad should be furnished within the limits of current legislation and appropriations. This stipulation effectively restricted arms transfers to sales of excess equipment under the Surplus Property Act of 1944, the only general authority for providing arms to foreign nations following the expiration of lend-lease.[49] Although surplus inventories were enormous at the end of the war, they often consisted of unbalanced or incomplete sets of equipment. Furthermore, many countries with immediate needs could not afford to purchase arms even at a nominal price. As a result, surplus sales could not serve as an effective method, especially over time, of supporting most foreign military establishments. The overall effect of the SWNCC report was confusion. It opened the door to arming most of the world's nations but, unaccountably, did not determine how the United States could most effectively distribute its resources.[50]

Some State Department officials vigorously objected to the draft report. Opposition centered in the Division of International Security Affairs (IS), which was concerned with American participation in the Security Council of the United Nations and which had not been consulted in the preparation of the report. In a long memorandum to his superiors, IS officer James M. Ludlow attacked the SWNCC study for placing undue emphasis on arming foreign nations while ignoring the United Nations' collective efforts to maintain the peace. Ludlow also criticized the SWNCC paper for its "piecemeal consideration" of foreign military requirements and its failure to establish a permanent standard for judging requests for military assistance. He argued that the only reasons for sending arms abroad were to help a country carry out decisions of the Security Council and to strengthen "a satisfactory military ally." To fulfill the latter purpose, he advocated the provision of "such armament aid as wisdom and time dictate" only to Great Britain, France, China, and perhaps India, and the withholding of such assistance from the Soviet Union—the only conceivable military enemy—and those less powerful states, such as Korea, Iran, Turkey, and Afghanistan, that might "fall prey to our military enemy." Ludlow made clear, however, that national security would benefit far more from an American backing of Security Council decisions with armaments and, if necessary, armed forces. He urged revision of the SWNCC report so that the Joint Chiefs would be "under no illusions as to the significance we place on any re-armament programs" and would be fully aware of "the emphasis we propose to place on military coopera-tion . . . under the United Nations Organization."[51]

The changes that the SWNCC approved were not so extensive. At the insistence of the State Department, the committee noted that the conclusions of its report would be revised to accord with any policy on the regulation of armaments that the United Nations might approve. The committee also agreed that the State Department could weigh each request for armaments aid in light of current national policy, an altera-tion that severely diminished the value of the paper's guidelines. Finally, at the State Department's urging, the SWNCC agreed that it was not desirable to establish a reserve of equipment or disrupt exist-ing procedures for the disposal of surplus property in order to meet possible requests for armaments.[52] Following these changes, the three departments gave their consent on 21 March 1946 to SWNCC 202/2, the administration's first comprehensive statement of policy on postwar military aid.[53]

SWNCC 202/2 actually had far less influence on American arms transfers, however, than did a set of guidelines, known as SC/R-184, that the State Department had adopted six weeks earlier. On 5 Febru-ary Byrnes's Staff Committee agreed to limit the supply of surplus armaments to Great Britain, France, China, the Philippines, Latin America, and Canada.[54] Far more restrictive than SWNCC 202/2, these guidelines more accurately reflected the State Department's thinking. During testimony on 5 February 1946 before the Senate Special Com-mittee Investigating the National Defense Program, Under Secretary Acheson declared that the administration planned sales of surplus munitions only to those countries listed in SC/R-184. While not ruling out future transactions, he made clear that the administration had no intention of furnishing such equipment to other nations despite the more permissive paper that the SWNCC was about to approve.[55]

The restrictive guidelines of SC/R-184 prevailed even though the Truman administration shifted in early 1946 toward a policy of getting tough with Russia. This reorientation came at the direction of the president himself. A series of events—Soviet pressure on Iran and Turkey, police-state methods of Soviet occupation authorities in Bulgaria and Rumania, and the arrest of a Canadian spy ring attempting to steal atomic secrets—had shaped Truman's desire for a harder line against the Soviets. So had vociferous criticism from the press and from congressional Republicans, who compared the accommodationist diplomacy of Secretary of State Byrnes at the Moscow Conference of Foreign Ministers to appeasement. Truman tried to disarm these critics by announcing that he was in command of American foreign policy and instructing Byrnes to make no further concessions to the Soviets. Dramatic evidence of the change came in March 1946 when Byrnes vehemently denounced the failure of the Soviets to honor their agreement for the withdrawal of their troops from Iran and when former British prime minister Winston Churchill—with Truman at his side—delivered his famous Iron Curtain speech. This tough anti-Soviet rhetoric had no effect on the arms assistance guidelines in SC/R-184, however. In fact during the crisis over the removal of Soviet troops, the State Department ruled out the provision of military equipment to Iran.[56]

The State Department tried to adhere strictly to the guidelines in SC/R-184. A controversy over the sale of 100 surplus P-51 fighter aircraft to Sweden revealed the strength of the department's commitment. State's Office of European Affairs urged approval of the sale "in view of our extremely cordial relations with Sweden" and the "pacific influence in Europe" of Sweden's Social Democratic government. Byrnes, however, rejected the proposed transaction because it was inconsistent with SC/R-184.[57] Despite this disapproval, the Foreign Liquidation Commission mistakenly signed a contract on 16 April 1946 for the delivery of the planes to Sweden. For the next five months Acheson made every effort to cancel the contract. Unable to do so, he informed the Special Committee that the administration would carry out the sale as an exception to its general policy. The secretary's Staff Committee finally authorized the release of the aircraft on 1 October, but Acheson emphasized to the department's Policy Committee on Arms and Armaments that SC/R-184 should continue to guide decisions on arms transfers.[58]

With the exception of this transaction with Sweden and several minor surplus sales, arms aid during the first year of peace did not exceed the limits of SC/R-184. The administration sold considerable excess equipment to France and England in 1946. After protracted internal debate, the State Department approved limited transfers to Latin America but gave only tepid support to a bill for continuing inter-American military cooperation, which died in the Seventy-ninth Congress. Truman authorized substantial military help to the Nationalist Chinese, but in August 1946 the president's special representative in China, General George C. Marshall, suspended deliveries of military equipment because of the lack of progress toward an internal settlement. American officials agreed in principle to sales of surplus equipment to Canada to further joint defense, but none took place in that first year after the war.

Finally, the administration furnished substantial quantities of surplus armaments to the Philippines under the authority of the only military assistance legislation enacted during the first year of peace. Congress approved this measure because it helped perpetuate U.S. influence in the Philippines after the granting of its independence on 4 July 1946, and did so without requiring—at least immediately—any new appropriations since extensive stocks of equipment were left over from World War II and stored in American depots in the Philippines. On the eve of Philippine independence the United States transferred to them $100 million in surplus munitions, the first installment in a program to equip small armed forces that could maintain internal security. These transfers provided the newly independent republic with the means to fight the Hukbalahaps, peasant revolutionaries who began to clash with government troops in the first half of 1946. Filipino leaders tried to undercut support for the Huks by charging that they were controlled by Communists, an allegation that was undoubtedly exaggerated. Although the Huk resistance was limited and scattered, the Philippine government could not suppress it without American military aid, General W. H. Arnold of the War Department's Operation Division told the House Foreign Affairs Committee. In return for this help the United States maintained the friendship of the Philippine government and, more important, secured the rights to "a keystone in the foundation of a base system essential to the security of the United States." According to an agreement signed on 14 March 1947, the United States acquired the rights to maintain sixteen bases and military facilities in the Philippines for ninety-nine years and to establish seven others at designated sites should military necessity require.[59]

While Congress approved the Philippines Military Assistance Act, it balked at the sole administration request for global authority to aid foreign military establishments. This legislation, which Truman sent to Congress in February 1946, would have allowed the president to send military and naval advisory groups to any nation that desired such help. By the autumn of 1945 Turkey and Syria had requested American military advisers; Iran had asked for the continuation of the army and gendarmerie missions that had been established during World War II under emergency executive powers. Yet existing legislation, which allowed the dispatch of service advisory groups only to the other American nations and the Philippines, not only precluded action on the Turkish and Syrian requests but also tacitly supported the perpetuation of spheres of influence, according to the SWNCC, which drafted the missions bill. "The foreign policy of the United States, devoid of imperialistic design upon the sovereignty of any nation," declared the SWNCC, "leads many of the smaller nations to prefer American assistance." Despite such altruistic justifications, some congressional conservatives remained unmoved. Representative Karl E. Mundt (R-S.D.) complained that the American advisory groups provided the Soviet Union with an excuse for keeping its troops in Iran. The United States, he asserted, would never consent to similar Russian missions in Mexico. Although Mundt could not prevent the bill from passing the House, Robert A. Taft (R-Ohio) killed the legislation in the Senate. Until the United Nations had a chance to establish its authority, Taft argued, "we should not be sending military missions all over the world to teach people how to fight in American ways."[60]

Those measures that the Truman administration did implement during the first year of peace did not constitute an integrated program of military assistance. Although they shared common goals, such as preparing for a future war, checking the spread of Communist influence, and advancing bureaucratic interests, no single objective predominated. No coherent purpose yet transcended conflicts within the government. SWNCC 202/2 all but ignored the general goals of military aid programs in favor of a country-by-country catalog of policy. Indeed the debate within the government focused not so much on general policies as on specific programs of military aid. Not until the Truman administration launched its policy of containment in late 1946 and early 1947 did military aid programs gain the overriding purpose that carried them deep into the fabric of national security policy.

2 | Military Aid and Hemispheric Defense

I think it is fundamental that we should do everything within our power in a reasonable manner to unify the entire Western Hemisphere, so far as we can, in our thinking and in our arrangements, for our own security, for our own well-being.
—Secretary of State George C. Marshall, 23 June 1947

The Latin American armed forces contribution to U.S. security would be relatively small. The chief gain to the U.S. from a Latin American military aid program would be the continued alinement of these countries with the U.S., their greater willingness to furnish bases and strategic materials and the increased security of certain critical strategic areas.
—Army staff memorandum, 16 January 1949

World War II proved to U.S. policymakers the interdependence of national and hemispheric security. "The fact has been well established during this war," wrote one State Department expert in Latin American affairs in early 1945, "that the American republics constitute a single strategic defense area. Neither the United States nor any other American republic can be secure against aggression from overseas unless the security of all other republics is also safeguarded."[1] The Joints Chiefs of Staff commented a year later that "the Western Hemisphere is a distinct military entity, the integrity of which is a fundamental postulate of our own security in the event of another World War."[2] Although political and military authorities shared these convictions, they clashed repeatedly over a program of Latin American military assistance designed to consolidate the defenses of the hemisphere. Their conflicts revealed how sharply the services and the State Department could differ during the early postwar period over using military aid as a major instrument to build U.S. influence overseas.

At the end of World War II the State, War, and Navy departments agreed in principle that the United States should send equipment and advisers to the Latin American nations to promote the standardization of hemispheric armaments. Equally important was the obverse of standardization, the exclusion of European arms and military missions from the hemisphere. Washington officials remembered the influence that German advisers commanded in Latin American military circles on the eve of the war. They also recalled the difficulties of inter-American military collaboration at a time when the hemisphere faced the dangers of Axis subversion and invasion. Mindful of these lessons of the past, the SWNCC concluded in July 1945 that "the United States must take measures to prevent such a situation as confronted it at the outset of this war from again arising to hamper and jeopardize the common defense."[3]

Political and military officials differed, however, over the urgency and importance of standardizing the military establishments of the hemisphere. Because of revolutionary changes in the technology of warfare and sweeping realignments in international power, service authorities believed that the security of the United States depended more than ever before upon hemispheric solidarity. In an era of total war, they argued, the United States should not merely uphold the Monroe Doctrine but must also insulate the hemisphere from all foreign military influences. At the end of World War II they advocated swift passage of an inter-American arms bill and large-scale military aid before European advisers and arms traders could reestablish their prewar ties to Latin America. The purpose of this Western Hemisphere Defense Program, the War Department concluded, was not to prepare the Latin American forces to fight in a future conflict but to secure goodwill and maintain the orientation of the other American nations toward the United States.

The State Department, on the other hand, saw dangers in the ambitious arms programs proposed by the War and Navy departments. In the absence of an immediate military threat to the hemisphere, political officials favored only limited military aid, in order to avoid fueling local rivalries and reinforcing authoritarian regimes. For two years the State Department battled with War and Navy over military aid to Latin America. The intensification of the Cold War helped end the State Department's resistance in early 1947, but it also brought a new awareness of the limits on U.S. resources and a clarification of global priorities that pushed the Latin American program to a low priority. Stalled at first by conflicting views within the government, the early plans for military assistance to Latin America eventually gave way to a recalibration of interests against resources.

The Western Hemisphere Defense Program sprang from the desires of the army and navy to preserve and extend the influence that the United States had been building in Latin America since the eve of the Second World War.[4] By the late 1930s President Franklin D. Roosevelt feared that Hitler aspired to world conquest and posed a real threat to the security of the Western Hemisphere. Alarmed by Germany's extensive political and economic penetration of Latin America, Roosevelt attached new importance to inter-American relations. Beginning in 1938 he approved ambitious programs of economic aid, cultural exchange, and public works aimed at tying the Latin American nations closely to the United States. As Germany swept first to diplomatic triumphs and then to military victories in Europe, Roosevelt repeatedly warned that the American nations faced the common danger of invasion. After the outbreak of war he also worried about ominous reports of subversion and fifth-column movements that might turn Brazil, Argentina, Uruguay, and Paraguay into Nazi satellites. To meet the threat of German aggression, Roosevelt announced in November 1938 that the United States would use its armed forces to protect all American nations, a declaration that inspired a shift in military planning from national to hemispheric defense. At inter-American conferences in Lima (December 1938), Panama City (September–October 1939), Havana (July 1940), and Rio de Janeiro (January 1942), U.S. representatives urged continental solidarity against the Axis threat. The delegates cooperated by agreeing in Havana to consider an attack against one nation an attack against all and by voting at Rio to recommend to their governments the severance of diplomatic relations with Germany and Japan. Such actions marked a new high in inter-American unity under U.S. leadership.[5]

The establishment of close military relations with Latin America was an important part of the Roosevelt administration's effort to promote hemispheric solidarity. There was much room for improvement in these relations, since on the eve of the war U.S. armed forces had little interest and even less influence in Latin America. European nations dominated the training and supply of Latin American armed forces. Germany and Italy played leading roles, their long-established advisory missions instilling respect for Axis military might and winning the favor of admirals and generals who dominated Latin American politics. In early 1938 the State Department began urging the army and navy to counteract these Nazi and Fascist influences by increasing contacts with their Latin American counterparts. The services responded first with symbolic gestures—goodwill visits, demonstration flights, and training of Latin American officers in U.S. schools. The prodding of Under Secretary Sumner Welles, the State Department's foremost advocate of Pan-American cooperation, and the approval of new RAINBOW war plans encompassing hemispheric defense brought more ambitious efforts, including the eventual stationing of military attachés or advisers in every Latin American nation. The withdrawal of German and Italian missions after the outbreak of war provided the United States with an extraordinary opportunity, unimaginable only a few years earlier, to forge strong links with most Latin American military leaders.[6]

The Roosevelt administration accelerated its efforts to secure these ties in mid-1940, as German armies swept France from the war. The German blitzkrieg caused new fears of a transatlantic strike launched from French West Africa, and Roosevelt urgently directed the army and navy to plan for the dispatch of an expeditionary force to protect the bulge of Brazil. He also authorized bilateral staff talks, held during the summer of 1940, to arrange for military collaboration with the Latin American nations in the event of an emergency. Because they doubted that the Latin American forces could serve as "effective allies in war," War Department authorities aimed instead during these conversations at "better mutual understanding" by "impressing Latin American officers with our military preparedness and our determination to uphold the Monroe Doctrine." This understanding, they hoped, would lead to cooperation with U.S. defense plans, primarily by providing access to base facilities in Latin America. This basic decision, to use military aid primarily to secure goodwill rather than to raise the military capabilities of Latin American forces, guided U.S. policy throughout the war.[7]

In return for their cooperation in defending the hemisphere, the Latin American nations requested substantial military aid from the United States. Their need for such assistance became urgent after the outbreak of war all but halted the flow of arms from the European nations that had equipped most of their armed forces. Although Roosevelt and Welles recognized the advantages of providing military aid, legal restrictions made difficult the transfer of anything but antiquated coastal-defense equipment, which the Latin American nations refused to purchase. The passage of the Lend-Lease Act in March 1941 removed the legal obstacle but did not alleviate the scarcity of materiel, which proved to be the greater impediment to meeting Latin American demands. At a time when it could not satisfy the requirements of its own rearmament programs and the enormous demands of Great Britain and the Soviet Union, the War Department was not about to divert scarce resources to much less urgent needs. If the Latin Americans could not understand such reasoning, Secretary of War Henry L. Stimson privately fumed, they had no intelligence.[8]

Thus at the time of greatest danger to the hemisphere, the United States provided Latin America with token shipments of armaments—valuing only $125 million by mid-1943. The failure to meet even minimal requests for arms occasionally strained relations with a few Latin American nations, such as Brazil, whose leaders thought that their enthusiastic and extensive support of hemispheric defense measures merited a special relationship with the United States. Yet War Department analysts found, on balance, that this limited assistance was enough to achieve the fundamental objective of inducing cooperation with the United States. "Primarily, it [lend-lease to Latin America] has tided us over a period of uncertainty and anxiety when it was not known which way the several countries were going to lean. It is believed to have been a contributing factor in stabilizing internal conditions, it has developed an added feeling of confidence in their ability to resist aggression and it has served to arouse an interest in American made munitions."[9]

This assessment reflected the sharp change that had occurred in the War Department's thinking about Latin America. Despite earlier reservations, many uniformed officers became convinced of the value of strong hemispheric military ties. Through the furnishing of arms, the dispatch of military missions, and the creation of an Inter-American Defense Board, the services developed close relationships with most of the Latin American military establishments. Those relationships yielded, in their view, important benefits—access to bases and strategic raw materials, cooperation in economic warfare, and support of U.S.

defense plans. Eager to preserve these advantages, military authorities replaced political officials as the principal advocates of inter-American military cooperation. Even with the end of any important strategic danger to the hemisphere, efforts to provide military aid to Latin America actually gained momentum.[10]

In December 1943 the services revealed their principal postwar objective in Latin America when the Joint Army and Navy Advisory Board on American Republics recommended the use of lend-lease to encourage the standardization of hemispheric armaments. Although European nations had equipped most of the Latin American military establishments before the war, the Joint Board now insisted that the United States should settle for nothing less than a monopoly over the supply of arms within the hemisphere. Otherwise, it predicted, the end of the war would bring an unrestrained arms trade as former belligerents, including the Axis powers, dumped surplus munitions throughout the continent. The result would be the inflammation of local rivalries and the reappearance of hostile military influences in an area now deemed vital to the security of the United States. Because it would avert these presumed dangers, the Joint Board considered the standardization of hemispheric armaments "of first importance to the peace and safety of the Western Hemisphere" and proposed a major revision of lend-lease policy that reflected this assessment. While urging new restrictions on lend-lease for wartime projects, the Joint Board advocated limited military aid to promote the postwar standardization of hemispheric armaments. A major objective of this new lend-lease policy, the War Department explained, was "to dangle before the American Republics just sufficient equipment to maintain that interest [in U.S. armaments] which now exists."[11]

Even though the Joint Chiefs of Staff and Acting Secretary of State Edward R. Stettinius, Jr., endorsed the Joint Board's report, conflict soon erupted between the services and the State Department over restricting wartime aid and planning postwar assistance. One of the sharpest disagreements concerned the control of lend-lease allocations for the remainder of the war. Since there was no longer any major Axis threat to the hemisphere, the State Department maintained that political considerations should govern the provision of military supplies to Latin America, except Brazil and Mexico, the two countries that were preparing small forces to fight outside the hemisphere. By regulating the assignment of lend-lease munitions, the State Department hoped to establish its control over Latin American policy. But the War and Navy departments jealously guarded the influence over Pan-American affairs that they had gained during the war and insisted that the State Department was encroaching on *their* prerogatives. Admiral Ernest J. King, the chief of naval operations, complained that "the whole object in having a policy on this subject [the distribution of lend-lease to Latin America] was to avoid the necessity of referring individual requests to the Department of State." Admiral W. O. Spears, the senior navy member of the Joint Board, bluntly asserted that the assignment of lend-lease munitions was beyond the purview of the State Department.[12]

This dispute came to a head in the summer of 1944 over a Peruvian request for twelve dive-bombers. Spears insisted that these aircraft were necessary for coastal defense and declared that the navy would regard any State Department intervention in the matter as an "impingement" on its authority. Officials in State's Office of American Republic Affairs (ARA), on the other hand, thought that the planes exceeded legitimate military requirements and that their transfer would upset relations between Peru and its neighbors. Tiring of Spears's arrogant efforts to exclude his department from lend-lease decisions, Secretary of State Cordell Hull appealed to the president, who sustained Hull's position. After learning of Roosevelt's decision, service representatives finally admitted that considerations of foreign policy should prevail in the allocations of lend-lease armaments to Latin America. Despite this concession, the State, War, and Navy departments continued to quarrel for the duration of the war over their specific responsibilities for hemispheric arms transfers.[13]

The three departments encountered similar difficulties in establishing procedures for bilateral staff talks with the Latin American nations. The purpose of these conversations was to insure Latin American cooperation with U.S. postwar defense policies and to help the Roosevelt administration determine the amount of military assistance needed to standardize hemispheric armaments. Both diplomatic and military officials were eager to begin the staff talks but were divided over the role of the U.S. ambassador in the discussions. This dispute raised again the fundamental question of responsibility in making hemispheric policy, and both sides issued shrill warnings that the other was trying to usurp its authority. For example, General John E. Hull, the army's assistant chief of staff for operations, declared that the procedures for the staff talks advocated by the State Department would establish "a dangerous precedent . . . wherein military personnel in foreign countries would be subject to the overriding authority of the American Ambassador in military matters beyond the cognizance of the Department of State."[14] Spruille Braden, ambassador to Cuba, countered that the services' proposed instructions, by giving the army and navy undue influence over political matters, "would violate the fundamental law that the Department of State is charged with the conduct of our foreign affairs." Unable to reconcile these conflicting views, the three departments halted the staff talks in October 1944 after the first round of discussions with Brazil. Only after months of wrangling did they agree that the ambassador should have primary responsibility for the conduct of these conversations, an arrangement that allowed the staff talks to resume in January 1945.[15]

Despite progress in settling differences over the staff talks and lend-lease, hemispheric arms policy continued to arouse bureaucratic animosities. The services' most zealous advocates of inter-American military cooperation, such as General George H. Brett, army commander in the Caribbean, often regarded the State Department as an obstacle to the realization of their plans. Postulating "a common understanding . . . among all military men," Brett asserted that "the most effective method of approach in any Americanization program will be by the use of military establishments." He frequently visited Latin American military leaders and offered assistance, sometimes without first consulting either the State Department or the chief of mission. Occasionally his activities proved embarrassing, as when he promised aircraft to the Dominican Republic at a time when the State Department was trying to bring pressure on the dictatorial regime of Rafael Trujillo. Later, during the staff conversations, Brett charged that several chiefs of mission were ill-prepared and uncooperative. "We are having our troubles," he complained to the War Department, "trying to get some of the Ambassadors in[to] the ball game."[16]

The commanding general of the army air forces, General Henry H. Arnold, was even more contemptuous of the State Department. In the autumn of 1944 Arnold recommended the disposal of between 4,000 and 8,000 surplus aircraft to Latin America to promote standardization, preempt foreign competition, and encourage requests for U.S. air missions. Although this extravagant proposal was never implemented, Arnold made arrangements on his own initiative to provide training and equipment on a lesser scale to several Latin American nations. At a War Department meeting Arnold justified his independent action by declaring that "any progress which we might make in furnishing Latin Americans with Air Force equipment, to the exclusion of foreign equipment, would have to be achieved through actions on our part without reference to the Department of State." Arnold also boasted that both Roosevelt and Stimson would support him in any controversy with the State Department. Confident of the backing of higher authorities, Arnold had his assistant, General Robert LeG. Walsh, inform ARA officials of his personal interest in the development of Latin American aviation—a move he undoubtedly hoped would intimidate his adversaries in the State Department. For good measure, Walsh also denounced ARA's efforts to restrain Brett.[17]

Behind this dispute over bureaucratic prerogatives was a fundamental disagreement over postwar policy toward Latin America. For service authorities, military measures were the key to building hemispheric solidarity. Comprehensive statements of regional policy, approved in early 1945, revealed that the services advocated a postwar program of military cooperation that exceeded even wartime measures. In addition to the standardization of hemispheric armaments, the Joint Chiefs of Staff desired permanent arrangements for U.S. forces to use naval and air bases essential to hemispheric defense. The War Department added to this agenda access to strategic raw materials and maintenance of "a spirit of friendly cooperation" with the Latin American armed forces. To secure these goals, the services intended to offer extensive military aid, including arms, training missions, and instruction of Latin American personnel in U.S. service schools. These measures of military collaboration, their proponents argued, would not only safeguard the hemisphere but also solidify U.S. military prestige and prevent the revival of European influences in Latin American military circles.[18]

These ambitious proposals for inter-American defense went far beyond strictly military requirements. Aware of the dominant position of the armed forces in many Latin American governments, service authorities believed that military cooperation would insure friendly political relations. The goodwill of hemispheric military leaders was vital not only to gain access to bases and strategic resources but also to maintain the orientation of Latin America toward the United States. Brett, for example, believed that there was "the greatest opportunity in Central and South America to establish a very solid and basic friendship through the medium of the military." Along with other uniformed officers, he also thought that U.S. arms and training would help preserve internal security and enhance stability throughout the continent. In short, military officials believed that extensive inter-American military cooperation would result in stable, cooperative, even compliant regimes insulated from hostile influences and tied closely to the United States. Indeed, in the opinion of Robert P. Patterson, who became secretary of war in September 1945, the reasons for extending military assistance to Latin America were "frankly . . . more political than military."[19]

Economic considerations also shaped the services' thinking. Convinced that there would be little time to mobilize before the next war, the Joint Chiefs concluded that the United States should maintain armaments industries that could rapidly meet emergency needs. Latin American orders would help support such productive capacity. It was no accident that the army air forces, for which the maintenance of a large and modern aircraft industry was a paramount concern, aggressively sought to dominate Latin American markets. Indeed, the War Department maintained that one of the benefits of standardization was making Latin America "dependent on the United States aviation industry." For the services, then, standardization served both military and economic ends.[20]

This blurring of traditional distinctions between political, economic, and military objectives reflected a new ideology of preparedness, a belief that the nation must mobilize its full resources to protect its security. More than fears of any current or future adversary, the experience of total war created this anxiety about the nation's well-being. As they shaped postwar goals, military planners repeatedly referred to the weaknesses in hemispheric defense that had existed at the beginning of the war, vulnerabilities that appeared even more frightening in a world in which the United States was no longer immune to sudden attack. For military officials the lessons of the past were clear: they could not allow the recurrence of these weaknesses because the next war, they feared, would come with little, if any, warning. Their solutions were extreme. Determined to prevent another hostile power from gaining a foothold in Latin America, they wanted to seal off the hemisphere from all foreign military influence. Alarmed by the appeal of Nazi ideology, they sought "to reorient the military thought of Latin America from European influence to the democratic lines of our military doctrine." Distressed by the inability of most neighboring countries to take on even minor military missions at the beginning of the war, they endeavored to make the military establishments of the other American republics adjuncts of U.S. forces in the protection of the hemisphere. Believing the security of the United States in jeopardy, they argued that nothing less than an unquestioned—and unprecedented—military hegemony in Latin America would suffice.[21]

Although they too were concerned about the nation's security, State Department officials objected to the services' grandiose proposals. Some political analysts feared that U.S. efforts to become the exclusive supplier of armaments within the hemisphere might encourage other nations, such as the Soviet Union or Great Britain, to seek similar arrangements in other areas of the world.[22] The department's Latin American experts criticized the extravagance of the services' plans. John C. Dreier, chief of the American Republics Analysis and Liaison Division, pointed out that the arming of some Central American countries of minor strategic significance clearly exceeded the requirements of hemispheric security. Ellis O. Briggs, ambassador to the Dominican Republic, dismissed as naive the claim that military missions might inculcate democratic principles in Latin America. ARA officials instead worried that the services' plans would lend prestige to dictators and provide them with the means to put down legitimate opposition. Rather than relying so heavily on military aid and building up the armies of dictators, the ARA urged continuation of the Good Neighbor Policy, which had encouraged "the political, economic and social advancement of the other republics" and had been responsible for wartime solidarity. Dreier thus saw a basic conflict between the policies of the State Department and those of the War and Navy departments, even though all three aimed at strengthening the security of the hemisphere.[23]

Yet the State Department was reluctant to provide what most Latin American governments considered essential to the postwar continuation of the Good Neighbor Policy—economic assistance. As the war came to an end in 1945, the Latin Americans expected U.S. help in the form of commodity agreements and loans to cushion the shocks of transition to a peacetime economy and to promote economic development. They believed that they had earned such aid by their wartime cooperation in providing the United States with bases and vital raw materials. Furthermore, such assistance was in the U.S. interest, explained Mexican Foreign Minister Ezequiel Padilla, since it would remove the principal cause of anti-Americanism—resentment of the U.S. economic position—and destroy the appeal of ideologies that threatened democracy in Latin America. The State Department promised to hold an international meeting to discuss the hemisphere's economic matters on 15 June 1945, but then postponed the conference indefinitely. Instead U.S. diplomats counseled Latin American governments to promote economic development by eschewing all forms of economic nationalism, eliminating trade barriers, and attracting capital from private foreign investors.[24]

Such advice seemed to many Latin Americans nothing more than a prescription for continued underdevelopment and dependence on U.S. corporate interests. Generous postwar programs of assistance for other regions only exacerbated the Latin American sense of betrayal. In fact, the failure to secure a long-term development loan of $1 billion eventually caused Brazilian Ambassador Carlos Martins to throw a tantrum in which he accused the United States of abandoning the Good Neighbor Policy. By relying mainly on private investment rather than government assistance to meet Latin America's economic needs, the State Department undermined its goal of perpetuating the Good Neighbor Policy and providing an effective alternative to the services' plans to cement hemispheric solidarity through military assistance.[25]

The SWNCC attempted to settle the dispute between the State Department and the services by issuing a statement of principles to guide postwar inter-American military cooperation. It endorsed assistance and training programs designed to encourage the standardization of hemispheric armaments along U.S. lines and agreed to request the necessary congressional authorization at the earliest possible time. The committee also resolved not to help the Latin American nations support military establishments that exceeded their economic means and to withhold training and equipment from nations that were likely to use such aid to threaten aggression or deny their citizens democratic rights and liberties. Finally, the SWNCC gave the State Department the power to veto arms aid programs proposed by the War and Navy departments that conflicted with foreign policy objectives.

But these conclusions, which Truman approved on 29 July 1945, did little more than provide guidelines for continuing conflict, since political and military officials still disagreed about using military assistance as a major instrument for building U.S. influence in Latin America. Despite the SWNCC statement of principles, the issues over which the State Department and the services had battled for almost two years remained unresolved at the end of the war.[26]

With the end of the war and the termination of lend-lease, military officials were eager to begin the programs of assistance to Latin America that Truman had sanctioned. The bilateral staff talks, completed during the summer of 1945, were supposed to be strictly exploratory but nevertheless raised throughout the hemisphere expectations of extensive U.S. military aid. The uniformed officers who led these discussions often encouraged such thinking. For example, Admiral Jonas H. Ingram, speaking without authorization, promised Brazilian naval officers that the United States would provide free of charge all the vessels that they requested. Brett and General Ralph H. Wooten, the commander of army forces in South America, reported that because of the staff talks government authorities in Paraguay, Uruguay, Chile, and elsewhere believed that the United States was committed to supporting their postwar military establishments. Given such thinking, Brett and Wooten concluded that failure to furnish equipment and training promptly would damage relations with several Latin American nations and destroy the military prestige that the United States had gained during the war.[27]

On the basis of the information gathered during the staff conversations, the Joint Army and Navy Advisory Board on American Republics completed on 15 September a detailed plan for the standardization of hemispheric military establishments. Under this Western Hemisphere Defense Program the United States would over several years equip peacetime Latin American armed forces amounting to twenty-eight ground divisions and supporting troops and some seventy-five tactical air squadrons. This enormous infusion of assistance would not only standardize hemispheric armaments but also require substantial increases in several Latin American armies and in most of the air forces. The Joint Board did not justify the need for these armed forces in any strategic plan for hemispheric defense. But it urged the

Joint Chiefs of Staff to approve its recommendations promptly so that the United States would not squander "a splendid opportunity for integrating the defenses of the Western Hemisphere."[28]

Senior officials in the Navy Department, however, demurred. Long skeptical of the effectiveness of Latin American military establishments, Admiral King did not share the enthusiasm of Spears and others for arming Latin America. He informed the Joint Chiefs that the combat vessels proposed for transfer to Latin America—including light cruisers, light carriers, and submarines—would more likely be used to menace neighbors than to protect the hemisphere. He also criticized the Joint Board for recommending excessive programs of assistance out of an exaggerated fear that the Latin American military leaders would turn to European sources of supply if the United States failed to meet their ambitious requests for armaments. In King's view, the Joint Board's proposals aimed at "complete control by the United States over the armed forces of other American republics." Whatever the military advantages of such an arrangement, he warned, "the idea of establishing a hemispherical block [sic] of satellite armies and navies might set a precedent that we would not wish to see followed in regional arrangements outside the Americas."[29] Secretary of the Navy James V. Forrestal added to these reservations his fears that the Western Hemisphere Defense Program might provide the means for "wars and revolutions which would be advertised to the world as being fought with American weapons." He reminded Patterson and Secretary of State James F. Byrnes that Venezuelan insurgents had already used lend-lease munitions during a recent coup d'état. Because of the navy's misgivings, the three secretaries agreed on 20 November to postpone any decision on the Western Hemisphere Defense Program.[30]

While the three departments reconsidered this extended program, War sought State's permission to send a portion of the proposed military assistance to Latin America under the authority of the Surplus Property Act of 1944.[31] This interim program, designed to maintain the flow of armaments until the enactment of an inter-American military aid bill, also met strong opposition within the State Department. Latin American experts—including Braden, the new assistant secretary for ARA, and Briggs, the recently appointed director of ARA—reiterated that substantial arms aid conflicted with the department's policy of encouraging democracy in the other American states and reducing tensions among them.[32] Braden's special assistant, Carl B. Spaeth, summed up the outlook of many of his colleagues when he called the War Department's proposals "a tragic error." So distressed were Briggs and Spaeth that they helped revive a proposal, which had languished in the department since the beginning of 1945, for a one-year moratorium on the provision of military equipment to foreign nations, pending approval of long-term restrictions by the United Nations. Deploring the inconsistency of supplying "other countries with the weapons for another war while . . . proclaiming a policy of peace and of support for the United Nations," they urged prompt action to halt the worldwide disposal of surplus munitions.[33]

Patterson tried to rebut these criticisms. Distressed by the State Department's prolonged deliberations, he complained that the delay in furnishing arms was eroding U.S. influence in Latin America. "It is becoming increasingly apparent to the Governments of countries with whom staff conversations have been held that they cannot depend on our promises to furnish them with arms and training," he told Byrnes, even though no commitments to Latin America had yet been made. Echoing the warnings of Brett and Arnold, he predicted that unless the Truman administration quickly took some "positive action," foreign arms and missions would again prevail in Latin America. To avert this "grave danger to the military security of the United States," Patterson asked that the State Department speedily consent to the interim allocations.[34]

Faced with the opposing views of ARA and the War Department, Byrnes approved a compromise on the interim program. The secretary and his advisers rejected an embargo on arms exports because, as Under Secretary of State Dean Acheson later explained, the United States had incurred "a moral commitment of a sort" to provide military aid to Latin America as a result of the bilateral staff talks.[35] At the same time the department's senior officials heeded the warnings of ARA and sought to minimize the adverse political effects of furnishing such assistance. Acheson informed Patterson on 19 December that the State Department would approve interim allocations only to countries that agreed not to purchase military equipment from other nations, a condition that would lessen the chances of an arms race in Latin America and insure progress toward the standardization of hemispheric armaments. Acheson also requested the War Department to withhold or reduce interim shipments to several authoritarian or unstable regimes—the Dominican Republic, Haiti, Honduras, Nicaragua, Bolivia, and Paraguay. Argentina, which had been excluded from the staff talks because of its pro-Axis sympathies, was ineligible for any assistance. Finally, after further consideration, the State Department decided in January 1946 to prohibit the transfer of bomber aircraft to all Latin American nations except Brazil and Mexico.[36] Acheson explained to Acting Secretary of War Kenneth C. Royall that the misuse of bombing planes in internal strife or international disputes would alienate "those people of Latin America who are devoted to the cause of peace and of stable democratic government" and whose support was crucial to "our position of leadership among the American republics."[37]

Although the War Department accepted these conditions, Arnold refused to abide by them. He denounced the State Department for what he considered its characteristic obstructionism in hemispheric military affairs. He was particularly enraged over the restrictions on bombers, which threatened to embarrass his efforts to arrange for the transfer of aircraft during an impending visit to several Latin American countries. Just as he had on previous occasions, Arnold appealed to the president, and Truman, who apparently had little patience with the State Department's scruples, overruled the diplomats. Before his departure for Latin America in January 1946, Arnold met with Braden and approved a revised interim program of 566 aircraft, which was approximately the same size as the War Department's original proposal, and included bombers. Braden did manage to salvage some of the State Department's restrictions by persuading Arnold to withhold any deliveries, because of current political conditions, to Argentina, Bolivia, the Dominican Republic, Haiti, Honduras, Nicaragua, and Paraguay. Arnold also agreed that the new interim program would discharge any implied commitment arising from the staff conversations.[38]

Cheered by the approval of these interim allocations, service leaders spoke with new unity and vigor in the defense of the Western Hemisphere Defense Program.[39] Conceding that the navy had "dragged its feet," Forrestal now joined Patterson in advocating immediate action on an inter-American arms bill, especially since the British and Canadians were offering to sell vessels to several Latin American countries.[40] The Joint Chiefs of Staff also reaffirmed their support for the standardization of hemispheric armaments, noting that the invention of the atomic bomb, the development of long-range aircraft, and the advent of the Soviet Union as the dominant power in Eurasia meant that "the ultimate security of the United States has become far more dependent than heretofore upon the maintenance of the strategic unity of the Western Hemisphere."[41] The army's new chief of staff, General Dwight D. Eisenhower, met on at least two occasions with Acheson to assure him that the War Department had no intention of supplying "guns, tanks and airplanes indiscriminately to the Latin American countries, either to unload surplus equipment for cash or with any desire to build up a military hegemony in the hemisphere."[42] Yet without significant reductions in the Western Hemisphere Defense Program, Eisenhower's words could not have provided much comfort to Braden and his staff.

Despite the Joint Chiefs' concern over the Soviet threat, policymakers expressed few worries about the immediate ambitions of the USSR in Latin America. Even when a new attitude of firmness toward the Soviet Union took hold in Washington at the beginning of 1946, military analysts only infrequently mentioned the possibility of Communist subversion in Latin America or Soviet arms sales to the other American states. In one exceptional instance, the Military Intelligence Service warned as early as March 1945 that Communist penetration posed "a positive threat to the United States' military, political and economic position in Latin America." Yet this alarmist report made little impression on War Department officials and apparently had no significant effect on planning postwar military cooperation. The State Department also considered the Soviet Union a possible competitor for postwar political and economic influence in Latin America but dismissed any danger to U.S. leadership in the hemisphere as remote.[43] Born of the experiences of World War II, the Western Hemisphere Defense Program, in the eyes of both its critics and its defenders, was not a Cold War measure.

Advocates of hemispheric military aid fretted not about Soviet challenges but about the resumption of Great Britain's long-standing arms trade with Latin America. Service attachés and ambassadors in Brazil and Chile reported that British efforts to sell ships and munitions were embarrassing the U.S. military missions and jeopardizing plans for inter-American defense.[44] Disturbed by this situation, the army and navy suggested in December 1945 that the State Department ask the British to abstain from the Latin American arms trade as part of a settlement of outstanding financial issues between the two countries. Political officials rejected this proposal even though they worried about a potential Latin American arms race stimulated by British and American competition. Byrnes, however, raised the issue with British officials, and Foreign Minister Ernest K. Bevin replied that his government was prepared to explore with the Truman administration ways of regulating the Latin American arms traffic. Bevin had already shown his willingness to cooperate when he joined with Byrnes in October 1945 in a gentleman's agreement to withhold combat materiel from Argentina. But the State Department did not pursue Bevin's suggestion of bilateral discussions, and military leaders called for timely action to exclude British military influence from the hemisphere.[45]

The State, War, and Navy departments continued to debate the Western Hemisphere Defense Program until Byrnes's Staff Committee voted on 25 April to sponsor an inter-American arms bill. The Staff Committee made its decision even though ARA officials were as convinced as ever that additional military assistance would only aggravate political and economic instability in Latin America. Eisenhower apparently played a pivotal role in persuading the State Department's senior officials to overrule the objections of the Latin American experts. He met with Acheson on 22 April, and as one official in ARA later recollected, "The Department gave its reluctant support . . . on the assurance of the Chief of Staff that the bill was essential for the security of the United States."[46]

As the price of its support, the State Department insisted on major changes in the legislation drafted by the War Department. The Inter-American Military Cooperation Act (IAMCA), which Truman proposed to Congress on 6 May 1946, authorized the president to furnish equipment and training to the other American nations according to terms that he deemed satisfactory, provided that the United States received full value for new procurement. In order to satisfy the State Department's desire to hold to a minimum any increase in the level of hemispheric armaments, the bill allowed the Latin American nations to exchange nonstandard items in their possession for equivalent amounts of U.S. materiel. Also at the department's request, the proposed legislation stipulated that all transfers would be subject to any international arms accord to which the United States adhered. To meet the State Department's final objection, Truman assured the Congress that his administration would implement IAMCA so as to reduce the chances of either an arms race or the misuse of equipment and to avoid placing an undue burden on the Latin American economies.[47]

Despite these concessions, some State Department officials still had strong misgivings about the bill. One critic, a former director of ARA, sensing the incompatibility of the services' military goals in Latin America with the State Department's political desires, doubted that the administration would adhere strictly to the restraints that ARA demanded. He thought that the services would prevail upon the president to relax these restrictions once the IAMCA was enacted, because otherwise "not many of the Latin American countries would receive any military aid whatever."[48]

Although the State Department agreed to sponsor the IAMCA, it refused to make more than a perfunctory effort to secure its passage. Byrnes testified before the House Foreign Affairs Committee, as did Eisenhower and the chief of naval operations, Admiral Chester W. Nimitz. Both Eisenhower and Nimitz emphasized that the proposed legislation would prevent the recurrence of the weaknesses in hemispheric security that existed at the beginning of World War II. The committee reported the bill unanimously, but the full House never considered the measure because of the press of business to attend to before adjournment. The bill fared less well in the Senate. The Foreign Relations Committee, apparently unimpressed by the administration's case for arming Latin America, took no action at all. At the end of the congressional session, Eisenhower reaffirmed his strong personal support of the bill. But Byrnes's Staff Committee recommended that the State Department make no last-minute push for the enactment of the proposed legislation. Commenting on the Staff Committee's decision, Briggs wrote, "Good. . . . It's a War-Navy project. I prefer not to get too enmeshed." The IAMCA died with the adjournment of the Seventy-ninth Congress on 2 August. Delayed by the State Department's opposition, the Western Hemisphere Defense Program was now also frustrated by congressional inaction.[49]

In August 1946 Acheson informed Patterson and Forrestal that the State Department would support the resubmission of the IAMCA to the Eightieth Congress, but by December the department's position had changed. Warning again of the baneful effects of arming Latin America, Braden and the staff of ARA persuaded Byrnes to reconsider the department's sponsorship of the proposed legislation. Braden emphasized that most of the Latin American nations could not afford even the modest quantities of surplus equipment offered under the interim program. Complete standardization, according to a recent estimate, would cost almost $1 billion, a sum "infinitely beyond the economic resources of Latin America." If carried out, such a program would halt social progress and promote an arms race that would jeopardize the peace and security of the hemisphere. ARA urged Byrnes to withhold support from the IAMCA unless the State, War, and Navy departments could agree to measures for hemispheric armament standardization that would neither impose substantial costs on the United States nor bankrupt Latin America. Such a recommendation was tantamount to suggesting that the United States provide no more than token quantities of military equipment to the other American nations.[50]

To the objections of his advisers, Byrnes added his own. Although the War and Navy departments counseled against further delays on the proposed legislation, Byrnes told Patterson and Forrestal on 18 December that he did not consider the extension of military assistance to Latin American an urgent matter. He realized that European arms manufacturers, particularly the British, coveted the Latin American trade, but he doubted that their activities would upset the services' plans for standardization since most of their prospective clients lacked funds for substantial purchases of military equipment. Nor was he worried about the establishment of a British military or naval mission in Latin America. Only the Soviet Union, in his increasingly bipolar view of international affairs, could challenge U.S. security interests in the hemisphere, but there was no reason to fear that any Latin American country would request Russian advisers in the near future. Byrnes instead believed that the United States should use its resources to assist countries that faced an immediate Soviet threat. Greece, where Communist-led guerrillas threatened to topple the rightist government, was "our real problem today," he emphasized.[51]

Byrnes then asked Patterson and Forrestal to define U.S. military interests in Latin America. He inquired, according to the minutes of their meeting, "What is our real objective there? Is it because [sic] we feel that a Latin American fighting force would be of any value to us or is it merely to keep others out?" Patterson replied that the exclusion of foreign influences was the army's primary goal, and Forrestal basically agreed, while noting that the Latin American navies might assist the United Sates in antisubmarine warfare. Since the principal argument of his colleagues was "the negative one of keeping others out," Byrnes asserted that the United States could achieve that objective by maintaining and establishing military and naval missions in the hemisphere without necessarily supplying arms. Despite these reservations, Byrnes postponed a final decision on the IAMCA until he received a report on the costs of the Western Hemisphere Defense Program and a written statement of the views of the War and Navy departments.[52]

Patterson had anticipated Byrnes's objections, and at the end of the meeting he handed the secretary of state a letter that explained in detail his department's thinking. Patterson wrote that the nation's principal strategic concerns in Latin America were to protect the Panama Canal and gain access to raw materials. But the predominant military interest, in his analysis, was "simply . . . having a stable, secure, and friendly flank to the South, not confused by enemy penetration— political, economic or military." He reminded Byrnes "that the penetration of non-hemispheric nations during the years preceding World War II resulted in a situation so dangerous at the outbreak of hostilities that we were forced to devote considerable effort and resources to counteract the threat. It is to insure that this situation is not repeated that the War Department is so strongly in support of the Inter-American Military Cooperation Act." The War Department contributed to hemispheric solidarity by sending advisory missions overseas and training Latin American officers in U.S. schools. These activities provided opportunities "to introduce and demonstrate, to individuals in key positions, U.S. democratic principles." This work would cease, however, if the United States failed to supply Latin America with military equipment. Belgian and Czechoslovakian arms dealers, Patterson reported, had already offered or sold materiel to Argentina, Chile, Peru, and Venezuela, and French officials were trying to reestablish their prewar military advisory groups in Bolivia, Brazil, and Peru. These activities proved that "the European nations are only too willing to fill the vacuum in missions and munitions of war which would be created by our failure to . . . secure passage of the legislation."[53]

Patterson's arguments failed to impress officials in ARA and consequently had little effect on Byrnes, who was not deeply concerned with Latin America and usually accepted Braden's advice.[54] Byrnes resigned in January 1947, however, and his successor, George C. Marshall, held far different views about inter-American military cooperation. As army chief of staff in 1945, Marshall had approved the plans for the postwar standardization of armaments. Less than a month after becoming secretary of state, he appeared before the Senate Foreign Relations Committee and agreed emphatically with Chairman Arthur H. Vandenberg (R-Mich.) that "Pan-American solidarity" was "a highly essential military need at the moment."[55]

Hopeful that Marshall would choose to renew the State Department's sponsorship of the IAMCA, Patterson pressed for a decision. In a letter to Marshall on 24 January he maintained that failure to proceed with the standardization of armaments might force some Latin American nations to turn to "a potentially hostile power" for arms and advisers and "the infiltration into Latin America of that power's military philosophy and, ultimately, its political ideologies, would inevitably follow." To these familiar dangers Patterson added a new threat, one that he had dismissed only a month earlier in his letter to Byrnes. He now warned that foreign possession of even a small base in Latin America might permit an air or missile attack on major U.S. cities. Patterson also listed six regions in Latin America vital to U.S. security: the Panama Canal and its approaches within 100 miles; the Straits of Magellan; Northeast Brazil; Mexico; the River Plate estuary and its approaches within a 500-mile radius; and Mollendo, Peru and Antofagasta, Chile. Patterson declared that, because of their location or resources, these areas were "so important in their own right that the threat of attack on any of them would force the United States to come to their defense," even if there was no certainty of a subsequent attack on the United States itself. If Patterson thought that Marshall, because of his military background, would be more sympathetic to these arguments, he was disappointed. Unwilling to change policy or reject the counsel of ARA so soon after taking office, Marshall, like Byrnes, reserved his decision until the State Department completed its study of the economic effects of the proposed legislation.[56]

State Department officials focused their attention on the economic implications of the IAMCA because they had learned just recently that the costs of standardization would greatly exceed their previous expectations. Plans for arming Latin America were made at a time when, in the words of one State Department analyst, there was "more naval, air and ground force military equipment than we know what to do with."[57] In 1945 the War Department expected to provide the materiel for standardization from these surplus inventories, and the IAMCA would allow the Latin American nations to compensate the United

States with nonstandard equipment in their possession. But by early 1947 the rapid depletion of surplus stocks forced the War Department to rely heavily on new procurement to carry out the Western Hemisphere Defense Program, and the Latin American countries would have to pay full price for such equipment. Adding to the cost of standardization, the Navy Department reported, was the expense of reconditioning vessels stripped during demobilization.[58] Braden estimated that, based on this new information, the cost of the Western Hemisphere Defense Program, even under the most favorable terms, would approach $1 billion. Detailed studies by the War and Navy departments soon confirmed the accuracy of that figure.[59]

This $1 billion price tag was the basis of the long-awaited State Department study's conclusion that the costs of standardization were prohibitive. Only five countries—Cuba, the Dominican Republic, El Salvador, Panama, and Venezuela—could meet the expenses of the Western Hemisphere Defense Program without difficulty. All other Latin American nations would experience some financial strain, which might force the postponement of their plans for internal development or the deferral of their payments on existing foreign debts. Six countries—Bolivia, Chile, Costa Rica, Ecuador, Nicaragua, and Peru—faced such acute problems with foreign exchange and recurring internal deficits that their participation in the proposed arms program was nearly impossible. The State Department was not the only agency that reached such pessimistic conclusions. The Caribbean Defense Command, using information gathered by U.S. military attachés, confirmed many of the State Department's findings. The passage of the IAMCA, Acheson wrote Patterson, would necessarily yield two undesirable results: it would exacerbate conditions of political and economic instability in Latin America, and it would encourage requests for costly subsidies that the economy-minded Eightieth Congress did not wish to provide.[60]

Patterson disagreed totally. He did not dispute the State Department's financial analysis, yet he insisted that enactment of the IAMCA would not place new burdens on the Latin American economies. By using "good judgment" in implementing the Western Hemisphere Defense Program, Patterson argued, the State Department could insure that the cost of armaments did not exceed the means of the recipients. He also maintained, somewhat contradictorily, that the United States could not dictate to the other American nations the size of their military establishments. "Thus, the question we face in Latin America," he declared, "is not 'Shall they have arms?' . . . [but] 'Shall they have United States or foreign arms?' " Patterson strongly urged Marshall to render his decision immediately. [61]

Rising Cold War tensions reinforced Patterson's determination to break the stalemate on the arms bill. On 12 March 1947 Truman called for aid to Greece and Turkey on the grounds that it "must be the policy of the United States to support free peoples who are resisting attempted subjugation by armed minorities or by outside pressures."[62] Impressed by the sweeping promise of the Truman Doctrine, service leaders tried to fit military aid to Latin America into a global context of containing communism. Frustrated by the State Department's opposition and congressional inaction, they undoubtedly hoped that an emphasis on the Soviet threat would strengthen their case for the arms bill. The Joint Chiefs of Staff, for example, added to their reasons for close hemispheric military ties the growing strength of the Latin American Communist parties.[63] The intelligence agencies of the War and Navy departments endorsed a report by the Central Intelligence Group that emphasized Soviet efforts "to undermine U.S. hegemony in the Hemisphere and make inter-American military cooperation difficult to achieve."[64] Assistant Secretary of War Howard C. Petersen concluded that, compared to Europe and Asia, "Latin America can be preserved for Western democracy at a far less cost and with considerably less effort."[65] Patterson expressed the same theme when he wrote to Acheson on 27 March that the Western Hemisphere Defense Program was designed "to prevent the very type of crisis which has arisen in Turkey and Greece."[66]

Eager for "preventive and forehanded" action to thwart the spread of communism, military officials took their case to the White House.[67] The three service delegates on the Inter-American Defense Board notified the president's secretary for legislation that the Western Hemisphere Defense Program was "of substantial importance" to national security. A memorandum to Truman on 26 March blamed the State Department's obstructionism for inaction on the IAMCA and suggested that the president might intervene to end the impasse. Although he lacked any deep interest in Latin America, Truman was receptive, in the wake of his strong stand on assistance to Greece and Turkey, to appeals for a bold assertion of American leadership within the hemisphere. The president promptly informed Acheson that he wanted the State, War, and Navy departments to settle their differences so that the United States could provide military equipment to Latin America. "I'm of the opinion that striped pants are trying to run So. Amer.," Truman commented simplistically. "They won't be able to do it."[68]

Truman's intervention was decisive.[69] Only a few days after his discussion with the president, Acheson shifted IAMCA responsibility within the department from Braden to General John H. Hilldring, chairman of the Policy Committee on Arms and Armaments, who War Department officials described as "very receptive" to their views. With Braden "out of the picture," as one army officer noted with relief, Acheson informed Patterson and Forrestal on 23 April that he would ask Marshall to renew the State Department's sponsorship of the IAMCA. The only restriction was that the three departments find some means of implementing the standardization program without adding to the debts of the recipient countries, a condition that was impossible to satisfy without subsidies from Congress. Nevertheless, Marshall accepted this recommendation. Having just returned from the stalemated Moscow meeting of the Council of Foreign Ministers, he was apparently convinced that Soviet intransigence in Europe made the consolidation of hemispheric defenses imperative. On 1 May the State, War, and Navy departments formally agreed to resubmit the Latin American arms bill to Congress.[70]

As they ended the opposition to the IAMCA, Truman and Marshall also reversed the State Department's position on military cooperation with Argentina. Since the beginning of World War II, the United States had withheld military assistance from Argentina because of its unwillingness to participate in hemispheric defense measures. In large measure, Argentine noncooperation was the product of traditional nationalism and neutralism, policies that arose from strong cultural and economic ties with Europe and fear of U.S. domination of the hemisphere. Cordell Hull, however, viewed Argentina's neutrality after Pearl Harbor mainly as the product of pro-Axis sympathies. Hull condemned Argentina as "the Nazi Headquarters of the Western Hemisphere" because of its toleration of German agents and efforts to subvert neighboring governments and forge them into a neutralist bloc. As sanctions for this contemptible behavior, Hull insisted on restrictions on trade and aid.[71]

Following Hull's retirement, the State Department in March 1945 relaxed its hard line against Argentina at the inter-American conference at Chapultepec Palace in Mexico City. Argentine President Edelmiro Farrell accepted the Act of Chapultepec, which required the elimination of all Axis influences, and declared war against Germany and Japan. The State Department, in turn, lifted economic sanctions and supported Argentina's admission to the United Nations. But these steps toward rapprochement halted abruptly in mid-1945 because of the Farrell regime's outrageous new campaign to suppress human rights and its sheltering of Nazi subversives. In response, the Truman administration excluded Argentina from the staff conversations and continued its ban on the shipment of combat materiel. Byrnes added to the pressure on the Argentines when he secured British Foreign Secretary Bevin's pledge, under the Gentlemen's Agreement of October 1945, to join the embargo.[72]

The official most responsible for the reimposition of hard-line policies toward Argentina was the new assistant secretary of state for inter-American affairs, Spruille Braden. Although not a career diplomat, Braden had considerable experience in inter-American affairs. After making a fortune as a mining engineer in Chile and then losing it during the Great Crash, Braden held a succession of diplomatic posts in Latin America, during which time he built a reputation both for tenacity and pugnacity. He patiently participated in the lengthy negotiations that finally settled the Chaco War between Bolivia and Paraguay in 1938. But he also admired the swagger of Theodore Roosevelt's "big stick" policy as much as the noninterventionism of Franklin Roosevelt's Good Neighbor Policy. As ambassador to Cuba during World War II, for example, Braden so vociferously decried governmental corruption that President Fulgencio Batista requested his recall. At the end of the war he served briefly as ambassador to Argentina and concluded that Farrell and his charismatic vice-president, Juan D. Perón, were unrepentant fascists. After becoming assistant secretary of state, Braden declared that the Good Neighbor Policy would not restrain U.S. actions against Argentina, since "it would be the grossest perversion to pretend that it requires us to respect Fascism in any of its guises."[73]

At Braden's urging, the State Department got tough with Argentina. Braden persuaded Byrnes and Truman in September 1945 to postpone the impending conference at Rio de Janeiro for the negotiation of an inter-American defense treaty because of Argentina's failure to meet its obligations under the Act of Chapultepec. Braden and his staff elaborated their case by preparing a documentary history of Argentine collaboration with Nazi Germany. The State Department released this Blue Book to the public in February 1946, just two weeks before the Argentine national elections. Braden's apparent goal was to embarrass Perón, one of the two leading candidates for president, but his strategy backfired. Perón shrewdly turned popular resentment against Braden's undiplomatic intrusion in Argentine politics into support for his candidacy and won a clear victory. Perón's triumph only reinforced Braden's determination to demand strict compliance with the Act of Chapultepec before lifting the arms embargo or calling the Rio Conference, a policy that Truman and Byrnes continued to endorse.[74]

But Braden's stern policy also aroused strong criticism. The most bitter adversary was George S. Messersmith, Braden's successor in Buenos Aires. Messersmith maintained that, although the Argentine government was making a sincere effort to purge Axis influences, Braden was trying only to antagonize Perón with provocative statements and unrealistic demands. Messersmith harangued Truman and Byrnes with lengthy indictments of Braden's conduct and even tried to stir opposition to Braden in the press and on Capitol Hill.[75] Messersmith's accusations reinforced the opinions of leaders of the Senate Foreign Relations Committee, such as the senior Democrat, Tom Connally of Texas, who urged a rapprochement with Argentina and restoration of hemispheric solidarity under U.S. leadership. Vandenberg, the ranking Republican, publicly denounced the postponement of the Rio Conference and privately disparaged " 'the Braden policies' which smack entirely too much of the old 'big stick' days when we used to dictate to our Pan-American neighbors." Concurring in this line of reasoning were advocates of the Good Neighbor Policy, such as former Under Secretary of State Sumner Welles, who bemoaned the division of the Americas and the squandering of U.S. influence within the hemisphere.[76]

The strongest challenge to Braden's policies came from the War and Navy departments. Forrestal, among others, complained that the arms embargo was encouraging Argentina to look to Europe for military equipment, thereby jeopardizing standardization. The Joint Chiefs of Staff worried that delay in negotiating a hemispheric defense treaty was leaving the southern flank of the Unites States dangerously weak. The War Department informed ARA that the United States could not afford strained military relations with Argentina because of the strategic importance of the Straits of Magellan, an area that the United States would have to control in a future war, owing to the increasing vulnerability to attack of the Panama Canal. Latin America experts in the army's Operations Division objected so vehemently to what they considered unwarranted interference in Argentina's internal affairs that they began urging Eisenhower in early 1946 to press for Braden's removal. Although Eisenhower rejected this advice, he openly challenged Braden's hard-line approach. When asked to comment on the State Department's paper, "Foreign Policy of the United States," the Joint Chiefs of Staff, at Eisenhower's insistence, replied that Argentine cooperation was essential to hemispheric solidarity, "accomplishment of which must in the end over-ride other, more transitory, political considerations."[77]

Concern over Soviet expansionism reinforced these objections. Vandenberg, for example, worried about "a potential Communist menace throughout Central and South America which *could* be far more dangerous than the Fascist problem in the Argentine."[78] Welles noted that the Soviet government had extended diplomatic recognition to Argentina and warned that policies that alienated Latin America from the United States only opened the door to Russian meddling. The Operations Division agreed that mounting difficulties with the Soviets required a united hemisphere. The Joint Chiefs of Staff went even further in May 1947 in an assessment of countries requiring military assistance. Because of the growing strength of Communist parties in Latin America, they argued that "anything less than complete rapprochement between the United States and every one of her neighbors to the south is entirely unacceptable from the viewpoint of United States security."[79] All of these critics agreed that the United States could no longer forfeit influence in Latin America to the Soviets because of Braden's preoccupation with the remnants of Nazism in Argentina.

Yet it was British moves, not Soviet actions, that finally precipitated a change in policy toward Argentina. On 27 January 1947 the British ambassador notified the State Department that his government was lifting its ban on the sale of combat materiel to the Perón regime. Bevin explained to Marshall that Britain's urgent need to trade for Argentine foodstuffs was the principal reason for his withdrawal from the Gentlemen's Agreement. He also hinted that dissatisfaction with the U.S.

plans for the standardization of hemispheric armaments influenced his government's action. British arms manufacturers were determined to continue their long-established trade with Latin America, and especially with Argentina, which possessed large foreign-exchange reserves and was willing to pay cash for modern armaments. Even though Bevin still hoped to cooperate with the United States to avert an arms race in Latin America, he felt that the Gentlemen's Agreement no longer served British interests.[80]

The British announcement immediately forced the Truman administration to reconsider its policy toward Argentina. Braden recommended that the State Department continue to deny military equipment and attempt to discourage the sale of British munitions to Perón. But at a Cabinet meeting on 7 February, Truman said that he favored an end to the embargo on arms exports to Argentina. He agreed with Forrestal, who pointed out that Argentina was trying to purchase several new combat vessels, the construction of which would contribute to the health of the U.S. shipbuilding industry, a vital concern of the navy. Forrestal wrote in his diary, "The President remarked that if the ships were not built in this country they would be built probably by the British or by the French or Dutch. He told the Secretary of State that he would like to see the business come here if possible and Marshall said that he would act accordingly."[81] Matthew J. Connelly, the president's secretary, summarized Truman's views more pointedly. According to his notes, Truman declared, "They [the Argentines] have 5 billion cash. Would like to get some of it."[82]

In accordance with the president's wishes, the State Department reduced its demands upon Argentina. Marshall decided to accept reasonable and substantial progress toward the elimination of Nazi influences, rather than Braden's more exacting standard, as a basis for reconciliation with the Perón regime. He indicated the change in the State Department's outlook when he told the Senate Foreign Relations Committee in executive session on 11 February 1947 that he expected that the United States and Argentina would settle their differences shortly. Truman also took a conciliatory position when he informed the Argentine ambassador, Oscar Ivanessevich, on 31 March 1947 that only the deportation of approximately two dozen Nazi agents who remained in Argentina stood in the way of normal relations.[83]

British actions, however, again disrupted the Truman administration's plans. Although the British ambassador had previously promised that his government would provide only "a trivial program" of naval assistance to Argentina, the State Department learned in May that the Hawker Siddeley Aircraft Company of London had signed a contract for the delivery of 100 jet fighter planes. Shocked by this transaction, Acheson explained to Truman that the sale would diminish the chances of Argentine cooperation in the expulsion of Nazi agents and upset the military balance in Latin America, perhaps even triggering an arms race. He also worried that the administration would appear, for insubstantial reasons, to be denying business opportunities in Argentina to American firms. Although Truman approved a letter of protest, Bevin refused to yield. Indeed, he informed Marshall of an additional British sale of thirty bombers to Argentina.[84]

Unable to dissuade the British, the Truman administration rapidly ended its dispute with Argentina. Despite the failure of the Perón regime to deport several important Nazi agents, Truman still announced on 3 June the restoration of normal relations and the U.S. readiness to attend the postponed Rio Conference for the negotiation of an inter-American defense treaty. At the same time, Marshall disposed of the department's principal antagonists on Argentine policy by recalling Messersmith and announcing Braden's resignation.[85] On 26 June 1947 Truman formally approved the change in policy he had requested almost five months earlier when he concurred in the Committee of Three's recommendation to allow the Argentines to contract with U.S. shipbuilders for the construction of naval vessels. The following month the State Department formally lifted the arms embargo and sanctioned Argentine participation in the Western Hemisphere Defense Program.[86]

The decisions on Argentina and the IAMCA were part of a fundamental shift in the State Department's position on military aid to Latin America. Beginning in mid-1947 the department dropped its objections to interim allocations not only for Argentina but also for other countries, such as the Dominican Republic and Haiti, that it had denied government surplus for political reasons. During the fall of 1947 the department's Policy Committee on Arms and Armaments stopped discouraging the commercial sales of weapons to Latin America, provided that those transfers conformed to the recommendations of the staff conversations of 1945. Accompanying these revisions of policy were sweeping changes in the leadership of ARA. Following Braden's resignation, two of his most important subordinates—Briggs and

Thomas C. Mann, the chief of the Division of River Plate Affairs—were assigned to South American embassies. These changes insured the cessation of the State Department's protracted opposition to the Western Hemisphere Defense Program.[87] In defending the arms bill, Marshall expressed his department's new position: "I think it is fundamental that we should do everything within our power in a reasonable manner to unify the entire Western Hemisphere, so far as we can, in our thinking and in our arrangements, for our own security, for our own well-being."[88]

At the same time that it helped change the State Department's position on arming Latin America, the deepening of Soviet-American antagonism provoked a review of military aid policy, which diminished the importance of the Western Hemisphere Defense Program. Inspired by the global sweep of the Truman Doctrine and abandoning their piecemeal, country-by-country approach to planning, State, War, and Navy department analysts made a worldwide survey of possible demands for U.S. foreign aid. In an interim report of 21 April 1947 they called for a comprehensive, integrated program of military assistance aimed primarily at containing Communist expansion and building American influence overseas. Accordingly, the State-War-Navy planners gave highest priority to emergency requests for help in stopping Communist coercion and penetration. They ranked second in importance long-term projects, such as the Western Hemisphere Defense Program, even though they thought that such assistance more efficiently preserved international peace and security.[89] The distinction was crucial, since additional studies revealed that possible demands for assistance would be far in excess of available resources.[90]

To facilitate the allocation of scarce equipment, policymakers established priorities among programs of arms aid during the first half of 1947. Forced to choose for the first time among competing requirements, both political and military officials placed the Western Hemisphere Defense Program low on their lists. First in March and again in June the State Department ranked Latin America last among current recipients—behind Greece, Turkey, Italy, Iran, China, Canada, and the Philippines—almost all of which faced immediate Communist threats. Using different criteria, the Joint Chiefs of Staff reached a similar conclusion. They argued that the United States should extend military aid only to nations that might become effective allies in the event of a war with the Soviet Union. Even a plea by Eisenhower that Latin America deserved special consideration did not prevent the Joint Chiefs from placing it eleventh among sixteen potential recipients, based on urgency of need and importance to national security.[91] These new calibrations of interests against resources, more rigorous and formal than previous efforts, undercut arguments for arming Latin America just when political and military leaders finally agreed to seek enactment of the IAMCA. If Cold War fears provided a new rationale for the Western Hemisphere Defense Program, they also persuaded American planners to concentrate their limited resources elsewhere.

Without urgent backing, the IAMCA again failed to make much headway in Congress. After Truman submitted the legislation on 26 May 1947, Vandenberg predicted that it would precipitate a "first-class fight" in the Senate, led by those who feared the remnants of fascism, rather than the beginnings of communism, in high government circles in Latin America.[92] Senator Robert A. Taft (R-Ohio) used his powerful influence against the legislation because he felt that it would make wars and revolutions in Latin America more destructive than ever before. Taft also objected to the creation of another costly foreign aid program, a sentiment so strong in Congress in mid-1947 that the Truman administration had to struggle to secure appropriations for an authorized program of military and economic aid to Greece and Turkey and shelve plans for a Korean aid bill. Because of this opposition, the proponents of the IAMCA decided to defer action on the bill rather than risk an embarrassing defeat on the eve of the Rio Conference. Although the House Foreign Affairs Committee approved the legislation, Vandenberg and Marshall agreed on 19 June to postpone consideration of the IAMCA until the next session of Congress.[93]

During the following year the IAMCA, overwhelmed by more important Cold War measures, sank into oblivion. Congress took no action on the proposed legislation while it approved the European Recovery Program and considered an accompanying emergency aid bill. Later in the session, Vandenberg balked at holding hearings on the IAMCA because of its controversial nature and its secondary importance. Even the *bogotazo*—the riot that occurred in April 1948 following the assassination of Colombian opposition leader Jorgé Eliécer Gaitán and that disrupted the Inter-American Conference at Bogotá—failed to provide new impetus for the passage of the IAMCA.[94] Temporary fears of Communist revolution in Latin America quickly receded as Colombian troops restored order and the Bogotá Conference completed its business. Despite Marshall's personal appeal to congressional leaders, neither chamber voted on the IAMCA before adjournment on 19 June 1948. At the end of the year the administration finally abandoned its efforts to gain passage of the measure.[95]

The failure to secure Latin American arms legislation forced the Truman administration to rely primarily on the sale of surplus property to promote the standardization of hemispheric armaments. Difficulties plagued even these transactions. Administrative problems and Latin American dollar shortages prevented all but token sales before mid-1947 and delayed final deliveries under the interim program until 1950.[96] The depletion of surplus inventories hampered the military establishment's ability to meet requests for even small amounts of armaments. In December 1947 the Argentine minister of war submitted a list of materiel he desired for immediate delivery, but the army found that it could provide less than one-fifth of the equipment. Even after Argentine officials pared their request, Secretary of the Army Kenneth C. Royall had to obtain Truman's approval for the sale since the items were not in surplus stocks.[97] By mid-1948 the three services had practically no armaments to furnish Latin America. A lack of authority and equipment brought the Western Hemisphere Defense Program to a halt.[98]

The Cold War thus had a dichotomous effect on the plans for postwar military aid to Latin America. On one hand, concern over Soviet expansionism helped persuade Marshall and Acheson in early 1947 to join with their colleagues in the military establishment in sponsoring the IAMCA. Anxiety over the Soviet threat also reinforced the services' conviction that the United States could no longer afford to postpone its long-standing plans for inter-American military unity. Eisenhower reminded the Joint Chiefs in May that the Western Hemisphere was "the main base" of the war potential of the United States.[99] Safeguarding the security of the hemisphere through the negotiation of an inter-American defense treaty and the provision of arms aid, in his view, was one of the essential tasks of national security.

On the other hand, the worldwide scope of the Truman Doctrine—

raising the prospect of substantial new programs of foreign assistance—relegated the Western Hemisphere Defense Program to a low
priority. Concerned about over-taxing national capacity, administration officials decided that the standardization of armaments, however
desirable, was beyond their means. Convinced that they could not meet
Communist challenges on every front, they concentrated their resources in the principal theaters of the Cold War—Europe and the
Eastern Mediterranean—not Latin America. Although bureaucratic
conflict and congressional inaction bedeviled plans for postwar military assistance to Latin America, it was the hardening of Cold War
attitudes in the spring of 1947 that insured the demise of the Western
Hemisphere Defense Program. Often an impetus to interventionism,
Cold War thinking actually restrained, albeit temporarily, U.S. military
aid to Latin America.

3 | The Limits of Aid to China

Our major objectives with respect to China are: effective joint prosecution of the war against Japan; and from a long-range standpoint, the establishment of a strong and united China as a necessary principal stabilizing factor in the Far East.
—State Department policy statement, 18 April 1945

There has been much loose talk about China's becoming the stabilizing influence in the Far East. We have never felt that this was a possibility in the reasonably near future but we have hoped that China would not become an unstabilizing influence—which is an entirely different thing.
—Acting Secretary of State Dean Acheson, 23 November 1946

In several ways American plans to furnish military assistance to China at the end of the Second World War resembled those for Latin America. In both cases lend-lease and wartime military cooperation provided the foundation for postwar assistance. Also in both instances and for similar reasons service officials were the leading advocates of such help. In China as in Latin America military officials hoped to promote standardization on American armaments, exclude European military influences, and insure China's friendly orientation toward the United States in the event of a future conflict. Much like the Western Hemisphere Defense Program, their extravagant plans for long-term material and advisory assistance to China encountered strong opposition from regional experts in the State Department, who feared the establishment of "a *de facto* protectorate with a semi-colonial Chinese army under our direction."[1] These divisions between diplomatic and military officials, like those over arms aid to Latin America, were sharp and persistent.

Like the Western Hemisphere Defense Program, the ambitious plans for lavish and continuing assistance to China never were fulfilled, although for different reasons. The eruption of civil war in China in 1945 provoked extended debate within the administration of Harry S. Truman over the extent of American support for the Nationalist government of Chiang Kai-shek and the role of arms aid in bringing a solution to Chiang's internal problems. Truman backed Chiang, while hoping that military assistance would both enable the Nationalists to extend their control and encourage the generalissimo to compromise with his Communist opponents. When Chiang proved recalcitrant, Truman, on the recommendation of his special representative in China, General George C. Marshall, halted American arms transfers to the Nationalists. As the civil war expanded, administration officials first scaled down and then all but abandoned plans for extended military cooperation, which assumed a peaceful, unified China. By early 1947 the Truman administration had retracted but not yet redefined its policy on military aid to China.

Military assistance to China had been a persistent and vexing problem for the United States since the beginning of the Second World War. The decision of President Franklin D. Roosevelt and his advisers to concentrate American resources on the defeat of Germany angered Chiang Kai-shek. Instead of receiving the substantial military supplies that he had expected, Chiang had to settle for meager lend-lease allocations. Roosevelt tried to ease Chiang's distress by treating China as a great power and emphasizing that it would play a major role in maintaining peace in Asia after the war, but the generalissimo was not appeased. He complained bitterly in May 1942 that China was "treated not as an equal like Britain and Russia, but as a ward," and hinted that his government might sue for peace if greater aid was not forthcoming.[2] Responding to Chiang's demands, Roosevelt tried to increase the flow of supplies to China without diminishing American efforts in more important theaters of operations. He also granted Chiang's request for a $500 million loan and looked the other way when members of Chiang's inner circle used the funds for their personal enrichment. Chiang's dissatisfaction with American aid policies, however, remained a continual source of friction between the United States and China until the end of the war.[3]

No one was more deeply involved in shaping wartime plans for military aid to China than General Joseph W. Stilwell, the commander of American troops in China, Burma, and India and chief of staff to

Chiang. Stilwell arrived in China in March 1942 carrying orders to help improve the combat capabilities of the Chinese army, and he quickly proposed sweeping reforms. He advocated the training and equipment under American supervision of a thirty-division force that would assist in the reconquest of northern Burma, thereby reopening an overland supply route to China. Attaining this objective was critical because the only Allied line of communication to China since the fall of Burma in May 1942 was the air route over the Hump of the Himalayas between Assam in India and Kunming in China. Stilwell's plans also called for the creation of a second group of thirty divisions that would participate in a campaign to open a port in Japanese-occupied East China. Stilwell eventually hoped for American assistance in establishing a third thirty-division force. Together, these troops would provide Chiang with a formidable and efficient army for waging war against Japan as well as bolstering his power against domestic rivals.[4]

Stilwell's proposals involved major changes in Chinese military organization. The Nationalist armies consisted of approximately 3.8 million men organized in over 300 divisions, most of which were understrength and ill-equipped. Many of the local commanders were virtually autonomous; many, as well, were venal and placed personal gain above military efficiency when it came to paying and outfitting their troops. Chiang maintained their loyalty by shrewdly distributing supplies and patronage. Furthermore, he managed the Nationalist armies with political considerations firmly in mind. Many of his best troops blockaded areas of Communist strength throughout the war; others that were resisting Japanese advances failed to receive vital supplies.[5] Stilwell's reforms threatened to sweep away this system, thereby weakening Chiang's hold on his primary source of power.[6]

While Stilwell pressed for the reorganization of the Nationalist armies, Chiang resisted. He delayed sending troops to the training center that Stilwell established in Yunnan. He also embraced proposals advanced by General Claire L. Chennault, the commander of a small air task force in China, that challenged Stilwell's plans. A zealous advocate of air power, Chennault promised Roosevelt in October 1942 that he could bring Japan to its knees with a force of just 147 planes. Chennault's air strategy appealed to the generalissimo since it in no way jeopardized Chiang's system of political and military control. Chennault's ideas also interested Roosevelt, who hoped that an air offensive might inflict immediate and substantial losses on the Japanese at little cost to the United States. Roosevelt also feared a Chinese collapse and was unwilling to use lend-lease, as Stilwell recommended, to prod Chiang into reform of the army. In May 1943, despite contrary advice from General Marshall, the army chief of staff, and Secretary of War Henry L. Stimson, he ordered that supplies for Chennault's air force receive top priority in the Hump airlift. This decision, which held the flow of ground force equipment to a trickle, was a major blow to Stilwell's program.[7]

During the next year, Stilwell's plans collapsed. The reorganization and training of Nationalist units in Yunnan progressed slowly, hampered by lack of equipment and Chiang's erratic cooperation. "I have told him [Chiang] the truth," Stilwell fumed. "All of this he ignores and shuts his eyes to the deplorable condition of his army." Infuriated by Chiang's stubbornness, Stilwell barely concealed his contempt from the man he privately called Peanut. By the autumn of 1943 American military authorities shared Stilwell's conviction that the Nationalist armies would be unable to make a major contribution to the defeat of Japan. When Soviet Premier Josef V. Stalin stated in October that his armies would enter the war against Japan after the surrender of Germany, China's importance in American strategic planning declined even further. Although Roosevelt casually approved Chiang's request at the Cairo Conference in November 1943 to equip ninety Chinese divisions, military officials actually scaled down plans for aid to China. By early 1944 any hope of building a modern army in China had vanished.[8]

American officials instead worried about averting the collapse of the Nationalist war effort. In April 1944 the Japanese launched a powerful offensive in East China that overwhelmed the Nationalist defenders. The advancing forces seized Chennault's forward bases and appeared to threaten Kunming, the eastern terminus of the Hump route, and Chungking, the Nationalist capital. "What I am trying to find out," Roosevelt complained, "is where is the Chinese Army and why aren't they fighting, because the Japanese seem to be able to push them in any direction they want to."[9] On the advice of the Joint Chiefs of Staff, Roosevelt made an extraordinary proposal: he asked Chiang on 6 July to place Stilwell in command of all Chinese forces, including the Communists. He explained to the generalissimo that such a drastic measure was necessary because "the future of all Asia is at stake along with the tremendous effort which America has expended in that region."[10]

At stake for Chiang was his leadership of China, and he refused to cooperate. He was unwilling to surrender control of his armies to Stilwell—his bitter, personal antagonist—or to acquiesce in lend-lease aid to the Communists. After temporizing until the end of September, he demanded Stilwell's recall. Roosevelt reluctantly complied and named General Albert C. Wedemeyer as Stilwell's replacement. The president and his top advisers now abandoned all hope of persuading Chiang to step up his military effort against the Japanese. Roosevelt did not want Wedemeyer to command the Chinese armies; the Joint Chiefs of Staff did not order him, as they had Stilwell, to attempt to strengthen the Nationalist ground forces. "If Chiang Kai-shek had supported Stilwell, we should have had a well-trained nucleus of . . . Chinese troops to meet them [the Japanese]," Stimson wrote bitterly in his diary. "As it is, they are still impotent Chinese, untrained and badly led."[11]

The Nationalists' military disabilities, however, were a marginal concern in Washington during the last months of the war. After Stilwell's recall, American interests in China increasingly focused on postwar objectives. Roosevelt continued to believe that despite its "temporary weakness," China "would someday . . . be the most important factor in the whole Far East."[12] He worried that a civil war, which might encourage Soviet intervention or bring to power a Communist regime, would destroy his plans for postwar Russian-American cooperation. His remedy was a coalition between the Nationalists and the Communists, an arrangement he considered the best hope for unity and stability in China.[13]

The State Department's China experts also thought that the United States should try to promote a settlement between the Nationalists and the Communists, but cautioned against overcommitment to Chiang. Foreign Service Officers John P. Davies, Jr., and John S. Service reported that the Nationalist government, dominated by Chiang's Kuomintang party, was corrupt and decadent and concerned only with preserving, rather than sharing, its declining power. The Communists, by contrast, possessed popular appeal, dynamic leadership, and waxing military strength. They warned that Chiang's unwillingness to relinquish one-party rule would only hasten the onset of a civil war that the Kuomintang could not hope to win. Service and Davies recommended that the United States should not exclusively support Chiang's increasingly reactionary and repressive regime but instead should induce the generalissimo to carry out reforms and make meaningful concessions to the Communists. They also urged American military cooperation with the Communists in the war against Japan. By working with both the Kuomintang and the Communists, Service explained, the United States could avoid alignment with either party and preserve friendly relations with any government that might eventually come to power.[14]

Such thinking was anathema to Patrick J. Hurley, the new American ambassador in Chungking. Hurley had been President Herbert C. Hoover's secretary of war and Roosevelt's diplomatic troubleshooter in the Middle East. Although he possessed only a slim knowledge of Chinese affairs when he assumed his post in November 1944, Hurley was so certain of the Kuomintang's vitality and so optimistic about the prospects for unity under Chiang's leadership that he suppressed embassy reports to the contrary. The breakdown of his mediation efforts at the end of 1944 did not shake his conviction that he could compose the differences between the two major Chinese factions. Hurley thought that the Communists, whose strength he greatly underestimated, would eventually have to come to terms with Chiang. He vehemently opposed any American military cooperation with the Communists without Chiang's consent, because he worried that their leader, Mao Tse-tung, might become intransigent in negotiations. Despite a growing belief in the State Department that the United States was tying itself too closely to a faltering regime, Hurley adamantly insisted that his mission, for which he claimed presidential sanction, was to prevent the collapse of the Nationalist government and to sustain Chiang's leadership.[15]

The State Department nevertheless continued to advocate a flexible policy toward Chiang's regime. John Carter Vincent, the chief of the Division of Chinese Affairs, advised the War Department in January 1945 that the United States should distinguish between the immediate goal of mobilizing China's resources against Japan and the eventual goal of helping to develop a "united, democratically progressive, and cooperative China." Current support of Chiang, Vincent asserted, should not preclude future cooperation with another leader who might have a better chance of creating a unified and democratic China.

Accordingly, he recommended that Wedemeyer avoid strengthening Chiang's armies for postwar purposes. Lend-lease aid should be given only to those Nationalist forces that contributed to the war effort.[16]

The conflict between the State Department and Hurley peaked in March 1945 over the extension of military aid to the Communists. Distressed by the failure of Hurley's renewed mediation efforts and the outbreak of skirmishes between Nationalist and Communist forces, Vincent argued that Chiang's reluctance to offer the Communists more than token representation in his government was preventing an internal settlement. Setting aside his earlier reservations, Vincent now advocated the provision of arms to the Communists without first securing Chiang's consent. He thought that this action would not only strengthen the war effort against the Japanese, but also prod Chiang into making genuine concessions to the Communists.[17] The embassy staff in Chungking agreed. While Hurley was en route to Washington for consultations, his subordinates reported on 28 February that Chiang's liberal critics believed that no American action could do more to make the generalissimo come to terms with the Communists. Acting Secretary of State Joseph C. Grew sent a copy of this message to Roosevelt with the suggestion that it serve as a basis for discussion with the ambassador.[18]

Hurley was enraged. He considered the dispatch from Chungking an act of disloyalty by his subordinates. Furthermore, he vehemently maintained that their recommendations, if implemented, would destroy his efforts to arrange an accommodation between the two Chinese parties. Roosevelt supported Hurley, but for different reasons. The president was banking on Soviet cooperation, rather than Hurley's negotiations, to bring peace and unity to China. At the Yalta Conference in February, Roosevelt agreed to territorial concessions in East Asia in return for Soviet entry into the war against Japan and Stalin's support of the Nationalist government. He reasoned that the Communists, unable to count on Moscow's assistance, would have to compromise with Chiang. Military aid to the Communists, Roosevelt feared, would make them less compliant and so increase the chances of civil war. Assured of Roosevelt's backing, Hurley purged the embassy staff. Policymakers in Washington gave no further consideration, for the duration of the war, to arming the Communists.[19]

Soon after Roosevelt's decision to furnish wartime military aid solely to the Nationalists, defense and diplomatic officials discussed postwar military assistance. The army air forces took the lead. On 21 March General Henry H. Arnold, the commanding general of the army air forces (AAF), approved a tentative plan based on the recommendations of Chennault and Wedemeyer for extensive American help in building a Chinese air force of forty and one-half air groups—a total of 1,922 planes—which amounted to a six-fold expansion of Chinese air strength.[20] The AAF plan also called for the establishment of an American advisory group of 1,895 officers and men to train Chinese pilots and ground crews. Arnold thought that this extravagant air force was necessary "to assure a stable government [in China] capable of taking a prominent position among the Allied Nations in an effort to maintain world peace."[21]

Parochial interests strongly influenced Arnold's China proposals, just as they had affected his plans for Latin America. A large Chinese air force standardized on American equipment would help the AAF achieve one of its most important postwar objectives: the maintenance of a large domestic aircraft industry. Staff planners, however, felt that the United States would face stern competition from other nations, especially the Soviet Union, that wanted to sell military and commercial aircraft to China. In their view, one of the main reasons for offering the Chinese abundant air assistance was to prevent such competition. The planners stated bluntly, "We should be prepared to meet all offers by other nations." American generosity, they added, could also forestall "for some years" the construction of Chinese aircraft and engine factories. In China, as in Latin America, the AAF aggressively sought to dominate postwar markets for aircraft.[22]

The State Department quickly urged restraint. They argued that any postwar military obligations to the Nationalist government would make Chiang even more intractable and deprive American policy of any continuing freedom of action. The State Department also discounted the AAF's anxieties that other nations were eager to equip the Chinese air force. They averred that Great Britain lacked the resources, and that the Soviet Union would probably extend any military help to the Communists. While hoping that a strong and united China with modern armed forces would eventually become an anchor of stability in East Asia, the State Department believed that the United States should confine its measures of military aid to wartime projects until China solved its internal problems. At State's request the State-War-Navy Coordinating Committee (SWNCC) and the Joint Chiefs of Staff agreed in May to defer planning for postwar military assistance to China.[23]

Although the State Department refrained from making any new commitments to the Nationalists, American military support of Chiang's armies increased during the final months of the war. Because of the opening of a supply route through Burma and the expansion of the Hump airlift, military aid flowed to the Nationalist armed forces in larger amounts than ever before. Wedemeyer used these supplies to build thirty-nine Chinese divisions. By V-J Day most of the American-sponsored (Alpha) units had completed several weeks of training; many also benefited from an improved system of rations that helped relieve malnutrition, a major problem in the Nationalist armies. But only five divisions received full equipment before the Japanese surrender, and even these troops the Nationalists could not support reliably in battle.[24] Even though Chiang's forces made some gains against the Japanese near the end of the war, American advisers had no illusions about the Nationalists' military strength. "Our small successes," Wedemeyer knew, "were due as much to the enemy decision to withdraw as to increased Chinese spirit and military effectiveness."[25]

The political consequences of American military support of Chiang's armies were far greater. Confident of American backing, the generalissimo refused to share power with his domestic rivals. Mao, on the other hand, grew increasingly mistrustful of American policy. Despite their aim of peace and unity in China, American actions actually encouraged division and conflict. "While favoring no political faction, we continue to support the existing Government of China, headed by Chiang Kai-shek," the State Department informed President Truman shortly after he took office. At war's end neither Truman nor his top advisers appreciated the contradiction in that statement.[26]

The Japanese surrender of 14 August 1945 brought the end of one war in China and the renewal of another. Conflict erupted immediately between the Nationalists and the Communists over the reoccupation of areas under Japanese control. Allied directives required the Japanese in China proper to lay down their arms only to Chiang or his representatives. General Chu Teh, the Communist commander, angrily protested these arrangements and asserted that the Communists would not be prevented from sharing in the victory for which they had fought.

Aware that the future of China hung in the balance, both sides rushed troops into strategic areas of North and Central China. Clashes between Nationalist and Communist forces inevitably followed.[27]

Chiang relied heavily on American assistance in this race for supremacy in China. On 10 August the Joint Chiefs of Staff authorized Wedemeyer to help Chiang's armies reoccupy important areas held by the Japanese. At the same time, the service leaders specifically prohibited Wedemeyer, while discharging this mission, from backing the Nationalists in civil strife. Yet American aid inevitably supported Chiang's efforts to vanquish his Communist foes. With the help of Wedemeyer's staff, members of the National Military Council worked out a plan to rush Nationalist troops, concentrated in South China, to ports and cities in the North before Communist forces could arrive.[28] In early September American transport aircraft began ferrying Nationalist armies to Shanghai and Nanking, the area to which planners assigned highest priority. At the end of the month 50,000 American marines came ashore to secure ports, airfields, and railroad lines in Tientsin, Tsingtao, and Chefoo. Although the mission of the marines was not clearly specified before their deployment, one of the principal effects of their presence was to help Chiang's armies extend Nationalist control.[29]

Lend-lease also kept flowing to the Nationalist armed forces. The Joint Chiefs authorized the continuation of lend-lease in response to Wedemeyer's pleas that the United States do everything possible to avert the outbreak of civil war in China, even to the point of ranking China ahead of Japan in the allocation of occupation troops and supplies. The service chieftains rejected Wedemeyer's priorities, but agreed to the continuation of lend-lease to enable the Nationalists to take control of Japanese-occupied areas. In the first two months after V-J Day, military lend-lease amounted to some $430 million, more than half the value of wartime arms aid. This timely and extensive material assistance, along with troop support and transportation aid, enabled Nationalist forces to establish their authority in the major cities of North and Central China.[30]

Chiang also sought long-term commitments for American military assistance that would further strengthen his position against the Communists. He reminded Hurley on 11 August of Roosevelt's statement at the Cairo Conference that the United States would equip ninety Chinese divisions. Chiang insisted that this obligation did not expire at the end of the war and asked for the outstanding equipment so that the Nationalist government would be able "to sustain itself against armed factions in China." Chiang also desired the establishment of an American military advisory group, which he hoped Wedemeyer might head, to help the Nationalists build modern armed forces and reorganize their arsenal and supply services. Premier T. V. Soong presented these requests to Truman on 30 August and announced that he was prepared immediately to discuss arrangements for their implementation.[31]

Service officials were almost as eager to provide military assistance as the Nationalists were to obtain it. Wedemeyer recommended approval of the military advisory group and supported the continued supply of American equipment to the Nationalist armed forces, although he had reservations about meeting Chiang's extravagant demands for a ninety-division force.[32] Admiral William D. Leahy, Truman's chief of staff, urged the president to help Chiang build "a well armed and well trained army."[33] Secretary of the Navy James V. Forrestal responded with alacrity to Chiang's desire for American naval assistance. He forwarded to Truman on 24 August draft legislation for the creation of a naval advisory group and the transfer of surplus vessels.[34]

The AAF pressed even more vigorously for extended military cooperation with the Nationalists. On 23 August Arnold approved a new plan, known as PALMYRA, for American support of thirteen and one-half Chinese air groups. Although less ambitious than the previous AAF proposal, PALMYRA still involved a major expenditure of resources: supply of 311 additional aircraft, training of 7,700 Chinese personnel, and establishment of an American air mission of 1,300 men. AAF planners thought that these measures of assistance would help the Nationalist government consolidate its power and bring stability to postwar China. PALMYRA thus aimed at the same objectives that Wedemeyer had in assisting Chiang in reoccupying Japanese-held territory. The AAF reiterated many earlier warnings about foreign designs on the Chinese market for aircraft and voiced new fears of possible Soviet military aid to Chiang if the United States failed to act swiftly. Wedemeyer, too, supported PALMYRA and emphasized both its military and economic benefits. "Stated bluntly," he told the War Department, "we are today on the ground floor and should not lose [the] existing opportunity to insure full American participation" in the development of military and commercial air facilities in China.[35]

Reflecting the services' desire to expand their military influence in China, the State, War, and Navy departments recommended to Truman on 13 September that he reply favorably to Chiang's request for long-term assistance. The president called in Soong the next day and told him that the United States would help the Nationalists develop armed forces of moderate size for the maintenance of internal security and the assumption of control over liberated areas. He dismissed Soong's request to arm ninety Chinese divisions by replying evasively that he could find no record of Roosevelt's pledge at Cairo to provide such assistance.[36] He promised instead, pending further studies by the Joint Chiefs, supplies to complete the thirty-nine-division program begun during the war, equipment for an air force of commensurate size, and naval craft for coastal and river operations. This assistance, Truman admonished Soong, would be furnished on the condition that it "not be diverted for use in fratricidal warfare or to support undemocratic administration."[37]

Uniformed officers quickly pointed out that this stipulation was unrealistic. General George A. Lincoln, the army's chief strategic planner, told his colleagues on the Joint Staff that Chiang's regime was undemocratic and there was great doubt that any government in China would enjoy widespread popular support. Requiring foreign governments to conform to standards of liberal democracy, a solution that appealed to most Americans, simply would not work in China. Wedemeyer also had reservations about American objectives in China. He told the War Department that he was deeply perplexed by the contradiction between American military backing of Chiang's bid to unify China, and simultaneous instructions to avoid intervention in China's civil conflict. But his attempts to secure a clarification from Washington during the first weeks of peace proved unavailing.[38]

Detailed proposals by the Joint Chiefs of Staff for prolonged assistance to the Nationalists pointed up the need for a more precise definition of American policy toward China. The Joint Chiefs recommended the creation of a military advisory group of some 4,000 army and navy personnel. In return they sought extensive concessions, some of which—such as American supervision of Chinese commercial aviation and communications, and preferential treatment of American business interests—had no relation whatsoever to the operation of the advisory group. The service chiefs also proposed that the United States plan to equip a Chinese army of fifty divisions, an air force of eighteen groups, and a navy adequate to police the coast and inland waterways. Anxious that the Nationalists might look elsewhere for assistance and eager to dispose of surplus materiel in East Asia, the Joint Chiefs asked for prompt implementation of these measures of assistance.[39]

The scope of the Joint Chiefs' plans disturbed John Carter Vincent, the new director of State's Office of Far Eastern Affairs. Vincent was concerned that the services were aiming at establishing what amounted to a protectorate over China, with a semicolonial army under American supervision. He also suggested that the contemplated military assistance might redound against American security interests by creating friction with the Soviet Union. Most troubling to him was the probable effect of such assistance on the prospects for Chinese unity. With extraordinary prescience, Vincent warned Secretary of State James F. Byrnes that "if the Group serves simply to encourage Chiang to seek a settlement of his difficulties by means of force and if the maintenance of unity in China were to become dependent upon American military assistance in the form of materiél [sic] and advice, we would find ourselves in an unenviable, and perhaps untenable, position."[40]

Reports from Wedemeyer also called attention to the perils of American military involvement in China. As hostilities between Nationalist and Communist forces spread through North China, Wedemeyer informed the War Department that the United States could not continue to furnish Chiang military support without participating directly in civil strife. Mindful of instructions to avoid such intervention, he refused in early November to transport additional armies to North China because Chiang intended to use them not to disarm the Japanese but to fight the Communists. (Indeed, the generalissimo was in no hurry to repatriate the Japanese since he was using former enemy troops to protect lines of communication against Communist guerrillas.) Wedemeyer also recommended the withdrawal of the marines beginning on 15 November, since they had discharged their mission of guarding important installations in North China pending the arrival of Nationalist forces.[41]

Wedemeyer's request for guidance from Washington started a major review of American policy toward China. At issue, Assistant Secretary of War John J. McCloy told a meeting of the Committee of Three on 6 November, was "how far we should back Chiang in his efforts to unify the country." McCloy believed that the United States already had "a considerable investment" in the Nationalists. Evacuation of the marines, even if they had fulfilled the original mission, would be a blow to Chiang's prestige. The generalissimo needed their help to repatriate the Japanese, but even more "to increase his Army's strength in North China against the communists." McCloy worried that Chiang's inability to maintain internal order might provide Soviet troops, which occupied Manchuria during the last week of the war, with an excuse to delay their withdrawal. Despite his mistrust of Russian ambitions, McCloy hesitated to endorse unrestricted military backing of Chiang. Although he considered American support of the Nationalists essential to stability in China, he also cautioned that similar Russian aid to the Communists would result "in a real mess."[42]

Far less subtle and much less informed was Truman's analysis. A note found with his daily appointment sheets revealed that the president remained wedded to the fiction that "we are not mixing in China's internal affairs." Showing startling ignorance of the history of the China theater in World War II, Truman declared that Chiang's armies had fought "side by side with us against our common enemy." The Communists, by contrast, "not only did not help us but on occasion helped the Japs." Furthermore, the president reasoned, the Nationalist government had been recognized by most major powers, including the Soviet Union. Because of the presence of large numbers of Japanese troops in Central China, Truman concluded, the United States was providing assistance for nothing more than "mopping up the war."[43]

Before top officials in Washington could reach any decisions about the continuation of aid to China, Chiang made new demands. His ambitions soaring, the generalissimo pressed Wedemeyer for the transportation of troops into Manchuria. Wedemeyer counseled against such a move out of concern that the Nationalists would stretch their forces dangerously thin. He also advised Marshall that the diversion of government armies from North China to Manchuria would prolong the stay of the marines indefinitely. Once again, he asked the War Department for instructions.[44]

A preliminary reply to Wedemeyer on 19 November revealed that the administration was caught on the horns of a dilemma. Secretary of State Byrnes, the War Department informed Wedemeyer, wished neither "to support the National Government directly against the Communists" nor to abandon "a policy we have long supported which contemplated unifying China and Manchuria under Chinese National Forces." For the time being, Byrnes desired the retention of the marines in North China, but ruled out military backing of the Nationalists "except in so far as necessary to get the Japanese disarmed and out of China." Before making further decisions, the secretary of state wanted Wedemeyer's estimate of Chiang's need for American help in clearing the Japanese from North China and Manchuria.[45]

Wedemeyer submitted a series of long and discouraging analyses of the growing chaos in China. He reported to the War Department that Chiang's reach far exceeded his grasp. Without large-scale assistance, the Nationalists might not be able to establish their authority in North China, to say nothing of Manchuria, for years. Wedemeyer blamed the disorder in China not only on the Communists, whose guerrilla operations disrupted transport and communications in the North, but also on the Nationalists, whose corruption and incompetence alienated local inhabitants. Wedemeyer told the War Department that Chiang was counting heavily on American help to relieve his difficulties. The generalissimo contemplated using the marines "as a base of maneuver" while mounting a campaign against the Communists. His aim was "to create conditions that render our military assistance against the Chinese Communists, and possibly the Soviet Communists, mandatory or inevitable."

The possibility of a Soviet-American confrontation in China troubled Wedemeyer. Despite the signature of a treaty of friendship between Moscow and Chungking on 14 August 1945, Wedemeyer was suspicious of Soviet ambitions. He told the Joint Staff Planners during a visit to Washington in October that the Russians were "determined to penetrate North China and to set up a buffer area there similar to what they have done in Europe."[46] Indeed, the Russians were exploiting the industrial and natural resources of Manchuria and appeared to oppose the extension of Nationalist control into the provinces bordering the Soviet Union.[47] In mid-November Wedemeyer repeated his earlier warnings and expressed new fears about the expansion of Soviet power: "If China were to become a puppet of the Soviet which is exactly what a Chinese Communist victory would mean, then Soviet Russia would practically control the continents of Europe and Asia. . . . We were determined to prevent Japan from making China a puppet power. It is believed even more important, if we are to realize our policies with reference to China, that Russia not be permitted to do so." Yet Wedemeyer knew that opposition to Russian aspirations in China carried grave risks, including war with the Soviet Union.

Wedemeyer emphasized that the administration would have to decide quickly whether it was willing to accept these consequences because the current American position in China was "untenable." He asserted once more that the retention of the marines in North China to help with the evacuation of the Japanese would not result merely in incidental assistance to the Nationalists but in "definite participation in fratricidal warfare." Owing to the Communists' desire to obtain Japanese weapons and to arouse opposition to the presence of American military forces, "armed conflicts between Americans and Chinese" were unavoidable. Wedemeyer thought that administration officials had to choose among three alternatives: withdrawal of all American troops from China, direct and extensive intervention to unify China under Nationalist rule, or establishment of a trusteeship over Manchuria and repatriation of the Japanese under the auspices of the United Nations, after which the Chinese would determine their own future "through processes of evolution or revolution." Wedemeyer made no definite recommendation to his superiors, but implied that he favored the third course of action.[48]

Forrestal and Secretary of War Robert P. Patterson opted instead for continued military backing of Chiang. In a memorandum to Byrnes on 16 November they discounted Wedemeyer's contention that the Nationalists had little chance of gaining control of North China and Manchuria.[49] Forrestal and Patterson doubted that the Communists could mount a strong challenge to the Nationalist armies and insisted that Chiang, despite his weaknesses, still had the best chance of unifying China in the near future. Defining America's goal in East Asia as "a unified China, including Manchuria, friendly to the U.S.," they favored keeping the marines in China, stepping up efforts to repatriate the Japanese, and speeding arrangements for the establishment of a military advisory group. Although conceding that these measures constituted intervention in China's civil conflict, they maintained that the consequences of halting military assistance to the Nationalists were far more serious. Echoing Wedemeyer, they warned that withdrawal of American support from China might lead to the disintegration of China into several states or the expansion of Soviet power until "Russia will have achieved in the Far East approximately the objectives Japan initially set out to accomplish." Containing the expansion of Soviet power, Forrestal and Patterson asserted, was the most important reason for furnishing military aid to Chiang.[50]

Like their colleagues in the military establishment, State Department officials also weighed several options in China policy. At the request of Under Secretary Dean Acheson, Vincent drew up a comprehensive memorandum on 19 November that discussed four possible courses of action: withdrawal of marines, continuation of present policies, expansion of military assistance to the Nationalists, and initiation of measures to end the civil strife in China. Vincent preferred the last alternative. Because of his conviction that the United States had an obligation to help in establishing a progressive government that could unify China, Vincent wanted to encourage the Chinese to solve their problems through political rather than military methods. Accordingly, he thought that the administration should accelerate its efforts to repatriate the Japanese while putting pressure on the Nationalists and the Communists to accept a truce and negotiate a settlement. Once the Japanese were cleared from China, Vincent favored a suspension of economic and military assistance until the two Chinese parties resolved their difference.[51]

Vincent's memorandum and Wedemeyer's reports strengthened the State Department's opposition to major military intervention in China. During a meeting of the Committee of Three on 27 November, both Byrnes and Acheson urged restraint on their service colleagues. Byrnes, who was more concerned about the situation in China than that in any other country, suggested that the wisest course of action was to press for an accord between the Nationalists and the Communists, partly by using military aid as a lever to gain Chiang's cooperation. Acheson outlined a tentative approach that drew on the recommendations of both Vincent and the service secretaries. He proposed American assistance in supplying additional armies and transporting them to North China, arranging a truce in areas cleared of Japanese, and establishing a coalition government, especially by exerting pressure on Chiang to make meaningful concessions. While the policymakers reached no agreement at this meeting, Byrnes hoped that they might soon decide on a program that Hurley, who was in Washington for consultations, could take back to China.[52]

But only hours later, Hurley abruptly resigned. Since returning to the United States in September, Hurley had tried to quit his post on several occasions, but Byrnes had dissuaded him. On the morning of the twenty-seventh he assured the secretary of state that he would soon depart for Chungking. Then new fears about State Department opposition to his policy of supporting Chiang beset him, and he suddenly changed his mind. Without warning, he released a vitriolic letter of resignation that blamed subversives within the Foreign Service for the failure of his efforts to mediate the dispute between the Nationalists and the Communists. "See what a son-of-a-bitch did to me," Truman cried that afternoon as he showed his cabinet news reports of Hurley's outburst. Secretary of Agriculture Clinton P. Anderson suggested that the appointment of General George C. Marshall, who possessed towering prestige, would help avert a furor over Hurley's spectacular charges. Later that day, Marshall, who only a week earlier had retired as army chief of staff, dutifully accepted Truman's request to become the president's personal representative to China.[53]

During the next two weeks the State and War departments debated Marshall's instructions. Political and military officials agreed that Marshall should continue Hurley's efforts to bring about a coalition government under Chiang's leadership. Byrnes warned that a divided China would be an invitation to Soviet intervention, a fear shared by other senior policymakers, including Truman.[54] Both State and War analysts also advocated continued American help in clearing the Japanese from China and establishing Nationalist authority in North China and Manchuria. They disagreed, however, about the timing of these measures. Marshall and his uniformed advisers wanted to rush Chiang's troops northward without delay. Vincent and State's China experts thought that a political settlement should precede further military assistance to Chiang.[55]

At a meeting on 11 December Truman, Marshall, Byrnes, and Leahy settled these differences. They decided that the United States would furnish military assistance to speed the removal of the Japanese from China and, despite Wedemeyer's warnings, to enable Chiang to take control of Manchuria. The services would prepare to transfer additional Nationalist troops to North China but would keep these arrangements secret for the time being. If the Communists blocked negotiations toward an internal settlement—the eventuality Marshall considered most likely—Marshall would authorize the movement of Chiang's forces into North China. But if the generalissimo stalled the discussions, Marshall thought that the administration "would have to swallow its pride and much of its policy" and continue to back Chiang. Otherwise "there would follow the tragic consequences of a divided China," leading to Russian hegemony in Manchuria and "the defeat or loss of the major purpose of our war in the Pacific." Byrnes, who had earlier suggested that the administration withhold military and economic aid from Chiang should he refuse to make reasonable concessions to the Communists, now deferred to Marshall's position, as did Truman. Three days later the president confirmed the general's instructions. Marshall would pressure Chiang, but not to the point of withdrawing military assistance. Once again American policymakers refused to call Chiang's bluff.[56]

"I know very little about Chinese politics," Truman told Secretary of Commerce Henry A. Wallace in January 1946. "The one thing I am interested in is to see a strong China with a Democratic form of Government friendly to us."[57] The Marshall Mission aimed at this objective but also pursued a contradictory policy: military support for Chiang against the Communists. Vincent was one of the few government officials who recognized the incompatibility of these goals. He predicted that movement of Chiang's troops into the North would not prevent civil war but would simply allow the Nationalists, like the Japanese, to take over the main urban centers and lines of communication while the Communists held the countryside. With equal foresight, a member of the American Observer Group at Yenan wrote to Wedemeyer that Chiang would not negotiate seriously as long as he felt that he could count on American aid to help him subjugate the Communists. These warnings were ignored or rejected. Only after several months in China did Marshall realize that American military aid policy was impeding rather than fostering peace and unity in China.[58]

The Marshall Mission began auspiciously. After listening to representatives of all Chinese factions, Marshall entered into negotiations with Chang Chun, Chiang's emissary, and Chou En-lai, Mao's envoy. These discussions led to a cease-fire on 10 January 1946 and the creation of an Executive Headquarters made up of American, Nationalist, and Communist commissioners to supervise the armistice. Marshall also persuaded Chiang to convene a Political Consultative Council, which passed resolutions granting equality to all political parties and providing for the adoption of a new constitution. Marshall considered his most important achievement the agreement of both parties on 25 February to the establishment during the next eighteen months of a unified peacetime army consisting of fifty Nationalist and ten Communist divisions. By the time Marshall returned to Washington in March for consultations, success in China appeared to be within reach.[59]

During his first months in China Marshall relied heavily on military assistance as an instrument of persuasion. He offered military aid to both parties as an inducement to cooperation. To overcome Mao's hesitations about an integrated army, the general promised equipment and training for ten Communist divisions so that they would not be at a disadvantage with the American-equipped Nationalist units. Marshall also constantly dangled the prospect of American assistance before Chiang to gain concessions from him. He repeatedly emphasized China's critical need for economic and military aid, but made clear that without an internal settlement the generalissimo could not expect additional American help. Marshall strongly believed that American assistance was essential to unity in China. "Without the most liberal kind of American aid," Marshall's attaché told Truman, "the chances of the new coalition Government to succeed are dismal."[60]

Yet American military aid policy was by no means evenhanded. While Marshall used the promise of military aid to foster negotiations, the United States gave Chiang critical military backing that reinforced his preference for conquest rather than compromise. Perhaps the most important measure of assistance was the transportation during the first five months of 1946 of 225,597 Kuomintang soldiers into Manchuria.[61] Wedemeyer outfitted these troops and supplied their operational needs, and such help counted as a charge on the thirty-nine-division program.[62] Without this assistance Chiang's bid for control in North China would have been impossible. Added to this lend-lease aid was the sale of surplus combat equipment. The first such transfer occurred in November 1945, when the United States sold a substantial stockpile of materiel in West China for the nominal price of $20 million.[63] Finally, the marines continued to guard important supply depots and communications routes for the Nationalists. Many of Truman's top advisers agreed with Forrestal that during the first half of 1946 the marines were "the balance of order" in China. Indeed, Acheson told the Cabinet on 2 August that withdrawal of the marines would be "foolhardy" because they were helping to prevent "some other country from interfering in China to our own regret."[64]

In early 1946 the Truman administration also established the military advisory group that Chiang had requested at the end of the war.

Soon after Marshall left for China, representatives of the War and Navy departments urged SWNCC to approve the Joint Chiefs' plan for a mission of approximately 4,000 American personnel. In a memorandum to the SWNCC Assistant Secretary of War Howard C. Petersen reiterated the services' conviction that prompt action was necessary to prevent Chiang from turning to the Russians for assistance and to avoid dissipating the military influence that the United States had developed in China during the war. Patterson expressed similar views and Marshall added his support, pointing out that the early creation of the advisory group would hasten the deactivation of the China Theater, thereby putting pressure on the Russians to remove their troops from Manchuria.[65]

The State Department, however, continued to oppose the services' plan for an advisory group. Drawing on Vincent's views, Byrnes complained to the SWNCC that the Joint Chiefs aimed at creating not an advisory mission but "a military training group which would permeate throughout the Chinese Army on an operational level." He also thought that the Joint Chiefs had disregarded larger American security interests: their plans, if "construed as a projection of U.S. military power onto the Asiatic continent rather than as simply aid to China in modernizing its Army," might invite a comparable extension of Russian power. Unwilling to consent to the services' extravagant proposals, Byrnes asked the Joint Chiefs to review their recommendation.[66]

The Joint Chiefs, concerned that further delay in establishing an advisory group might cause Chiang to accept Russian or British assistance, did so.[67] Drawing on suggestions from Wedemeyer and Marshall, the service chiefs now urged the immediate creation of a military mission with an initial strength of 750 army and 165 navy personnel, whose primary function would be to advise the higher staffs of the Chinese defense establishment on organizational and training matters. Although Vincent worried that the services still desired eventually to expand the advisory group, he did not challenge the Joint Chiefs' revised proposals. On 25 February Truman authorized the creation of an American military group in China with a strength of 1,000 officers and men.[68] Even though intended to help in the training of a unified Chinese army, this mission offered assistance exclusively to the Nationalist military forces.[69]

Chiang also received American help in building up his air force. Again under pressure from the State Department, the services pared down their earlier proposals for air assistance. Wedemeyer submitted in January 1946 a revised plan, which the Joint Chiefs promptly approved, for American assistance to a Chinese air force of eight and one-third groups. In carrying out this program, he assigned highest priority to the development of two troop-carrier groups because of their value to Chiang in his efforts to unify the country. Parochial service interests also shaped plans for the Chinese air force. AAF officials, for example, pressed for the establishment of a heavy-bomber (B-24) group because the Chinese would then have to build and maintain facilities that the United States might need to use in the event of an emergency.[70] Under lend-lease and surplus property arrangements, the United States transferred in the spring of 1946 $40 million worth of air force equipment and provided training for approximately 3,500 Chinese pilots and technicians.[71]

These various measures of military assistance encouraged the Kuomintang hard-liners who wanted to eliminate the Communists by force of arms. Bolstered by approximately $700 million in lend-lease aid in the year after the Japanese surrender, the 3-million-man Nationalist army was superior to the Communists in manpower, equipment, and training. The Communists, with 300,000 regulars, half of whom were armed, received indirect help from the Soviets, who abandoned to them captured Japanese weapons in Manchuria. Estimates of this Japanese materiel varied, but there was no doubt that the Communists lacked the equipment and the manpower to stand in pitched battle with the Nationalists. Discounting the effectiveness of Communist guerrilla operations, Kuomintang leaders believed that they could achieve an easy military victory over Mao's forces even if, as T. V. Soong once boasted to Forrestal, the United States withdrew its troops from China.[72]

Chiang's confidence in his ability to win on the battlefield undermined Marshall's negotiations. While the general was in Washington, widespread fighting broke out in Manchuria as both Nationalist and Communist forces attempted to fill the vacuum left by departing Soviet troops. Marshall returned to China in April 1946, but was unable to do more than piece together fragile truces. Deferring to the extremists in his party, Chiang showed almost no desire to compromise, despite Marshall's repeated warnings that the Nationalists could not unify China by force. He told Marshall that all-out civil war would be preferable to continued negotiations, an opinion that Soong echoed in conversations with Forrestal. "At least war did provide definite direction and objectives," Soong insisted, "whereas the present situation would enable the Communists to drag down the government piecemeal and by degrees." Following the expiration of a cease-fire on 30 June, Marshall could do little to stem the fighting in China. Chiang, however, was anything but discouraged by the failure of Marshall's peace efforts. In time, he confidently predicted, victory would fall to the Nationalists like ripe fruit.[73]

After returning to China in April, Marshall found that American military aid policy was hindering his efforts to repair the shattered accords. Communist leaders complained that American assistance was sustaining the Nationalist war effort. Chou pointed out that transportation of troops into Manchuria, guarding of Nationalist railroad lines by American marines, and continued supply of lend-lease munitions were at odds with the American desire to restore peace. While those measures disturbed the Communists, they emboldened the Kuomintang irreconcilables, as Marshall reported to Truman, "to push forward with a campaign of determination against the Communists." Marshall explained to both sides that although American military aid aimed at cementing rather than destroying unity, the effect of such assistance was just the opposite. The Communists feared and the Nationalists hoped that the United States would continue to back Chiang whether or not he made meaningful concessions to his adversaries.[74]

Nationalist bellicosity and Communist protests at last made Marshall aware of the contradictions in American military aid policy. During the spring and summer of 1946 he began to limit American military help to the Nationalists. Because of the fighting in Manchuria, he refused in early May to transport additional Kuomintang armies to the Northeast, and during the next two months he cut off shipments of troops and supplies in American vessels to North China as well.[75] Marshall also did nothing to prevent the death of an administration bill authorizing continuing military aid to China, fearing that its passage would further strengthen the reactionaries in the Nationalist government. Most important, Marshall arranged on 29 July for the imposition of an embargo on private and governmental transfers of combat equipment to the Nationalists.[76] These actions constituted a major reversal of American tactics. Instead of furnishing military aid to induce a settlement, Marshall now hoped that the withholding of such assistance would force the Nationalists to compromise.[77]

He was wrong. The changes in military aid policy did not make Chiang more compliant. Neither did a stern message from Truman on 10 August threatening a redefinition of American policy "unless convincing proof is shortly forthcoming that genuine progress is being made toward a peaceful settlement of China's internal problems." After months of futile negotiations, Marshall asked on 28 December to be recalled. Upon his departure from China on 7 January 1947, he issued a statement that castigated extremists on both sides for the failure to achieve peace and unity. "The salvation of the situation," he believed, lay in the formation of a new, liberal government, an attitude that reflected an all-too-common belief in the universal applicability of American institutions and values. Marshall was also keenly aware of the limits of American influence, however, and realized that the Chinese would have to settle such matters by themselves.[78]

"There has been much loose talk about China's becoming the stabilizing influence in the Far East," Acheson reminded Marshall in November 1946. "We have never felt that this was a possibility in the reasonably near future but we have hoped that China would not become an unstabilizing influence—which is an entirely different thing." Acheson's concern had been Roosevelt's as well, and since the beginning of 1945 American policy had aimed at encouraging Chinese unity in order to contain the growth of Russian power and avoid a possible Soviet-American confrontation in East Asia. Although Marshall failed to mediate the conflict between the Nationalists and the Communists, he was still determined to preserve a Soviet-American equilibrium in the Far East. Further American military assistance, Marshall believed, would not enable Chiang to defeat his foes; worse, such help might invite comparable Russian intervention.[79]

This concern about the extension of Communist power was a critical difference in the policy debates over postwar military aid to China and to Latin America. Administration officials worried about whether the provision, or restriction, of American arms assistance would affect the growth of Russian power in East Asia; they had little reason to fear Soviet penetration of Latin America. This difference accounted in large measure for the extension of far larger amounts of military assistance to China, even though American strategic interests were greater in Latin America. The Joint Chiefs considered U.S. predominance in Latin America an essential requirement of national security, but they thought that American interests in East Asia could be protected from the strategic frontier of the offshore islands. The prospect of Chinese disintegration or, even worse, the triumph of a Communist regime, however, made it imperative that the United States use its diplomatic influence and military resources to prevent the Soviet Union, as Truman feared, from taking "the place of Japan in the Far East."[80] Latin America, where there was no immediate danger, had to wait for American arms.

However different the magnitude of American assistance, the bureaucratic divisions over arms aid to China and Latin America were remarkably similar. In both cases, military planners clashed sharply with the State Department's regional experts. The former were eager to use arms assistance to secure bases, strategic resources, or customers for U.S. defense industries; the latter feared that such aid would prevent the development of democratic regimes and liberal institutions in Latin America and China. Marshall's military background and his enormous prestige kept the debate over aid to China during 1946 somewhat less acrimonious than the battles over the Western Hemisphere Defense Program. Yet the fundamental issue was the same: how much to rely on military aid as a means of securing American influence abroad.

Shortly after returning to the United States, Marshall became secretary of state and so continued to grapple with this question as the principal shaper of American policy toward China. Guided by a first-hand appreciation of Nationalist weaknesses and the limits of American ability to influence China's internal affairs, Marshall tried carefully to regulate the flow of American armaments to China. But events in other parts of the world complicated his efforts. A major reorientation of American arms policy, precipitated by events in Iran, Turkey, and Greece, helped create new pressures for increased American intervention in China.

4 | The Reorientation of American Arms Aid Policy: The Near East and the Truman Doctrine

Greece is our real problem today.
—Secretary of State James F. Byrnes, 18 December 1946

The choice is between acting with energy or losing by default.
—Secretary of State George C. Marshall, 27 February 1947

In the long run, the U.S. must depend upon forehanded action in its foreign policy because of the high price of a continuous series of crises, and because the failure to prevent them will contribute to the continuation of international instability and expansionism.
—General Dwight D. Eisenhower, 10 May 1947

On 12 March 1947 Harry S. Truman went before a joint session of Congress and sternly delivered the most famous speech of his presidency. The occasion for Truman's address was his request for $400 million in military and economic aid for Greece and Turkey. The lasting importance of his message was his sweeping justification for this assistance, soon known as the Truman Doctrine: "It must be the policy of the United States to support free peoples who are resisting attempted subjugation by armed minorities or by outside pressures."[1] Truman's address was remarkable for its effect not only on the Cold War but also on military aid policy. His appeal for arms aid to Greece and Turkey—the first instance of a president seeking such appropriations other than in wartime—accelerated the emergence of military assistance as a major instrument of containment.

Although the immediate cause of his message was a British decision to curtail aid to Greece and Turkey, Truman's proposals were the product of months of growing concern over events in those countries. By the late summer of 1946 Washington officials saw Soviet demands for concessions in Turkey, a Communist-led guerrilla movement in

Greece, and a separatist regime in northern Iran as parts of a concerted Soviet effort to dominate the Near East. When Moscow proposed joint Soviet-Turkish defense of the Black Sea straits in August 1946, Truman and his advisers reacted with alarm and resolved to "resist with all means at our disposal any Soviet aggression."[2] During the next two months, the administration lifted restrictions on the transfer of arms to Iran, Greece, and Turkey and agreed to share with Great Britain the burden of economic and military aid to the latter two nations. These decisions insured that the Truman administration would respond affirmatively to Britain's appeal of 21 February 1947 to take over chief responsibility for aiding Greece and Turkey.

In contrast to their division over military aid to Latin America and China, political and military officials united in support of the provision of armaments to Greece and Turkey. The Joint Chiefs of Staff emphasized that Greece and especially Turkey were important to the control of the Eastern Mediterranean; political analysts added that they were the keys to the future orientation of the entire Near East. Both defense and diplomatic authorities believed that military aid would stiffen the resolve of the Greeks and Turks to resist Communist pressures. They also regarded such aid, conversely, as a symbol of American determination to stop Soviet expansion by "back[ing] our policies to the hilt."[3]

Following the enunciation of the Truman Doctrine, State, War, and Navy department planners considered the possibility of providing similar assistance to other countries facing Communist threats. Their studies called attention to the enormous gulf between potential demands for military assistance and the means to meet those requests and forced more careful distinctions between vital and peripheral interests and the assignment of priorities to existing military aid programs. Equally important, State-War-Navy committees urged new legislation and better logistical planning so that the United States could sustain current military aid projects and promptly extend assistance to countries with urgent needs. In these ways, the Greek-Turkish crisis was responsible for the first important steps toward a comprehensive military aid program.

At the end of World War II, State Department officials regarded the Near East as an area of intense—and possibly explosive—great-power rivalry. Astride vital communications routes and possessing vast oil reserves, this region had enormous strategic and economic importance to Great Britain, the United States, and the Soviet Union. State Department planners hoped that the United States, through the vigorous pursuit of commercial and investment opportunities and the extension of economic and technical assistance, would soon replace Britain as the leading Western power in the Near East. They also expected that the Soviet Union, concerned about the security of its southern rim and eager to prevent the spread of British and American influence, would assert its interests vigorously in that region. Already, in August 1945, the State Department's Office of Near Eastern and African Affairs (NEA) predicted that competition between the United States and the Soviet Union in the Near East, if unchecked, might even lead to another world war.[4]

Although Truman thought that the United States could avoid such a conflict, he became increasingly concerned, as did many of his advisers, about Soviet actions in the Near East.[5] American misgivings first arose over Soviet aspirations in Turkey. In June 1945 Moscow revealed that its conditions for the renewal of a Russo-Turkish treaty of friendship included joint fortification of the Black Sea straits, bases on Turkish soil, and cession of border territories, terms that Turkey flatly rejected.[6] Reacting to the Soviet proposals, the American ambassador in Ankara, Edwin C. Wilson, reported that the real Soviet objective was the installation of a subservient regime in Turkey. Secretary of the Navy James C. Forrestal also concluded that the Russians wanted to turn Turkey into a satellite. The Joint Chiefs of Staff recommended that the Truman administration resist Soviet efforts to secure base rights in the straits. So did Wilson, who considered a strong stand against Soviet expansionism in the Near East imperative since, in his opinion, Eastern Europe had already "been lost to [the] USSR."[7]

Despite such counsel, Truman believed at first that diplomacy could produce an agreement that would preserve Turkish sovereignty and accommodate legitimate Soviet security interests. At the Potsdam Conference, Truman advised Soviet Premier Josef V. Stalin to settle any territorial questions with Turkey through bilateral negotiations. He also urged the internationalization of the Black Sea straits and major inland European waterways, such as the Danube River. But when his proposal failed to make any headway, he endorsed, as did British Prime Minister Winston S. Churchill, a Soviet request for revision of the

Montreux Convention, which governed passage through the straits, and agreed that each nation should take up the matter directly with Turkey.[8] The American proposals, submitted to Turkey on 2 November 1945, called for opening the straits at all times to the warships of the Black Sea nations and generally closing them to those of other countries, except with the consent of the riparian powers.[9]

Following this initiative, however, the Truman administration rapidly lost hope that negotiations could settle Russo-Turkish differences. Soviet officials quickly condemned the American proposals and reiterated demands for direct control of the straits and territorial concessions. During the autumn of 1945, a Soviet press campaign embittered relations with Turkey, and Soviet troop movements in the Balkans aroused acute anxiety in Ankara.[10] Such actions also caused consternation in Washington. As early as 13 October, Truman wrote to Secretary of State James F. Byrnes, "I am of the opinion if some means isn't found to prevent it, Russia will take steps by direct action to obtain control of the Black Sea straits." A Soviet assault on the straits, NEA informed Byrnes on 5 January 1946, could come "in a matter of weeks or months" and so the time had come to "stand shoulder to shoulder with the other Powers opposed to aggression . . . in preventing an attack on Turkey." To do otherwise, warned NEA Director Loy W. Henderson, might "bring about the restoration of an era in which a series of unchecked aggressions will result in world war."[11]

Such dire predictions also arose from distress over Soviet policy in Iran, a nation in which uneasy wartime cooperation among the great powers dissolved into postwar confrontation. Russian and British forces occupied that oil-rich country in August 1941, and American troops arrived fifteen months later to supervise the transshipment of lend-lease supplies to the Soviet Union. Both the Soviets and the British, imperial rivals in Iran for over a century, treated the weak government of Shah Mohammad Reza Pahlavi with disdain. In their occupation zone in the north, the Soviets encouraged the Communist-led Tudeh party and abetted traditional separatist movements. In their sphere of influence in the south, the British followed commercial policies that amounted to "pillaging," according to the Iranian foreign minister. The United States, on the other hand, supported the Shah's government by distributing lend-lease supplies, providing financial and military advisers, and reiterating support for the independence and territorial integrity of Iran. By no means disinterested, these policies helped advance American objectives in Iran, which included stimulating trade, securing an oil concession, and preventing the development of any threat in the Persian Gulf area to American petroleum interests in Saudi Arabia. By the end of the war, the Iranian government looked primarily to the United States for help in consolidating its authority and reducing British and Russian influence. On 23 August 1945 NEA issued a policy statement that went a long way toward fulfilling Iranian desires. It asserted that the State Department would "make every effort to prevent the development of any situation which might constitute a limitation on Iranian sovereignty . . . or any attempt by a third power to exploit the internal difficulties of Iran for its own expansionist purposes." At the same time, NEA called for the establishment of a tripartite commission to supervise the stabilization and development of Iran.[12]

But any hope of great-power harmony in Iran vanished during the autumn of 1945 when insurgents demanded autonomy for the northwestern province of Azerbaijan. The Soviet occupation authorities openly supported the separatists and prevented Iranian security forces from moving against the armed insurrectionists. The American consul in the provincial capital of Tabriz reported that the Azerbaijani uprising was more an expression of genuine discontent with the Iranian government than the product of Soviet intrigue.[13] But Ambassador Wallace Murray and the State Department's experts in Near Eastern affairs disagreed. They also doubted that the Soviets were simply exploiting the turmoil in Azerbaijan to extract an oil concession from the reluctant Iranian government. Instead they thought that the Soviets, who bluntly rejected American requests for the immediate withdrawal of troops, might next try to install a subservient regime in Tehran.[14]

So troubling were Soviet intentions in the Near East that Loy Henderson warned of an impending crisis. Henderson, a career diplomat and Soviet specialist who became director of NEA in early 1945, considered Stalin an even greater threat to world peace than Hitler had been. In a long memorandum written at the end of 1945, Henderson worried that the traditional barriers to Soviet expansion were crumbling. The Second World War had eliminated Germany in the west and Japan in the east; Russia was now trying to remove "a third barrier in the south," so that its power could flow unimpeded into the Eastern Mediterranean and the Persian Gulf. Any appeasement of Soviet aspirations, Henderson cautioned, would "make a mockery of the principles on which the United Nations Organization rests . . . [and] might eventually give birth to a third World War." Henderson favored the calling of a Big Four conference in order to persuade the Soviet Union to "abandon its present unilateral approach towards Near East problems." He conceded that prospects for such a settlement were dim. Still, a great-power meeting, even if it failed, would at least postpone a "supreme test" for the United Nations, one it might not survive "at the very outset of its existence."[15]

Henderson's memorandum was one of many appeals for firmer and more consistent opposition to Soviet ambitions. Under the direction of James F. Byrnes, American diplomacy had followed an erratic course. Byrnes's demands for democratic reforms in Eastern Europe and ominous references to the atomic bomb had contributed to the breakdown of the first meeting of the Council of Foreign Ministers (CFM) in London in September 1945. At the next CFM conclave in Moscow three months later, Byrnes abruptly shifted tactics and eagerly accepted token concessions as justification for the negotiation of peace treaties with the Soviet-dominated governments of Rumania and Bulgaria. Byrnes's conciliation of the Russians elicited vociferous protests. Republican leaders of Congress, notably Senator Arthur H. Vandenberg of Michigan, the ranking member of the Foreign Relations Committee, denounced as "one more . . . American 'give away' " the agreement in principle that Byrnes had reached in Moscow on international control of atomic energy.[16] Even influential Democrats on Capitol Hill, such as Senator Tom Connally of Texas, the chairman of the Foreign Relations Committee, similarly complained to Truman that Byrnes was all too willing to endanger American interests in his zeal to cultivate Soviet goodwill. Within the White House, Admiral William D. Leahy, the chief of staff to the commander-in-chief, reproached Byrnes for turning the Moscow conference into "a veritable Munich," at which the secretary of state appeased a nation that behaved in Eastern Europe and the Near East more like a potential enemy than a former ally.[17] Less influential, but equally vehement, was the criticism of career foreign-service officers. The most contemptuous assessment came from George F. Kennan, counselor of the embassy in Moscow, who excoriated Byrnes for hoping only to achieve "some sort of agreement, he doesn't much care what."[18]

In early 1946 Truman placated these critics by ruling out further compromise with the Soviets. To a great extent, Truman acted in order to calm the turbulent political waters agitated by Byrnes's diplomacy. In addition, Truman shifted toward a firmer policy because he no longer believed, as he had at the Potsdam Conference, that he could do business with Stalin. While Byrnes was in Moscow, Truman told his staff that the Soviets understood only one thing—"divisions." Such thinking permeated a letter that Truman addressed, but probably never read, to Byrnes after the secretary of state returned from Moscow. After declaring that he was in charge of foreign policy, Truman announced his preference for tough opposition to the Soviets, particularly in the Near East. Only "an iron fist and strong language" would prevent a Soviet "invasion of Turkey and seizure of the Black Sea Straits." Against the "outrage" of Russian policy in Iran, Truman asserted, "I think we ought to protest with all the vigor of which we are capable. . . . It is a parallel to the program of Russia in Latvia, Estonia and Lithuania . . . [and] in line with the high-handed and arbitrary manner in which Russia acted in Poland."[19] Truman concluded what historian Robert L. Messer has called his "personal declaration of the cold war" by exclaiming, "I'm tired of babying the Soviets." Even though Byrnes probably never heard these words, he quickly became aware of the new orientation in foreign policy and the president's expectation that he should change his way of dealing with the Soviets. Truman, for example, informed his staff on 27 February 1946 that he had instructed Byrnes "to stiffen up and try for the next three months not to make any compromises."[20]

Byrnes heeded this advice during a confrontation over the removal of Soviet troops from Iran. By treaty, Britain and the Soviet Union had promised to remove their occupation forces from Iran within six months after the end of the Second World War. But when the Soviets failed to meet the deadline of 2 March 1946, Byrnes quickly sent a strong note of protest to Moscow and released its text to the public. Tension mounted in Washington the next day, 6 March, when the State Department received a report from the vice-consul in Tabriz that Soviet troops were advancing toward Tehran and the Turkish border.[21] Fearing that the Soviets were "adding military invasion to political subversion in Iran," Byrnes exclaimed, "Now we'll give it to them with both barrels."[22] He strongly encouraged the Iranians to put aside their hesitations and argue their case before the United Nations. George V. Allen, the deputy director of NEA, even made sure that Hussein Ala, the Iranian ambassador to the United Nations, went well beyond his instructions in issuing a strong denunciation of Soviet policy. Byrnes himself led the American delegation to the Security Council and repeatedly opposed Soviet efforts to remove the Iranian question from the agenda, even after Moscow announced on 25 March that its troops would depart in five or six weeks. The crisis ended ten days later when the Soviet and Iranian governments released an agreement that called for the evacuation of the Russian forces in early May in return for an oil concession in northern Iran. Byrnes, who won widespread public support for his vigorous stand against the Soviets, concluded that "firmness and the United Nations won."[23]

The Iranian crisis and the continuing dispute over the Turkish straits helped focus attention within the Truman administration on American strategic interests in the Near East. In a letter to Byrnes on 13 March 1946, the Joint Chiefs of Staff warned that the Soviets aimed at domination of the entire Middle East and Eastern Mediterranean. This objective, which endangered Great Britain's position as a world power, indirectly threatened American military interests. "The defeat or disintegration of the British Empire," the Joint Chiefs explained, "would eliminate from Eurasia the last bulwark of resistance between the United States and Soviet expansion." Such a collapse would also, in a future war, prevent the military potential of the United States and its probable allies from matching the Soviet Union's. Thus, the Joint Chiefs found that the Soviet pressures on Turkey and Iran, although not an immediate threat to the United States, would "definitely impair our national security."[24]

Preliminary planning for a future war with the Soviet Union suggested more direct American military interests in the Near East. A series of Joint Staff studies code-named PINCHER, the first of which were completed in March and April 1946, pointed to the advantages of using the Caucasus Mountains–Black Sea region, rather than Central Europe or the Balkans, as a corridor for a major offensive against the "industrial heart" of the Soviet Union. These planning papers, although highly tentative, revealed the central importance that the Near East was assuming in American strategic thinking.[25] Further indication came when Forrestal arranged for a show of force in the Mediterranean; the battleship *Missouri* arrived at Istanbul on 5 April, ostensibly to return the body of the Turkish ambassador who had recently died in Washington.[26]

The *Missouri* also called at Athens, an expression of the Truman administration's growing interest in the political and economic stability of Greece. Following its liberation by British troops in October 1944, Greece suffered from the bitter legacies of German occupation. Its transportation and communications systems were practically destroyed, famine ravaged the countryside, and inflation soared out of control.[27] To add to the country's plight, civil war erupted between the British-backed government, which was committed to the restoration of the monarchy, and the National Liberation Front (EAM), a coalition of republican resistance groups led by the Communist party (KKE).[28] Determined to prevent the extreme left from seizing power, Churchill poured British troops into Greece. An armistice halted the fighting in February 1945, but it did not end the country's political strife. There were reprisals against the EAM by rightist vigilantes, often with the assistance of the army and the national guard, both of which came under royalist control. Economic turmoil also continued unabated. Despite British assistance, a series of right-wing governments proved completely unequal to the enormous task of repairing the devastation of war.[29]

During the autumn of 1945, American officials became concerned about the lack of progress in rebuilding Greece's shattered economy. Ambassador Lincoln MacVeagh and officials of the United Nations Relief and Rehabilitation Administration warned that a financial collapse would occur unless the United States provided advisers and credits. British military authorities also stated that they needed American help to prevent chaos in Greece.[30] Byrnes ruled out stationing American troops in Greece or sharing responsibility with the British for training and supplying the Greek army or national guard; he did, however, secure Truman's approval to strengthen American efforts to stabilize the Greek economy. In January 1946 the State Department announced the approval of a $25 million Export-Import Bank loan and hinted that further funds would become available if Greece adopted major financial and administrative reforms.[31] During the next six months, the Truman administration coupled gestures of support, such as the visit of the *Missouri,* with appeals for internal changes that would hasten recovery.

The State Department recommended such assistance even though it had reservations about the Greek government. Officials in NEA deplored the corruption and inefficiency of the Athens regime, failings they considered major impediments to effective reconstruction. When, for example, a Greek mission came to Washington in August 1946 to seek new loans, Henderson and Acting Secretary of State Dean Acheson expressed their displeasure over the failure to use the $25 million already granted and reiterated the need for stringent reforms before any new aid could be effective.[32] But fears of a Communist dictatorship outweighed reservations about the rightist regime. Mac-Veagh stressed that the EAM was "under Moscow-trained and directed leadership" and could count on help from Greece's Soviet-dominated northern neighbors. An economic collapse, he predicted, would probably lead to a government of the extreme Right and then to the seizure of power by the EAM.[33] Such concerns, however, did not become acute until the civil war resumed in earnest in the last summer of 1946.

Despite the alarm over Communist pressures on Greece, Turkey, and Iran, American financial assistance to those countries during the first year of peace was extremely modest. Greece received only a $10 million surplus-property credit in addition to the $25 million Export-Import Bank loan; Turkey received just $38 million in loans and credits; and Iran got nothing at all.[34] On several occasions, Henderson appealed for the exertion of American economic power in the Near East, but to no avail. In October 1945 he advocated the creation of a $100 million fund from which loans could be made to Near Eastern countries at the discretion of the president. In June 1946 he recommended that the Export-Import Bank earmark $120 million for those nations. Byrnes, doubting that Congress would approve, rejected the first suggestion. The State Department's financial officers opposed the second proposal on the grounds that Export-Import Bank loans should promote economic recovery, not American political objectives.[35]

American assistance to the armed forces of Near Eastern nations was also quite limited. Only Iran received help from American military advisers. Two advisory missions—one commanded by General Clarence S. Ridley to assist the army, the other headed by Colonel Norman H. Schwarzkopf to train the gendarmerie—had been established in 1942 at the request of the Iranian government. The State Department hoped that these missions would strengthen Iran's internal security, counteract "pro-Axis feeling," and build "a firm foundation for future relations." In pursuing these goals, however, Ridley and Schwarzkopf encountered persistent obstacles, including shortages of training supplies and political interference in army and gendarmerie reforms. By mid-1944 Ridley doubted that his mission could continue to be effective and recommended its recall. But the State Department prevailed upon the War Department to maintain both the Ridley and Schwarzkopf advisory groups through the end of World War II and indefinitely afterward. Both missions, Byrnes explained, helped bolster the authority of the central government, check Soviet influence, and protect American interests in Iran.[36]

Even more limited than training assistance was arms aid. Indeed, the United States provided only negligible quantities of military equipment to Iran, Greece, and Turkey during the first year of peace. The guidelines that Byrnes's Staff Committee established in February 1946 for the sale of surplus armaments precluded all but token transfers to Near Eastern countries. Although the State-War-Navy Coordinating Committee endorsed a less restrictive policy one month later, the State Department guidelines prevailed in practice. Even during the confrontation over the removal of Soviet troops, the Staff Committee refused to ease the restraints on the transfer of arms to Iran. Byrnes replied to Ridley's informal inquiry of 12 March about the possibility of Iran's purchasing tanks, machine guns, and other internal security equipment by stating that current policy barred such transactions. When Turkish officials asked about fighter and bomber aircraft the following July, the State Department refused to authorize their sale. Although the Truman administration had decided to stand firm against Soviet expansion in the Near East, it relied mainly on diplomatic and limited economic measures to implement that policy.[37]

Rising apprehensions over Soviet ambitions in the Near East during the last half of 1946 led to the reformulation of American arms policy. The catalyst for change was a Soviet note on 7 August 1946 proposing revision of the Montreux Convention. The Soviets advocated a new regime for the Turkish straits limited to the Black Sea powers, and joint Russo-Turkish defense of the straits. Turkish officials found these terms unacceptable and looked to the United States for support. Because there was no explicit demand for bases on Turkish soil, however, Foreign Minister Hasan Saka actually breathed a sigh of relief after reading the Russian démarche. Not so Ambassador Wilson. The Soviet initiative, he cabled the State Department, was a thinly disguised attempt to use the straits question to remove the last obstacle to Soviet penetration of the Near East. According to Wilson, the United States faced the choice of protecting a vital interest—Turkish independence—or acquiescing in the "closing [of the] one remaining gap in [the] chain [of] Soviet satellite states from [the] Baltic to [the] Black Sea."[38]

Top officials in Washington agreed. Indeed, a crisis atmosphere enveloped the State Department and the Pentagon as diplomatic and defense authorities assessed the Soviet démarche. A memorandum prepared in NEA emphasized that the Soviet proposals would exclude Western nations from control of the straits and recommended that the United States continue to insist on revision of the Montreux Convention under the aegis of the United Nations. Military authorities pointed out that effective defense of the straits required control of their approaches for several hundred miles. "The same logic which would justify Soviet participation in the defense of the Dardanelles," the Joint Chiefs reasoned, "would also tend to justify further Soviet military penetration through the Aegean."[39] Such extrapolation transformed the Soviet note from a diplomatic initiative in accord with the Potsdam agreements into a bid to dominate the Near East and Eastern Mediterranean.[40]

At a White House meeting on 15 August, Truman heard this alarmist analysis from his top advisers. Acheson, Forrestal, and Secretary of War Robert P. Patterson foresaw the inexorable growth of Soviet power—a decade later this outlook would be called the "domino theory"—should the Turks accede to the Soviet proposals. "In our opinion," they wrote, "the establishment by the Soviet Union of bases in the Dardanelles or the introduction of Soviet armed forces into Turkey on some other pretext would, in the natural course of events, results [sic] in Greece and the whole Near and Middle East . . . falling under Soviet control and in those areas being cut off from the Western world." Hegemony in the Middle East, in turn, would give the Soviets control over the region's oil resources and enable them to sever British imperial communications. The Soviets, then, would be in a far better position to attain their goals in India and China. According to such concatenated reasoning, then, at stake in Turkey was control of nothing less than the entire Asian mainland. Never before had the Truman administration seen such enormous stakes, however exaggerated, riding on a single decision.[41]

Truman's advisers thought that diplomacy was all but useless. They remembered only the futility of previous negotiations with the Soviets, which, they insisted, invariably ended in American capitulation. The reason for this supposed one-sidedness was that the Soviets were immune to persuasion and unwilling to compromise. What diplomacy could not accomplish, however, firmness could—according to Acheson, Forrestal, and Patterson. The only thing that would prevent the Soviets from pressing their demands upon Turkey, the three secretaries told Truman, would be an awareness that the United States was "prepared, if necessary, to meet aggression with force of arms." Viewing the Turkish question in a global context, the three secretaries maintained that "the time has come when we must decide that we shall resist with all means at our disposal any Soviet aggression and in particular . . . any Soviet aggression against Turkey."[42] Truman wholeheartedly agreed. Only a few weeks earlier he had told White House aides Clark M. Clifford and George M. Elsey that he was "tired of . . . being pushed around" and prepared to take a strong stand against further Soviet "chiseling." Truman thus resolved to follow the recommendations of his advisers on Turkey "to the end," and declared "that we might as well find out whether the Russians were bent on world conquest now as in five or ten years."[43]

Truman vastly exaggerated the danger of war. At the beginning of the straits crisis, Stalin asserted that he had no intention of using force to gain Soviet objectives in Turkey, and analyses by the Central Intelligence Group (CIG) confirmed those assertions. CIG Director Hoyt S. Vandenberg informed Truman on 24 August that the Soviets had not positioned their troops to strike against Turkey, but instead had slightly speeded up their demobilization program. On balance, Vandenberg concluded, the Soviets were conducting "an intensive war of nerves," probably to "test U.S. determination to . . . sustain its commitments in European affairs." The Soviets still showed no inclination toward military action after the United States and Turkey rejected their proposals for defense of the straits. Another exchange of notes followed, but Soviet pressure for revision of the Montreux Convention subsided by late October.[44] The only significant deployment of force during the straits crisis came not through Soviet action but through American dispatch of a naval task force to the Eastern Mediterranean.[45]

The dispute over the straits, however, made a lasting impression on American arms policy. At the height of the crisis on 23 August, the Joint Chiefs of Staff recommended the sale of defensive armaments to Turkey. They considered Turkey "the most important military factor" in the Near East because of its strategic location and its apparent determination to fight, if necessary, to preserve its independence. Properly equipped, the Turkish army could mount strong resistance against a Russian attack. Even more important in the Joint Chiefs' view, the extension of American military aid would stiffen Turkey's will and prevent its yielding to Soviet demands. In addition, American assistance to Turkey would indirectly fortify other nations on the periphery of Soviet power. In the short run at least, the Joint Chiefs advocated the transfer of armaments to Turkey largely to achieve the political goals of reassuring friendly nations and strengthening American credibility.[46]

For similar reasons, the State Department now began to reverse its stand on the sale of military equipment to Turkey. In a letter to Byrnes, who was attending the Paris Peace Conference, Acting Secretary William L. Clayton explained that the Soviet Union's persistent efforts during the previous six months to undermine the stability and gain control of Turkey, Greece, and Iran were responsible for the change in the department's thinking. He warned that the refusal to provide military equipment to those countries would create the impression that the United States did not have a deep interest in the preservation of their independence and thereby weaken their resolve to resist Soviet pressures. Clayton proposed "in the light of the Dardanelles decision" that the State Department alter its policy to allow the transfer of armaments to countries, "the maintenance and integrity of which are considered to be of important interest to the United States."[47]

Byrnes, too, believed that assistance to countries facing Soviet threats was a highly important matter. "The world is watching the support . . . which we furnish our friends at this critical time," he wrote to Clayton from Paris, "and the future policies of many countries will be determined by their estimate of the seriousness . . . with which the US upholds its principles and supports those of like mind."[48] Byrnes and British Foreign Minister Ernest K. Bevin agreed, however, that Great Britain should provide military equipment to Greece and Turkey while the United States rendered all feasible economic assistance. Patterson, who had originally favored direct arms sales to Turkey but had changed his mind, pointed out that this arrangement would be less provocative because of Britain's long-standing interests in those two countries. Some of Truman's advisers also believed that the administration should try to build public support before it undertook a deeper commitment in Greece and Turkey.[49]

Although they wanted to avoid provocative actions, top policy-makers were convinced of the need for stronger measures to stop Soviet expansion. A long report on Soviet-American relations, which White House counsel Clark M. Clifford completed in September, reflected the outlook of most of Truman's principal advisers.[50] "The language of military power," Clifford wrote, "is the only language which disciples of power politics [i.e., the Soviet Union] understand." He therefore recommended maintaining military power sufficient to deter Soviet attack on areas vital to American security and providing support to "all democratic countries which are in any way menaced or endangered by the U.S.S.R."[51] Clifford's proposals went beyond Byrnes's concept of "patience with firmness," by which the secretary of state meant refusing to make concessions in negotiations with the Soviet Union. Clifford expressed the view, which began to prevail in discussions of Near Eastern policy in the late summer of 1946, that the United States should draw far more heavily on its economic and military resources to protect its interests abroad.[52]

The State Department took an important step in that direction when it completed the review of its armaments policy at the end of October. Rather than establishing new general guidelines, Byrnes's advisers recommended that the secretary of state have the power to "depart from the existing policy when it was clearly in the interest of the United States to do so."[53] Following his return from Paris in mid-October, Byrnes exercised this authority for the first time. According to the agreement with Bevin, the United States would furnish Britain, for transfer to Greece and Turkey, any arms that Britain could not provide those two countries from its own inventories. For Iran, whose leaders were deeply suspicious of any expansion of British influence, Byrnes approved direct military aid in the form of a $10 million credit for the purchase of surplus armaments. These changes in policy indicated the Truman administration's new willingness to use military aid to contain Soviet expansion.[54]

The decision to provide military assistance to Iran clearly illustrated the Truman administration's shift toward a tougher policy in the Near East. In the preceding months, the United States had provided little aid to the beleaguered government in Tehran. An autonomous regime in Azerbaijan, which remained in power after the evacuation of Soviet troops, posed a major challenge to Tehran's authority. Labor strife exploited by the Soviet-backed Tudeh party and a revolt of southern tribes added to the central government's problems. Iranian Prime Minister Ahmad Qavam had been under strong pressure from the new American ambassador, George V. Allen, to abandon his conciliatory policy toward the Azerbaijani separatists and to expel the Tudeh ministers from his cabinet. But Allen had little to offer Qavam beyond diplomatic support. A policy statement drafted in the State Department on 15 July ruled out loans to Iran that would be used for political purposes and restricted military assistance to maintaining advisory missions to the army and gendarmerie and helping the Iranian government obtain essential noncombat equipment. In early September the State Department's Policy Committee on Arms and Armaments (PCA) refused to permit sales of combat materiel to Iran to help maintain internal security because such transactions were at odds with current policy.[55]

But several weeks later, in the aftermath of the Turkish straits crisis, there was strong support within the administration for lifting these restraints. When Qavam asked Allen on 30 September for American military supplies and financial credits, officials in NEA urged approval of his request. "We feel that Qavam is making concession after concession to the Russians," Henderson wrote to Acheson on 8 October, "and that one reason for his course of action is our inability to take concrete steps to assist Iran economically or politically."[56] The Joint Chiefs of Staff also recommended the provision of limited military aid to Iran. "It is . . . to the strategic interest of the United States," they advised the State Department, "to keep Soviet influence and Soviet armed forces removed as far as possible from oil resources in Iran, Iraq, and the Near and Middle East." Military aid to Iran would advance this interest by strengthening the government in Tehran and creating goodwill toward the United States.[57]

A cabinet crisis in mid-October increased the pressure to ease restrictions on American arms transfers to Iran. Allen used his skill in palace intrigue and his influence with the Shah—his doubles partner in tennis—to force Qavam to dismiss the Tudeh members of the Cabinet. "It would be most helpful at this juncture, when [the] Iranian Government has made [a] gesture of independence from foreign domination by eliminating members of [the] Cabinet who were under foreign control," Allen implored the State Department, "if I could be authorized to offer some encouragement on [the] subject of credits." Officials in NEA echoed Allen's plea. Henderson informed Acheson that the

Truman administration could no longer delay answering Qavam's request for military aid. Without "concrete acts" that demonstrated serious American interest, Henderson argued, "the Iranian Government and people will eventually become so discouraged that they will no longer be able to resist Soviet pressure." Added to the urgency of these warnings was a suspicion that the Iranians were prepared to accept Soviet military equipment in repayment for a wartime debt.[58]

Byrnes accepted the recommendations of his advisers and on 29 October authorized the provision of military aid to Iran for the purpose of protecting that nation's internal security. Bolstered by this expression of American support, Qavam decided to send troops into Azerbaijan. Despite blunt warnings from the Soviet Union that it could not remain indifferent to military action so close to its borders, Qavam, with Allen's encouragement, refused to cancel his orders. The result was an astonishingly easy victory for the central government: the separatist regime collapsed within hours after Iranian troops entered Azerbaijan on 11 December. The Soviets, their threats notwithstanding, did not intervene.[59] The promise of military aid—American arms actually did not reach Iran for more than two years—helped bring the United States an important diplomatic success that reinforced the State Department's preference for stronger measures to contain the Soviet Union.[60]

The policy of indirect aid to Turkey yielded less satisfactory results. By assisting the Turks in this manner, Acheson explained to Wilson, the State Department hoped to achieve conflicting goals. The aim of indirect aid was to silence critics who charged that the United States was "fanning the embers of a possible Soviet-Turkish war" while reassuring the Turks that American support was not "limited to words." The latter goal was critical since the State Department believed that Turkey was "the stopper in the neck of the bottle through which Soviet political and military influence could most effectively flow into the eastern Mediterranean and Middle East." Any weakening of Turkish resistance might lead to a row of falling dominoes that could seriously weaken American security.[61]

Nonetheless, difficulties impeded the transfer of armaments to Turkey from British and American sources. In early November the Turkish government inquired about credits for modernizing several of its warships, purchasing American frigates, and completing construction of a naval yard. Eager to reduce British expenditures in the Near

East, Bevin encouraged Byrnes to assist the Turks. But American officials hesitated. Military and naval officers questioned whether such aid would significantly strengthen Turkey's defenses against a Soviet attack. Political officials doubted that the Turkish government could afford to go into debt for naval armaments since it was already experiencing some financial difficulty in maintaining its large military establishment. Wilson reported from Ankara that Turkey's requests for assistance reflected a lack of planning, and suggested a survey of the country's economic and defense requirements. In November a State-War-Navy working group endorsed this proposal.[62]

On 10 January 1947, however, Byrnes informed Wilson that the State Department had decided not to send the survey mission. The Export-Import Bank lacked funds for a new loan to Turkey, and Byrnes was afraid that an official American mission would raise hopes for immediate assistance that the United States would be unable to fulfill. After receiving this news, Wilson urged direct American military aid to Turkey. He had not yet informed the Turks of the Byrnes-Bevin agreement and feared that American inability to provide economic aid, and reluctance to furnish military assistance, would discourage Turkish leaders. He also argued, as did a few military and naval officers, that the direct supply of arms to Turkey would make a stronger impression in Moscow. On 20 January Byrnes replied that the State Department was reconsidering its arms policy toward Turkey.[63]

Administration officials were even more concerned about providing effective aid to Greece, a nation in which another round of civil war began in late 1946. The escalation of the fighting between leftist guerrillas and government forces coincided with a plebiscite on 1 September that restored the Greek monarchy. Contributing far more to the violence was the inefficiency and repression of Greece's right-wing government. Despite extensive British aid, the Greek economy remained in a shambles. According to the chief of the British economic mission, the state of the Greek economy was largely due to the government's "well-known propensity to do nothing." Far more energetic were the government's efforts to suppress its leftist opponents through mass arrests, summary justice, and the incarceration of the wives and children of fugitives. Ambassador MacVeagh complained to King George II that toleration of political dissent and respect for civil liberties would reduce the strength of the guerrillas by at least 70 percent. But MacVeagh's pleas for moderation brought only ineffective gestures toward reconciliation. And despite the dismissal in November 1946 of the odious Defense Minister Petros Mavromichalis, who helped finance royalist vigilantes, and the reshuffling of cabinet ministries in January 1947, the Right remained firmly in control of the government. Even the CIG concluded that the intransigence, intolerance, and inertia of the Greek government were major reasons for the renewal of civil war.[64]

While deploring the excesses of the rightist regime, the Truman administration worried more about the growth of Soviet influence in Greece. The KKE led the insurgency and received help from Greece's northern neighbors. The best evidence indicates that Stalin neither instigated the fighting nor aided the rebels.[65] But State, War, and Navy officials, believing in monolithic communism, could not conceive of international action by Yugoslavia, Bulgaria, or Albania independent of Soviet direction. Hence they insisted that Moscow was deeply involved in the Greek civil war, to the point, as one army planner wrote, of "giving direct military assistance to elements seeking to cause the fall of the Greek government."[66] MacVeagh also concluded that the "Soviet Government in [the] final analysis must be 'assigned responsibility for [the] continued strife.'"[67] A statement of policy prepared in NEA and approved by Byrnes at the end of October described Greece as a pivotal nation in the struggle to contain Soviet influence. "If Greece were allowed to fall victim to Soviet aggression," the memorandum warned, "there could not fail to be the most unfavorable repercussions in all of those areas where political sympathies are balanced precariously in favor of the West and against Soviet communism." The State Department considered Greece important less for its intrinsic value than for the effect its collapse might have on Western Europe and the Near East.[68]

Determined to arrest the spread of Soviet influence, Byrnes, in the aftermath of the Turkish straits crisis, agreed with Bevin that the United States would underwrite Britain's military aid to Greece. In doing so, Byrnes accepted a major responsibility. The Greek National Army (GNA)—poorly supplied, inefficiently organized, and severely demoralized—required substantial assistance in order to conduct effective antiguerrilla operations.[69] British Field Marshall Bernard L. Montgomery warned in December that Greece would be lost unless the GNA was retrained and reequipped. General Stephen J. Chamberlin, the director of War Department Intelligence, concluded that only large-scale British or American aid could prevent the rebels from establishing control over much of northern Greece. MacVeagh, too, stressed the urgency of supplying the GNA and worried that British efforts would fall short. On MacVeagh's recommendation, the State Department emphasized to the British government on 20 December the need for prompt action to meet Greece's essential military requirements and asked for a list of items that the United States might have to furnish.[70]

During the winter of 1946–47, however, American officials were frustrated in their efforts to hasten the delivery of military equipment to Greece. Not only were most items the GNA requested unavailable in the War Department's domestic stocks but also problems arose in channeling available equipment through the British.[71] Citing the heavy financial burden that they were already carrying in Greece, the British refused to pay, as required by law, for American surplus supplies that they planned to deliver to Greece. (An acute dollar shortage made it impossible for Greece to reimburse Britain for such costs.) The State Department, therefore, had no choice but to sell the equipment on credit directly to the Greek government. Acheson approved such a sale of training aircraft on 5 February as an exception to existing policy.[72] But this transfer did little to compensate for the inability of the strapped British government to provide Athens with subsidies for an increase in the GNA and new equipment for a spring campaign against the guerrillas. On 20 February Henderson recommended that the State Department alter its policy and furnish direct military aid to Greece.[73]

By that time many American officials believed that Greece was on the verge of collapse. Paul A. Porter, the chief of a special American survey mission, painted a grim picture of financial chaos, administrative incompetence, and widespread demoralization. Economic and political stability in Greece, he told the State Department, would be impossible without an all-out American effort.[74] Mark F. Ethridge, the American representative on a U.N. commission investigating the fighting along Greece's northern borders, reported that the "Soviets feel that Greece is [a] ripe plum ready to fall into their hands in a few weeks."[75] MacVeagh joined with Porter and Ethridge on 20 February in describing the situation in Greece as "so critical that no time should be lost in applying any remedial measures."[76] After reading these alarming reports, Secretary of State George C. Marshall authorized Acheson to prepare legislation for a loan to Greece and to plan for the direct supply of armaments. It was clear to State Department officials that henceforth the United States would have to shoulder the major responsibility for aid to Greece.[77]

During late 1946 and early 1947, then, the Truman administration incorporated military assistance into its efforts to check Soviet expansion in the Near East. Within six months American policy shifted from restricting arms shipments to Greece, Turkey, and Iran, to sharing responsibility with the British for such transfers, to preparing to assume primary responsibility for arming those nations. Both defense and diplomatic officials believed that military assistance would strengthen local resistance to Soviet demands and demonstrate American toughness and dependability. Although the amount of armaments actually transferred to Greece, Turkey, and Iran was small, the changes in American policy were substantial.

A British démarche helped complete the transformation in American armaments policy that had begun six months earlier. On the afternoon of 21 February 1947 the British government notified the Truman administration that it intended to discontinue its economic and military aid to Greece and Turkey at the end of March. American officials learned of the impending cutoff from two urgent notes that the British embassy delivered to the State Department. The first, much like the reports of MacVeagh, Ethridge, and Porter, warned that Greece was on the verge of financial collapse and estimated that it needed approximately $250 million in foreign aid during 1947 and an indefinite amount for several years thereafter. The second stated that Turkey, lacking outside help, could not strengthen its armed forces sufficiently to resist Soviet pressure without abandoning plans for economic development. Both documents explained that Britain, because of its own financial woes, could no longer offer assistance to Greece and Turkey and expressed the hope that the United States would furnish the necessary support.[78]

The British notes did not particularly surprise administration officials. The British government had long considered Greece "a bottomless well," and the State Department had known for at least six months that Bevin was considering retrenchment in Greece as a way of easing the drain on scarce foreign aid funds. During the Paris Peace Conference, Bevin emphasized that Britain was stretching its resources thin in the Near East. In December 1946 he told Byrnes that he was eager to remove British troops from Greece. In February 1947, when severe winter weather and a coal shortage aggravated Britain's acute financial problems, Chancellor of the Exchequer Hugh Dalton proposed "the most ruthless economy in overseas expenditure . . . [to] begin at once by cutting off the Greeks." Although the Cabinet did not authorize such a drastic step, Bevin approved a message to the United States suggesting that it actually had, "for the sole purpose of bringing matters to a head."[79]

The State Department responded with exceptional speed. Marshall, who was preoccupied with other matters, assigned responsibility to Acheson and Henderson, both of whom considered strong and swift action imperative. Both, as well, unhesitatingly accepted the British notes at face value since, as Henderson recollected, they had believed for some time that "the British could not indefinitely continue to carry the burden of Greek and Turkish assistance." At Acheson's direction, Henderson and his staff began to work on a series of planning papers shortly after the British notes arrived on Friday afternoon. Over the weekend they completed a memorandum recommending that the United States extend all necessary military and economic aid to Greece and Turkey. Acheson approved this document on Sunday, 23 February. The Committee of Three and the president endorsed a slightly revised version three days later. Exhilarated officials could not recall when State had moved so quickly on a matter so grave.[80]

Such swift action was possible because the administration's decision was never in doubt. During the straits crisis, Truman and his top advisers had resolved to spare no effort, including the use of force, to preserve the independence of Turkey; this policy, Henderson now asserted, applied as well to Greece. In October 1946 Byrnes had agreed with Bevin that the United States would be the guarantor of Britain's military aid to Greece and Turkey. By mid-February 1947 the State Department's experts on Near Eastern affairs believed that only direct American military and economic assistance could prevent the collapse of Greece. In view of the administration's previous commitments and its growing concern over the Eastern Mediterranean, Truman and his principal advisers hardly even deliberated over whether to seek the authority and funds for aid to Greece and Turkey. As Acheson realized, "under the circumstances there could be only one decision."[81]

There were few dissenters. One was General James K. Crain, the deputy chairman of the PCA, who argued unpersuasively that excessive foreign aid expenditures accounted for Britain's financial distress. To prevent the United States from suffering a similar fate, he recommended conservation of resources for "the final trial of strength" with the Soviet Union. To protect Greece and Turkey, he suggested that Truman issue a warning that the United States would fight, if necessary, to prevent those nations from falling under Communist control.[82]

State Department officials paid a bit more attention to Paul Porter's objections to arming the Greek government. Porter wanted to avoid American intervention in a civil war in support of a government he found "reactionary . . . incredibly weak, stupid and venal." So he proposed that Truman make negotiation of an armistice a prerequisite for the provision of American economic aid to Greece. In a letter to Acheson, MacVeagh dismissed Porter's suggestion as the product of "a 'new deal' enthusiast . . . with little knowledge of the outside world beyond the USA." MacVeagh insisted that the Truman administration could not afford "being sentimental about what is happening in Greece" because that was "playing into the hands of the Russians." The only way to establish lasting peace in Greece, he continued, was to "stop Russia on the Greek frontiers" and defeat the Communist-led guerrillas. In a final denunciation of Porter, one that captured the prevailing mood of the State Department, MacVeagh declared, "Omelets are not made without breaking eggs, and the time has come when we must be tough."[83]

Preliminary planning for the Greek military aid program also caused few disagreements. The most significant difference of opinion arose between the War and State departments over the urgency of the Greek situation. General Stephen Chamberlin, the head of War Department Intelligence, took issue with the conclusion of MacVeagh and Ethridge that Greece might fall under Soviet domination in a matter of weeks. Like most of his colleagues in the State Department, Chamberlin believed that the Soviet Union ultimately bore responsibility for the fighting in Greece because it was channeling aid to insurgents through Albania, Yugoslavia, and Bulgaria. But he did not think that Moscow would permit the guerrillas to receive the assistance they needed to overthrow the Greek government as long as Stalin desired American cooperation in the settlement of more important matters, such as the future of Germany. In a second estimate of 26 February, Chamberlin pointed out that the guerrillas operated only in northern border regions and controlled no more than 10 percent of Greek soil. Although the military situation was deteriorating for the Greek government, he reiterated, it was not yet critical.[84]

Chamberlin agreed with State Department experts, however, that

American military aid could have a decisive effect on the Greek civil war. Political and military officials blamed the difficulties of the 100,000-man Greek National Army on a lack of equipment, poor morale, and reliance on conventional tactics. Reequipped and reorganized for mobile warfare, the GNA could exploit its estimated eight-to-one numerical advantage over the guerrillas and bring the fighting to an end, perhaps in six months. Planners, too, easily discounted any suggestion that the extension of American aid would redound against the Greek government by stimulating guerrilla recruiting or encouraging additional outside support of the revolutionaries. Instead they predicted that the Greek population would take a firm stand against the insurgents. Terrorist methods, Chamberlin argued, not economic woes, political grievances, or government repression, accounted for the strength of the guerrillas among the northern Greek peasantry. "In the final analysis," concluded a memorandum by the SWNCC, "the situation is more psychological and political than military. Morale and the superficial manifestations of force, such as possession of weapons and equipment, are the important elements." American military advisers would not even have to provide operational advice, but only determine the equipment the GNA needed and educate Greek soldiers in its use. By extending military aid and rendering technical advice, the Truman administration all too optimistically hoped to alter the perceptions of power in Greece so dramatically that the GNA would quickly gain the upper hand in the civil war.[85]

Policymakers differed more sharply over military aid to Turkey. Kennan objected strenuously to such assistance. Emphasizing that Turkey faced neither "serious Communist penetration" nor domestic strife, Kennan wanted "the accent . . . on internal morale and firmness of diplomatic stance, not on military preparations."[86] He recommended to Acheson that the president refrain from asking Congress for aid to Turkey, and failing this, that Truman make clear that there was no cause for alarm over the situation in Turkey. Kennan got some support for his views from Patterson, who thought that Turkey should receive only economic aid.[87]

Even the Joint Chiefs of Staff, up to a point, concurred in Kennan's analysis. Like Kennan, the Joint Chiefs doubted that the Soviets would use military force to gain their objectives in Turkey. The main problem, they reiterated, was to maintain the Turks' political and psychological resolution and prevent their yielding to Soviet demands. Unlike Kennan, the Joint Chiefs felt that the Turks required "positive assurances" of American support, including military assistance. Such aid would be provided, they asserted, "to stiffen the Turkish will and ability to . . . continue a firm national posture against Soviet pressure" and only secondarily to improve Turkish military capabilities to resist a Soviet attack. Acheson and Forrestal agreed with the service chiefs and brushed aside Kennan's objections. The Committee of Three tentatively agreed that all the aid Turkey received during the coming fiscal year should be reserved for military purposes.[88]

Despite the strong support within the administration for aid to Greece and Turkey, the prospects for prompt congressional approval were problematical. Republican majorities controlled both the House and the Senate for the first time since 1931, and they proclaimed as one of their paramount goals the restoration of economy in government. A GOP policy committee endorsed a 20 percent cut in income taxes, and in February 1947 a joint congressional committee endorsed a budget ceiling of $34.7 billion—$3 billion less than Truman proposed. New proposals for foreign assistance obviously were at odds with these Republican fiscal goals. Henderson predicted "grave difficulties" in obtaining the necessary legislation for aid to Greece and Turkey not only because many members of Congress were bent on economy but also because they were unaware of the vital interests that Truman and his advisers believed were at stake in those two nations.[89]

Consultation with congressional leaders revealed that the only way to overcome these obstacles was through an extraordinary effort to build public support for aid to Greece and Turkey. At a White House meeting on 27 February, a bipartisan group of legislators gave the administration's proposals a chilly reception. Only a dramatic presentation by Acheson transformed the reaction of the congressional delegation. A fervent and persuasive advocate, Acheson drew heavily on arguments that had appeared in dozens of State Department memoranda and gave them stunning force. The United States, he declared, was facing a crisis unparalleled in modern times. The situation in Greece was the result of a Soviet bid for the control of three continents. "Like apples in a barrel infected by one rotten one, the corruption of Greece would infect Iran and all to the east," he asserted. "It would also carry infection to Africa through Asia Minor and Egypt, and to Europe through Italy and France, already threatened by the strongest domestic Communist parties in Western Europe." Only the United

States was in a position to thwart this Soviet challenge. The issue was not saving British interests or extending charity, but protecting American freedom and security. After a long pause, Senator Vandenberg, the new chairman of the Foreign Relations Committee, replied gravely, "Mr. President, if you will say that to the Congress and the country, I will support you and I believe most of its members will do the same."[90]

Under Acheson's leadership, administration officials began to prepare such a message for Truman to deliver to Congress. Acheson informed a State-War-Navy working group on 28 February that the president's proposals for aid to Greece and Turkey "must be put over forcefully. . . . We must stress the necessity of maintaining those areas of the world that are now free and in which there are individual liberties." General Archibald V. Arnold, the army's assistant chief of staff for plans, agreed, noting that the only thing that could sway the public was the necessity of holding the line against communism. Building on these ideas, Francis H. Russell, the director of the State Department's Office of Public Affairs, suggested that the president explain his decision to help Greece and Turkey "in terms of [a] new policy . . . to go to the assistance of free governments everywhere."[91] Four days later, the State-War-Navy group handed Acheson a paper that recommended that the administration adopt as the major theme of its public information program on Greece and Turkey "the world conflict between free and totalitarian or imposed forms of government."[92] This memorandum served as the basis for the first working draft of Truman's message. During the next week, administration officials revised the speech for maximum effect on public and congressional opinion. As Truman explained to his Cabinet on 7 March, he had taken on "the greatest selling job ever facing a President."[93]

With domestic considerations firmly in mind, the drafters of the president's speech decided to play down American military aid to Greece and Turkey. When a navy planner urged the administration to emphasize military assistance in order to dramatize the depth of its concern for Greece and Turkey, NEA Assistant Director John D. Jernegan replied that the public would react adversely to the idea of military aid; the administration should stress instead the "economic side."[94] This view prevailed. On 12 March Truman asked Congress to vote funds for "financial," "material," and "economic" assistance, but did not mention "military" aid. Several paragraphs of his message described how these funds would help restore the shattered Greek economy, but only two sentences explained that they would also pay for equipment for the GNA. Yet $172 million of the $300 million that the administration sought for Greece was allocated for military purposes. Truman told Congress that the administration's goal was to help Turkey "in effecting that modernization necessary for the maintenance of its national integrity." Such oblique phrases were at best uninformative, at worst deceptive. All of the $100 million requested for Turkey was intended for defense.[95]

Concern over public and congressional reaction also helped limit the scope of the president's request for funds and authority to render foreign aid. Early drafts of Truman's speech not only proclaimed a worldwide policy of support for non-Communist governments but also contained an appeal for legislation to implement such a policy. A special State Department committee similarly recommended to Acheson on 4 March that the president ask Congress for authorization "to furnish assistance to any country for the purpose of promoting its stability and independence whenever he finds such assistance is in the interest of the national security." Marshall, however, feared that such a request would arouse strong opposition on Capitol Hill. Instead he ordered the preparation of a bill that covered only Greece and Turkey. On 6 March Acheson informed Joseph M. Jones, the State Department's principal drafter of Truman's message, that the president would make a statement of global policy but confine his request for funds, for the time being, to Greece and Turkey.[96]

Some officials wanted the president to temper his rhetoric as well. Kennan objected to placing aid to Greece and Turkey "in the framework of a universal policy rather than in that of a specific decision addressed to a specific set of circumstances." He was so displeased with the State Department's working draft of the president's message that he submitted a new version, stripped of all sweeping language, to Acheson on 6 March.[97] En route to the Moscow foreign ministers' meeting, Marshall also counseled moderation by cabling his dissatisfaction with the "flamboyant anti-Communism" of the draft speech. His desire to avoid such provocative language arose mainly from his appreciation of the limits on American military power arising from postwar demobilization.[98] George M. Elsey, an administrative assistant to the president, recommended to Clifford that the president restrict the scope of his message. The Soviet Union, he explained, had not recently committed any overt act that would justify an "all-out speech," nor was the public prepared for such a stern message.[99]

These objections came too late: Truman held firmly to the understanding he had reached with Vandenberg. On 12 March he went before Congress and explained American interest in Greece and Turkey not on the basis of strategic or political considerations but in terms of a global ideological struggle. Each nation, Truman asserted, had to choose between two ways of life; one was based on majority rule and free institutions, the other on the forcible suppression of the popular will and personal freedoms. "I believe," he proclaimed, "that it must be the policy of the United States to support free peoples who are resisting attempted subjugation by armed minorities or by outside pressures." Truman's alarmist language and simplistic portrait of a global conflict between good and evil aimed "to bring people up to [the] realization that the war isn't over by any means," according to Clifford.[100]

The speech had the desired effect. On 13 March Representative Carl Vinson (D-Ga.) told Forrestal that Truman had put many conservative opponents in an untenable position: "They don't like Russia, they don't like Communism, but they don't want to do anything to stop it. But they are all put on the spot now and they all have to come clean."[101] Vandenberg also thought that Congress had little choice but to accept Truman's proposals. He explained to members of the Foreign Relations Committee that they faced a situation similar to a "Presidential request for a declaration of war . . . there is precious little we can do except say 'Yes.'"[102] Substantial, if not necessarily enthusiastic, majorities in both houses approved the Greek-Turkish Aid Act, which Truman signed into law on 22 May. Congress provided the full appropriation of $400 million, but not until more than two months later, largely because of the dilatory tactics of archconservative John Taber (R-N.Y.), the obstructionist chairman of the House Appropriations Committee. One conservative Republican, Representative Francis H. Case of South Dakota, wrote to Truman that at least seventy-five members of Congress, himself included, voted to authorize the assistance only because they feared "pulling the rug out from under you or Secretary of State Marshall."[103]

Although many members of Congress felt an obligation to support the president, they still expressed misgivings about military assistance to Greece and Turkey. Vandenberg, for example, fretted over the section of the legislation that authorized the dispatch of military advisers to those two countries. He thought that it constituted "a blank check that comes pretty close to a potential act of war."[104] Republican representatives Karl E. Mundt of South Dakota and Jacob K. Javits of New York voiced similar concerns, but Patterson and Acheson turned back Mundt's efforts to limit to 100 the number of military advisers to each nation and Javits's to restrict their functions to training and logistical assistance.[105] Senator H. Alexander Smith (R-N.J.) questioned the ultimate effectiveness of military aid. Such assistance to Turkey, in his view, was "a palliative rather than a cure." He voted for the legislation in the hope that a strong stand on Greece and Turkey would hasten a settlement of Soviet-American differences. Acheson, however, was discouraging; he believed that successful negotiations would be the result of a consistent policy of firmness.[106]

The most frequent objection—both public and congressional—to the Greek-Turkish Aid Act was that it ignored the United Nations. Those who expressed this criticism, according to a sampling of public opinion that was submitted to the White House by Elmo Roper, feared that unilateral American action undermined the authority of the United Nations. Many members of Congress voiced similar concerns. Senator Edwin C. Johnson (D-Colo.) proposed an amendment to reaffirm the basic American policy of referring to the United Nations all situations that endangered world peace. Senator Claude R. Pepper (D-Fla.) went even further. He advocated that the United States limit its aid to a $250 million contribution to a U.N. relief fund for Greece. Vandenberg was sympathetic to these congressional and public demands for U.N. involvement, even though he considered unilateral American action imperative to prevent "a chain reaction around the world which could very easily leave us isolated in a Communist-dominated earth."[107] He thus secured passage of an amendment that called for the termination of American aid if the General Assembly or Security Council determined "that action taken . . . by the United Nations makes the continuation of such assistance unnecessary or undesirable." Acheson dismissed the amendment as "window dressing," but the Roper analysts thought it would increase support for the Greek-Turkish Aid Act from a "bare majority" to "between two-thirds and three-fourths" of the public. Vandenberg also predicted that his amendment would not only appease but also educate public and congressional opinion by drawing attention to U.N. impotence brought on by Soviet obstructionism.[108]

Even more troubling to some legislators was the possibility that the Greek-Turkish legislation would establish a precedent for assistance to other countries facing Communist threats. During the congressional hearings, Acheson repeatedly attempted to clarify the implications of Truman's sweeping language. He told the Senate Foreign Relations Committee that future requests for aid would be considered on the basis of a country's need for help, the extent to which American resources might alleviate that nation's problems, and the consistency of the proposed measure of assistance with the administration's foreign policy. "It cannot be assumed, therefore," he assured the committee, "that this Government would necessarily undertake measures in any other country identical or even closely similar to those proposed for Greece and Turkey."[109]

Acheson, however, reaffirmed Truman's principle of support for foreign peoples resisting subjugation. "If there are situations where we can do something effective, then I think we must certainly do it," he explained to the Foreign Relations Committee.[110] Acheson also agreed with Vandenberg that, although the United States would not necessarily react in the same way to every challenge to a non-Communist government, "We propose to react." So, Acheson's testimony, while it left no doubt that there were limits to the administration's efforts to resist communism, confirmed the possibility of additional programs of military assistance.[111] Indeed, even as Acheson spoke, administration planners had begun a major review of military aid policies.

Military aid to countries other than Greece and Turkey was a frequent topic in the February and March 1947 discussions that followed the presentation of the British notes. Political and military officials were convinced that the retreat of British power and the expansion of Soviet influence would cause new unrest that might necessitate American intervention. Marshall, for example, informed Truman on 26 February that the State, War, and Navy departments were concerned about the development of "similar situations requiring substantial aid from this Government." On 5 March Acheson referred this matter to the SWNCC for urgent study. The resulting reports helped consolidate and extend the changes in American armaments policy.[112]

The SWNCC began its study at a time when military aid policy was mired in conflict between the State, War, and Navy departments. The dispute concerned the revision of SWNCC 202/2, the first interdepartmental statement on postwar armaments assistance.[113] The revision originated in the PCA, a body that Byrnes established in May 1946 to enable the State Department "to assume leadership in armament matters by formulating the policy first." Faithful to its charge, the PCA quickly decided to rewrite existing guidelines on arms transfers because they were narrow, inconsistent, out-of-date, and, in the case of SWNCC 202/2, flawed by unacceptable concessions to the War and Navy departments. Months of drafting produced a comprehensive statement of policy that encompassed the supply of armaments to foreign nations from all domestic sources, government and private. In January 1947 the State Department presented this document, designated SWNCC 202/4, to the SWNCC for approval.[114]

According to SWNCC 202/4, the long-term objective of the United States should be "to limit drastically" the flow of American munitions to foreign nations. Such a restrictive policy would hold to a minimum the diversion of human and economic resources from "creating a peaceful and orderly world," encourage the settlement of international disputes through the United Nations, and conform to the General Assembly Resolution of 14 December 1946 calling for the "regulation and reduction of armaments and armed forces." SWNCC 202/4 thus gave standing approval only to transfers of military supplies under existing programs for France, Latin America, Canada, and the Philippines.[115] But until the United Nations effectively regulated the international arms trade and preserved world peace—difficult and distant goals, at best—SWNCC 202/4 allowed the provision of military equipment to other nations as well. Such transfers were justified when they helped a country in maintaining internal order, defending against armed attack, or discharging international responsibilities. SWNCC 202/4 gave the secretary of state sole authority to determine whether foreign requests for armaments satisfied these conditions. Therefore, the paper's authors did not fear that these provisions constituted a blank check for distributing munitions. Instead, any new programs of military aid, such as the recent one for Iran, would be "carefully weighed exceptions rather than generally permissible."[116] Consequently, SWNCC 202/4 satisfied both State Department officials (such as Alger Hiss and others concerned with U.N. affairs) who hoped for international regulation of arms transfers and those (such as Henderson) who intended to use military aid to demonstrate American firmness toward the Soviet Union.

The War Department resisted the State Department's attempt to take control of armaments policy. Military officials objected vehemently to the goal of eventual drastic limitation of American arms transfers. Uniformed officers feared that the restrictive language of SWNCC 202/4 would prevent the completion of the Western Hemisphere Defense Program and the resumption of military assistance to China. The War Department proposed instead the long-term goal of drastic *regulation*, a standard that implied close scrutiny, but not reduction, of the flow of American military supplies abroad. Even more important, drastic regulation would not necessarily interfere with the services' efforts to secure bases and other foreign concessions in return for arms aid.[117]

The War Department also criticized SWNCC 202/4 for its failure to recommend more effective procedures for sustaining approved military aid programs. The greatest problem was the lack of any general authority for government transfer of armaments, except the Surplus Property Act of 1944. The inadequacies of that measure as a means of arming foreign nations became apparent during the first months of peace. As early as March 1946, the army informed the State Department that it could no longer provide from excess stocks many essential maintenance items and spare parts. As inventories dwindled, Patterson notified Byrnes on 1 July that the War Department did not have on hand all the equipment proposed for transfer to Latin America, China, and the Philippines. He also warned that the department's ability to meet the requirements of new programs of military aid from surplus resources would soon be "practically negligible."[118]

The failure of Congress to pass the Inter-American Military Cooperation Act and the administration's decision to defer action on the China Aid Act exacerbated these supply problems. Also, the difficulties that arose after the November 1946 extension to Iran of the $10 million credit for surplus armaments convinced service authorities that existing arrangements all but precluded timely and effective military assistance to foreign nations. Logistics experts found that Iranian needs could be met only at the expense of other approved programs. Furthermore, the War Department, already chafing under budgetary limitations, had to bear the costs of repairing, packing, handling, and transporting the equipment for Iran.[119] With the approval of Patterson and Eisenhower, Assistant Secretary of War Howard C. Petersen asked that the SWNCC help overhaul "the present awkward machinery" by establishing priorities among existing military aid programs and preparing legislation that would provide the president with general authority to arm foreign nations.[120]

Finally, and most important, the War Department sought to preserve its influence over arms policy. Rather than allow the secretary of state to decide whether to approve foreign requests for armaments, as provided in SWNCC 202/4, the War Department wanted to give that power to the SWNCC, with the secretary of state retaining a veto. Defense officials also recommended the addition to SWNCC 202/4 of a country-by-country listing of policy on arms transfers—much like the one in SWNCC 202/2—that would be kept current by the Rearmament Subcommittee of the SWNCC. The War Department maintained that such a catalog would facilitate planning for new programs of military aid. At the same time, this listing would give the SWNCC, rather than the State Department, primary responsibility for determining policy on the provision of military equipment to foreign nations.[121]

SWNCC 202/4 in this way provoked another battle in the continuing interdepartmental warfare over arms transfers. Political officials reacted with alarm to the War Department's unwillingness to agree "that the determination of arms policy lies with the Secretary of State and that the implementation of such policy is a function of the military." For example, Elmer T. Cummins, executive secretary of the PCA, warned that the proposed amendments to SWNCC 202/4 constituted "an attempt by the War Department to inject itself into the formulation of foreign policy." Specialists in U.N. affairs viewed this threat to State Department prerogatives as part of a War Department effort to change completely the emphasis of SWNCC 202/4. "The effect of the [War Department] revisions," complained John C. Elliott, "would be to open the door to transfers of arms to almost every country in the world at a time when the United States is engaged in complex negotiations in the Security Council for the regulation and reduction of armaments and armed forces."[122] The two departments, in short, were unable to agree either on the goals of armaments policy or their responsibilities in formulating them. On 26 February the Rearmament Subcommittee, which had been considering SWNCC 202/4, reported that it had reached a deadlock.[123]

The Greek-Turkish crisis, however, abruptly ended the debate over SWNCC 202/4. On 5 March Acheson asked the SWNCC to study "situations elsewhere in the world which may require analogous financial, technical and military aid on our part." His request was a pivotal event since it provided the impetus for a far more ambitious survey of foreign aid requirements than the State Department had previously contemplated; it was geared toward the enlargement, rather than the reduction, of American arms transfers. To prepare the report, the SWNCC appointed on 11 March a Special *Ad Hoc* Committee chaired by the State Department representative, Colonel William A. Eddy, an expert on the Middle East from the Office of Strategic Services, who was temporarily assigned as a special assistant to Marshall. The selection of Eddy—someone who was "in but not of the State Department"— insured that this foreign aid study would differ substantially from SWNCC 202/4. SWNCC directed Eddy's committee to address the following subjects: considerations of national interest that should govern decisions to provide aid; forms of assistance that each country required; arrangements for supervising the use of aid; and consequences of failure to provide assistance. As Joseph M. Jones recollected, "The scope of the committee's terms of reference was breathtaking."[124]

The special committee worked swiftly. Drawing mainly on the expertise of those at the middle and lower levels of the three departments, it completed on 21 April an interim report, designated SWNCC 360, on countries that might need American assistance during the next several months. According to its authors, SWNCC 360 was a "highly tentative" analysis prepared from "fragmentary data" and written under such intense pressure that its contents could not be fully cleared with senior officials. Nevertheless, it contained the broadest examination to date of American military aid programs. It also revealed that staff planners in the State Department as well as the armed services were now beginning to think of military aid as a major, continuing instrument of global policy.[125]

The spirit of the Truman Doctrine pervaded SWNCC 360. The report asserted: "The broad purpose of U.S. aid and assistance is to extend . . . the objective recently enunciated by the President for Greece and Turkey, by supporting economic stability and orderly political processes, opposing the spread of chaos and extremism, preventing advancement of Communist influence and use of armed minor-

ities, and orienting other foreign nations toward the U.S. and the UN."
Rather than endorsing, as did SWNCC 202/4, the goal of drastic limitation of arms transfers, SWNCC 360 concluded that the principal concern of American policymakers should be to insure that foreign
assistance strengthened American security. Rather than emphasizing
the eventual hope of international arms regulation, the report urged
unilateral action to meet immediate threats to American overseas interests. "A realistic appraisal of the world situation," the paper explained,
revealed that many countries faced dangers, such as subversion and
war-of-nerves tactics, that were beyond the purview of the United
Nations. Direct American aid was necessary to strengthen the determination of these imperiled nations—including several that were precariously balanced between East and West—to preserve their independence and remain friendly to the United States. Containing Soviet
expansion and building American influence, in short, should be the
fundamental objectives of foreign aid.[126]

The SWNCC planners viewed military assistance as a powerful
instrument toward these ends. Such help could strengthen a country's
internal security forces and bolster it against outside attack, as well
as orient its military establishment toward the United States. The
SWNCC analysts added that nations seeking modern armaments had
to rely largely on either "the Soviet Union and its satellites, or the U.S.
supplemented by Britain." This assertion, of course, was simplistic and
misleading. British and American arms policies often came into conflict—in Latin America, for example. The United States and the Soviet
Union were not directly competing for the armaments business of all
foreign countries. The SWNCC planners, though, ignored these quali-
fications and maintained that failure to meet requests for military
equipment provided the Soviets with an opportunity to extend their
military influence, to the detriment of American security. On the other
hand, the provision of munitions to foreign nations strengthened the
American armaments industry, which was an important advantage,
especially in the event of mobilization for war.[127]

To advance American interests most effectively, the SWNCC planners urged the allocation of military aid in a "positive, forehanded and
preventative" manner. Behind this recommendation was a concern
that Communist minorities might foment a succession of crises—much
like the current situation in Greece—that would deplete American
resources. The ad hoc committee stressed that the "timely provision of

moderate amounts of assistance" could forestall such emergencies, thereby avoiding "urgent, much larger expenditures."[128] Military leaders, anxious about the dwindling supply of armaments on hand for foreign aid programs, agreed emphatically. Eisenhower, for example, wrote, "In the long run, the U.S. must depend upon forehanded action in its foreign policy because of the high price of a continuous series of crises, and because the failure to prevent them will contribute to the continuation of international instability and expansionism." He also concurred in the SWNCC's recommendation that urgent demands for assistance should not preclude sustained programs of military collaboration, such as the Western Hemisphere Defense Program, that would help to avert costly emergencies.[129]

Despite their emphasis on economy, the SWNCC planners recommended an expansion of current efforts to arm foreign nations. The ad hoc committee found that seven countries needed or might soon request emergency aid to counter Communist threats. Five of them—Greece, Turkey, Italy, Iran, and France—had been offered or had already received American arms. According to the SWNCC staff, two others—Korea and Austria—should receive military aid to maintain internal security and strengthen their orientation toward the West. The committee also recommended the continuation of approved programs for China, the Philippines, Latin America, and Canada. Finally, the planners urged preparation for possible assistance to Spain—even though current policy barred arms shipments to Franco's reactionary regime—as well as Norway and unspecified countries in the Middle East. The SWNCC staff did not estimate the cost or duration of such aid, even though it was clear that the War and Navy departments would not be able to provide the necessary equipment from existing stocks alone.[130]

The special committee consequently proposed several measures to bring available resources and potential commitments into balance. Most important was the passage of new legislation. The committee urged prompt action on pending bills, such as the proposed Inter-American Military Cooperation Act and the China Aid Act, and on the submission of new legislation that authorized the service departments to produce new equipment for transfer to foreign governments. In the meantime, the SWNCC recommended the establishment of a system of priorities to govern the allocation of available supplies. In general, the planners thought that countries resisting aggression or coercion should have first priority, after which remaining resources should be distributed among the long-term programs of military collaboration. Current rankings in the former category were Greece, Turkey, Italy, Iran, Korea, France, and Austria, and in the latter category were the Western Hemisphere and the Philippines, the Middle East and Europe, and the Far East. Finally, and most important, the planners urged central planning and monitoring of individual military aid programs so that they conformed to "broad national policy." "A comprehensive program must be developed," they argued, "on the basis of a careful judgment and consideration of the many and complex U.S. interests, both political and military, involved."[131]

Military authorities commented extensively on these recommendations. The most detailed analysis came from the Joint Chiefs of Staff, who praised SWNCC 360 but suggested that the paramount objective of any comprehensive aid program should be the advancement of American strategic interests. They argued that the United States should extend aid only to nations that might become effective allies in the event of a war with the Soviet Union. As a result, their priorities for assistance differed markedly from the SWNCC's. Great Britain, France, and Germany headed the list. Germany was included because the revival of its military power was essential to resisting a Soviet attack in Europe prior to the commitment of American troops. Conversely, China, Korea, and the Philippines ranked near the bottom of the list.[132] The Joint Chiefs urged "that assistance in each instance should be sufficient to positively assist [sic] the nation aided to achieve, or retain, a sound economy, to maintain the armed forces necessary for its continued independence, and to be of real assistance to the United States in case of ideological warfare." Equally important to the Joint Chiefs was withholding assistance from nations that might threaten American security. No aid of any sort, they insisted, should go to countries in which the Soviet Union exercised a predominant influence.[133]

Several top army officers also endorsed the recommendations in SWNCC 360, but expressed concern that the special committee had overestimated available means for providing military aid. They had good reason for their doubts. Truman and his budget director, James E. Webb, abhorred deficits and their inflationary consequences. For fiscal year 1948 they sent to Congress the first balanced postwar budget, an equilibrium achieved only by limiting the proposed new appropriations for national defense to $9.5 billion, including $6 billion for the War Department. The latter figure had been determined after the secretary of war had reduced the army's and the army air forces' request for new funds from $10 billion to $8.4 billion, and Webb had slashed that amount by another $2.4 billion. Although Eisenhower told Congress that the administration budget "already reflected . . . drastic curtailments," Congress imposed upon the army an additional cut of $200 million; these reductions gutted the army's procurement program. The restrictions on defense spending, combined with Congress's willingness to support Greek-Turkish aid only under pressure, made service leaders certain that neither the authority nor the funds would be available to carry out the special committee's recommendations.[134]

Because of the restraints on defense spending, many army leaders worried that new commitments to provide military aid might stretch their limited resources perilously thin. General LeRoy Lutes, the director of service, supply, and procurement, predicted that Congress would approve new appropriations for military assistance only at the expense of the budgets of the War and Navy departments. As a result, Lutes thought that the fundamental question at issue was, "Do we wish to purchase a certain amount of security for the United States through foreign aid programs or should this money and effort be directed toward building a strong United States military establishment?" General Charles P. Hall, the director of organization and training, also warned that new programs of military aid, owing to the lack of surplus materiel and the difficulties in procuring new equipment, might dangerously diminish the inventories set aside for the army's reserve forces. General Lauris Norstad, the director of Plans and Operations, doubted that Congress would soon pass broad military aid legislation. In the interim, he suggested, the army would have to rely on more careful planning to balance commitments against resources. Together these comments revealed a new awareness among army officers, particularly those concerned with logistics, that military aid programs could endanger as well as advance service interests.[135]

The SWNCC staff took account of these views in its speculative report of 10 July on the growth of the military assistance program during the next three to five years. Combining the strategic arguments of the Joint Chiefs with the political outlook of the Truman Doctrine, the planners recommended that military aid should aim at creating "a condition of goodwill and common military orientation which would provide a basis for continued collaboration in event of war." Assistance for such purposes was "clearly indicated" for Great Britain, France, Italy, Austria, Greece, Turkey, Iran, Korea, the Philippines, China, and Latin America and might be required for eight other nations.[136] Yet the SWNCC staff, reacting to the warnings of Lutes, Hall, and Norstad, urged caution in making new commitments to arm these nations. The army program alone might amount to the equivalent of equipment for 169 light divisions, and furnishing even a portion of this materiel would necessitate at least partial mobilization of industry. Without a definite limit on military aid programs, the study concluded, "the industrial effort necessary to meet them may approximate a war condition." Furthermore, since many countries lacked dollars, the United States would have to provide grants and credits, which could amount to a staggering financial burden. The SWNCC staff doubted that Congress would approve such subsidies. To these economic and financial difficulties, the planners added their political reservations about the effectiveness of military aid as a means of maintaining friendly governments in power. Hence, while reiterating their support for an integrated program of arms aid and new legislation, they concluded that the United States, "in the light of existing realities," might have to rely more heavily on other instruments, such as economic aid or mutual assistance treaties, to advance its interests abroad.[137]

That is precisely what the Truman administration did during the next year. In his famous commencement address at Harvard University on 5 June 1947, Secretary of State Marshall announced that the United States was prepared to extend substantial assistance to alleviate the crisis arising from "the dislocation of the entire fabric of European economy." To fulfill Marshall's pledge, State Department planners formulated a program that aimed not only at restoring European prosperity but also at encouraging the integration of European economies, halting the spread of communism, and fortifying Europe's shaken confidence in democratic institutions. On 9 December 1947 Truman asked Congress for $17 billion during the next four years to carry out this Marshall Plan. Compared to this enormous sum, military assistance accounted for only a small portion of the foreign aid expenditures, despite the inauguration of the programs for Greece and Turkey. This heavy reliance on economic aid forced the Truman administration to defer any requests for authority or funds for new programs of military aid until the Marshall Plan had safely cleared Congress.

Instead the State Department hoped to rely on current legislation and existing resources, despite their inadequacies, to meet urgent foreign needs for armaments. As a result, in October 1947 the SWNCC postponed indefinitely further consideration of the *Ad Hoc* Committee's report on military assistance.[138]

Still, the review of military aid policy that followed the Truman Doctrine speech had major consequences. One of the most important was that it encouraged more systematic treatment of military assistance matters. However tentative or questionable their conclusions, the planning papers of 1947 were the first to consider military aid programs from a global perspective, to weigh their relative significance, and to appraise their political, strategic, and logistical consequences. The approach reflected a nascent conviction—as yet stronger among military than political officials—that the United States should develop an integrated, worldwide program of arms aid. After the Truman administration opted instead to concentrate American aid on the reconstruction of the European economy, military officials urged consideration of the relationship between economic and military assistance. On 5 August 1947 Assistant Secretary of War Petersen wrote presciently to the SWNCC, "The maintenance of expensive armed forces, particularly by nations now economically bankrupt, can be a substantial factor in retarding purely economic rehabilitation. In one form or another," he argued, "the support of such armed forces must be financed, and the simplest solution is to ask the U.S. to bear this burden. . . . It is, therefore, self-evident that the question of armaments assistance must be thoroughly . . . integrated in overall U.S. programs for assistance."[139] Political and military planners addressed this issue repeatedly while implementing the Marshall Plan.

The SWNCC reports also stimulated efforts to solve the supply problems that impeded the provision of military aid. The Rearmament Subcommittee echoed the complaints of uniformed officers when it warned that "the U.S. is already over-extended in its plans for military assistance to foreign nations." By mid-1947 this disparity between commitments and resources forced the allocation of materiel among competing programs. The State Department established priorities among recipients of arms aid similar to those recommended by the SWNCC. Greece, Turkey, Iran, and Italy ranked highest, followed by China, Canada, the Philippines, and Latin America. At the same time, the army approved a system of distributing scarce equipment between these foreign requirements and its own domestic needs. But these expedients still left the Truman administration unable to fulfill current obligations, much less new demands, for arms aid. Moreover, these arrangements jeopardized the army's fighting capabilities. Alarmed logistics officers worried that one of the principal effects of the Truman Doctrine would be the allocation of precious armaments to nations facing Communist threats at the expense of combat inventories for army reserve units designated for mobilization in a national emergency. To concerned army division chiefs, such as Lutes, Norstad, and Hall, the SWNCC studies revealed that the Truman administration could not adequately meet either foreign or domestic military needs without further changes in military aid policies and procedures.[140]

Consequently, and perhaps most importantly, the SWNCC studies stimulated further planning. On 30 July the SWNCC directed its Rearmament Subcommittee to submit specific recommendations concerning military aid legislation, to determine an order of priority for military aid to foreign countries, and to examine national capabilities for supporting long-term measures of military assistance. In November 1947 the State-Army-Navy-Air Force Coordinating Committee, the successor to the SWNCC, appointed another ad hoc committee to formulate a new policy governing all transfers of American military supplies to foreign nations. The resulting reports figured prominently in the development of a worldwide program of military assistance during the spring of 1948.[141]

In the year between the Turkish straits crisis and the delivery of the first armaments under the Greek-Turkish Aid Act, American military aid policy had changed remarkably. In August 1946, when the Soviet notes arrived in Istanbul, administration guidelines prohibited the transfer of substantial quantities of armaments to the Near East. State Department policy aimed at limiting the flow of military equipment abroad, and the Surplus Property Act provided the only means for supplying materiel to the Near East. In August 1947, when the first American ship unloaded its cargo at Piraeus, State Department regulations not only allowed the transfer of armaments to Greece, Turkey, and Iran but also to any nation "whose independence and territorial integrity are important to the security of the United States." The Greek-Turkish Aid Act authorized the first grants for arms aid since lend-lease, and planning committees urged enactment of even broader legislation that would create a worldwide program of military assistance to counter the spread of Communist influence. Even though in October 1947 the Truman administration deferred submission of a global arms bill, many national security officials had learned during the previous year to think of military aid as an effective—and potentially extensive—instrument of containment.[142]

Accompanying this change in outlook was a shift in bureaucratic alignments. By mid-1947 service authorities, who had previously been the foremost advocates of military aid, often regarded such assistance as a threat to their interests. Because of the dwindling of surplus stocks and the possibility of enormous foreign demand for American armaments, military authorities began to direct their energies toward establishing a balance between commitments and resources. Diplomatic officials, who had earlier tried to limit the efforts of the services to send arms overseas, now took the lead in planning programs of military aid. In their view, such help was primarily a political and psychological instrument that raised foreign morale and strengthened ties to the United States. The emergence of containment, in short, generally shifted the initiative in military assistance from the soldiers to the diplomats.

Despite such changes, military assistance policy still suffered from a fundamental contradiction. Although military aid assumed new importance in American national security policy by mid-1947, the Truman administration did not take adequate steps to enlarge its global capabilities to transfer armaments. The expansive rhetoric of the Truman Doctrine raised foreign expectations of ambitious new programs of arms assistance; but administration officials worried about the heavy burden of overseas commitments and the perils of securing funds from a parsimonious Congress. Military assistance programs, then, while gaining new purpose and coherence from containment, were in danger of losing their effectiveness because of administrative, logistical, and financial difficulties. Not until it faced a crisis over European security in the spring of 1948 did the Truman administration act to close the gap between means and ends.

5 | The Decision for a Global Military Assistance Program

For the U.S. to embark on a potentially world-wide program of providing military assistance to free nations is an action of transcendent importance in U.S. history.
—Foreign Assistance Correlation Committee, 16 February 1949

By late 1947 American military aid programs had reached a crisis. Despite the efforts of the State-War-Navy Coordinating Committee, there was no "national policy governing the broad subject of U.S. military assistance to foreign nations," observed Colonel H. G. Sparrow of the army Plans and Operations Division, nor were there established governmental procedures for making decisions on arms aid. Emergency assistance on a country-by-country basis, Sparrow continued, prevented systematic efforts to balance commitments against resources and postponed consideration of permanent solutions to foreign armament needs. The depletion of surplus materiel, the sharp contraction of munitions industries since 1945, and the lack of "broad legislative authority under which the President, in time of peace, may exercise discretionary authority" in transferring military equipment threatened not only current programs but also future efforts to arm foreign nations. Sparrow concluded that drastic reforms were needed to maintain military assistance as an effective, continuing instrument of national policy.[1]

The problems of providing armaments to Europe confirmed the accuracy of these warnings. Convinced that a decisive political struggle for the control of the continent had begun, the Truman administration made ambitious plans for economic and military assistance to several European nations in late 1947 and early 1948. State Department officials took the lead in advocating expanded arms aid to Greece and emergency help to Italy, Denmark, and Norway in the hope of strengthening their resistance to Communist pressures and insuring their orientation toward the United States. Legal and logistical obstacles, however, delayed, restricted, or prevented these transactions. Military authorities spared no effort in explaining to the State Department the reasons for their inability to supply arms to these countries and in proposing sweeping changes. Their suggestions, which had previously yielded few results, now impressed diplomatic officials, who increasingly considered military assistance an important instrument of containment.

The final impetus for a major revision of military assistance policy and procedures came in the spring of 1948 when the Truman administration decided to negotiate a North Atlantic defense treaty and to provide the signatories with extensive arms aid. The National Security Council (NSC) promptly urged Truman to seek from Congress not simply a North Atlantic arms bill but a broader measure that would provide the president with the general authority and funds he lacked to arm foreign nations. The NSC also proposed the development of a coordinated military assistance program—one in which Western Europe would have first priority—aimed at strengthening "political resistance to communist aggression now, and military resistance later if necessary."[2] Truman's acceptance of these recommendations represented the culmination of efforts, begun in the wake of the Truman Doctrine speech, to establish an integrated, worldwide program of military assistance.

During the late summer and early autumn of 1947, the Truman administration became acutely apprehensive over Soviet ambitions in Europe. The most immediate danger, according to high-ranking civilian and military officials, was a desperate Soviet attempt to frustrate the prospective Marshall Plan for the reconstruction of Europe. Although discounting the possibility of Soviet military action, these top policymakers feared that local Communist parties would step up their efforts to seize power in countries such as Italy, Greece, and France, where economic distress was severe and political stability fragile.[3] The formation in September 1947 of the Cominform, a central directorate of Communist parties under Moscow's control, reinforced the belief in Washington that the European Communists had begun a "concerted effort to subvert democratic governments before . . . a cooperative recovery program can get under way."[4] The Central Intelligence Agency summed up the prevailing view within the administration by declaring on 26 September that "the greatest present danger to U.S. security lies, not in the military strength of the U.S.S.R. and the possibility of Soviet armed aggression, but in the possibility of the economic collapse of Western Europe and of the consequent accession to power of elements subservient to the Kremlin."[5] "The margin of safety in Europe," added the State Department's Policy Planning Staff, "both from an economic and political viewpoint, is extremely thin." Rather than easing tensions in Europe, the promise of Marshall Plan aid had helped increase them.[6]

To meet this critical situation, the Truman administration resolved to consolidate the opposition to Soviet expansion. Charles E. Bohlen, one of the State Department's leading experts on Soviet affairs, emphasized to a group of senior officials—including Secretary of War Kenneth C. Royall, Army Chief of Staff Dwight D. Eisenhower, and Acting Secretary of State Robert A. Lovett—at a Pentagon meeting on 30 August 1947 that the administration should base its policies on the "complete disunity" between the Soviets and the rest of the world. To counter the "centralized and ruthless direction" of the Soviet bloc, these top officials agreed that the United States should use its foreign aid to increase the political, economic, and military unity of the "non-Soviet world." While forging these links, Bohlen cautioned, the Truman administration had to act carefully so as to avoid criticism for dividing Europe into hostile camps. The success of this effort to build an anti-Communist bloc would determine the outcome of "a major political showdown crisis" between the United States and the Soviet Union, which Bohlen believed would come to a head during the next several months.[7] Secretary of State George C. Marshall presented a similar analysis to a Cabinet meeting on 7 November, as he urged the strengthening of local resistance to communism. "Our policy," Marshall asserted, "must be directed toward restoring a balance of power in Europe and Asia." The State Department believed that negotiations with the Soviets were all but futile.[8]

As a step toward restoring stability, Truman asked a special session of Congress to provide emergency economic aid to Europe. At a White House meeting in September, he explained to leaders of Congress his reasons for requesting such assistance. "We'll either have to provide a program of interim aid relief until the Marshall program gets going," Truman declared, "or the governments of France and Italy will fall, Austria too, and for all practical purposes Europe will be Communist.

The Marshall Plan goes out of the window, and it's a question of how long we could stand up in such a situation. This is serious. I can't overemphasize how serious."[9]

These acute fears of a Communist Europe helped the administration overcome much of the partisan opposition within the Republican-controlled Eightieth Congress. Truman gained no more valuable ally on Capitol Hill than Senator Arthur H. Vandenberg, (R-Mich.), chairman of the Foreign Relations Committee, who worried that "if our friends in Western Europe are allowed to starve and freeze to death this winter, the Commies will be completely back in the saddle." Like many fiscal conservatives, Vandenberg was concerned about squandering precious resources in a futile attempt to prevent such a takeover. Still, he preferred the "calculated risk" of extending aid to "do[ing] nothing and ultimately find[ing] ourselves isolated in a Communist world."[10] On 17 December Truman signed the Foreign Aid Act of 1947, which authorized $597 million in emergency assistance for Austria, Italy, and France.[11] On the heels of this victory, he proposed to Congress a far more ambitious measure of containment: Marshall Plan aid amounting to $17 billion during the next four years.[12]

Although these actions fortified some beleaguered governments, they also helped deepen the European crisis. By late 1947 the Truman administration believed that the prospect of American aid had blunted Communist efforts to gain power in Western Europe through legitimate political processes. In a series of estimates, the CIA repeatedly proclaimed the "marked deterioration" of the Communist political position in Europe. The State Department's Policy Planning Staff agreed that the "political advance of the Communists in Western Europe has been at least temporarily halted." Nevertheless, intelligence authorities took little comfort from this political victory since they expected that the European Communist parties would turn in desperation to more militant tactics. In France, the CIA reported, a wave of strikes and disorders in late 1947 was a harbinger of this shift. Although the government of Premier Robert Schuman had rallied sufficient support to quell these disturbances, the Communists could still cause economic dislocations through work stoppages and industrial sabotage. In Italy, according to the CIA, where the Communists had enough strength to launch a general strike or an armed uprising, the government's ability to meet either challenge was "questionable." The Policy Planning Staff predicted that "an intensified push against

Greece" might accompany Communist disturbances in France or Italy. American aid, then, might eventually bring economic recovery and political stability, but not unless several European countries survived a period of turmoil and even insurrection.[13]

To help these nations withstand these challenges, the Truman administration also expanded programs of military aid. The Greek government was one of the first beneficiaries. While planning the Greek program, administration officials had all too easily concluded that the simple extension of American assistance would enable government forces to seize the initiative in the civil war. Despite the arrival of American military advisers in May 1947 and the delivery of the first shipload of armaments in August, however, the military situation deteriorated sharply. Guerrilla recruiting soared, and insurgent strength by the end of 1947 reached 22,500 men, an increase of 50 percent over the number of soldiers at the time of the passage of the Greek-Turkish Aid Act. Rather than taking the offensive against the insurgents, the Greek National Army followed a defensive strategy of protecting villages. General William G. Livesay, the head of the American Military Advisory Group, concluded in frustration that the GNA would not be "properly and vigorously" used unless the United States consented to an increase in its size. In October 1947 the Truman administration did agree to the creation of a 21,000-man National Defense Corps (NDC) that could guard towns and villages and so enable the GNA to pursue the guerrillas. Funds originally earmarked for civilian projects instead paid for the establishment of the NDC. So worried were American policymakers about the insurgency by late 1947 that they believed that internal security must take priority over economic reconstruction.[14]

To insure the vigorous prosecution of the war, Truman authorized American army officers to furnish operational advice to Greek combat units. In approving this expansion of the American role in the civil war, Truman acted on the unanimous recommendations of military and diplomatic experts in Greece. Dwight P. Griswold, the chief of the American aid mission, first proposed this step in mid-September, owing to his belief that only American participation in the direction of combat operations could reverse the deterioration in the military situation. Ambassador Lincoln MacVeagh agreed, noting that "economic reconstruction cannot succeed in the absence of order and tranquility, while economic chaos favors the spread of Communism and the recruitment of the rebel forces." Perhaps most influential was the report of General Stephen J. Chamberlin, the chief of army intelligence, who visited Greece in September and urged that American army advisers help restore "the offensive spirit" in the GNA by "advising on planning and operations." Chamberlin justified this proposal by issuing a stark warning: "The United States has only two alternatives—they [sic] should get out of Greece or stay and be prepared to commit the means to win." Drawing on Chamberlin's analysis, the NSC recommended on 30 October that American military personnel furnish strategic and tactical advice to GNA units down to division level.[15]

Congressional opposition to this change in the advisory group's activities was limited and transitory. At first, Vandenberg was furious. In a meeting on 10 November with Secretary of the Army Royall, he even speculated that Congress might not have passed the Greek-Turkish Aid Act had it known that the small advisory group providing logistical aid that the administration contemplated in May would grow into a sizable mission furnishing operational advice by November. He then asked Royall for a written explanation for the change and announced that he intended to take up the matter the next morning with the Foreign Relations Committee. But after venting his fury, Vandenberg changed his mind about the committee meeting and the explanatory letter and acquiesced in the expansion of the American military role in Greece. His counterpart on the House Foreign Affairs Committee, Charles A. Eaton, (R-N.J.), expressed complete support. The Department of the Army issued a routine announcement about the change in the responsibilities of the military advisory group, and Congress took no action.[16]

The increase in military assistance occurred despite persistent American criticism of the Athens government. Both Livesay and Griswold deplored the inertia of the Greek General Staff. Livesay particularly resented the granting of subsidies for an increase in the Greek armed forces, a concession extracted from the United States, he insisted, only for political reasons. In spite of the September 1947 formation of a coalition government between the two largest parties, the Populists and the Liberals, Griswold continually used American economic aid as "a club" to mitigate political infighting and prevent the seizure of power by the extreme right. Even Truman denounced the excesses of the Greek leaders and considered them "accomplices" in creating the turmoil that engulfed Greece. He objected to the mass arrest in July of 14,000 people, many of whom had nothing to do with the insurgency. In a note to Admiral William D. Leahy, his chief of staff, Truman exploded: "Greeks and Jews suffer from an inferiority complex as well as a persecution complex. I've tried to help them both and so far they've only given me a pain in the—neck." Still, however detestable the policies of the Athens rulers, the consequences of a Communist insurgency gaining power were intolerable. According to the CIA, Greece was a critical test of the ability of the United States to contain Soviet expansion: "The continued ability of Greece to resist with US aid will therefore be closely watched by both the Eastern and Western blocs and will have an important influence on the future success of US foreign policy in Europe and the Near East."[17]

So critical did the Truman administration consider the Greek situation in late 1947 and early 1948 that the Joint Chiefs of Staff, the Policy Planning Staff, the CIA, and the NSC all studied the possibility of sending American troops to Greece. Such drastic action was contemplated because the deplorable state of the economy, "a feeling of insecurity among the people, friction among short-sighted political factions, selfishness and corruption in Government, and a dearth of effective leaders" had brought Greece to the edge of collapse. The only way to overcome such enormous difficulties, according to Loy W. Henderson, the director of the Office of Near Eastern and African Affairs, was for the Truman administration to resolve to use American armed forces, if necessary, to prevent an insurgent victory. Henderson argued that assurances of such support would raise Greek morale and galvanize resistance to the guerrillas. He also felt that such a strong stand would pay political dividends elsewhere since Greece was "the test tube which the peoples of the whole world are watching in order to ascertain whether the determination of the Western powers to resist aggression equals that of international Communism to acquire new territory and new bases for further aggression." While agreeing that "a Communist victory in Greece would be interpreted everywhere as a sign of American weakness," the Policy Planning Staff worried about deciding in advance to send troops and the difficulties of extracting them. To these reservations, Marshall added that, because of the lack of reserves, the dispatch of combat forces to Greece would foreclose action in other trouble spots, such as Italy and Palestine. Even stronger objections came from the Joint Chiefs. According to them, the commitment of American troops to Greece would be "militarily unsound," since the

United States needed to mobilize its strength before risking a major war. This view prevailed. Truman approved on 16 February 1948 one NSC paper, which deferred any decision about sending troops to Greece, and on 21 June another, which ruled out such a commitment barring a sharp change in the civil war. Instead, the Truman administration hoped that a one-year extension of its aid program and a new appropriation—$150 million for military assistance—would calm the turmoil in Greece.[18]

Even more alarming to Truman and his top advisers was the political and economic turbulence in Italy. Beset by high unemployment and a severe deficit in its balance of payments, Italy lacked the means to obtain many basic commodities—coal, foodstuffs, petroleum products—without substantial outside help.[19] Its political situation was equally precarious, owing to the conflict between the two principal rivals for power, the Christian Democrats and the Communists (PCI). With American encouragement, Alcide De Gasperi, the Christian Democratic prime minister, excluded the Communists from his government in May 1947.[20] The Communists in turn launched a campaign of propaganda, demonstrations, and strikes that, the Policy Planning Staff warned, might be the prelude to an armed insurrection and "the complete subjugation of Italy to Soviet control." Party leader Palmiro Togliatti privately favored greater moderation, but pressure from Soviet sponsors and PCI hard-liners forced him to endorse publicly the militant tactics that aroused American fears of a coup d'état.[21] Convinced that democracy in Italy—perhaps even in Europe—hung in the balance, the Truman administration responded not only with economic aid but also with military assistance.

Both the United States and Great Britain had been providing surplus armaments to the Italian armed forces since the end of the Second World War. In the spring of 1947, however, the British announced that they had exhausted their surplus stocks of many types of equipment and that financial difficulties prevented them from meeting the outstanding requirements of the Italian army from other sources. What made the British default serious was the impending ratification of the Italian Peace Treaty, which required the evacuation, within ninety days after it entered into force, of British and American occupation troops. Without additional equipment, allied military authorities reported, the Italian army would not "be capable of standing on its own feet once the Allies withdraw."[22]

The State Department stressed the political value of building up the Italian army. Deeply concerned about Communist strength in Italy, Marshall instructed Ambassador James C. Dunn on 20 May to offer De Gasperi additional surplus armaments, among other measures of assistance, as an inducement to reorganize his cabinet. Dunn urged speedy delivery of this military aid following the elimination of the Communists from De Gasperi's government. "The general political situation of the Government, and the deplorable inadequacy of the present Italian military forces to assume responsibility for the maintenance of order and even token protection of Italy's northeast frontier," he cabled on 19 June, "make it indispensable to hasten the Allied program of providing for the transfer to Italian troops of combat material in this theatre." Through his personal intervention, Dunn helped arrange an agreement on 21 July that provided for the sale to the Italian government of some $184 million worth of army and air force equipment for $18 million.[23]

War Department officials, however, were unwilling to fulfill the State Department's promises to Italy at the expense of further erosion of their limited reserves of equipment. Deep cuts in the army's procurement budget for fiscal year 1948, imposed by the Bureau of the Budget and approved by Congress, made some types of materiel scarce and impossible to replace. Secretary of War Robert P. Patterson informed Marshall on 23 June that medium tanks and howitzers in American depots in Italy were needed for other War Department programs. Disregarding Marshall's plea that a well-equipped Italian army was "important to the national interest," the War Department ordered the return to the United States of armor and artillery that the Italian army required. The War Department tried to provide the Italians with substitutes, but in most cases they were inadequate, unserviceable, or unavailable. Legal and financial obstacles added to these difficulties, since the War Department lacked authority to sell nonsurplus armaments to Italy or to obtain reimbursement for replacement and handling costs. Dunn reported with chagrin on 11 September that even the transfer of all available surplus materiel in Europe would not prevent critical deficiencies in the Italian army.[24]

The problems of providing military aid to Italy became more urgent with the proclamation of the Italian Peace Treaty on 15 September 1947. The Central Intelligence Group asserted that the withdrawal of American and British occupation troops would harm American security interests because the De Gasperi government was ill-prepared to cope with the Communist party. Using a powerful but dubious analogy, the intelligence analysts warned of the possible eruption of a civil war in northern Italy "similar to that prevailing in northern Greece." Doubtful that Italian security forces could handle such a situation, they recommended additional American equipment and training for the Italian army.[25] This analysis prompted War Department officials to reconsider what they might do, within their resources, "to check the present deterioration of the political situation, . . . from which might emerge a totalitarian regime firmly inimical to the U.S." General Dwight D. Eisenhower, the army chief of staff, dispatched a survey mission to Italy to investigate possible measures of military assistance.[26]

Like the CIG, the army survey mission stressed the similarities between Italy and Greece. Armed Communists were present in their northern provinces—guerrillas in Greece and paramilitary groups in Italy. Both shared a border with Communist Yugoslavia, which aided the Greek insurgents and might go so far as to intervene in an Italian civil war, partly because of the Yugoslavs' frustrated ambitions for the disputed region of Venezia Giulia and the city of Trieste. On the basis of this questionable analogy, the army analysts maintained that "the situation in Northern Italy is *potentially* comparable to that in Greece." They recommended the passage of military aid legislation similar to the Greek-Turkish Aid Act to forestall this threat. Because of the depletion of surplus stocks, such legislation was needed to equip and maintain the Italian army for the preservation of internal order and the defense of national frontiers. The survey mission cautioned, however, that military aid alone could not solve Italy's problems and should be closely integrated, as in Greece, with other forms of assistance—particularly Marshall Plan aid. In reply to Dunn's contention that such legislation might embarrass the De Gasperi government by pointing up its dependence on the United States, the army officers confidently predicted "that a program of U.S. military assistance to Italy openly undertaken at this time as a corollary to similar assistance being given to Greece and Turkey would emphasize the U.S. policy of firmness toward the advance of Communism, and would be more likely to avert than to evoke a crisis."[27] Relying on an increasingly familiar justification, the army analysts believed that the extension of military aid would produce major psychological gains by reassuring the Italians while deterring and demoralizing their Communist adversaries.

This exchange revealed the widening differences between the State Department and the army over military aid to Italy, even though both considered such assistance necessary. Officials in State's Office of European Affairs agreed with Dunn that congressional involvement would bring lengthy and public scrutiny of a matter that required swift and secret action. Army officials, on the other hand, demanded new legislation and appropriations before releasing precious armaments to Italy. For example, during deliberations in the NSC, Secretary of the Army Royall prevented approval of a draft report that did not call for an Italian Aid Act, yet recommended the transfer to Italy of additional equipment "now in the hands of, or being prepared for, our own armed forces."[28] The revised final version suggested only technical assistance to the Italian armed forces.[29]

As the deadline for the withdrawal of American occupation troops approached, a crisis atmosphere enveloped Rome and Washington. Dunn reported in late November and early December that De Gasperi and his advisers believed that the Communists were desperately afraid of losing the elections scheduled for April 1948 and so might launch a coup. Dunn agreed that the "strategically planned strikes and civil disturbances" were "preliminary skirmishes leading to an attempt to overthrow the government." At first De Gasperi thought an insurrection imminent. So great was his anxiety that he secured Truman's consent to delay the departure of American occupation troops by ten days until 14 December, the deadline established by the peace treaty. He also urged the United States to strengthen its forces in Austria and to station troops in the Mediterranean for quick intervention in Italy. Even before De Gasperi's request, Truman approved an NSC report that called for countering a Communist insurrection by extending "the strategic disposition of United States armed forces in Italy and other parts of the Mediterranean." On 1 December the Italian situation appeared so ominous to the State Department's Office of European Affairs that Acting Secretary Lovett asked the armed services to prepare at once to carry out this action.[30]

Despite their understandable fears, De Gasperi and Dunn overestimated the danger of armed insurrection. Togliatti actually intended the campaign of strikes and disorders not to be a prelude to armed insurrection but a way of forcing De Gasperi to take the Communists back into the government. Togliatti did not want to prevent Marshall Plan aid from reaching Italy—he doubted that the nation's economy could survive without it—but wanted to help determine its allocation. Badly conceived and easily misinterpreted, the campaign of disruption and violence instead produced greater efforts—Italian and American—to isolate and confront the Communists. In mid-December De Gasperi took the center-left Social Democratic and Republican parties into his government, thereby gaining a solid majority in Parliament. Upon the departure of American occupation troops, the White House issued a strong statement suggesting American intervention should the Communists threaten Italian freedom or independence.[31]

American officials, however, continued to worry about a Communist revolution, especially since Dunn warned that the Italian armed forces lacked the equipment to quell such an uprising. Based on Dunn's reports, army intelligence, which had previously believed that the Italian armed forces could handle a strictly internal uprising, abruptly revised its estimate. The CIA concurred, noting that the Italian government's ability to put down an armed insurrection was, "at the moment, in doubt."[32] When the Italian regime submitted a new request for arms, Dunn urged "an extraordinary effort" to fulfill it.[33]

Officials in Washington reacted quickly. On 9 December Truman personally instructed Secretary of Defense James V. Forrestal to do everything possible so that Italy would receive the military equipment it needed to combat "totalitarian inspired unrest."[34] Army officials promptly notified the State Department that they could furnish from existing stocks many items the Italians most urgently required. Forrestal, however, reminded Marshall that Congress would have to provide the authority and funds for this transaction since little equipment was surplus. A few days later Royall emphasized to the State-Army-Navy-Air Force Coordinating Committee (SANACC), which was beginning a new study of military aid to Italy, the need for legislation similar to the Greek-Turkish Aid Act. The army, in short, remained determined to secure congressional authority and appropriations before making any new commitment to Italy.[35]

The State Department, nevertheless, still did not want to place this matter before Congress. Officials in State's Office of European Affairs agreed with Dunn that such a move would embarrass the De Gasperi government to the benefit of the Communists. They also doubted that Congress could act swiftly enough so that Italy would receive armaments prior to the April elections. Determined to speed arms to Italy, Acting Secretary Robert A. Lovett decided instead to offer De Gasperi a modest quantity of available surplus, primarily small arms and ammunition, at a cost of $3.75 million. But De Gasperi demurred. He protested that Italy lacked the dollars for this purchase and that any such expenditures would occasion the "strongest kind of attack from the left." Because of the prime minister's hesitations and legal restraints in Washington, the debate over military aid to Italy reached an impasse. But as Dunn reminded Marshall on 4 February 1948, there had been "no significant developments tending to make any less urgent the provision of those arms and equipment for the Italian armed forces."[36]

The SANACC proposed a new solution to the problem of emergency military aid to Italy. In its report of 16 January 1948, the committee found that the army could furnish not only many of the small arms that the Italians urgently requested but also several other items, including rocket launchers, grenades, and tanks. Yet there was no specific legislative authority that would allow the transfer of this equipment, only a small part of which was surplus. Accordingly, the SANACC recommended that the president provide these munitions under "his plenary powers as Commander-in-Chief and as head of the State in its relations with foreign countries and for the purpose of protecting primary security interests of the United States."[37] The NSC promptly endorsed this suggestion, and Truman accepted it on 13 February. Truman still required the Italians to pay for the equipment, handling, and transportation, which amounted to $10 million, since he had no discretionary or unvouchered fund that might be used to defray those expenses.

His action pushed the powers of the presidency beyond previous limits. Never before had a chief executive invoked such constitutional powers for the transfer of armaments to a foreign nation.[38] Truman then used his presidential authority on 10 March to override federal law by ordering the immediate delivery of military equipment to Italy even though the United States had not received payment.[39]

Notwithstanding Truman's extraordinary action, the bulk of American military supplies did not reach Italy before the elections. De Gasperi was responsible for the delay. Reversing his previous position, he told Dunn on 12 March that the delivery of American armaments would now hurt his campaign. De Gasperi's statement reflected a shrewd assessment of the rapidly improving electoral prospects of the Christian Democrats, who had been trailing in public-opinion polls and the estimates of political experts. The change was the result of the Communist coup in Czechoslovakia in late February, a dramatic event that suddenly shifted support to the Christian Democrats. De Gasperi now managed to deflect public attention away from Italian economic woes, difficulties exacerbated by the fiscal policies of Minister of the Treasury Luigi Einaudi. Instead he insisted that the only issue for the Italian electorate was to choose between democracy and total-itarianism. De Gasperi also benefited from an elaborate campaign of propaganda and covert funding of the Christian Democrats orches-trated by the United States, and from an army of campaign workers provided by the Vatican. Sensing victory and increasingly doubtful that the Communists would stage an insurrection, De Gasperi feared that the benefit of delivering American military supplies before the election would be outweighed by the political damage from new Com-munist charges that the Christian Democrats were American puppets.[40]

This assessment stunned State Department officials. John D. Hickerson, the director of State's Office of European Affairs, com-plained to Dunn that De Gasperi was playing into the hands of the Communists: their propaganda campaign, Hickerson believed, aimed precisely at preventing aid to the Italian armed forces. Only defeatism or false security, not political canniness, could account for De Gasperi's decision. Indeed, according to an outraged Hickerson, De Gasperi was now endangering an *American* interest that the State Department had worked so hard to protect—a stable, independent Italy. Under pres-sure, De Gasperi consented to secret deliveries, beginning on 3 April, of American surplus armaments then in Germany and of other equip-ment from the United States after the election. Because of these arrangements, American military aid had no direct effect on the Chris-tian Democrats' astounding victory at the polls on 18 April, a triumph that provided De Gasperi's party with a clear majority in Parliament. Nor was it needed, as De Gasperi had anticipated, to put down an attempt by the defeated Communists to seize power.[41]

Nevertheless, American policy in Italy demonstrated a growing reliance on military aid as an instrument of containment. Although economic assistance was the administration's principal weapon against communism, many of Truman's top advisers believed, partly from their experience in Italy, that economic recovery was inseparable from inter-nal security. Making easy analogies with the situation in Greece, they exaggerated the Communist threat in Italy and used military means to combat it. They concluded that arms aid was useful not only in strengthening the Italian army but also in stiffening the morale of democratic forces. State Department officials in particular found military aid a versatile tool, since they stressed the psychological importance of maintaining Italy's Western orientation. Convinced that the danger in Italy was both political and military, State Department officials regarded arms aid as an essential element in preventing the Soviets from extending their sphere of influence.[42]

Just as important, the problems in providing arms to Italy focused attention on deficiencies in existing arrangements for handling foreign requests for military assistance. Army officials had pointed out in the spring of 1947 that excess equipment could no longer sustain new programs of military aid, but the Surplus Property Act remained the only general authority for furnishing arms abroad. The difficulties with the Italian program confirmed the worst fears of those army officials who had worried that the State Department would make new commitments that exceeded current capabilities. Not only did the State Department veto the presentation of new legislation to Congress but also it prevailed on the army to transfer to Italy several million dollars of equipment from its war reserves. Nothing proved more conclusively to army officials that the military aid machinery needed a drastic overhaul. Uniformed officers redoubled their efforts to secure new legislation and appropriations. In addition, irked by the prevailing country-by-country approach, logistics experts demanded more systematic planning of arms aid. This drive for the consolidation of military assistance programs gained even greater momentum in the spring of 1948, as policymakers weighed the possibility of rearming Western Europe.[43]

The impetus for American rearmament of Western Europe came from European efforts, beginning in late 1947, to protect against Soviet expansion. Following the failure of the December 1947 London Conference of Foreign Ministers to make any progress toward a German treaty, British Foreign Secretary Ernest K. Bevin told Marshall, "There is no chance that the Soviet Union will deal with the West on any reasonable terms in the foreseeable future. The salvation of the West depends upon the formation of some form of union, formal or informal in character, in Western Europe, backed by the United States and the dominions, such a mobilization of moral and material force [as] will inspire confidence and energy within and respect elsewhere."[44] Elaborating these ideas before the House of Commons on 22 January 1948, Bevin proposed a network of bilateral alliances, modeled on the Dunkirk Treaty of 4 March 1947, embracing Britain, France, and the Low Countries.[45] Bevin purposely left vague the American relationship to this Western union, although he indicated that he was counting on American "power and resources." He also emphasized that this Western union would be broader in conception than a conventional military alliance, that it must be "a spiritual union as well," which derived its strength "from the basic freedoms and ethical principles for which we all stand."[46]

Reaction within the State Department was mixed. Hickerson enthusiastically supported Bevin's proposal, but thought the extension of the Dunkirk Treaty a "highly dubious" first step since it would preclude Germany's eventual participation. He urged instead a multilateral security pact modeled on the Rio Treaty and insisted that American participation was essential to its success. "I don't care whether entangling alliances have been considered worse than original sin ever since George Washington's time," he exclaimed to one of his subordinates on New Year's Eve in 1947. "We've got to negotiate a military alliance with Western Europe in peacetime and we've got to do it quickly." Hickerson promptly won influential support for his views—John Foster Dulles, the Republican expert on foreign affairs, was one of his first converts—and remained throughout 1948 the State Department's most fervent advocate of a North Atlantic Treaty.[47]

George F. Kennan, the director of the Policy Planning Staff, was far more circumspect. Like Hickerson, he applauded Bevin's initiative since it held out hope of establishing a new European equilibrium in which Germany was not the predominant power. He also agreed with Hickerson that the Dunkirk Treaty was a poor starting point for a Western union because it would exclude Germany and focus the alliance far too narrowly on military defense. Kennan thought that military union should be the consequence of, rather than the stimulus for, political, economic, and spiritual ties. Unlike Hickerson, however, he opposed formal American participation in a European alliance. Kennan believed that if the Europeans forged an effective Western union there would be "no real question as to our long-term relationship to it, even with respect to the military guarantee."[48] As he explained later, "military policy would flow correctly of its own accord—it needed no legal obligations or prescriptions."[49]

Because of their uncertainty over the relationship of the United States to the proposed Western union, administration officials gave only scant consideration to supplying arms aid. Marshall thought at first that American participation in any Western defense system would be restricted to furnishing material assistance to its members, but did not elaborate his views.[50] Theodore C. Achilles, Hickerson's deputy for Western European affairs, also raised the possibility of military aid, but maintained that the Europeans far more urgently needed public assurance of American determination to defend their soil. Only American adherence to a multilateral security pact, in Achilles's view, would ease their doubts about the future.[51] Kennan agreed that the Europeans lacked confidence, but ridiculed their anxieties. "What in the world," he asked, "did they think we had been doing in Europe these last four or five years? Did they suppose we had labored to free Europe from the clutches of Hitler merely in order to abandon it to those of Stalin? . . . Why did they wish to divert attention . . . [to] a danger which did not actually exist but which might indeed be brought into existence by too much discussion of the military balance and by the ostentatious stimulation of a military rivalry?"[52] Because he believed that the Soviets did not contemplate a military offensive in Europe, Kennan did not even consider the possibility of American military aid during the first weeks of 1948.[53]

Washington's response to Bevin's initiative thus was both encouraging and cautious. Marshall replied to Bevin on 20 January that the United States would do everything it properly could to assist in the formation of a Western union, but made no commitments of any sort. Under Secretary Lovett later informed Lord Inverchapel, the British ambassador, that there were two main reasons for Marshall's hesitation. First, the prospect of "new and extensive military and political commitments" might harm the chances for congressional approval of the European Recovery Program (ERP). Second, Marshall believed that any statement about the American relationship to the proposed Western union was premature. "You are in effect asking us to pour concrete before we see the blueprints," Lovett told Inverchapel. Although British officials protested that they could not make the Western union a going concern without American participation, Marshall was unmoved. He was determined that the initiative remain in Europe, not pass to Washington.[54]

These discussions of European security were transformed by a dramatic series of crises that began in late February with the Communist seizure of power in Czechoslovakia. Exploiting a governmental crisis, the Communists transformed a coalition regime into one-party rule in the last European state that was precariously balanced between East and West. The mysterious death on 11 March of the eminent Czech Foreign Minister Jan Masaryk profoundly shocked Western public opinion, which was already anxious that Soviet ambitions knew no limits. More than three months earlier, Kennan had warned Marshall and Truman that American efforts to throttle Communist influence in Western Europe would provoke the Soviets to tighten their grip on their own sphere and particularly "to clamp down completely on Czechoslovakia."[55] Yet Kennan's prescient analysis was apparently forgotten by early 1948, and the Czech coup was generally interpreted not as a defensive reaction but as part of an ominous pattern of Soviet expansion—in Eastern Europe, Greece, and Italy. Comparisons abounded, both publicly and privately, between the current Czech crisis and the one of a decade earlier. Truman, for example, asserted, "We are faced with exactly the same situation with which Britain and France were faced in 1938–9 with Hitler."[56]

Soviet moves in Scandinavia seemed to confirm such fears. Immediately after the Czech coup, the Soviets pressured Finland, a nation that generally followed their lead in foreign affairs, to conclude a mutual defense treaty, and despite Finnish reluctance such an alliance was signed on 6 April. Even more alarming to Western leaders were apparent Soviet designs on Norway. Since the end of the Second World War, Norway had made support for the United Nations the fundamental tenet of its foreign policy and ruled out participation in any regional alliance. Norwegian military authorities, however, recognized that the United Nations could not guarantee Norwegian security and based their defense plans on British assistance in the event of war. By early 1948, however, they had begun to doubt whether they could depend on British military help and asked about American assistance in the event of an attack. This inquiry coincided with rumors that Soviets were trying to force Norway to accept a nonaggression pact similar to the treaty with Finland.[57]

The rumors proved false, but not before they provoked a strong reaction in Washington and London. Marshall, after clearing his response with Truman, informed the embassy in Oslo that it was "imperative that Norway adamantly resist . . . [Soviet] demands and pressure" and implied that the United States would support such a strong stand. The British were almost in a panic over the prospect of Soviet advances in Norway. Bevin told Marshall that "the pace set by Russia in Czechoslovakia, then Finland, and now Norway, shows clearly that there is no time to lose." Only "a bold move," in Bevin's view, could avert the destruction of "all efforts to build up a Western Union" and the consequent "extension of the Russian sphere of influence to the Atlantic."[58]

These anxieties accelerated Western defense planning. Following the Czech coup, the French government, which had been preoccupied with the threat of a revived Germany, agreed to accept a multilateral alliance directed against Soviet aggression. On 17 March representatives of Great Britain, France, and the Benelux countries signed a fifty-year treaty in which they pledged "all the military and other aid and assistance in their power" in the event of an attack on one of the signatories.[59] That same day, Truman hailed the creation of the Western Union and promised "that the United States will, by appropriate means, extend to the free nations [of Europe] the support which the situation requires."[60] Even before he made this pledge, Truman authorized Marshall to accept a British invitation to discuss the establishment of an Atlantic security system. Among the ideas that representatives of the United States, Britain, and Canada considered during these secret Pentagon talks in Washington at the end of March was "a military ERP," but the conferees failed to reach any firm conclusions.[61]

The administration's willingness to discuss an Atlantic security system and the rearmament of Western Europe did not derive from a belief that there had been a fundamental change in Soviet policy, despite some warnings to the contrary. The most sensational prediction came from General Lucius D. Clay, the commander of American occupation troops in Germany. Clay cabled the Department of the Army on 5 March that he had previously thought war unlikely for at least ten years, but had recently "felt a subtle change in Soviet attitude which I cannot define but which now gives me a feeling that it may come with dramatic suddenness."[62] Intelligence analysts, though, found no basis for Clay's suspicions. Only a day after receiving Clay's telegram, the Intelligence Division assured top army officials that "the Soviets will continue their expansionist policy taking care to avoid war."[63] On 16 March the CIA informed Truman that there was no "reliable evidence that the USSR intends to resort to military action within the next sixty days." Two weeks later, in a more detailed report, the CIA declared that available evidence and "the logic of the situation" suggested that the Soviets would not launch a war during 1948. State Department experts and army officials independently reached similar conclusions; they reckoned that Soviet miscalculation, rather than design, carried the greater risk of war. In spite of their alarm over recent developments, most American officials did not think that the Soviets would resort to force of arms.[64]

Indeed, policymakers doubted that the Soviets would change tactics precisely because their current methods had been so successful. "By exploiting the postwar political and economic instability in Europe and the rest of the world along traditional Marxist lines," the CIA argued, "Soviet leaders have already obtained very substantial results." Although the Soviets were capable "of overrunning all of Western Europe and the Near East to Cairo within a short period of time," their current tactics, the CIA analysis maintained, were "the cheapest and safest method by which Soviet leaders can obtain their objectives."[65] General Chamberlin thought that the Soviets could continue to draw on a variety of means short of general war—"military, diplomatic and propaganda pressure, subversion, infiltration of labor and security forces, and civil war"—to gain their objectives. In its annual estimate of Soviet intentions, the American Embassy in Moscow succinctly summarized the prevailing view by asserting that in Europe and elsewhere the Soviets had "no reason to change present methods of extending Communist influence."[66]

Given their assessment of Soviet intentions, American officials were as concerned about reassuring the Europeans as deterring the Russians. The Czech coup kindled in Europe fears of relentless Soviet expansion that threatened to undermine the Marshall Plan and weaken democratic governments. Regardless of the formation of the Western Union, the CIA warned that "without the prospect of active and effective US support, the present tendency toward stiffer resistance might give way to despair and to a rush for the Communist bandwagon." Military officials expressed similar views. While urging a variety of measures, including extensive arms aid, to build up the military establishments of Western Europe, the army's Plans and Operations Division (P&O) declared that the immediate purpose of such assistance should be strengthening the will to resist in Western Europe. The State Department was especially concerned about European morale. With Kennan temporarily overseas, Hickerson's counsel now prevailed. One of the greatest dangers in Europe, Hickerson wrote to Marshall, was "that too many people in the remaining free countries will be intimidated by the Soviet colossus and the absence of tangible American support to the point of losing their will to resist." Administration officials believed that the crisis in Europe was a crisis of confidence.[67]

Only American military commitments, policymakers concluded, could allay European anxieties. Despite the passage of the Marshall Plan on 3 April 1948 and the subsequent appropriation of $5 billion for its first year, European leaders maintained that their nation's security depended on American military help as well as economic aid. They reasoned that the United States alone could neutralize the threat of force that made Soviet tactics of infiltration and intimidation so effective. The French were especially concerned about American assistance in the defense of Western Europe, since only such help could save them from the twin horrors of Soviet occupation and subsequent liberation. High French military officials told Ambassador Jefferson Caffery that, without assurances of American arms, the French people "with the conviction of going to certain defeat," would meekly surrender to any Communist challenge. Although not as jittery as the French, the British insisted during the Pentagon talks that the most important issue was the American attitude in the event of a Soviet invasion of Europe. The American response, although still measured, was far more encouraging than it had been only a few weeks earlier. At the conclusion of the Pentagon talks, working levels of the State Department recommended that the United States take the lead in negotiating a North Atlantic defense arrangement and in the meantime open military conversations with the Western Union. The NSC soon explained that such actions would help increase the confidence of European nations in their ability to resist Soviet aggression.[68]

Service officials had additional reasons for favoring military cooperation with Western Europe. In their view, recent events in Europe—the Czech coup, Soviet moves in Scandinavia, the tension in Italy—necessitated increased defense appropriations, which they had long thought necessary to check Soviet expansion. "The apparently unlimited extent of Soviet Communistic ambitions, heretofore recognized only by a few, is now apparent to all who are capable of recognizing the truth," declared the P&O. In addition to calling for a military aid program modeled on the Marshall Plan, P&O advocated the expansion of the armed forces to meet possible overseas commitments, including the defense of Western Europe. In a similar report, Chamberlin specifically recommended an increase in troop levels, intensified strategic planning, and restoration of the draft. The chief of naval operations, Admiral Louis E. Denfeld, urged partial mobilization. Although service leaders undoubtedly exaggerated the Soviet threat, they were not merely exploiting the March crisis to advance parochial interests. They firmly believed that, without increased military strength, any effort to deter the Soviets or reassure the Europeans would be a hollow gesture.[69]

While staff planners hurriedly completed the first joint war plan since the end of World War II, Secretary of Defense Forrestal led the campaign for domestic rearmament. In doing so, he appealed to Truman and James E. Webb, the director of the Bureau of the Budget, to ease the restraints they had imposed on defense spending in their attempt to curb inflation and reduce the public debt. For fiscal year 1949, Truman had asked Congress for military appropriations of just $9.8 billion, a sum, the president conceded, that sufficed "only for the minimum requirements."[70] Forrestal disputed even that modest claim. Troop shortages were so severe that the army had only one division in reserve to meet an emergency and the navy had to immobilize 107 ships. Noting the decline of American military capabilities at a time of rising Cold War tensions, Marshall told the NSC that "we are playing with fire while we have nothing with which to put it out."[71] To help increase military readiness, Forrestal secured from Truman a commitment to ask Congress for the reinstitution of the draft, which had expired in 1947, and a supplemental appropriation of $3.2 billion for the National Military Establishment.[72]

Truman's decision on the latter issue came only after wrangling among the services and with the congressional military affairs committees over the amount of the additional funding and its allocation—particularly over whether the air force should be the principal beneficiary. Webb blamed Forrestal for these difficulties because he had been "bulldozed" by the Joint Chiefs and "lost control."[73] So did Truman, who bemoaned the inability of his secretary of defense to secure the agreement of the three services to "a balanced sensible defense for which the country can pay."[74] Such restraint was imperative because Congress had passed a $4.8 billion tax cut over Truman's veto. Drawing on Webb's counsel, Truman dressed down his military chiefs and informed them that he would not support an expansion of the armed forces that could be maintained only through "large-scale deficit financing" that would trigger inflation. Truman thus continued to place high priority on the maintenance of a sound economy through a balanced budget and to hope that extensive foreign assistance, rather than a major military buildup, could contain communism.[75]

Forrestal also took the lead in pressing for changes in military assistance policy. Convinced that the existing arrangements for furnishing arms to foreign countries were cumbersome and inefficient, he told Royall on 7 March that the army and the State Department should more closely coordinate their activities. As a first step, he appointed an assistant responsible for handling military aid matters and recommended that Marshall do the same.[76]

Forrestal's initiative gave the army a chance to express anew its growing discontent with current procedures for supplying arms abroad. In response to Forrestal's suggestions, a special army committee recommended on 1 April a detailed division of responsibility between the National Military Establishment and the State Department to remedy the confusion that often hampered programs of military aid. The army planners went further, however, and urged the enactment of legislation that would broaden the authority of the president to arm foreign countries. Equally important, in their view, were appropriations to reimburse the services for expenditures in the implementation of military assistance programs.[77] Finally, because of the exhaustion of surplus stocks and the demands of new Department of the Army programs, the army committee suggested limited expansion of the domestic armaments industry. The service planners believed that, taken together, these actions would provide a sound basis for the continuing supply of military assistance to foreign nations.[78]

Even before the army committee completed its report, Congress began to consider new military aid legislation. During hearings on the European Recovery Program, the House Foreign Affairs Committee suddenly asked the State Department to submit a bill authorizing the president to supply military equipment to foreign nations whenever he thought such transfers were in the national interest. This measure was to have become part of comprehensive foreign aid legislation, authorizing not only the Marshall Plan but also military and economic assistance to Greece, Turkey, and China. House Republicans favored such an omnibus bill because of their distress over "receiving from the administration a long succession of 'piecemeal' programs, each with a separate timetable of emergency, without any adequate total program either as to scope or commitments." Drawing on previous SANACC studies, diplomatic and military officials hurriedly drafted a military assistance bill, known as Title VI, and sent it to the Foreign Affairs Committee in early March.[79]

The State Department, however, firmly opposed the merger of European recovery and military assistance legislation. Marshall feared a new round of congressional hearings that would delay help to the beleaguered nations of Europe. Hickerson also noted that incorporation of Title VI in an omnibus bill would "change the whole emphasis of ERP from a program to promote positively European recovery to a program of defense against Soviet aggression." Such a shift, he warned, might alienate European neutrals such as Sweden and Switzerland. Vandenberg, the floor leader of the European Recovery Program in the Senate, also objected to the coupling of economic and military aid for fear that such legislation might fail to pass the upper chamber. He prevailed on his colleagues in the House to compromise. Despite its broad sweep, the Foreign Assistance Act of 1948, which Truman signed on 3 April, did not contain the controversial Title VI.[80]

But military assistance legislation was by no means dead. As soon as the Foreign Affairs Committee tabled Title VI, the military establishment began to press for the introduction of a separate arms bill. Forrestal wrote to Marshall on 24 March that he understood that Truman was "generally familiar" with Title VI and supported the presentation of similar legislation to Congress.[81] So did several State Department officials. Hickerson, for example, declared that such a measure "would undoubtedly strengthen the resistance of non-Communist forces throughout Europe." A departmental committee, however, recommended legislation more limited in scope than Title VI. Such a bill, the committee explained, would have a better chance in Congress while meeting the administration's most pressing need— expanded authority to fulfill emergency requests for arms.[82]

At the end of April and the beginning of May 1948, Washington was rife with speculation that Truman would ask for legislation to arm

Western Europe. White House officials denied this rumor on 1 May, but privately railed about the failure of the State Department and the National Military Establishment to inform them of their plans. The reason for this lack of communication was that Pentagon officials were trying to assess the mood of Congress. Marx Leva, one of Forrestal's deputies, predicted that, because there were so many false stories circulating on Capitol Hill about an impending administration proposal for a multibillion-dollar military assistance program, a request for interim authority to spend $750 million would actually ease the anxieties of many legislators and aid in the passage of other pending defense measures, such as the supplemental appropriation and selective service. Most of the uniformed and civilian service leaders, however, reached antithetical conclusions about the probable congressional reaction. Certainly the opposition of Budget Director Webb was by no means tempered when he learned that the Defense and State departments were contemplating only an interim program of military aid. Webb told officials from those two departments that all the loose talk about spending billions for arms assistance was "very dangerous and . . . already out of hand." The president, he declared, would not support such a program. Webb doubted that Truman would endorse even a more limited measure, although the president would withhold his final decision until reading the draft legislation.[83]

Marshall and Forrestal finally sent the proposed Military Assistance Act of 1948 to the White House on 7 May. Based on Title VI, it would have allowed the president to provide emergency help to any foreign government until 30 April 1949, by which time administration officials hoped to submit more comprehensive arms legislation. The bill's prospects in Congress were actually quite poor, and not merely because of legislative reluctance to approve another costly national security program. Vandenberg, whose support was critical, thought that the Europeans should first pool their military resources before requesting American help. Truman, however, never even sent the legislation to Capitol Hill; he and Webb shared a conviction that the budget could not accommodate another major foreign aid expenditure during the current fiscal year.[84]

Despite the failure to secure an interim arms bill, planning for comprehensive military assistance legislation moved ahead quickly, hastened in part by the administration's efforts to carry out Truman's pledge of support for the Western Union. During the spring of 1948, the State Department informed several European countries that it wished to develop a regional approach to military assistance; it no longer preferred to grant individual requests for arms on a piecemeal basis. Such thinking influenced the NSC report on 13 April on American assistance to the Western Union. Although primarily concerned with the negotiation of a North Atlantic defense treaty, the NSC paper recommended that the United States promptly coordinate its military production with the Western Union nations. Such a suggestion implied substantial transfers of arms to Europe, which, as administration officials realized, would require new legislation and appropriations.[85]

State Department officials worked closely with Vandenberg, the chairman of the Senate Foreign Relations Committee, in planning measures of assistance to Western Europe. Indeed, so heavily did they rely on his advice that Vandenberg became one of the architects of the North Atlantic Treaty.[86] During a series of meetings in April with Acting Secretary Lovett, Vandenberg firmly opposed any "unlimited, open-ended offer of aid," concerned that it might encourage the majority of countries either "to fold their hands and let Uncle Sam carry them" or, conversely, to take "so firm an attitude as to become provocative." He preferred instead a military assistance program modeled on the Marshall Plan; that is, one requiring the recipients first to integrate their defenses, rather than "inviting countries to come to us with their shopping lists."[87] This principle was embodied in the Vandenberg Resolution, approved by the Senate on 11 June by a vote of sixty-four to four, which affirmed support for "association of the United States, by constitutional process, with such regional and other collective arrangements as are based on continuous and effective self-help and mutual aid, and as affect its national security." The Senate was well aware of the implications of this general language. By an overwhelming margin, the upper chamber rejected an amendment offered by Claude R. Pepper (D-Fla.) that would have struck from the resolution any reference to the possibility of American military assistance.[88]

The Truman administration shaped policy on military aid to Western Europe to conform to the principles of the Vandenberg Resolution. The NSC recommended on 28 June that American uniformed officers join the Western Union military conversations in London and "make clear throughout that the ERP precedent should be followed." Only after the European nations had combined their military resources, the NSC declared, should the United States consider their requests for supplementary assistance. In return, the United States should request reciprocal assistance, perhaps in the form of base and air-transit rights. Truman promptly approved these recommendations, and in mid-July the Joint Chiefs named General Lyman L. Lemnitzer as their representative to the London talks. A central task of Lemnitzer's mission was to stress to the Europeans that they would receive American military aid only if they adopted strategic concepts that offered "reasonable promise of success," held to a minimum their demands on American resources, and envisioned not only "the defense of Western Europe" but also "the rapid and complete defeat of aggression." Once the Europeans had met these conditions, the president would seek military assistance legislation from Congress.[89]

Just as the possibility of rearming Western Europe shaped the administration's legislative agenda, so did the army's persistent desire to establish a sound basis for continuing programs of military assistance. Throughout the spring of 1948, General Henry S. Aurand, the director of logistics, bombarded his superiors with requests for more systematic handling of arms aid. Typical was his suggestion on 19 March to Bradley and Royall that the army oppose new commitments to furnish arms until the approval of "an integrated total military aid program" and the enactment of a bill modeled on lend-lease. Because of the depletion of surplus stocks, Aurand was eager to arrange for the orderly and efficient procurement of military supplies for transfer overseas. He also recalled that the SWNCC had estimated in the summer of 1947 that requests for American military aid might total as much as $22 billion. Aurand was determined to prevent such an overextension of national capacity and to insure that any new commitments brought the greatest possible return to American security. Until his recommendations were carried out, Aurand warned army officials, "every piecemeal commitment for foreign military aid fritters away our limited assets and jeopardizes the main result we are trying to accomplish."[90]

Aurand's importuning influenced army policy. His appeal for legislation and appropriations reinforced the army's staunch support of these measures. His insistence on an overall program of military aid resulted in plans for a new survey of potential demands for American equipment and the mobilization of industry to meet those requirements. Although army authorities rejected his suggestion to deny all requests for military aid pending the enactment of legislation, they did stress more vigorously than ever to the State Department that a lack of authority, equipment, and funds hamstrung the military establishment's ability to arm foreign nations.[91]

Aurand's influence shaped the army's reaction to requests from Denmark and Norway for military aid. The State Department was eager to provide armaments to both these countries to discourage their adherence to a neutral Scandinavian bloc championed by Sweden and to increase their interest in a Northern Atlantic defense treaty.[92] The army, however, demurred. After consulting with Aurand, Wedemeyer told Hickerson that the army could furnish only token quantities of small arms to Denmark—not even the types the Danes had requested—but emphasized his opposition to the transfer of this material. "A strategic analysis of Europe would indicate that Denmark might be overrun should the Juggernaut to the East decide to move Westward," Wedemeyer declared. "If the Juggernaut does not roll, the equipment would not be required in Denmark." The army also balked at even minor assistance to Norway, despite the Joint Chiefs' desire to encourage Norway's Western leanings. "Furnishing aid on the piecemeal basis presents the possibility that we shall give away equipment which may be requested later by nations more vital to the security of the United States," Royall asserted in a memorandum drafted by Aurand. The army's point was clear: the administration could no longer postpone a solution to the problems of providing military aid to foreign nations.[93]

Studies by the SANACC, begun in the wake of the Truman Doctrine speech and completed in early 1948, supported the army's view. In one report, the SANACC concluded that "there is a definite requirement for legislation which will broaden the authority of the President to implement U.S. military assistance to foreign nations under appropriate conditions." The initiation of new programs of military aid, the committee noted, was now "difficult and in some instances impossible." In another paper, the SANACC warned that the inability to provide maintenance items and spare parts "could tend to drive some nations into the orbit of Soviet influence." Even though the president could seek congressional approval of each arms transfer, this method was usually too slow and often led to an exhaustive public inquiry, which the administration had every desire to avoid. To overcome these problems, the SANACC recommended the enactment of legislation that would allow the president to furnish military equipment to foreign

nations whenever he thought such transfers were in the national interest.[94] Such a measure would consolidate all military assistance programs under a single authority for the first time since lend-lease.[95]

The SANACC also approved, after more than a year of deliberation,
a new arms policy. The committee agreed that the primary purpose of
sending arms abroad was to further the interests of the United States.
This conclusion seemed self-evident and empty, except when compared to earlier policy statements, such as SC/R-184 and SWNCC
202/4, which stressed that the *restriction* of arms transfers generally
furthered American objectives. The committee emphasized that military assistance should be consistent with the nation's primary security
interest, "supporting resistance to immediate or potential communist
aggression."[96] Most top administration officials agreed. In April Royall, for example, wrote to the former secretary of war, Henry L. Stimson, that "our current thinking indicates that it will eventually be to
our interests to assist . . . foreign armed forces . . . in order that
aggressive Communist action cannot so easily overcome, one by one,
other free nations now outside the Soviet orbit." Conversely, partly
because of the absence of an immediate Communist threat, the administration refused to furnish military aid to India, and the Western
Hemisphere Defense Program sank into oblivion. Since the end of
World War II, checking the spread of Soviet influence had been an
important objective of American military assistance programs; by
mid-1948 it was the overriding purpose.[97]

Anticommunism pervaded the NSC report of 1 July on military
assistance to "nations of the non-Soviet world." This report, the product of more than a year of study and debate of American military
assistance, asserted that "the success of certain free nations in resisting
aggression by the forces of Soviet directed world communism is of
critical importance to the security of the United States." Drawing on
familiar arguments, the NSC analysts maintained that American military help would raise the "moral and material" strength in recipient
nations, which was essential to "political resistance to communist
subversion from within and Soviet pressure from without." Political
considerations might occasionally dictate provision of arms to nations
for other reasons, the NSC planners allowed, but the containment of
Communist expansion should be the guiding principle of military aid
policy.[98]

Toward this end, the NSC advocated the consolidation and expansion of American military assistance programs. Like the SANACC planners, the NSC staff considered imperative the passage of legislation, similar to Title VI, which broadened the authority of the president to furnish military aid. "On the basis of legislation along these lines," they explained, "it would be possible to work out . . . a coordinated military assistance program in which the quotas of each recipient would be related to overall needs, production capabilities, political considerations and strategic concepts." Western Europe, they believed, should receive first priority in any future program of arms aid, yet the planners placed no limit on the scope of such an effort. The NSC also urged that the United States insist on self-help and mutual assistance among the recipient nations and on reciprocal assistance, perhaps in the form of strategic raw materials. Truman ratified this new consensus on military aid by approving these recommendations on 10 July. Propelled by a desire both to maintain the effectiveness of an instrument on which it had repeatedly drawn since the end of World War II and to embark on a new program of assistance for Western Europe, the Truman administration was now committed to the development of a comprehensive, worldwide program of military aid.[99]

6 | The Dilemma of Aid to China

You can help any government but one which does not know how to govern.
—George F. Kennan, February 1948

I am unable to understand General Marshall's apparent willingness to become involved in saving the Greek and Turkish Governments in view of his present attitude toward the Government of China," Admiral William D. Leahy, the president's chief of staff, confided to his diary on 6 March 1947. "The two situations seem to be identical."[1] Leahy's complaint reflected the widespread perplexity within the service departments and Congress and among the public over the State Department's attitude toward military assistance to China. At the same time that President Harry S. Truman proclaimed his determination "to support free peoples who are resisting attempted subjugation by armed minorities or by outside pressures," he backed the efforts of Secretary of State George C. Marshall to limit American military help to the Nationalist regime of Chiang Kai-shek.[2] Marshall ultimately prevailed over his bureaucratic and congressional adversaries: he was able to brake the momentum of commitment to Chiang, which by 1947 promised to imperil rather than advance American global security interests. Yet his victory left a residue of bitterness and misunderstanding that not only exacerbated divisions over China policy but also aroused opposition to the administration's plans in 1949 for a worldwide program of military aid.

Although partisan Republicans and die-hard Asia-firsters generated most of the controversy over military aid to China, Truman and his top foreign policy advisers contributed to their own difficulties. Their expansive rhetoric of containment raised expectations of a major effort to stop communism in East Asia, an area they ranked in strategic importance behind Western Europe, Latin America, and the Middle East. Their conviction that the United States must prove its credibility led to the continuation of arms aid to Chiang even after they thought that such help could not prevent a Communist victory. Truman and Marshall at times found it easier to appease Chiang's congressional supporters than to risk reductions or delays in vital programs of economic or military aid to Western Europe. Administration spokesmen frankly acknowledged the dangers of commitment to Chiang behind closed doors, but, not wanting to be accused of dealing a death blow to the Nationalist government, refused to do so publicly. By these actions, the Truman administration helped turn a policy that aimed at proving American reliability into one that seemed to demonstrate irresolution and perfidy.

Soon after returning from China in January 1947, Marshall asked the State Department's Office of Far Eastern Affairs (FE) to review American policy toward China. The memorandum that John Carter Vincent, the director, presented to the new secretary of state on 7 February stressed the importance of preventing China from becoming a major area of Cold War confrontation. Vincent reaffirmed his view that a unified and democratic China was a means toward the "larger objective" of maintaining a Soviet-American equilibrium in East Asia. He therefore counseled against large-scale assistance to Chiang as long as the Soviets made no attempt to provide material support to the Communists. The United States, in short, could most effectively contain Russian influence in China for the time being by minimizing its own involvement in the civil war.[3]

Vincent in particular urged Marshall to continue to deny combat equipment to the Nationalist government. He argued that no amount of military assistance short of an unrestricted commitment of American resources—a burden the administration had no desire to assume—would enable Chiang to defeat the Communists. "Limited amounts of munitions of war," he reasoned, "might then serve only to encourage the Kuomintang military leaders to wage an inconclusive war which might cause the collapse of the National Government for economic reasons." Furthermore, he warned that the resumption of arms shipments would strengthen the position of the Kuomintang reactionaries, whom Marshall blamed for the failure of his mediation. "In the absence of evidence that the civil war may soon cease," Vincent concluded, "it would be preferable from our standpoint to let the opposing Chinese military forces reach some kind of solution or equilibrium without outside interference." Only then might there be a chance for genuine reform of the government, "which is the only practical method of combatting the challenge of the Communists."[4]

Although Vincent was convinced that American munitions ultimately could not solve Chiang's problems, he did not close the door completely to further military aid. "It would be manifestly unrealistic to withhold arms from National Government forces," he wrote, "if such action condemned them to a degree of military anemia which would make possible a successful offensive by Communist forces." Vincent doubted that such a situation would occur during the next few months, but recognized that maintenance of the embargo might soon render ineffective some of Chiang's American equipment. "This situation," he cautioned, "will take the most careful day to day watching."[5]

Marshall basically agreed with Vincent's analysis but emphasized that the Nationalists' dependence on American military supplies was a major problem. He told the Senate Foreign Relations Committee on 14 February, "If we give them ammunition we are participating in the civil war directly. On the other hand, if we never give them any ammunition we have disarmed them, because they have American equipment." This was a dilemma, he confided, that he had hoped would never arise.[6]

It was also one that he could not escape. Despite the current embargo, the United States had provided more postwar military assistance to China than to any other nation and had made an extraordinary effort, through Marshall's year-long mediation, to end the civil war. Such actions had linked American prestige to the continued quest for a stable postwar international order in East Asia and had raised expectations of additional American help for the Nationalist government. But as much as he wanted to avert the collapse of Chiang's government, contain the expansion of communism in East Asia, and strengthen American credibility, Marshall—perhaps more than any American—appreciated the dangers of deep involvement in the Chinese civil war. With no good alternative, Marshall was eager to defer action on the provision of further arms aid to China.

Not so his colleagues in the service departments. Both Secretary of War Robert P. Patterson and Secretary of the Navy James V. Forrestal advocated a stronger commitment to the Nationalist regime. Forrestal warned that Soviet influence would increase in China as "the United States withdrew its support from the Central Government." Patterson agreed and declared that he was not ready "to accept with equanimity the military collapse of the National Government." Concerned over the deterioration of stockpiled equipment reserved for China, he called for a prompt decision on the resumption of arms deliveries and recommended that the three secretaries request the views of the Joint Chiefs of Staff.[7]

Marshall, however, resisted suggestions that the administration step up its military aid to China. On 27 February he told Truman, who was concerned about the possibility of Russian military intervention in Manchuria, that the resumption of ammunition shipments would foreclose any chance of a liberal reform of the Chinese government.[8] He wrote to Patterson five days later that, although he agreed that the Joint Chiefs should review American military aid policy, he still preferred to encourage the Chinese to solve their problems by peaceful methods.[9] Marshall's attitude did not arise from any false hopes about the prospects for Chinese unity, but from the conviction that "the U.S. was definitely in a negative position" and should avoid being drawn deeper into a potentially disastrous situation.[10]

The administration's strong response to the Greek-Turkish crisis of February and March 1947 complicated Marshall's efforts to limit American involvement in the Chinese civil war. Encouraged by the global rhetoric of the Truman Doctrine, some of the president's top advisers, such as Forrestal and Leahy, argued that the administration should do more to prevent China from falling under Communist influence. When this issue arose at a Cabinet meeting on 7 March, Acheson explained that the principle of containing Communist expansion guided the State Department's thinking on China as it did on Greece; the vast differences in the two countries accounted for the variations in specific policies. Speaking far more bluntly, Truman declared that further military aid to Chiang Kai-shek under prevailing circumstances would be like "pouring sand in a rat hole."[11]

Representatives of the service departments nevertheless continued to press for increased aid to China under the Truman Doctrine. The divisions between political and military officials on this issue were especially clear in the SWNCC report of 21 April on urgent foreign requirements for American assistance. State Department planners thought that American aid to China during the next few months should be focused on selected reconstruction projects that would help to meet urgent economic needs. War and Navy officials, however, felt that these limited measures fell short of Truman's public promise of support for besieged free peoples. Unlike the State Department analysts, they were neither pessimistic about American ability to influence events in China nor convinced that any attempt to do so would ultimately require an enormous expenditure of resources. Instead of the State Department's "wait and see" attitude, the service planners favored "a more crystalline and positive policy including carefully controlled economic and military aid," designed to head off "a crisis similar to that in Greece." The SWNCC was unable to reconcile these conflicting views.[12]

The SWNCC, however, did agree that the issue of further aid to China had global implications. "If the U.S. supports a freedom-loving people whose independence is threatened," the committee argued, "other nations may be stiffened in their determination to remain free; conversely, if the U.S. neglects to support a free people, other nations may be profoundly dismayed and may lose faith in the leadership of the U.S." At stake in China, then, was American credibility as a dependable ally of nations determined to resist Communist pressures.[13]

A surge of criticism from Republican legislators added to the pressure on the State Department to alter its attitudes toward China. Senator Arthur H. Vandenberg of Michigan, the new chairman of the Foreign Relations Committee, urged the Truman administration in January to "shift its emphasis" from promotion of a coalition government to firm support of the Nationalist regime. "It seems to me," he explained, "that we might just as well begin to face the Communist challenge on *every* front."[14] When Truman called congressional leaders to a meeting at the White House on 10 March during the Greek-Turkish crisis, Vandenberg deprecated the administration's policy toward China, a country he thought far more important to American security than Greece. Senator Styles Bridges of New Hampshire, the chairman of the Appropriations Committee, also appealed for a vigorous American effort to prevent China from falling into the Soviet orbit. During the hearings on the Greek-Turkish Aid Act, Representative Walter H. Judd of Minnesota, a former medical missionary to China and an influential champion of the Nationalists, rebuked the administration for encouraging Chiang to negotiate with the Communists while helping the Greeks to fight them. After several bitter exchanges with Acheson, he announced, "I do not think we can have one kind of policy in Europe with respect to the danger of Communist-dominated governments and another policy in Asia."[15] Increasingly, the thrust of this criticism was that the administration was failing to carry out the Truman Doctrine in China.[16]

Events in China helped bring to a head the issue of further arms assistance to the Nationalists. During April and May, Chiang's overextended armies suffered a series of stunning reverses. The most serious occurred in Manchuria, where the Communists launched a general offensive—bolder than any of their previous efforts—that quickly immobilized large bodies of government troops in isolated towns and cities. The Communists' advances sapped the Nationalists' morale, dissipated their supplies, weakened their already tenuous popular support, and exposed what American observers agreed was their "fantastically inept leadership" in all command echelons.[17] The fighting in Manchuria ended Chiang's fatuous hopes, which he had expressed to American officials only a few weeks earlier, of defeating the Communists by September. His armies now faced, as Ambassador John Leighton Stuart reported on 7 June, "a military debacle of large proportions."[18]

Chiang looked to Washington for help. He told American officials that he was seriously concerned about shortages of ammunition and informally requested an end to the embargo on arms shipments to China. Information from the Chinese Ministry of National Defense appeared to corroborate his fears. American military experts estimated from this data that as of 31 March the Nationalist forces in Manchuria possessed only 52 days worth of supplies of cartridges for their American rifles and anywhere from 5 to 160 days worth of shells for various types of mortars: these inventories could not sustain prolonged operations.[19] Chiang and his associates implied that the United States had a responsibility to prevent the Alpha units from becoming ineffective and appealed for help in obtaining ammunition for their American weapons.[20]

Nationalist officials also renewed their efforts to obtain 130 million rounds of 7.92 mm rifle ammunition from army surplus stocks. The Chinese had sought these munitions, manufactured to their specifications in American arsenals during World War II, since the summer of 1946, but the State Department had refused to issue an export license because of the embargo.[21] State also had frustrated Chinese efforts in early 1947 to obtain this type of ammunition from American and Belgian manufacturers.[22] But by early April Vincent thought that the department should reverse its position. Upset by reports of the Nationalists' depleted munitions inventories, he told Marshall that, while he believed that the administration should continue to discourage Chiang from seeking a military solution to China's problems, "complete withholding of ammunition might impair [the] defensive effectiveness of [the] Chinese Army." He urged the secretary of state to approve the sale of the surplus cartridges as an exception to the embargo.[23]

The Nationalists' mounting military difficulties in Manchuria at last persuaded Marshall to act. At the end of April, he authorized the marines to abandon to the Nationalists 6,500 tons of ammunition—most of it, however, unserviceable or suitable only for training purposes—as they withdrew from Tsingtao.[24] A month later, he relaxed the embargo and declared that the Chinese should have normal access to the American arms market. He also authorized the sale of the surplus 7.92 mm ammunition and the resumption of deliveries of transport aircraft and spare parts under the Chinese Air Force Program. He declined, however, to approve transfers of additional bomber and fighter planes or to allow the Chinese to purchase other combat materiel from government surplus stocks.[25] Marshall eased the restrictions on arms transfers to China quietly, a further indication that he had not abandoned his efforts to limit American involvement in the civil war. He had no illusions that these limited measures would solve the Nationalists' serious military problems—he told the Chinese ambassador earlier in May that Chiang was "the worst advised military commander in history"—but he apparently hoped that they would at least ease the pressure for further military aid.[26]

Marshall's hopes were not fulfilled. On 9 June the Joint Chiefs of Staff challenged the State Department's China policy by issuing a strong appeal for increased military and economic aid to the Nationalist government. They argued that such assistance was necessary to thwart a Soviet bid, much like similar efforts in Europe and the Near East, to seize control of China. The service chieftains discounted arguments that the Chinese Communists were independent of Moscow. In their view, Mao and his followers subscribed to "the same basic totalitarian and anti-democratic policies" that motivated other Communist parties and "should be regarded as tools of Soviet policy." Mao's victory in the civil war, the Joint Chiefs warned, not only would result in Russian domination of China but also would lead to Communist penetration of neighboring areas—Indochina, Malaysia, and India—and "eventual Soviet hegemony over Asia." A Communist victory, therefore, would significantly affect the world configuration of power, the Joint Chiefs concluded. "The United States must seek to prevent the growth of any single power or coalition to a position of such strength as to constitute a threat to the Western Hemisphere," they declared. "A Soviet position of dominance over Asia, Western Europe, or both, would constitute a major threat to United States security." Hence the need for "an over-all plan," of which military support of China was an essential part, to contain Communist expansion.[27]

Indeed, the Joint Chiefs asserted that only a small amount of American military aid could have a decisive effect on the Chinese civil war. Service leaders believed that American assistance had so far failed to yield satisfactory results because it was "piecemeal and uncoordinated" and given in support of a policy with "no firm objectives" other than to effect a peaceful settlement between two parties with irreconcilable differences. The Joint Chiefs urged instead the strengthening of the Nationalist government "to the extent necessary to prevent Soviet expansion." Although unfamiliar with the specific military requirements of the Nationalist forces, they nonetheless thought that simply a public declaration of firm support for the Nationalists would have such a pivotal effect on the morale of the opposing forces that the Communists would have to come to terms with Chiang. According to the Joint Chiefs, if the promise of American aid could not produce a negotiated settlement, small quantities of munitions would enable Chiang's armies to defeat their foes. In short, they believed that a modest investment could produce major results in a global struggle against communism.[28]

The State Department's China experts recoiled at this analysis. They vigorously disputed the Joint Chiefs' assertion that military support of the Nationalists was a wise and effective investment of American resources. Vincent wrote to Marshall on 20 June that aid to help Chiang defeat the Communists would not be cheap. Instead, it "would lead inevitably to direct intervention in China's civil war" to the extent that American officials would have "to take over direction of Chinese military operations and administration and remain in China for an indefinite period." Such an enormous effort, as the Joint Chiefs themselves had pointed out only a month earlier in a review of American military assistance policy, was all out of proportion to American security interests in China.[29]

Vincent and his colleagues also felt that the Joint Chiefs had greatly underestimated the obstacles to Soviet control of China. In view of China's administrative inefficiencies, its lack of industrial and material resources, and its resentment of foreign interference, as well as the Soviet Union's inability to provide the vast amounts of aid that China required, Vincent concluded that a Russian-dominated China was "not a danger of sufficient immediacy or probability" to justify intervention on behalf of the Nationalist government. The issue was not whether to contain the growth of Soviet power in East Asia, but how to do so.[30]

Marshall also disagreed with the Joint Chiefs' conclusions, especially their assertion that a relatively small amount of arms aid would enable Chiang to eliminate the Communists. He viewed the disintegration of the Nationalist war effort—reversion to a static defensive strategy, collapse of army morale, huge losses of manpower and materiel to the Communists—with despair and disgust.[31] He described to Patterson and Forrestal on 26 June "the dilemma created by the incompetence, inefficiency and stubbornness of the Central Government—qualities which made it very difficult to help them. He cited the military ineptitude of their leaders, the cashiering of the only generals who had produced successful campaigns, the instability of their leadership and the appalling lack of an organization to deal with the vast and complex economic and social problems of China."[32] For these reasons, Marshall considered the Joint Chiefs' analysis "not quite realistic" and their recommendations "somewhat impracticable, particularly as to implementation in China."[33] On 3 July he asked Ambassador John Leighton Stuart to inform Chiang that, despite his concern over the spread of hostilities and the resulting economic deterioration, he believed that "lasting solution of China's problems must come from the Chinese themselves. The US cannot initiate and carry out solution of those problems and can only assist as conditions develop which give some assurance that the assistance will have practical beneficial results."[34]

Although Marshall rejected extensive intervention, he pondered limited measures aimed at preventing the collapse of the Chinese armies. At the meeting of the Committee of Three on 26 June, he discussed the resupply of the Alpha divisions, an issue that still troubled him. Marshall felt a moral obligation to provide ammunition for these units, but worried about expanding American involvement in the civil war and provoking similar action by the Soviet Union, which had so far refrained from furnishing direct military aid to the Communists. These considerations bothered neither Forrestal, who opposed withdrawal from China no matter what difficulties arose, nor Patterson, who added the flimsy argument that military aid, because it would be going to the recognized government, would not constitute intervention in China's internal conflict. Marshall, however, remained unpersuaded and undecided.[35]

After several days of reflection, Marshall informed Truman that he wanted to send General Albert C. Wedemeyer back to China on a special mission. Marshall conceived of the Wedemeyer Mission, he later explained, as "a last resort," a final effort to find some realistic and effective way of helping Chiang's faltering regime.[36] Marshall had wrestled for weeks with the question of aid to China. "I have tortured my brain and I can't now see the answer," he told a group of business leaders on 11 June.[37] He informed Patterson and Forrestal two weeks later that "he had been searching for a positive and constructive formula to deal with the Chinese situation."[38] A product of this reflection was the idea of sending Wedemeyer to China. Similar proposals from several Republican legislators, including Walter Judd, persuaded Marshall to approach Wedemeyer.[39] In mid-July the general and a small group of assistants left for China to investigate political, economic, and military conditions and to prepare recommendations for future American assistance.[40]

The appointment of Wedemeyer, who was esteemed in Nationalist circles, temporarily disarmed the critics of the administration's China policy. Forrestal "heartily concurred" in the dispatch of the Wedemeyer Mission, and Vandenberg expressed satisfaction that the administration was "now making progress in the right direction."[41] So did Admiral Leahy, mistakenly convinced that Marshall had completely reversed his stand on China. Reassured by Wedemeyer's impending departure, the Joint Chiefs tabled on 9 July a new appeal for urgent military aid to the Nationalists.[42]

Marshall apparently hoped that Wedemeyer's report would further strengthen his hand against the advocates of substantial military assistance to Chiang. He explained to Truman that he thought that the Joint Chiefs' recommendations were based on a faulty estimate of conditions in China and for that reason desired Wedemeyer's assessment. Furthermore, Wedemeyer's instructions made clear that additional American aid depended on the Nationalists' adoption of internal reforms, a stipulation that Marshall and Stuart—just like Stilwell and many others—had repeatedly and futilely urged on Chiang. Although conclusive evidence is lacking, Marshall may well have felt that Wedemeyer's endorsement of such conditional aid would help him resist more ambitious proposals for extensive support of the Nationalist regime. At the very least, he hoped that the Wedemeyer Mission would buy some time on the China issue and allow him to focus his attention on the European meetings concerning the Marshall Plan and preparation for the Rio Conference on Inter-American Security.[43]

Whatever Marshall's expectations may have been, Wedemeyer's dispatches from China surprised and disappointed the advocates of a stronger military commitment to Chiang. Appalled by the chaos he observed, Wedemeyer sent back a series of bleak reports, harshly critical of Nationalist rule. Soon after arriving, he cabled Marshall that Chiang's corrupt and ineffective government, bereft of popular support, could not survive without drastic reforms and a purge of top officials. "I feel that the Nationalist Chinese are spiritually insolvent," he cabled. "They do not understand why they should die or make any sacrifices. They have lost confidence in their leaders, political and military, and they foresee complete collapse."[44] Such alarming accounts of the Nationalists' woes echoed the reports that the embassy had been sending to Washington for months. Wedemeyer's liaison in the War Department, who hoped that the mission would recommend "a new, positive approach to the China problem," commented gloomily that the general's messages were reinforcing the administration's "negative and pessimistic" thinking on China.[45]

Wedemeyer's analysis of Chiang's military plight was especially discouraging. He informed Marshall on 8 August that the Nationalists had practically no chance of retaining a grip on Manchuria: "The Communists have the initiative and are able to conduct operations when and where they will, restricted only by their own limitations, communications, terrain and weather." Wedemeyer felt that if Chiang moved reinforcements into Manchuria he risked rapid deterioration in the weakened areas of North and Central China. Wedemeyer believed that the Soviets, through their Chinese Communist agents, had taken long strides toward the establishment of "satellite or puppet" regimes in Manchuria, Sinkiang, and Inner Mongolia. And, in the face of this dismemberment of China, he considered especially disturbing "the apathy and ineptitude of the Chinese Government."[46]

Wedemeyer also found that the Nationalist leaders regarded American aid as a panacea for their ills. Their all-out campaign for American assistance accelerated with the appointment of Wedemeyer, who was given the usual dire warnings of imminent collapse.[47] Wedemeyer, however, paid no attention to these warnings and resisted Chinese efforts to curry favor. One member of the embassy staff recorded in his diary that Wedemeyer was "visibly annoyed by Chinese pressure tactics, especially the justly famous charm act of Madame Chiang. He may well be the only living human being on whom it does not work."[48] Wedemeyer angrily dismissed as "child-like" and "naive" Chinese efforts to plant evidence purporting to show that the Soviets were rendering assistance to the Chinese Communists. (He was nevertheless convinced that the Soviets were backing the Communist war effort.) "Every artifice will be resorted to on their part to compel United States aid and to minimize concurrently [the] Chinese contribution," he told Marshall. Wedemeyer thought that the Nationalists, by exploiting fears of Soviet expansion, hoped to persuade the United States to make a major effort in China while avoiding any reforms that might weaken the reactionary cliques in government.[49]

Wedemeyer tried to disabuse the Nationalist leaders of these misguided notions by openly criticizing their failings. Addressing them before his departure, he denounced official corruption, suppression of civil liberties, neglect of popular reforms, preoccupation with securing foreign assistance, and excessive reliance on military force as a solution to the Communist challenge.[50] "Promises," he declared, "will no longer suffice. Performance is absolutely necessary." These statements, intended to rouse the Nationalists from their lethargy, did not sit well in Kuomintang ruling circles, especially since Wedemeyer gave no indication that he planned to recommend substantial assistance to China. To Wedemeyer's surprise, Premier Chang Chun replied that the Nationalists would not alter their foreign or domestic policies as a result of the Wedemeyer Mission.[51]

Yet neither the Nationalists' recalcitrance nor their pervasive corruption and inefficiency dissuaded Wedemeyer from recommending in his final report of 19 September a major American effort to prevent China from falling under Communist control. He called for programs of economic aid that would last for at least five years and military assistance that would continue for an indefinite period, both to be supervised by an American mission similar to the one in Greece. He hoped that, by making this help contingent upon the adoption of sweeping reforms, the United States could induce the changes that Chiang had consistently resisted. Wedemeyer indulged in this wishful thinking partly because he could imagine no other alternative that would preserve American interests in China. The current "wait and see" policy, he argued, would lead either to the collapse of the Nationalist regime or to an internal settlement that would eventually bring the Communists to power. In either case, Wedemeyer believed that the establishment of a Communist government whose leaders had close ideological ties to the Soviet Union would be a major blow to American prestige and security and would pave the way for the spread of Soviet influence in Asia and elsewhere. Moreover, an unfriendly China would deny to the United States important air and naval bases, facilities that the Soviet Union might use in the event of war to launch short-range attacks on American installations in the Philippines, Ryukyus, and Japan.[52]

Much like the Joint Chiefs of Staff, Wedemeyer thus advocated "sufficient and prompt" military assistance to the Nationalists as part of a worldwide effort to contain Soviet expansion. He urged the provision of surplus ammunition, motor vehicles, and naval vessels, the completion of the Chinese Air Force Program, and the extension of credits for the purchase of new military equipment in the United States. Accompanying this material support, he thought, should be broader American military advice. He suggested help in training combat units outside areas of hostilities and in organizing Nationalist supply services, but ruled out direct participation in military operations because it was "contrary to current American policy." Wedemeyer believed that this assistance would help stabilize a grave military situation, provided the Nationalists adopted sweeping political and economic reforms. The United States should use its military aid as a lever "to foster the emergence of a regime which would develop along lines satisfactory to the United States, at the same time engaging in a holding operation against the progressive spread of militaristic Communism."[53]

Wedemeyer conceded, however, that even this enlarged assistance would not enable Chiang's armies to hang on to Manchuria. The only way, in his view, to prevent that province from becoming a "Soviet satellite" was to place it, as he had recommended two years earlier, under a five-power guardianship or a U.N. trusteeship. This proposal caused consternation in the State Department. Convinced that any suggestion for the separation of Manchuria from the rest of China would greatly offend Chiang, Marshall and his assistants dismissed Wedemeyer's idea as completely impracticable. Furthermore, State Department officials did not want to risk an embarrassing public debate, which might lead to proposals for similar U.N. intervention in Greece. Unable to convince Wedemeyer to delete his recommendation on Manchuria, Marshall decided to suppress his report.[54]

In a larger sense, the Wedemeyer report was unacceptable to the State Department because it failed to make a persuasive case for the extensive aid it recommended. Its alarming description of Nationalist incompetence and corruption undercut its conclusion that conditional American aid could be effective. The report's assertion that Chiang would accept basic political and economic changes was at odds with his government's public rejection of Wedemeyer's advice and subsequent suppression of the Democratic League, one of the few opposition parties. Wedemeyer's insistence that Chiang would face up to China's grave problems was belied by the generalissimo's petulant complaint to visiting American congressmen that the difficulties in Manchuria were an American responsibility arising from the Yalta agreements. For all these reasons, Marshall and his assistants doubted Wedemeyer's argument that American assistance could help reverse the course of events in China.[55]

Foreign-policy planners also disagreed with Wedemeyer's estimate of China's importance to American security. George F. Kennan, the director of State's Policy Planning Staff, later recalled that "deterioration of the situation in China did not strike us as fatal, in itself, to American interests." Kennan based this judgment on China's lack of industrial development and its inability to project military power beyond the Asian mainland, and on a belief that the Soviet Union would have severe difficulty maintaining its influence over a Chinese Communist regime. For similar reasons, the CIA asserted in its review of the world situation on 26 September that East Asia ranked behind Western Europe and the Middle East "from the point of view of containing the U.S.S.R. and eventually redressing the balance of power." The intelligence analysts predicted that acute political and economic disorganization would prevail in China for many years, thereby preventing the consolidation of Soviet power. "Whatever the course of events in continental Asia," they concluded, "maintenance of effective U.S. control of the Pacific would afford a sufficient safeguard."[56]

During the autumn of 1947, the Truman administration's foreign aid programs conformed to these assessments of American interests. The State Department concentrated its efforts on meeting the acute economic needs of Western Europe—an area, political officials felt, that might soon become the focus of a major confrontation between the United States and the Soviet Union.[57] Concerned about making commitments that exceeded national capacity, foreign-policy planners had no desire to shoulder another major burden in China, a country where both the stakes and the chances of success were far smaller. Kennan summarized the prevailing outlook within the administration: "In China there is not much we can do, in present circumstances but to sweat it out and try to prevent the military situation from changing too drastically to the advantage of the communist forces."[58]

In late 1947 and early 1948 Marshall made several important decisions that guided military aid policy for the duration of the Chinese civil war. Marshall's actions increased assistance to the Nationalists, partly because the secretary of state believed that the United States must prove to friendly governments both in Asia and Europe that it upheld its commitments. At the same time, Marshall imposed strict limits on American obligations to China. In reaching these decisions, he faced pressure from the military establishment—particularly Forrestal and Wedemeyer—Republican members of Congress, and Ambassador Stuart. Yet, though he made some concessions to his critics, he avoided direct, large-scale military intervention in the civil war.[59]

The most pressing issue Marshall confronted was the Nationalist request for transfer of munitions from government inventories. Patterson informed Marshall on 23 July 1947 that the War Department could supply the munitions the Chinese requested, but only at the expense of other approved programs. He suggested that the War Department lend the Nationalists ammunition from its reserve stocks, which would be replaced by Chinese purchases from American industry. Uniformed officers, eager both to help the Nationalists and to build up the American arms industry, enthusiastically supported this proposal. After reading Wedemeyer's report, Marshall approved Patterson's recommendation and allowed the advance from government inventories to the Nationalists of 6.5 million rounds of .50 caliber ammunition in return for the Nationalist purchase of equivalent supplies to be manufactured by Olin Industries. He also agreed to remove the restrictions on the sale of government surplus, enabling the Nationalists to purchase, between December 1947 and May 1948, $95 million worth of ground and air force supplies for a trifling $6 million.[60]

Marshall continued to take such steps quietly in order to avoid fueling a public debate that might restrict his freedom of action. At first, he wanted to abandon surplus materiel in the Pacific to the Chinese, since that could have been done without a public announcement. But the army bridled at his suggestion. "The State Department . . . is hoping for a solution in which the U.S. government will not be involved," one army officer wrote with annoyance, by having "the Army, through some subterfuge, give the munitions to the Chinese."[61] Because of army objections, Marshall opted instead for sale through surplus channels, but with minimal publicity. He also decided not to inform the Nationalists of the availability of surplus munitions until 16 December, a day after the termination of the London meeting of the Council of Foreign Ministers.[62] He evidently desired to avoid stimulating either new appeals for or protests against deeper American involvement in the civil war.

Marshall and his assistants also discouraged the Nationalists from hoping for more extensive American arms aid. Chinese procrastination in procuring munitions from commercial sources and negotiating contracts for surplus property produced within the State Department the impression that Chiang was still counting on considerable American help. W. Walton Butterworth, the new director of FE, complained that the Nationalists were reluctant to take "small steps" because they were awaiting some "larger solution" to their military plight.[63] Butterworth's assistants, Robert D. Magill and Philip D. Sprouse, believed that the central government expected that apprehension over Communist gains in Manchuria would eventually lead the United States to assume the burden of the Nationalist war effort.[64] State Department officials repeatedly warned Chinese representatives that their foot-dragging was casting doubt on the urgency of their need for military aid. Marshall was even blunter. He told Ambassador V. K. Wellington Koo on 13 November that he doubted that Chiang would adopt the reforms needed to relieve "the parlous state of the military situation in China," and that he expected that public support for aid to China would soon wane.[65]

Marshall dealt with advisory assistance to the Chinese much as he handled arms aid. Throughout the summer of 1947, General John P. Lucas, the chief of the Army Advisory Group (AAG), pressed for an expansion of his mission, then limited to advising the higher staffs of the Chinese military establishment on organizational matters, to include helping the Nationalists plan strategy and tactics and train combat units.[66] Marshall, however, consented only to a far more modest increase in the scope of the advisory group's activities. He agreed that army personnel could assist in reorganizing the Nationalists' services of supply and also allowed the AAG to send instructors to a center on Formosa for the retraining of combat units. But he made clear that he did not share Lucas's opinion that further enlargement of AAG responsibilities could overcome the persistent stubbornness and inefficiency of the Nationalist leadership. Even the Formosan training center, he told Ambassador Koo, "would do little or no good" since Chiang had made no attempt, despite repeated American suggestions, to establish a system for supplying trained replacement troops for existing divisions.[67]

Such reservations about Chiang's willingness to cooperate determined Marshall's attitude on the critical question of furnishing operational advice to the Nationalist armies. Marshall confronted this issue in November when he arranged for General David G. Barr to replace Lucas, whom Chiang wished recalled. Although Lucas was, as John F. Melby of the embassy staff privately described him, "a sweet, incompetent old darling, [who] has been a thorn for some time now due to his fondness for extemporaneous public conversation on unauthorized topics," Chiang was apparently as discontent with the limits on AAG authority as he was with Lucas's personal shortcomings.[68] Stuart reported that the generalissimo expected that Barr would have authority to advise Nationalist military officials on strategy and tactics. But Marshall balked at this suggestion even though he had just consented to a similar expansion of the mission of the American Military Advisory Group in Greece. Worried about the Greek government's lethargy in the face of intensified guerrilla activity and its tendency to rely all too heavily on American assistance, he still thought that American advisers could influence Greek leaders far more readily than they could Chiang.

Consequently, Marshall was prepared only to let Barr provide strategic and tactical guidance to the generalissimo on a personal and informal basis, so that it would not appear that the United States was ready to accept responsibility for Chinese plans and operations. Such responsibility, he replied to Stuart, had "very far-reaching and grave" implications and was "in logic inseparable from authority to make it effective." "Whatever the Generalissimo may feel moved to say with respect to his willingness to delegate necessary powers to Americans," Marshall continued, "I know from my own experience that advice is always listened to very politely but not infrequently ignored when deemed unpalatable."[69]

In spite of Marshall's opposition, American military officials continued to advocate more extensive arms aid to the Nationalists. Shortly before returning to the United States, Lucas added to his proposals for expanded advisory assistance a plan for building up Nationalist ground and air units, measures that the army later determined would cost almost $1 billion. Only such drastic steps, Lucas felt, could reverse the steady deterioration of the Nationalists' military position.[70] Wedemeyer, who became the army's director of Plans and Operations soon after returning from China, held similar views. Still smarting over the suppression of his report, he passed up no opportunity to urge greater American assistance to Chiang. He went before the Senate Appropriations Committee on 17 December 1947 and recommended urgent military and economic aid to the Nationalists as part of an overall plan for containing communism. For good measure, he accused the administration of failing to honor its commitments to Chiang and lauded the generalissimo's record of fidelity to the United States.[71] Also, Wedemeyer privately pressed Secretary of the Army Royall, Army Chief of Staff Eisenhower, and Secretary of Defense Forrestal for a revision of Marshall's policy of limited assistance.[72]

Wedemeyer was especially concerned about the lack of surplus equipment to meet Chinese requests. Surveys of Pacific depots revealed that some 63,000 tons of surplus materiel was available for transfer to the Nationalists, but much of it was unserviceable or unsuited to meeting the Nationalists' requests for small-arms ammunition, communications equipment, motor vehicles, and spare parts. Military authorities determined that transfer of all available equipment would still leave the program to supply eight and one-third air groups only half completed. In view of the depletion of surplus stocks, Wedemeyer urged the passage of a military aid legislation for China that would be similar to the Greek-Turkish Aid Act.[73]

Service proponents of increased aid to China continued to enjoy the vigorous support of Forrestal. Eager to prevent the spread of Soviet influence in Asia, the secretary of defense took a special interest in the efforts of the military establishment to provide assistance to the Nationalists. In response to Forrestal's inquiry, P&O expressed deep concern at the beginning of 1948 over the Nationalists' faltering war efforts. Drawing heavily on the views of Lucas and Wedemeyer, P&O recommended immediate and substantial military and economic aid to China as part of a worldwide program aimed at halting Communist expansion. The psychological boost that the Nationalists would receive from the approval of such a program, the army planners speculated, might be even more important than the actual material assistance. "Continuation of the present policy," General C. V. R. Schuyler warned, "will lead to the inevitable triumph of the Communist Party . . . thereby threatening the long-range military security of the U.S."[74] This analysis impressed Forrestal, who worried that the administration lacked "a clearly defined position" on aid to the Nationalists. On 15 January he asked the NSC to prepare a new statement of policy toward China.[75]

The report, which the NSC staff completed at the end of March, revealed the wide and persistent differences of opinion between the National Military Establishment and the State Department over short-term aid to China. Army, navy, and air force staff members advocated limited military and economic assistance to the Nationalists. They now conceded that such help could not bring about the defeat of the Communists but could buy time, which the Nationalist regime desperately needed to restore a modicum of internal stability. The State Department staff planner, however, thought that the United States should furnish only economic assistance. He argued that a new program of military aid might "lead to deeper and deeper involvement of our national strength in an area of, at best, secondary strategic importance to us." Restriction of American help to limited economic measures, on the other hand, would avoid an unending drain on American resources and a complete underwriting of Chiang's regime. And, most important to the State Department, "The military responsibility for the survival of the National Government would be clearly placed upon Chinese shoulders."[76]

Senior political and military officials were almost as sharply divided as the NSC staff. Marshall praised the State Department's recommendations and reiterated his conviction that further military assistance to the Nationalists would inevitably lead to an unlimited commitment of resources and manpower, a course he unalterably opposed.[77] The Joint Chiefs of Staff, on the other hand, endorsed the services' position and reaffirmed their opinion that selective, well-supervised assistance would advance American security interests in China.[78] Wedemeyer thought that the service representatives could have put their case even more forcefully by arguing that a Nationalist collapse would lead to Soviet control of continental East Asia and, thus, enable the Russians to concentrate their efforts on overrunning Western Europe and the Middle East.[79] The only prominent service official who dissented from these views was Royall, who expressed "grave misgivings" over further military aid to the Nationalists because their position seemed "hopeless."[80]

The outcome of this debate within the executive branch was to a large extent determined by the actions of Congress. Republican criticism of the administration's China policy, which had subsided during the Wedemeyer Mission, resumed with new fervor in the autumn of 1947 when Truman asked a special session of Congress to provide emergency economic assistance to France, Austria, and Italy. During the hearings in the House Foreign Affairs Committee, Representative Walter Judd took the lead in denouncing the administration for overlooking China. "I think we have got to win in Asia, too," he asserted, "or we will ultimately lose in Europe."[81] Backed by Styles Bridges, Speaker of the House Joseph W. Martin of Massachusetts, and Governor Thomas E. Dewey of New York (the leading contender for the GOP presidential nomination), Judd's efforts gained for the Nationalists only $18 million in economic aid. But the Republican agitation helped elicit from Marshall a promise to submit promptly a bill for the relief of China. Although the State Department had been contemplating measures of economic assistance for China, the congressional pressure determined the timing of Marshall's announcement. Such a pledge seemed politic at a time when the administration was drafting Marshall Plan legislation.[82]

In addition to conciliating Republican legislators whose votes were needed for the European Recovery Program, Marshall had other reasons for requesting new funds for the Nationalists. The dilemma of aid to China continued to gnaw at him. He felt constrained by previous policy to extend some help, however modest, to the beleaguered Nationalist regime. "We are already committed by past actions and by popular sentiment among our people," he explained to the Foreign Affairs Committee in February 1948, "to continue to do what we can to alleviate suffering in China, and to give the Chinese Government and people the possibility of working out China's problems in their own way."[83] Marshall also believed that failure to respond to Chiang's pleas for assistance would be a fatal blow to the Nationalist government. Regardless of his disillusionment with Chiang's leadership, he did not want to precipitate the Nationalists' downfall—or to be held accountable for their demise. The latter charge might seriously impair American credibility at a time when the Truman administration was deeply concerned about raising European morale and confidence in American leadership. Indeed, Butterworth confided to the Foreign Relations Committee that a desire to avoid responsibility for a Nationalist collapse was Marshall's principal reason for seeking new appropriations for China.[84]

The bill that Truman sent to Congress on 18 February 1948 was largely a diplomatic and political gesture—little more than "three cheers for the Nationalist government," according to Vandenberg. It aimed only at "giving the Chinese Government a respite from rapid economic deterioration during which it can move to establish more stable economic conditions."[85] Although all of the $570 million that the president requested was reserved for financing essential civilian imports and reconstruction projects, State Department officials did not completely overlook the Nationalists' military requirements. They estimated that the China Aid Act would free between $50 million and $100 million in foreign exchange holdings, depending on the level of Chinese exports, for the purchase of military supplies. Marshall realized that this modest, indirect subsidy of the Nationalist war effort would not satisfy Chiang's die-hard supporters, but he strongly opposed special military aid appropriations for reasons that were "too serious and too obvious to require elaboration."[86]

During a closed meeting of the Foreign Affairs Committee on 20 February 1948, Marshall reminded the legislators that the Nationalists' military difficulties arose not from a shortage of materiel but from Chiang's stubborn and futile efforts to solve China's internal problems by force, his disregard of American counsel, inept leadership, corruption, and failure to adopt popular reforms. He added that substantial infusions of American aid had not saved the generalissimo from the perils of the course he had chosen. Chiang, not the United States, Marshall emphasized to the committee, was responsible for the Nationalists' current plight.[87]

Marshall did not believe that the United States could afford to be responsible for "the continued failures of the present Chinese Government." He warned the representatives that any effort to rid China of communism would eventually require the United States "to take over the Chinese Government, practically, and administer its economic, military, and government affairs." Such an enormous expenditure of American capacity, he predicted, "would involve this Government in a continuing commitment from which it would practically be impossible to withdraw, and . . . would very probably involve grave consequences to this Nation by making China an arena of international conflict." Such a heavy investment in China would jeopardize American efforts to contain Soviet influence in the more vital region of Western Europe. Because of these dire consequences, Marshall was certain that the American people would never knowingly accept the obligations of direct participation in the Chinese civil war.[88]

But Marshall never tested that assertion by putting the issue frankly before the public. As historian William Stueck has convincingly argued, Marshall's unwillingness to do so did not arise from a fear that he could not cultivate sufficient popular support for the administration's China policy. Public opinion polls in early 1948 showed that a small majority favored additional assistance to Chiang, but the administration had previously reshaped public attitudes on controversial foreign aid questions. Marshall, however, was firmly convinced that a frank public discussion would only complicate American efforts to contain communism throughout the globe. At a time when the Truman administration was trying to show resolve in the face of a crisis in Europe, an acrimonious debate about global priorities would raise embarrassing questions about American reliability at home and, perhaps, debilitating doubts abroad. Because of these concerns, Marshall confined his candid assessments of Chiang's failings to closed-door meetings on Capitol Hill.[89]

Marshall's stark warnings about the dangers of a military commitment to the Nationalists made less of an impression on the Foreign Affairs Committee than did the analyses of several military officers who considered the withholding of such support a far greater risk. Perhaps the most influential came in a telegram from General Douglas MacArthur, the commander of occupation forces in Japan. Disclaiming any expertise on China, MacArthur nevertheless asserted that the suppression of civil strife would have to precede internal reform and issued a bombastic appeal for military assistance "in equitable relation to such global aid as may be determined upon . . . without underrating the strategic importance to us, as to the world, of a free and peaceful China."[90] Wedemeyer took a similar line, largely reiterating his testimony of the previous December before the Senate Appropriations Committee.[91] The most sweeping proposals came from Claire L. Chennault, the retired air force commander who now operated an airline in China. He recommended the extension of $1.5 billion in military aid over the next three years and the assignment of American tactical advisers to the Nationalist armed forces down to the level of the infantry company and the air corps squadron. Taking a position antipodal to Marshall's, he told the representatives that the administration should assure the Nationalists that such assistance would continue until the defeat of the Communists.[92]

Although unwilling to go as far as Chennault suggested, a majority of the committee thought that China should receive additional military aid. The committee stressed the similarities between the situations in China and Greece: both countries were torn by civil war; both required, in the opinion of Judd and his colleagues, a minimum of military security before political reform and economic recovery could occur. Furthermore, the House panel believed that American interests in both countries were equally strong: "The United States can no more afford to see China become a coordinated part of another system than it can afford to see Greece and Turkey become part of another system." On the basis of this superficial analysis, the committee approved measures of assistance for China similar to those for Greece. Of the $570 million it recommended for China, the committee reserved $150 million for military aid. It also stipulated that this assistance should be administered as in Greece, where American military personnel helped with strategic planning and provided operational advice down to the division level. The House accepted these provisions on 31 March when it passed omnibus foreign assistance legislation that encompassed both the China Aid Act and the European Recovery Programs.[93]

The Senate Foreign Relations Committee was far more sympathetic to Marshall's views on China. Its members unanimously opposed further military commitments to the Nationalists. Tom Connally of Texas, the ranking Democrat, considered the proposed China aid program a "handout" that would probably do more to enrich corrupt Nationalist leaders than to improve conditions in China. Walter F. George (D-Ga.) agreed that further aid was "a complete waste of money if it is going to Chiang." Henry Cabot Lodge (R-Mass.), a staunch internationalist, expressed alarm over the House bill, which he felt would eventually lead to armed intervention in China. "I will be willing to vote to send them some money," he told his colleagues, "but I'll be damned if I want to send them manpower." Even the committee's most conservative Republican members, Bourke B. Hickenlooper of Iowa and Alexander Wiley of Wisconsin, took a similar line. "The military aid they need is American troops," the latter warned, "and we don't want to be sucked into that."[94]

While Vandenberg, too, wanted to avoid any military commitments in China, he believed that the Senate had to appease the House members who were "hell bent" on military aid. Otherwise, he feared that the lower chamber might not consent to the European Recovery Program. Acting as a legislative broker, Vandenberg had to overcome the hesitations of some influential Democrats. George, for example, thought that the time had come to "just . . . say 'No'" to Chiang. Connally thought that the Senate could cut off aid to the Nationalists without risking defeat of the Marshall Plan. If Vandenberg, however, thought military aid to China essential, Connally recommended a loan rather than a grant. Connally fully expected Chiang and the "crooks" surrounding him to squander these funds, thereby allowing the Congress "to wash our hands of it and say, 'Well, now, the hell with you.'" Vandenberg, though, proposed another formula as a substitute for the objectionable section in the House bill. He suggested the establishment of a special fund that the Nationalists could use at their discretion and on their own responsibility for the purchase of military supplies.[95] The Senate accepted this proposal, and Vandenberg prevailed on House leaders to give their approval as well. The China Aid Act, which Truman signed into law on 3 April 1948, authorized $338 million in economic assistance and $125 million for use "on such terms as the president may determine."[96] This arrangement, Vandenberg explained, avoided "any implication that we are underwriting the military campaign of the Nationalist Government."[97]

House Republicans mounted one more challenge to the administration over military aid to the Nationalists. Upon the recommendation of its Appropriations Committee, the lower chamber again voted to require supervision of the $125 million similar to that provided in Greece. Administration officials responded by closing ranks and pressing their case in the Senate. Royall, who personally disapproved of any further military aid to the Nationalists, told the Senate Appropriations Committee that such supervision would dangerously involve the United States in China's internal conflict. Under pressure from Royall not to oppose the State Department's position, Wedemeyer stated that monitoring of Chinese procurement would adequately protect against Nationalist misuse of the special fund. The Senate sustained the administration's view, as did a conference committee. The appropriations act, which Truman signed on 28 June, provided the full $125 million but did not commit the administration to any greater effort to support the Nationalists.[98]

The China Aid Act was an important victory for the State Department. The department triumphed over proponents of a literal interpretation of the Truman Doctrine, who were demanding a major effort to check communism in both Europe and Asia, and secured a legislative mandate for its global perspective of concentrating American resources on Europe. At the same time that Congress approved $400 million for China, it provided $5.3 billion for the European Recovery Program. Too, the cooperation of Republican leaders in defeating ambitious proposals for military aid to the Nationalists strengthened Marshall's hand against the critics of his policy of limited assistance. Finally, the China Aid Act foreclosed any possibility of large-scale intervention in Chiang's behalf. As Acheson later told the Senate, "This matter was laid before the Congress . . . the Congress understood it perfectly" and had the "sound judgment not to choose armed intervention."[99]

By mid-1948 the Nationalist government was approaching collapse. Stuart reported that Chiang was "universally condemned for his ineptness and reviled and excoriated for his *intransigeance* in prolonging civil war."[100] Bereft of popular support, Chiang's authority crumbled. Reflecting the widespread longing for peace, a reform faction within the Kuomintang led by Vice President Li Tsung-jen favored the reopen-

ing of negotiations with the Communists, a step that Chiang unalterably opposed. Another group of Kuomintang dissidents headed by
Marshall Li Chi-shen planned to establish a new regime in south-
western China, which would also try to reach an accommodation with
the Communists. Local political and military leaders increasingly disregarded the moribund central government. Chiang responded to
these challenges with renewed obduracy. He allowed only paper
changes in the government and chose subordinates on the basis of
personal loyalty, regardless of their incompetence or venality. Such
bankrupt personal rule only accelerated the fragmentation of power in
Nationalist areas. By the summer of 1948, American observers were
convinced that Chiang's days were numbered.[101]

The severe deterioration of the Nationalists' military position reinforced this bleak assessment. Once grossly inferior in manpower and
armament, the Communist forces had attained parity with the
Nationalists in both categories. In the spring of 1948 they consolidated
their hold on the Manchurian countryside, completing the isolation of
large Nationalist garrisons in Mukden, Changchun, and Chinchow. In
North and Central China, increasingly the theaters of major operations, Mao's troops seized the initiative and for the first time demonstrated their mastery of positional warfare as well as guerrilla tactics.
As Communist military strength waxed, the Nationalist armies continued to suffer from incompetent generalship and ebbing morale.
"While the Government's military situation has probably not yet
become critical," collapse could be averted only by "inspired and
dynamic military leadership," the embassy informed Washington in
June, "and there are no officers having such qualities in positions of
authority."[102]

Fearful that the Nationalists were headed for certain defeat, American military advisers in China made one more effort to persuade
Washington authorities to enlarge the scope of their mission. Barr
cabled Wedemeyer on 8 June that the Nationalists' critical problems
arose from "the complete lack of aggressiveness and offensive spirit
among the Nationalist Chinese troops from the theater commanders
down to the privates."[103] He nevertheless thought that American help
still could change this sorry situation and asked for immediate permission to furnish operational assistance to the Nationalist general staff
and principal field commanders. Vice Admiral Oscar C. Badger, the
commander of naval forces in the Western Pacific, enthusiastically

seconded Barr's recommendations. Despite the current "black outlook," Badger, too, believed that American assistance with plans and
operations could instill offensive spirit in Chiang's demoralized
armies.[104] Stuart also endorsed Barr's proposals, convinced that American supervision of the Nationalist war effort was necessary to turn the
tide "in our favor."[105]

But policymakers in Washington demurred. Marshall, as ever wary
of Nationalist efforts to draw the United States deeper into the civil
war, told a meeting of political and military officials that acceptance of
Barr's proposals increased the risk of "getting sucked in." Service
officials fretted about the same peril. Retreating from his earlier views,
Wedemeyer declared that he no longer favored the placement of American advisers with Chinese units in the field. Such action, he feared,
would now only allow the Nationalists to blame the United States—
particularly the army—for "the final debacle." Royall reaffirmed his
opposition to further military assistance to the Nationalists and General Omar N. Bradley, the army chief of staff, dismissed Barr's suggestions as "impractical and undesirable."[106] Following this meeting,
the Joint Chiefs of Staff ruled out further consideration of operational
advice to the Nationalist army. When the long-delayed joint military
advisory group was activated on 1 November 1948, its mission was
limited to advice on organization and training.[107]

As the discussion of Barr's proposals indicated, a shift had occurred
in the army's attitude toward military aid to the Nationalists. So concerned was Royall about an imminent collapse of Chiang's regime that
he suggested to Forrestal on 19 July that they talk to Truman about
withdrawing all aid to the Nationalists. Studies by P&O, however,
counseled against such a move. The abrupt cessation of American
assistance, P&O warned, would precipitate the fall of the Nationalist
government and place upon the United States the onus for Chiang's
demise. The army planners also asserted that such actions might cast
doubt on American determination to honor its commitments to other
nations. Instead they recommended the continuation of current aid
programs in order to delay the collapse of the Nationalist regime. The
Joint Chiefs of Staff agreed, arguing that "the buying of time by
expenditures within reason will constitute . . . true economy in terms
of our national security." The service chiefs, however, had all but
abandoned hope of a Nationalist victory in the civil war. Like the army

planners, they viewed military aid to China primarily as a means of postponing a Nationalist defeat.[108]

The CIA, however, challenged this analysis. CIA Director Roscoe H. Hillenkoetter warned Truman on 20 July that Chiang's government was "so unstable that its collapse or overthrow could occur at any time." Because of the deterioration of the Nationalist regime, Hillenkoetter thought that it was "very questionable" whether the China Aid Program could do anything to slow the Nationalist decline. "Thus the US may find itself in the near future actively supporting a government at Nanking which exercises merely nominal power," Hillenkoetter cautioned Truman. This situation "would gravely impair US prestige and interests in the Far East."[109]

As Nationalist prospects darkened, officials in Washington began implementing the China Aid Act. To no one's surprise, the Nationalist minister informed the State Department on 11 May 1948 that his government wished to use the entire $125 million grant for the purchase of military supplies. While deliberating the administrative terms for use of this special fund, Butterworth and his colleagues in FE emphasized that the United States should assume no responsibility for Nationalist expenditures. Upon State's recommendation, Truman approved on 2 June procedures governing the $125 million grant that limited American supervision merely to checking the invoices supporting Chinese requests for payments. In addition, military and naval officers in Washington provided only technical advice on procurement to their Chinese counterparts.[110]

Pressure from Chiang's supporters in Congress forced reconsideration of these arrangements. Senator Bridges accused the State Department on 28 June of dilatoriness in allocating funds for Nationalist military purchases. Three days later he joined with John Taber (R-N.Y.), chairman of the House Appropriations Committee, in urging Truman to step up the administration's efforts to see that the Nationalists used the $125 million fund to meet their pressing military needs. Walter Judd beseeched Lovett on 9 July to hasten the delivery of armaments to Chiang by arranging for the transfer of equipment from the inventories of the National Military Establishment. Owing to the depletion of surplus stocks and the long lead time in the commercial procurement of munitions, transfer from war reserves was the fastest way to meet Nationalist requirements. Responding to these appeals, Truman accepted Marshall's advice and on 28 July 1948 revised his earlier directive to allow the service departments to furnish military supplies directly to the Nationalists.[111]

But even these new procedures did not result in the prompt delivery of armaments to the Nationalists. On the recommendation of the State Department, the army assigned the Chinese program a priority behind Greece, Turkey, and Iran. This ranking meant that the army would give preference to the other programs in allocating scarce equipment and that the Chinese would have to pay either procurement or replacement costs for most of the items they requested.[112] By mid-August logistics experts determined that the army could provide from stock the small arms and ammunition that the Nationalists urgently desired and begin to ship these munitions within two months. Other supplies, such as materials for Nationalist arsenals, would have to be obtained from manufacturers and could not be delivered until the following spring. At the end of August General Henry S. Aurand, the director of logistics, set 1 May 1949 as a target date for the completion of the $125 million program. He noted, however, that if the deadline were not met, there was little more under present policies that the army could do.[113]

Upset by the slow pace of deliveries of military supplies, critics charged that the program fell victim to bureaucratic bungling or willful obstruction. Neither was the case. The army completed availability studies during August with uncommon speed. The time required to fill Chinese requests from stock was not abnormal: the technical services needed at least 120 days to provide equipment to regular army units. The priority accorded the Chinese program reflected the political and strategic outlook that prevailed within the administration, not any desire to delay the $125 million program.

Efforts by American officials in China to influence the use of the special fund complicated the planning in Washington. The aim of these officials was to strengthen the forces in North China under the command of Fu Tso-yi, one of the few effective, aggressive Nationalist generals. Because Fu was not a member of Chiang's clique of favored officers—his friendship with Li Tsung-jen accounted for his difficulties with the generalissimo—the central government ignored his requests for military supplies. So great were Fu's needs that he tried to obtain American equipment from foreign brokers by bartering local products. The passage of the China Aid Act offered a solution to Fu's plight, in the opinion of several American officials. Eager to keep alive Nationalist resistance in the critical area of Peiping and Tientsin, they attempted to secure for Fu a portion of the military equipment purchased with the $125 million grant.[114]

The driving force behind the effort to help Fu was Admiral Badger. He argued persuasively that the loss of North China would make the Nationalist position untenable. Yet his primary concern in urging support of Fu was protection of American naval facilities at Tsingtao. Badger informed the Navy Department in May that he was prepared to assist the Nationalists in the defense of that city, a course of action that the Joint Chiefs, under pressure from the State Department, overruled in favor of prompt withdrawal in the event of a Communist attack. According to an embassy official, Badger was "desperate at the thought that he might eventually have to evacuate Tsingtao and is moving heaven and earth . . . to avoid the possibility." His solution was to hasten the delivery of supplies to Fu and to Nationalist forces in Shantung. With unrelenting zeal, he pressed this proposal in Nanking and Washington and predicted magical results. "It could be the turning point," he cabled the chief of naval operations, Admiral Louis E. Denfeld, "which would ultimately lead to a strong united China friendly to [the] United States and an effective opponent of Communism."[115]

Badger gained support for his plans from Stuart, who also had a special reason for concern over the fate of North China. Lewis Clark, the minister-counselor of the embassy, reported that "the Ambassador's heart is most deeply involved in Yenching [University of Peiping] and consequently in the stability of North China, and . . . his judgment is influenced by his desire at almost any cost to avoid Communist dominance of the Peiping-Tientsin area." Melby wrote that Stuart "didn't give a damn what Washington thinks about anything. He is in effect China's Ambassador to China."[116] A July meeting with Fu and several conferences with Badger persuaded Stuart that modest amounts of armaments would enable the Nationalists to hold North China. Despite objections from the embassy staff, Stuart urged the generalissimo to agree to the provision of military aid to Fu, while assuring the State Department that such action involved no responsibility for the Nationalist war effort. Stuart ignored Badger's tendency to stretch the truth as he importuned Washington authorities to back his proposals to help Fu. "I am willing to close my eyes to that if he can accomplish the end sought," he confided to Clark.[117]

Officials of the Economic Cooperation Administration (ECA) also enthusiastically endorsed aid to Fu. Shortly after arriving in China in June 1948, members of the ECA mission expressed shock at the Nationalists' perilous military position and dismay over the central government's willingness to write off North China, where "the armies and the articulate groups . . . are full of spirit for the fight against the Communists."[118] Roger D. Lapham, the ECA chief in China, insisted that the United States could not afford to abandon North China, no matter what Chiang did. Convinced that the administration should no longer pin its hopes on the generalissimo's decadent regime, he urged the provision of American arms to Fu as the first step in an "affirmative" program of support for regional groups that actively resisted the Communists. Attempting to revive a dead issue, he recommended an expanded effort in China, modeled on American aid to Greece, as vital to the containment of "world" communism.[119]

The only senior American official in China who had reservations about providing military aid to Fu was General Barr. Conceding that such help might prolong Fu's resistance, he thought that the Nationalists should use the special fund primarily to train and equip a force in South China capable of taking the offensive. But, without consulting Barr, Badger persuaded Chiang to give first priority to strengthening North China and Shantung. He apparently swayed the generalissimo by virtually promising—without authority—the sale of American armaments at procurement, rather than replacement, prices and free transportation of these munitions to China in navy bottoms. Convinced that Chiang had made a firm decision and aware of the strong feelings of other American officials in China, Barr acquiesced in the plan to aid Fu. At the end of August, the generalissimo affirmed to Barr, Badger, and Stuart his decision to ask the National Military Establishment to furnish equipment under the $125 million grant for Fu's seven armies and for three reorganized Nationalist divisions at Tsingtao.[120]

Washington authorities promptly agreed to the delivery of military aid to North China. Such assistance appealed to the State Department not as a step toward strengthening local Chinese leaders but as a way of arresting the trend toward regionalism, which Chiang's neglect of North China was encouraging.[121] Problems arose, however, when the Chinese ambassador asked for equipment that would cost some $75 million, almost twice the unexpended balance in the special fund.

Although the navy eventually agreed to provide the free transportation that Badger had promised, the army refused to alter its pricing policy but made every effort to furnish items at the lowest possible cost.[122] At the request of the army, the Nationalists designated first-priority items, primarily small-caliber weapons and ammunition, which amounted to $37.8 million. By early October army officials ordered the preparation of these munitions for shipment to China in December and January.[123]

Truman intervened personally to hasten the delivery of this materiel. Responding to an appeal from Chiang, who lamely blamed recent military reverses on shortages of equipment, and undoubtedly thinking about Republican criticism of his China policy in the final weeks of the presidential campaign, Truman directed the army to expedite the delivery of the small arms and ammunition that the Nationalists had requested. Service officials responded by assigning these items top priority. They also made available from MacArthur's stocks in Japan some 1,200 tons of weapons and ammunition. These supplies arrived in China in mid-November 1948, while the rest of the equipment left American ports between 9 November and 16 December.[124]

Little of this materiel actually reached Fu. Because of major Communist gains, Chiang's representatives notified service authorities in mid-November that they wished further deliveries of military aid diverted from North China. This decision threw Badger into a frenzy. He apparently tried to extract from Fu a pledge to resist to "the bitter end." He also urged the general to write a letter, which he would rush to Washington, asking Truman for help. Fu wanted no part of these desperate measures. Instead he entered into peace negotiations and on 23 January 1949 surrendered in Peiping to the Communists.[125]

Fu's capitulation practically completed the Communist conquest of China north of the Yangtze. During October and November, Mao's forces took in rapid succession Chinchow, Changchun, and Mukden, thereby ending the war in Manchuria. At the end of the year, the protracted siege of Hsuchow eliminated the last Nationalist armies in the North save Fu's. These defeats cost Chiang huge bodies of troops— including his best armies—and enormous quantities of materiel. Marshall was especially furious over the Nationalists' failure to destroy their ammunition dumps and the arsenal at Mukden. Barr reported on 16 November that government forces had not lost a single battle since his arrival for want of equipment. "Their military debacles," he explained, "can all be attributed to the world's worst leadership and many other morale destroying factors that led to a complete loss of will to fight." Further infusions of American arms in the autumn of 1948 could not have altered the results of the fighting.[126]

As the "mandate of heaven" slipped from his grasp, Chiang launched a desperate campaign for all-out American assistance. In an interview with an American journalist, the generalissimo asserted, "The center of endeavor in the salvation of Asia must be China. . . . I hope that the American people and their statesmen will dedicate their lives to this task."[127] Two weeks later he appealed to Truman for increased military aid and the assignment of a general who could direct the Nationalist war effort. Lesser Nationalist officials repeatedly importuned Marshall and his assistants for public expressions of support. Marshall, however, was unmoved. He considered the appointment of a new military mission a "quixotic venture" and reiterated his belief that American arms could not save Chiang.[128] Upon his recommendation, Truman repeated his pledge to Chiang to hasten the implementation of the China Aid Act but ruled out further assistance. As Lovett explained privately, "Only the Chinese can save China, and . . . we must not feel that there is anything practical that we can do to restore the position there."[129]

Nonetheless, administration officials scrupulously avoided public expressions of such views. At the end of November, Marshall rejected a recommendation from the Policy Planning Staff that the president issue a frank statement aimed at alleviating "the confusion and bewilderment in the public mind regarding our China policy." He explained to the Cabinet, "The Nationalist Government of China is on its way out and there is nothing we can do to save it. We are faced with the question of clarifying the American people [sic] and by so doing deliver[ing] the knock out blow to the Nationalist Govt in China—or we can play along with the existing govt . . . [by] keeping facts from the American people and thereby not be accused later of playing into the hands of the Communists." Truman agreed with his secretary of state that the administration should follow the later course. For similar reasons, the Cabinet decided to allow Madame Chiang to come to the United States on a mission to secure further assistance. Truman and his advisers preferred to suffer any embarrassment she might cause the administration—her pleas for additional aid were politely but firmly refused—rather than risk charges that the United States was turning its back on the Nationalists.[130]

In retrospect, these decisions appear unwise. If concerns about American credibility had kept the Truman administration from issuing a frank public statement about its China policy, those strictures should no longer have applied by late 1948. In China, all hope of preventing a Nationalist collapse had vanished. In Europe, the crisis of confidence of the previous spring had passed, and Marshall Plan aid was beginning to reach the recipient nations. Support for a doomed regime could do little, in these circumstances, to enhance American credibility. Still, the continued provision of arms aid carried the implication that American help could somehow preserve the Nationalist government, a dangerous expectation that could only harm American prestige. By their silence, Truman and Marshall inadvertently played into the hands of partisan Republicans and extreme supporters of Chiang. They neither educated public opinion nor moderated the fury of critics who later claimed that the United States "lost" China.[131]

Concern over public reaction also influenced the administration's attitude toward the continuation of military aid shipments to China. By the end of 1948, the civil war had turned so severely against the Nationalists that Washington officials no longer believed that the central government could rally the remaining forces of resistance. Further deliveries of armaments purchased with funds from the $125 million grant could do nothing to stem the Communist advance. Indeed, political and military analysts feared that their principal effect might be to strengthen the victorious Communist armies. At Forrestal's request on 16 December, the National Security Council reviewed Truman's earlier decision to expedite military aid to the Nationalists and agreed to ask Stuart and Barr for their opinions on the suspension of arms shipments. Pending action by the NSC, Lovett requested the army to divert vessels en route to China to intermediate ports.[132]

Both Barr and Stuart counseled against the abrupt cessation of military aid to the Nationalists. Stuart, who "never gave up until there was no longer anything to give up," emphasized that such action would discourage those forces that intended to carry on the fight against the Communists.[133] In a long review of the situation in China, Barr concluded that additional American arms could do nothing to prevent a Nationalist defeat. "Only a policy of unlimited United States aid," he declared, "including the immediate employment of United States Armed Forces to block the southern advance of the communists, which I emphatically do not recommend, would enable the Nationalist

Government to maintain a foothold in Southern China against a determined communist advance." Still, Barr opposed a sudden halt of military aid as long as the Nationalist government continued to exist, since "such action would be widely condemned and would place the United States in an unfavorable light in the eyes of the world." He urged instead the continuation of military and economic aid to South China and Taiwan as long as the Nationalists held "any considerable portions of these areas."[134] Officials in the State Department and the National Military Establishment, including the Joint Chiefs of Staff, expressed similar views.[135]

Truman ratified the consensus that his advisers reached on further aid to China. On 31 December he authorized continued implementation of the China Aid Act as long as the Nationalist government or a legal successor remained in power and pursued "an anti-Communist policy" and as long as "our military authorities in China" continued to recommend assistance. Barr thus ordered two ships that had been detained at intermediate ports to proceed to Taiwan for unloading. Further deliveries would depend on the course of military and political events in China. The overriding goal of the administration's policy, as Barr put it, was to avoid "any action that would tend to force the abdication of the Generalissimo or the collapse of the government."[136]

The rapid decline of Nationalist power led to a reconsideration of further arms shipments only one month later. Chiang's relinquishment of the presidency to Li Tsung-jen on 21 January 1949, and Fu's surrender of Peiping one day later, dramatically demonstrated the hopelessness of the Nationalist cause. Barr reported that effective resistance to the Communists was now most unlikely and recommended the cessation of military aid to the Nationalists. Army officials sustained his views. General Ray T. Maddocks, Wedemeyer's successor as director of P&O, declared that further efforts to help the Nationalists would only put arms into Communist hands. Royall, who was touring East Asia, cabled from Japan that "any military aid now delivered to China would either go immediately to the Communists or would be so applied or misapplied by officials of the Nationalist Government that it might well reach anti-democratic forces in or outside of China." On 4 February 1949 Truman approved an NSC recommendation that he stop the flow of military supplies to the Nationalists after consulting with the leaders of the congressional foreign affairs committees.[137]

The legislators, however, strongly opposed the suspension of military aid to China. Vandenberg made an impassioned speech against the NSC recommendation. "If we take *this* step at *this* fatefully inept moment," he pleaded, "we shall never be able to shake off the charge that *we* are the ones who gave poor China the final push into disaster. . . . I beg of you, at the very least, to postpone any such decision for a few more weeks until the China question is settled *by China* and *in China* and not by the *American government in Washington.* This blood must not be on *our* hands."[138] Vandenberg's appeal was decisive. The Truman administration still had no desire to precipitate a fractious, public debate over aid to China or to antagonize Vandenberg, whose cooperation was essential for renewal of the Marshall Plan and approval of the North Atlantic Treaty. Three days later, Truman decided against the suspension of arms shipments but ordered the pace of deliveries slowed. During the spring of 1949, American supplies—now a symbol of futility rather than fidelity to a former wartime partner— trickled into China as the vestiges of Nationalist power were driven from the mainland.[139]

"I've been badly mistaken in Chinese governments," Truman reflected in November 1951. "When I became President of the United States I thought Chiang Kai-shek's Government was on the road to a real reform government in China. I found by experience that it was the most corrupt and terrible government that China ever had."[140] More than two years earlier, during the final months of the civil war, Truman fixed the blame for the Nationalist defeat on the "grafters and crooks" in Chiang's ruling circle who had no interest in the needs of the Chinese masses. He told David E. Lilienthal, the chairman of the Atomic Energy Commission, that the United States had given the Nationalists $2.5 billion in aid since World War II, and "I'll bet you that a billion dollars of it is in New York banks today."[141] Behind this exasperation was a feeling shared by most of Truman's senior foreign policy advisers: Chiang had lost the civil war because of his inability to govern.

Although Truman spoke bitterly of Chiang, he did not think that the generalissimo's failure had greatly harmed American security interests in Asia. Truman measured events in China against the larger standard of containing Soviet expansion and accepted Marshall's conclusion that the United States had little to gain and much to lose by making a major effort to sustain the Nationalists. Conscious of the limits of

American power, the Truman administration concentrated its resources instead on meeting Communist challenges in the more important theaters of Europe and the Near East, while relying temporarily on a defensive perimeter in the islands of the Western Pacific to protect American security interests in East Asia.[142] In the long run, Truman held out hope that friction between the Soviets and the Chinese Communists would allow the United States to rebuild its influence on the mainland. "The dragon is going to turn over," he told Lilienthal, "and after that perhaps some advances can be made out of it."[143]

Not all government officials shared these views. Military leaders in particular worried that the Soviets had gained a major victory in Asia that would strengthen their position in Europe. But this fear suggested the extent to which the military establishment actually accepted the State Department's assessment of American interests in China. The services urged a stronger commitment to Chiang not because they considered China more important to American security than Western Europe or the Near East—indeed they thought just the opposite—but because they believed that *limited* military aid could prevent a Communist victory. When it became clear that the Nationalists' days were numbered, the Joint Chiefs supported continued assistance only to delay the Communist triumph and demonstrate American resolution to friendly nations in Europe and the Near East, not to save Chiang from defeat. Even the Nationalists' warmest supporters within the administration did not think that American interests justified all-out military assistance. Rather, the critical issue over which policymakers divided was American capacity, within limited means, to influence events in China.

The provision of arms to China also revealed the difficulties of using military aid to fortify American credibility. Even those policymakers who feared excessive involvement in the Chinese civil war believed that continued military assistance to the Nationalists was an important measure of American dependability, one that friends and allies around the world would use to gauge American determination to contain Communist expansionism. Because of the concern about American credibility, the Truman administration did not halt deliveries of arms to Chiang even after the NSC concluded that more materiel would no longer help his armies avert defeat. Congressional involvement—no other military aid program had such strong and vociferous support on Capitol Hill—meant that arms aid to China could trigger an explosive political debate that might weaken foreign confidence in American resolve. Its symbolic importance, then, made military assistance to China extremely hard to control.

Although the State Department prevailed over its bureaucratic rivals, Marshall never solved the dilemma of aid to China. He avoided the unending, step-by-step involvement in the Chinese civil war that he so constantly dreaded, but he never publicly explained the dangers of commitment to the Nationalists. Only a determined effort to inform the public that events in China were beyond American control might have lessened the widespread confusion that fed the belief that the United States was responsible for Chiang's downfall.[144] But Marshall and Truman explicitly rejected this course, and Chiang's die-hard supporters, turning the rhetoric of the Truman Doctrine against the administration, clamored in 1949 for a last-ditch effort to prevent a Communist victory. Despite his tortuous efforts, Marshall by no means settled the issue of further military assistance to China.

7 | The Mutual Defense Assistance Program

The effect of the assumed military assistance program would be primarily psychological.
—Central Intelligence Agency, 24 February 1949

On 6 October 1949 President Harry S. Truman signed into law the Mutual Defense Assistance Act (MDAA), a landmark in the development of arms aid as a major instrument of containment. The first global military assistance legislation since lend-lease, the MDAA authorized $1.314 billion to arm thirteen countries and empowered the president to sell military equipment to other nations that joined the United States in defensive alliances and regional arrangements. Most aid went to signatories of the North Atlantic Treaty, but Greece, Turkey, Iran, Korea, and the Philippines also received grants of equipment, as did recipients in the "general area" of China, through the use of an unvouchered presidential emergency fund. The MDAA finally corrected the imbalance between the administration's desire and its capability to provide military assistance, a disparity that had hampered foreign policy planners since 1947. The new law, in short, was the culmination of a two-year effort to establish "a unified, cohesive military aid program" that could raise the morale of friendly nations and demonstrate American resolve to resist the expansion of Communist power.[1]

Although the MDAA met many of the Truman administration's pressing needs, it left unresolved some critical problems. Administration officials admitted that the $1 billion reserved for the North Atlantic allies constituted interim assistance, but they had determined neither the duration nor the ultimate objective of such help. In Western Europe as well as in other countries that received American arms, MDAA planners hoped to stiffen the will to resist Communist pressures. But they lacked reliable methods of determining whether American aid could actually achieve that goal or how much aid might be necessary. In its zeal to arm foreign nations, the Truman administration had ignored the question that one concerned official had raised: "If we once take on the obligation, establish the precedent, where do we wind up?"[2]

Fortified by the NSC recommendation in July 1948 to seek new military aid legislation "at the earliest feasible time," army officials pressed for the submission of a bill to Congress. In September Secretary of the Army Kenneth C. Royall asked Secretary of Defense James V. Forrestal to consult with Secretary of State George C. Marshall about calling a special session of Congress for that purpose. Because such action was out of the question with national elections less than two months away, Forrestal replied that enactment of general military aid legislation would be the National Military Establishment's highest priority when the Eighty-first Congress convened in January 1949. This decision did not satisfy General Henry C. Aurand, the director of army logistics, who continued to complain that delays in developing an overall military aid program with supporting legislation and appropriations were "ruining our own material situation." Army planners, however, once again rejected Aurand's appeal for a moratorium on foreign military aid until the Congress acted. Although they, too, were impatient for the passage of an arms bill, they believed that occasional provision of modest amounts of armaments, such as the recent reequipment of three French divisions from American stocks in Germany, served both the army's and the nation's interests.[3]

While new legislation promised to ease the army's supply problems, it also raised the troubling issue of the relationship between domestic military needs and foreign aid. The Joint Chiefs of Staff first expressed their concern about this matter in the spring of 1948 when the administration began to consider arms aid to the Western Union. Although recognizing the desirability of such assistance, the service leaders maintained that "its extent must be limited by the necessity for avoiding both undue reduction of resources essential to our national security and undue interference with our own military requirements." Determined to preserve the freedom in the event of war to respond at places of their choosing, they also cautioned that military aid decisions should never be "dictated by foreign demand rather than appropriateness to strategic plans." However much the Western Europeans wanted to hold the Rhine against a Soviet invasion, such a defense—at least in the short run—appeared impossible to the Joint Chiefs. Service leaders also were concerned that large expenditures on foreign aid might bring a cut in defense appropriations, a prospect they viewed with genuine alarm. Because of the Joint Chiefs' worries, the NSC concluded that the military assistance program should neither jeopardize the minimum material requirements of the armed forces nor be inconsistent with American strategic plans.[4]

Even these assurances did not relieve the Joint Chiefs' anxieties, however. General Hoyt S. Vandenberg, the air force chief of staff, wrote in July that current budget restrictions would not permit both substantial rearmament and an extensive military assistance program and asked for a study of how best to satisfy these competing requirements. The Joint Strategic Survey Committee promptly reported that the United States should restrict military assistance to amounts that did not interfere with domestic rearmament. Vandenberg criticized this study for failing to recommend limits on the services' reserve stocks. So did General Omar N. Bradley, the army's chief of staff, who also warned that "it would seem a great mistake to concentrate our entire resources on a United States rearmament program in the belief that such action alone will contribute most to our national security." The Joint Chiefs eventually decided in early 1949 that they would consider each request for assistance on its own merits. Agreeing in principle that military aid could contribute to American security, they remained uncertain about how to balance such help against domestic needs.[5]

Also troubling the Joint Chiefs was the potential scope of a worldwide military assistance program. They found especially distressing a draft report on military aid priorities prepared by the State-Army-Navy-Air Force Coordinating Committee in August 1948. The SANACC declared eligible for American military aid almost every non-Communist country—a total of fifty-nine nations—although it recommended substantial assistance to only the five nations of the Western Union and Canada. The Joint Chiefs were aghast at the breadth and magnitude of these potential obligations and urged the most careful consideration of "our national financial and industrial limitations and our own military requirements before specific decisions are made." They also reminded the SANACC that "limited military aid may well prove difficult to limit once it has been begun and . . . token aid, by definition, bears to the recipient the implication of more to come." It was precisely to avoid a diffusion of American aid overseas and to restore a balance between commitments and resources that most military leaders championed new legislation and a consolidation of the military assistance program. These goals remained preeminent in their thinking, and during the planning conferences in late 1948 and early 1949 military officials continued to urge caution and restraint in sending arms abroad as well as improved military readiness—particularly the mobilization of industry—to support foreign commitments.[6]

Officials in the Bureau of the Budget also fretted about the overextension of the nation's resources. The reason for their concern was the consummation in July 1948 of an agreement to provide $10 million in surplus armaments to Iran. The Truman administration had promised this materiel in November 1946 when Iranian troops marched into Azerbaijan, but difficulties in arranging for payment held up delivery, and by the summer of 1948, some 60 percent of the equipment was no longer surplus. Budget officials reluctantly authorized the transfer of these supplies when Under Secretary of State Robert A. Lovett invoked overriding political considerations, but they were nonetheless disturbed by "the current piecemeal basis" of foreign military aid because it was both expensive and inefficient. "Until the individual proposals can be dealt with as parts of an over-all program," Budget Director James E. Webb warned Lovett, "we run a real risk not only of unwarranted costs and less than maximum employment of our defense resources, but also of making commitments we cannot meet."[7]

Although Lovett accepted the need for systematic planning, other political officials considered prompt action to raise morale overseas far more important. In July 1948, shortly after taking up his duties as Truman's special representative in Europe for Marshall Plan affairs, W. Averell Harriman cabled from Paris that the "appeasement psychology" was "not deeply buried," and so, "strengthening the will to resist in Europe should be fundamental in our policy through the coming months." Essential to this objective, he believed, was the early delivery of American armaments. Harriman insisted that Truman authorize these shipments without awaiting the passage of legislation and promised that the effect on European public opinion would be "inspiring." The military value of these transfers was "not important." What mattered, according to Harriman, was a public demonstration of American resolve—"that we mean business when we say their security is our security."[8] In conversation with Forrestal during the autumn, he recommended once again immediate military aid to raise morale in France, the country he considered the political and military keystone of Western Europe. Harriman did not fear that the rearmament of Western Europe would interfere with the Marshall Plan. Rather, he thought that military aid would inspire the confidence essential to economic recovery. Without "tangible support for [the] Western Union in the security and military field," he wrote to Lovett on 12 November, "the success of ERP will be jeopardized."[9]

Marshall, too, stressed the psychological effects of military assistance on Western Europeans who were "completely out of their skin, and sitting on their nerves." He thought that it was imperative that the United States ease these anxieties, and token shipments would have an "electrifying" effect, particularly if accompanied by the proper publicity.[10] One month later Marshall reiterated to Forrestal the importance of getting weapons to the Europeans, particularly the French, and criticized the military establishment for worrying too much about balanced sets of equipment for ground forces. So great was his faith in military aid as a means of raising morale that Marshall all but ignored French military requirements. Even though the French urgently needed heavy equipment, he suggested that the United States concentrate on providing them small arms—weapons they would "put in their hands"—since such items would do more toward "creating the spirit and will of resistance."[11]

Marshall and Harriman were so concerned about the will to resist because once again France was in the throes of political and economic crisis. Despite significant increases in the production of basic industrial commodities in early 1948, new inflationary pressures triggered acrimonious disputes over wages, prices, and government spending. These economic and financial difficulties brought down the middle-of-the-road government of Prime Minister Robert Schuman in mid-July and threatened the new coalition regime headed by Henri Queuille. American observers worried that, if the French Center failed to hold, a rightist government headed by General Charles De Gaulle might take power and plunge France into even greater turmoil. John D. Hickerson, the director of the State Department's Office of European Affairs, derided De Gaulle for proclaiming a "mystical (and illusory) idea of France as a great power" and having "no real program." Using a snide, sexist simile, Hickerson sneered, "He talks about economics as a woman talks about carburetors." An even more objectionable alternative was the Communist party, which stepped up the pressure on the

Queuille government in the autumn by organizing demonstrations and a strike in the critical coal-mining industry. Marshall, Harriman, and other American observers believed that the Communists intended to wreak havoc in the French economy, sabotage the European Recovery Program, and force their return to power.[12]

Nevertheless, the French crisis, according to American experts, had deeper causes than inflation or Communist agitation. Also contributing to the current turmoil were problems endemic to French society. Since the late nineteenth century, the French political system had consisted of a welter of competing parties, and the current constitution, Hickerson asserted, made it "very difficult to have any stable government." Hickerson thought that this system of politics reflected the values of the French people, who were "temperamentally selfish, individualistic and reluctant to cooperate with anyone." Ambassador Jefferson Caffery also believed that the crisis of 1948 arose in part from a long-standing social problem—conflict between the middle and working classes over their fair share of national wealth. Caffery and Hickerson agreed that American aid could alleviate French financial and economic difficulties. They also recognized, however, that "there is little anyone outside of France can do toward obtaining a French Government in which anyone can have confidence."[13]

Because of their exasperation with French political instability, however, Hickerson and other State Department officials nevertheless proposed to use the threat of a reduction in Marshall Plan aid to hasten the formation of a government strong enough to solve France's economic problems. Hickerson asserted that the time had come to inform the French that, unless they started making more progress toward the goals established by the Economic Cooperation Administration, the Congress would cut back on French allocations when the ERP came up for renewal in spring 1949. Hickerson cautioned that any such warning would have to be delivered most carefully lest the French, "in their present state of jitters, . . . merely throw up their hands and give up." Henry R. Labouisse, Jr., the State Department's coordinator of foreign aid and assistance, advocated even stronger action. He recommended immediate notification to all leaders of French non-Communist parties that the allocation of Marshall Plan funds—even those already authorized—would depend on whether the French government undertook necessary measures to control economic problems. Harriman, Caffery, and David K. E. Bruce, the chief of the ECA mission, believed France was absorbing an unwarranted amount of American aid because of its inability to undertake necessary measures of economic and financial self-help. But they insisted, and Marshall agreed, that "we should *not* at this time lay it on the line with the French party leaders," as Labouisse had suggested.[14]

Instead, Marshall and Harriman wanted to use planned allocations of economic aid and the promise of military aid to restore the confidence of French democratic forces and encourage their cooperation with American political, economic, and military plans. They desired support for the creation of a West German state and its integration into the European economy, goals that necessarily raised French apprehensions. They also wanted to calm French fears of being "helpless pawns in an impending conflict between Russian and American juggernauts." Hastening the provision of arms aid, they reasoned, would help to create a sense of security that would stimulate greater French efforts to curb inflation and promote recovery. They believed that economic and military aid should be used as incentives "to increase France's self-confidence and the French confidence in the US."[15]

Moreover, both Marshall and Harriman by this time regarded the provision of military aid as a symbolic action whose consequences they may well have exaggerated or misconstrued. Both believed that European will to resist ultimately depended on American action. Both worried that, if the United States appeared irresolute or undependable, a kind of bandwagon effect would sweep Western Europe, bringing economic chaos, political turmoil, and perhaps Communist seizures of power. Even though they had good reasons for such fears—after all, the Western Europeans had issued ominous warnings in the spring of 1948 while asking the United States for military commitments and armaments—Marshall and Harriman still seemed unduly apprehensive about American credibility when the Truman administration was demonstrating its resolve by providing Marshall Plan aid, participating in negotiations for a North Atlantic Treaty, and conducting the Berlin Airlift. They also assumed that highly publicized, symbolic transfers of armaments would be seen as gestures of assurance rather than ominous indications of impending conflict, as Italian Prime Minister Alcide de Gasperi had warned when he asked for the postponement of American arms deliveries on the eve of his country's critical elections. But State Department policy reflected the views of Marshall and Harriman. As Lovett informed the latter at the end of 1948, "It is the psychological effect [of aid], rather than the intrinsic military value, which is of primary importance."[16]

The concerns of both the State Department and the National Military Establishment shaped discussions of military aid with European officials during the last half of 1948. These conversations proceeded on two fronts. In Washington, State Department officials and representatives of the Western Union held secret talks, which yielded in September a working plan for the negotiation of a North Atlantic treaty. In London, an American delegation participated in Western Union military discussions aimed at devising an overall plan for the defense of Western Europe. In both these forums, Europeans stressed their immediate need for American armaments. However, both Lovett in Washington and General Lyman L. Lemnitzer, the American observer at the Western Union military talks in London, made clear that the United States desired coordinated rather than piecemeal requests for military assistance. Lovett emphasized that Congress would not sanction a costly giveaway program; it would only approve one, based on self-help and mutual aid, that increased American security. Charles E. Bohlen, counselor of the State Department, added that the immediate purpose of these collective measures was to bolster European confidence in the future, a conclusion in which the conferees basically concurred.[17]

Problems arose immediately in carrying out these principles, especially with the French. Bent on obtaining American military supplies and anxious about getting its share of them, France opposed the inclusion in a North Atlantic treaty of European nations other than the present members of the Western Union. Indeed, the French could not understand American concern with a long-range treaty and suggested that the United States concentrate instead on the immediate reequipment of the forces of the Western Union, especially their own. Repeatedly during the summer and fall of 1948 they lodged requests, which were completely unrelated to the defense plans of the Western Union, for military and naval armaments. Because of the crisis that followed the Soviet blockade of Berlin, Truman invoked his plenary powers to transfer American munitions to French occupation forces in Germany, but at the end of 1948 the Joint Chiefs decided that further French requests should be channeled through the Western Union. Despite their concern over French morale, officials in State's Office of European Affairs also became impatient with what they considered high-handed requests for preferential treatment in arms aid. Hickerson wrote to Caffery in exasperation, "The French are in our hair."[18]

The Western Union's request for military assistance also fell short of American expectations. Unable to complete a coordinated supply plan in time for American officials to study it before the next session of Congress, the Western Union military committee instead submitted in November 1948 a request for help in bringing current military units to full strength. This request was based not on a detailed strategic concept but on a brief statement of defense policy, the object of which was "to convince the U.S.S.R. that war would not pay." Military analysts quickly found that the Western Union's hastily drawn planning papers were "obviously incomplete" and geared toward national rather than European defense. As such, they failed to meet the criteria that the Joint Chiefs and the NSC had established the previous summer. But, because of the enormous concern about European morale, service officials nevertheless agreed to use the Western Union's interim supply plan as a basis for preparing the Military Assistance Program (MAP) that they soon planned to place before Congress.[19] At least in the short run, then, the strictures about coordinated defense planning yielded to the political and psychological imperatives that justified the provision of arms aid.

Whatever their differences over foreign assistance, political and military officials agreed by the end of 1948 that centralized planning was essential to the development of an overall military aid program. The State Department acted first, pushed by geographic officers who complained that there was no "central point in the Department where all aspects of the military aid legislation are being pulled together." To remedy this situation, Lovett named Assistant Secretary Ernest A. Gross as coordinator for foreign assistance programs. Forrestal soon appointed Lemnitzer, who had returned from the Western Union military talks in London, to handle similar responsibilities within the military establishment. In January 1949 Lemnitzer and Gross joined Alexander I. Henderson, the general counsel of the ECA, to form the Foreign Assistance Correlation Committee (FACC), a working group that took charge of shaping the MAP.[20]

The committee faced a formidable task. To his dismay, Lemnitzer found that administration planners had concentrated on general principles rather than specific country programs. The FACC, therefore, had to weigh requests for aid from dozens of countries against American resources and security interests and fuse its recommendations into a comprehensive, worldwide program that met demands for systematic planning from Congress, the armed services, and the Bureau of the Budget. Complicating the committee's work were differences between the State Department and the service departments, especially over sponsorship of the arms legislation and administrative control of the MAP. And added to these burdens was the pressure of time. Administration officials hoped to present the Military Assistance Program and the North Atlantic Treaty, then under negotiation, to Congress by the middle of March 1949. Because of the need for haste, the FACC concentrated not on producing a new series of studies but on coordinating, synthesizing, and reconciling the planning papers of the State Department and the National Military Establishment.[21]

Budgetary considerations exerted a powerful influence on the committee's deliberations from the start. Truman was determined to take a strong stand against the Soviets but still hoped to restrict and eventually reduce spending on defense and foreign aid. The Bureau of the Budget, therefore, was wary of large increases in military assistance and warned Truman in November 1948 that substantial new expenditures, without offsetting tax increases, would deepen the prospective deficit in fiscal year 1950 and aggravate inflation. Congress also was concerned about the size of a new military aid program, especially since the Truman administration already planned to spend $4.5 billion on Marshall Plan aid during the coming fiscal year. Aware of these pressures for economy, the FACC set a tentative ceiling on the MAP of between $1.5 billion and $2 billion, the maximum amount that the committee thought the Bureau of the Budget and Congress would accept. Rather than allow foreign demand or long-range military goals to dictate the size of the MAP, the FACC fit its recommendations to a predetermined budget.[22]

Policymakers also imposed this budgetary ceiling because of their desire to conserve the nation's material and military resources. So great was the Truman administration's concern about the effect of the MAP on supplies of raw materials that Lovett asked the National Security Resources Board to study this question in October 1948, months before formal planning of the MAP began. The resulting analyses eased anxieties. An expenditure of $2 billion, the board concluded, would

Table 1. Comparison of Joint Chiefs' and Foreign Assistance
Correlation Committee's Budgets (in Millions of Dollars) for the
Military Assistance Program

Country or Purpose	Joint Chiefs	FACC
Western Union	$ 995.647	$ 830.850
Denmark	36.500	49.990
Norway	48.800	81.650
Italy	60.000	44.770
Portugal	9.000	7.980
Turkey	100.000	102.300
Greece	200.000	198.160
Austria	112.000	102.550
Iran	12.300	15.200
Korea	20.000	17.650
Latin America	86.060	0
Philippines	5.890	10.130
Additional military production	0	200.000
Contingency fund	100.000	100.000
Administration	0	25.000
Pipeline supplies financed with FY 1949 funds	0	–19.960
Total	$1,786.197	$1,766.270

Source: JCS 1868/62, 7 March 1949, file CCS 092 (8-22-46) sec. 20, JCS; and table,
"Proposed Military Assistance Program," [April 1949], file N7-1(1)-B.1 vol. 1, Asst.
SecDef FMA.

neither reduce the amount of critical metals—aluminum, steel, and
copper—available for domestic consumption nor interfere with other
security programs that required these resources. Nor would a military
assistance program of this size hamper American preparedness. Although the Joint Chiefs found that the demands of the MAP would
cause some delay in the mobilization of American ground units, they
believed that the arming of European allies would yield an overall gain
for American security.[23]

Working within these limits, the Joint Chiefs devised a tentative
program of $1.786 billion in military aid for fiscal year 1950. (See Table
1.) In determining recipients and amounts of assistance, the Joint Staff
planners relied on political guidance from the FACC and the State
Department, which consisted mostly of reiterations of approved policy
statements on military assistance and summaries of current attitudes
toward potential recipients. In balancing requests against resources,

the Joint Chiefs weighed strategic, political, and psychological considerations and tried to "concentrate the aid where it will contribute the
maximum to our national security." But the recommendations that they
sent to the FACC on 7 March 1949 were more a consolidation of new
and continuing projects than a carefully integrated program shaped to
a detailed political-strategic plan. Nevertheless, their proposals formed
the basis for the MAP.[24]

Not surprisingly, the service chiefs thought that the bulk of this
assistance ($995,647,000) should go to the Western Union. Such exten-
sive help reflected not only the high priority that the Truman administration accorded Western Europe but also organizational conve-
nience. Because the North Atlantic Treaty was still under negotiation in
early 1949, the membership of the alliance remained unsettled and the
contributions of individual countries to collective defense uncertain.
Although they urged assistance to other signatories of the pact, the
Joint Chiefs could more easily assess the needs of the Western Union,
which had at least begun to make plans, however sketchy, for a common defense of Europe. The aid that they proposed aimed primarily at
bringing up to full strength the combat forces that the members of the
Western Union maintained during 1949. While such assistance
obviously would bolster the military capabilities of the recipients, the
service chiefs particularly emphasized that it would also "stiffen the
will of the Western Union nations to resist."[25]

The Joint Chiefs stressed that they were proposing interim
assistance, a first step toward building up the defenses of the Western
Union. Army planners found that the Western Union nations would
require substantial additional infusions of American materiel, as well
as troop support, in order to meet their goal of holding the Rhine
against a Soviet invasion by mid-1952. Prior to that time, American
military authorities considered the defense of Western Europe all but
impossible. In the event of war during 1949 or 1950, strategic plans
called for the evacuation of American occupation troops from the
continent, except perhaps for a contingent that might maintain a
bridgehead on the Iberian Peninsula. The interim program of arms aid,
the Joint Chiefs believed, would do no more than help the Western
Union forces delay a Soviet advance. An effective defense of the continent would require $13 billion of additional American military
assistance during the next four years, almost as much as the cost of the
Marshall Plan.[26]

In spite of such estimates, the Truman administration was by no means committed to any continuing program of military assistance to the Western Union. Although the Joint Staff was preparing a long-range strategic plan and supporting program of arms aid, higher authorities had not yet settled the scope or duration of American military help to the Western Union. Nor was there any agreement about the eventual goals of such assistance. The interim program could help equally in building European armed forces capable of defending against a Soviet invasion, either by themselves or in concert with American troops, or in creating military establishments aimed only at deterring hostile military actions. Neither American nor European military experts knew the size of the defense forces that the Western Union nations could support without straining their economies once American military help had ceased. Hence interim arms aid was a first installment in a military program whose objectives and dimensions had not yet been determined.[27]

Military planners urged arms aid to other prospective members of the North Atlantic pact, such as the Scandinavian nations, as much to promote specifically American objectives as to further the collective defense of Europe. In September 1948 the Truman administration resolved to use military assistance "to strengthen the present tendency of Norway and Denmark to align themselves with the Western Powers" and "to influence Sweden to abandon . . . [its] attitude of subjective neutrality" toward the Soviet Union. Despite some vacillations in carrying out this policy, the State Department repeatedly informed Norwegian, Swedish, and Danish officials that participants in a neutral Scandinavian bloc could not expect significant American military help. So important were American military interests in Scandinavia, however, that the Joint Chiefs recommended the provision of military equipment to Norway and Denmark whether or not they signed the North Atlantic Treaty. The service chiefs wanted to deny the Soviets bases in Norway and the Spitzbergen Archipelago. They also considered base rights in Greenland, a Danish possession, vital to American security, as well as control of that island in the event of war. Military aid—$48.8 million to Norway, $36.5 million to Denmark—would help the United States achieve these objectives. Unaware, of course, of the Joint Chiefs' recommendations, the Norwegian and Danish governments decided to join NATO, and the prospect of obtaining American arms—materiel they could not otherwise afford—was a major consideration in their decisions. Sweden, less dependent on the United States for military equipment, remained outside the alliance.[28]

The Joint Chiefs hoped that military assistance to Portugal, another possible signatory of the treaty, would help obtain base rights in the Azores. Because those islands were "the key to our primary air line of communication" with Eurasia, the Joint Chiefs considered the Azores "essential to the security of the United States."[29] The signature on 2 February 1948 of an agreement granting the United States temporary transit facilities in the Azores fell short of their hopes for long-term rights. The service chiefs pressed the State Department to reopen negotiations and recommended the provision to Portugal, should it join the North Atlantic alliance, of $9 million in military aid, mainly antiaircraft and infantry equipment to strengthen the Azores' defenses. Such help would "in the end contribute to the overall defense of the North Atlantic area," but army planners candidly admitted that it should be furnished "largely for political purposes."[30]

Proposals for aid to Italy, another prospective member of the pact, were based on similar reasoning. Throughout the treaty negotiations, some State Department officials expressed reservations about Italian membership, out of concern that inclusion of a nation that did not abut the North Atlantic would lead to demands for the expansion of the alliance. "Beyond the Atlantic area," Kennan cautioned, "there is no logical stopping point in the development of a system of anti-Russian alliances until that system has circled the globe and has embraced all the non-communist countries of Europe, Asia, and Africa." Hickerson, the director of State's Office of European Affairs, countered that failure to include Italy in the North Atlantic Treaty would be a repudiation of its pro-Western government and would weaken Italian resolve to oppose communism. Both Secretary of State Acheson and Truman accepted this logic in order to avoid jeopardizing a two-year invest- ment in "strengthening Italy's western orientation and weakening the Communist threat in Italy." The Joint Chiefs, however, reminded the FACC that Italy, because of restrictions on the size of its armed forces, could make only a minor contribution to the defense of Europe. Even so, they thought that Italy should receive $60 million in military aid— mainly to strengthen its internal security forces—whether or not it joined the North Atlantic alliance. Such help would continue American efforts to thwart the expansion of Communist influence in Italy.[31]

The only new program of military assistance that the Joint Chiefs advocated for a European country definitely outside the North Atlantic alliance was for Austria. Behind their recommendation was concern over Soviet expansion. British, French, Soviet, and American troops had occupied Austria at the end of World War II pending the negotiation of a peace treaty. But after the coup in Czechoslovakia in February 1948, State Department officials were apprehensive that the conclusion of such an agreement and the subsequent withdrawal of the Western occupation forces "would make Austria susceptible to Soviet aggressive aims." The Joint Chiefs concurred, adding that the presence of American soldiers kept intact an unbroken front against the Soviet Union and its satellites from Italy through Austria and Germany to the North Sea. In addition to the supposed external threat to Austria, political and military officials also worried about Soviet instigation of an internal uprising. These dangers frightened American policymakers because of Austria's military weakness. The planned peace treaty provided for an Austrian army of 53,000 men but did not allow their training or equipment prior to the departure of the occupation troops. Under these circumstances, administration officials warned, the Austrian army would not be able "to oppose successfully any violent action which may be contemplated or attempted by the Communist minority or by Soviet agents."[32]

To avert these consequences, American officials decided to extend military assistance to Austria. In the spring of 1948, the Truman administration authorized the commander of American occupation troops to train Austrian gendarmes and to establish stockpiles of equipment for their use in the event of an emergency. At the same time, American and British military experts secretly began to discuss organization of the proposed Austrian army. In violation of four-power directives, Western occupation authorities encouraged Austrian leaders to begin "covert planning" for national defense, but as one army analyst reported, "partisan differences and fear of Soviet reprisals . . . made all efforts rather sketchy and ineffective." American planning for arms aid to Austria was more productive. In December 1948 Lovett and Forrestal agreed to include Austria in the MAP. Three months later, the Joint Chiefs recommended $12 million worth of military equipment for the Austrian gendarmes and $100 million worth of supplies for the army if the conclusion of a peace treaty was likely during the coming fiscal year. Because of the obvious need to maintain secrecy, administration officials strictly ruled out any public discussion of military assistance to Austria. No part of the proposed MAP was more sensitive.[33]

The Joint Chiefs' proposals also encompassed the continuation of current programs in the Near East. Both political and military officials agreed that Greece should receive further assistance, even though they conceded that American help had by no means relieved—and had perhaps even exacerbated—the "inefficiency and lack of sustained fighting spirit of the Greek Army [GNA]."[34] This assessment arose partly from the disappointment over the offensives the GNA mounted against the guerrillas during 1948. Using heavy firepower, including napalm, the GNA inflicted substantial losses on the insurgents during fighting in the Grammos Mountains, but then retreated after attacking rebel positions at Vitsi. Because of the guerrillas' ability to take refuge in neighboring Yugoslavia and Albania and to replace their losses, these campaigns, according to the CIA, "did not fundamentally change the situation in Greece." General James A. Van Fleet, the chief of the American military advisory group, hoped to build the forces for a decisive campaign by tripling the amount of military aid to $500 million. But Ambassador Henry F. Grady argued that more American money and arms would only reinforce the complacency in Athens, since "each numerical increase [in the GNA], with corresponding increase in supplies, has added proof to Greeks that this, in [the] first instance, is America's war rather than Greece's." Accepting Grady's advice, the State Department concluded that the United States should instead bring pressure on Greek leaders for a more vigorous prosecution of the war. Unwilling to divert scarce resources to a country that would never be able to resist successfully a Soviet attack in the event of global war, the Joint Chiefs also ruled out a large increase in military aid to Greece. Instead they recommended a limit of $200 million, an amount that would allow only the maintenance of existing Greek forces. Once the GNA had eliminated major guerrilla activity—an event that finally occurred in 1949 largely because of the closing of the Yugoslav border to the dissidents and the leadership of a new GNA commander-in-chief—the Joint Chiefs thought that military aid should be "reduced to that sufficient only to maintain Greece's internal security."[35]

Previous commitments shaped proposals for future aid to Turkey and Iran as well. Fearful that morale in Ankara would sag without new shipments of American arms, the Truman administration decided to keep building up the Turkish defense establishment until it could offer strong resistance to a Soviet invasion. Toward this extravagant goal— one that all but precluded the cessation of American help—the Joint Chiefs reserved $100 million in the MAP.[36] Political rather than military considerations accounted for the continuation of aid to Iran. The surplus armaments that the Truman administration had promised in late 1946 were just beginning to arrive in early 1949, and American military experts doubted that the Iranians could absorb additional military equipment. But to appease Shah Mohammad Reza Pahlavi, who held grandiose notions of creating a bastion against Soviet expansion, political and military officials agreed on token aid of some $12.3 million, the Joint Chiefs estimated. In both instances, the momentum of existing policies was responsible for the additional infusions of aid.[37]

The Joint Chiefs' proposals for token assistance to Korea and the Philippines reflected the low priority that the Truman administration accorded East Asia. Regarding Korea, MAP planners balanced economy against prestige. Military authorities were eager to withdraw American occupation troops from a country with little strategic significance, but State Department planners insisted that Korea had "symbolic importance" because it was "a testing ground of the validity of United States v. Soviet objectives." In order to strengthen the army and police forces that the United States had trained and equipped and demonstrate American interest in South Korean independence, the Joint Chiefs reserved $20 million in the MAP.[38] Similar considerations led to a token gesture in the Philippines. Backing away from earlier estimates of the islands' importance to American security, the Joint Chiefs assigned the Philippines only a minor role in American war plans. General Albert C. Wedemeyer, the director of the army's Plans and Operations Division, warned against dissipating "limited resources in unwarranted provisions for the defense of the Philippines, at the expense of effort at the main centers of resistance to the Soviet Communist imperialism." Turning aside Philippine requests for substantial military aid, the Joint Chiefs recommended only $5.89 million to provide maintenance supplies to the armed forces that the United States had previously trained and equipped. In light of the impending Communist victory in China, the Truman administration hoped that such modest assistance to the Philippines and Korea would help stave

off further Communist advances in Asia and recoup American prestige.[39]

Finally, the Joint Chiefs renewed their long-standing effort to obtain
appropriations for military aid to Latin America. As usual, they faced
opposition from the State Department. Officials in the Office of American Republic Affairs wanted to limit military assistance to "small
amounts" to meet "urgent requests" and to provide such help from
unrestricted funds in the MAP. Military authorities disagreed.
Although still eager to promote the eventual standardization of hemispheric armaments, the Joint Chiefs concentrated on the more modest
goals of strengthening local defenses and maintaining stability in
countries with strategic resources. Toward this end, they proposed a
formal program of $86 million for Latin America. In addition to these
allocations, the Joint Chiefs still urged the creation within the MAP of a
contingency fund of $100 million, which the president might use to
meet the emergency or additional needs of any country he considered
important to American security.[40]

In early April, the FACC made some important changes in the Joint
Chiefs' proposed allocations, although the total expenditures were
practically the same. (See Table 1.) These modifications generally
reflected the FACC's accommodation of State Department positions.
The committee substantially increased allocations for Norway and
Denmark, enough to fill the requests for arms aid that these two
countries had made a year earlier. Hickerson and other officials in the
Office of European Affairs had been distressed by their inability to
meet Norwegian and Danish needs and were eager to reward those
two countries for recently choosing to adhere to the North Atlantic
Treaty. The Philippines also benefited from the State Department.
Whatever the strategic significance of the archipelago, its political
significance had been elevated "as a result of the military debacle in
China." The State Department felt that it would be "damaging . . . to
U.S. prestige and interests if the Philippine experiment should fail,"
because of the waxing strength of the "communist-lead [sic] Huk-
balahaps." Such reasoning persuaded the FACC to increase the proposed arms aid to the Philippines by two-thirds. On the other hand,
the committee eliminated any allocation for Latin America because of
the State Department's willingness to countenance only minor transfers of armaments to those nations.[41]

The greatest changes, however, were that arms aid to the Western Union was reduced by one-sixth and a $200 million fund was created to help finance increased military production in the NATO countries. Officials from both the State Department and the ECA were eager to stimulate such production to enable the Europeans eventually to support their military establishments from domestic sources and to demonstrate to Congress that the nation's new allies had accepted the principle of self-help expressed in the Vandenberg Resolution. American assistance would defray the dollar costs of imported raw materials for arms production and compensate the Europeans for any diversion of resources from economic recovery. On the basis of scant information, the FACC estimated that a $200 million subsidy would allow the Western Union nations and Italy to produce military supplies valued at twice that amount.[42]

However beneficial to European rearmament, such subsidies raised troubling questions about their effect on the Marshall Plan. "It is our policy," the FACC stated emphatically, "that economic recovery must not be sacrificed to rearmament and must continue to be given a clear priority."[43] Yet American officials found that only a small amount of slack capacity in Europe might be turned to armament manufacturing. Moreover, the expenses of such production would further burden European finances and disrupt long-term economic planning, which was geared—with American encouragement—toward increased civilian production at the expense of military outlays. For these reasons, officials in the Office of the Secretary of Defense had doubts about subsidizing European defense production. But W. Averell Harriman, the president's special representative in Europe for economic affairs, brushed aside such reservations. Harriman's staff reported to Acheson that not only would the MAP not jeopardize economic recovery but also that the stimulation of armaments production would help develop "the level of confidence in Western Europe which is necessary to insure economic viability beyond the Marshall Plan in 1952." Impressed by such arguments and concerned about placating Congress, FACC planners approved the creation of an Additional Military Production Fund in their tentative budget of $1.766 billion.[44]

The FACC now faced the difficult task of persuading the Bureau of the Budget to approve the MAP. Unanticipated difficulties arose when Edwin G. Nourse, the chairman of the president's Council of Economic Advisers, declared in an address at the Pentagon that the United States could not afford to increase spending on national security programs during the coming fiscal year. His conclusion reflected his conviction that spending on education, health, and social services already was "far below the level" desired by the president and demanded by the public. Furthermore, even without the additional expenses of the MAP, Nourse and Frank Pace, Jr., Truman's new budget director, forecast a deficit for fiscal year 1950. Fearful of the revival of inflationary pressures, which had abated in late 1948, Truman asked for a tax increase in early 1949, but his proposal made little progress on Capitol Hill. Because of these fiscal difficulties, Nourse proposed not only to meet the expenses of the MAP from the current budget of the National Military Establishment but also progressively to reduce defense spending as the North Atlantic allies built up their armed forces.[45]

Nourse's speech caused a furor in the Pentagon, especially since it had been cleared with Truman. The new secretary of defense, Louis A. Johnson, told Lemnitzer that the MAP was not "in any respect a justification for a reduction in our own military budget." The modest increases in the defense capabilities of the North Atlantic countries, Johnson informed Truman, in no way lessened the need for American preparedness, which was now the minimum necessary in view of Russian "intransigence" and "the current level of international tension." Not for several years, until the Western Europeans could defend their soil against a Soviet invasion, would any reduction in American military forces be possible.[46]

Although the FACC was able to turn back any threat to the service budgets, the Bureau of the Budget insisted on substantial reductions in the MAP. (See Table 2.) After a searching review, Budget officials slashed the MAP budget by one-third to $1.155 billion, primarily by lowering aid to non–North Atlantic countries and eliminating funds for additional military production and emergency requests. After lengthy negotiations, FACC officials succeeded in reinstating the last two items, albeit in reduced amounts, as well as partly restoring some of the other deep cuts. Administration planners finally decided to delete only the program for Portugal and reduce drastically only aid for Austria, since there was no chance of a peace treaty during the coming year. Further savings of some $44 million, through elimination of any charge for surplus equipment, brought the final total for the MAP to $1.45 billion. The negotiations with the Bureau of the Budget, which forced the State Department and the National Military Establishment

Table 2. Comparison of Budgets (in Millions of Dollars) for the
Proposed Military Assistance Program

Country or Purpose	FACC	Bureau of the Budget	Administration Request
Western Union	$ 830.850	$ 817.630	$ 801.600
Denmark	49.990	49.990	48.920
Norway	81.650	81.650	79.720
Italy	44.770	44.770	44.190
Portugal	7.980	0	0
Turkey	102.300	75.000	102.300
Greece	198.160	150.000	178.160
Austria	102.550	12.000	11.620
Iran	15.200	4.070	15.200
Korea	17.650	0	10.980
Philippines	10.130	0	5.740
Additional military production	200.000	0	155.000
Contingency fund	100.000	0	50.000
Administration	25.000	15.000	11.370
Pipeline supplies financed with FY 1949 funds	–19.960	–19.960	–19.960
Reduced ocean transport charges	0	–30.000	a
Nonreimbursement for surplus	0	–45.000	–44.840
Total	$1,766.270	$1,155.150	$1,450.000

Source: Table, "Proposed Military Assistance Program," [April 1949]; and memorandum, Lemnitzer to Gruenter and others, 27 April 1949, both in file N7-1(1)-B.1 vol. 1,
Asst. SecDef FMA.

ᵃSavings in ocean transport included in country totals.

to close ranks, facilitated agreement on another outstanding matter. In
return for the cooperation of the State Department in protecting their
budgets, the service departments dropped their demands for an independent administrator and agreed to let the secretary of state control
the MAP. Preliminary planning of the MAP came to an end on 20 April
1949 when Truman ratified this agreement and also approved the
budget of $1.45 billion.[47]

FACC planners thought that the program they had designed would
serve important purposes. Fundamental was the containment of Soviet
expansion, an objective so elastic that it encompassed all the country
and regional programs within the MAP, in spite of their diversity. Arms

aid, FACC analysts explained, would improve the ability of the recipients "to resist Soviet-Communist aggression" as well as support and encourage the political orientation of "the free nations of the non-Soviet world" toward the United States. The MAP also would invigorate American defense industries, a benefit that solidified support for the program within the military establishment. And in return for sending armaments abroad, the United States could receive reciprocal assistance, usually base rights and strategic raw materials, another dividend that military leaders especially coveted.[48]

Administration planners emphasized more than any of these objectives, however, the psychological effects of furnishing military assistance. The FACC insisted that "the psychological factor is of major significance in that military assistance will increase the determination to resist and will raise the level of confidence in all countries stimulating them to greater efforts in their economic and military recovery and enabling them to diminish their dependence on the United States." Acheson emphasized that the immediate result of arms aid would be confidence that the United States was a full partner "in the preservation of the peace and security of Europe" and in a consequent stiffening of European resolve that would make aggression unlikely. The CIA also considered the MAP a "primarily psychological" measure, but cautioned that its effect would depend on whether it was regarded "as an essential step toward the achievement of peace and security or merely as preparation for a new war."[49] Apparently impressed by such warnings and unwilling to leave to chance public reaction, foreign policy planners now turned their attention toward selling the MAP both abroad and at home.

After visiting London and Paris in January 1949, Paul H. Nitze, the deputy to the assistant secretary of state for economic affairs, reported that the sense of security of many Europeans depended not so much on American military assistance as on an easing of tension between the Soviet Union and the United States. But by this time détente was all but impossible. Truman and his top advisers placed their hopes not in negotiations with the Soviets but in the reestablishment of the military and economic power of Western Europe. Indeed, at the Paris meeting of the Council of Foreign Ministers in May 1949, Acheson was as unyielding as his Soviet counterpart on the terms of a German peace settlement, partly from fear that any concessions might disrupt American efforts to build Western European unity. More generally, administration officials were concerned in the spring of 1949 about a Soviet peace offensive that, the CIA predicted, would "eventually weaken substantially public support for rearmament programs and other measures designed to improve the western military position relative to that of the USSR."[50]

Eager to nurture that public support, the Truman administration portrayed the MAP as a step toward world peace. FACC planners devised an ambitious propaganda program, including speeches, public statements, and official publications, whose central theme was to convince the public that "the Military Aid Program expresses the determination of the United States to help build a stable, peaceful community of nations capable of maintaining itself against any threat." With an eye toward the reaction in Europe, administration spokesmen emphasized that the MAP carried no risks and imposed no costs on the recipients. Official statements, for example, avoided calling attention to the disparity in conventional military forces between the North Atlantic allies and the Soviet Union, an imbalance that the MAP did little to change. They also tried to calm any fears of an aggressive Soviet reaction to the passage of the MAP. Rather, they stressed that American military aid would "promote world recovery" and help "achieve a timely security for the North Atlantic area . . . which will not be susceptible to the hot-and-cold, 'peace' propaganda of the Soviet Union and international communism."[51]

This public information campaign perhaps had the greatest effect on American policymakers themselves. Harriman and other senior American officials in Europe reported on 5 June 1949 that any lengthy delay in the enactment of the MAP would bring to the surface "a deep latent feeling of insecurity" in Western Europe and "resurrect old doubts and uncertainties as to dependability and consistency of US foreign policy." Although abundant information supported these conclusions, American officials ignored or dismissed contrary indications. The embassies in Paris, Copenhagen, Oslo, and the Hague, for example, found no evidence that recovery efforts were suffering because Congress had not yet passed military assistance legislation, but still insisted that American arms aid was essential to the achievement of economic stability. The Truman administration, in effect, saw Europe's needs through the prism of its own requirements. By the spring of

1949, foreign policy planners had turned the MAP into a critical test of American will to resist Soviet expansion.[52]

The Congress, however, was skeptical of these views. Difficulties arose on 21 April when Acheson, Harriman, and Johnson informed an executive session of the Senate Foreign Relations Committee about their plans for the MAP. The discussion focused on the relationship between the MAP and the North Atlantic Treaty, which had been signed on 4 April, and the topic clearly perplexed and distressed several Senators. Henry Cabot Lodge (R-Mass.) found the scope of the MAP excessively broad, since it encompassed countries that had not signed the pact. Tom Connally (D-Tex.), chairman of the committee, worried that a grant of arms would encourage most of the North Atlantic allies "to sit down and fold their hands" until the United States sent troops as well as arms to Europe. H. Alexander Smith (R-N.J.), a supporter of the North Atlantic Treaty, questioned the need for military assistance. Since the MAP was "a military move which we know is not adequate," Smith suggested instead that the United States rely on the pact itself to deter a Soviet invasion.[53]

The committee's reaction upset the administration's schedule for the presentation of arms legislation to Congress. State Department officials, who had previously hoped to send the MAP bill to Capitol Hill before the end of April, abruptly reversed their position. Concerned about jeopardizing approval of the North Atlantic Treaty, Truman accepted on 12 May Acheson's recommendation to delay transmission of the arms legislation until after ratification of the pact. When Senate deliberations dragged on into late June, Truman, worried that Congress would not have time to act on the bill before adjournment, reconsidered his decision. But legislative leaders dissuaded him. Vandenberg worried about placing the treaty "in the wrong light to the country" by making it seem "a mere prelude" to the arming of Western Europe. Vice President Alben W. Barkley, Truman's principal liaison with the Senate, also counseled delay. Bowing to this advice, Truman reaffirmed his earlier decision on 1 July to wait until the Senate had consented to the treaty.[54]

Finally, on 25 July, hours after ratifying the North Atlantic Treaty, Truman sent the Foreign Military Assistance Act of 1949 to Congress. Like the Title VI legislation on which it was based, the draft bill proposed an enormous grant of power to the president. Under its terms, the chief executive had the authority to arm those countries "whose increased ability to defend themselves against aggression is important to the national interest of the United States" and to furnish such assistance on terms he deemed appropriate. FACC planners considered this expansive language necessary for flexible use of the contingency fund. In addition, the bill specified only the total authorization, $1.4 billion, not the amounts that each country would receive.[55] Administration officials omitted this information to avoid disclosing their plans to arm Austria and to forestall complaints from nations that felt slighted in the allocation of funds.[56]

These provisions surprised and angered influential legislators and helped precipitate, according to Senator Connally, the greatest struggle over foreign policy legislation since the enactment of lend-lease. Particularly vehement was a bipartisan group of internationalists who favored an arms program but condemned the administration bill. Led by Vandenberg, who had been Truman's most important congressional supporter of the North Atlantic Treaty, they denounced the proposed legislation for conferring upon the president unduly broad powers to arm any nation on whatever terms he considered appropriate. "It's almost unbelievable in its grant of unlimited power to the Chief Executive," he fumed in a letter to his wife after reading the text. "It would virtually make him the number one war lord of the earth." Vandenberg made similar comments before the Foreign Relations Committee on 29 July and urged a sweeping revision of the legislation, because failure to pass an arms bill would be a "supreme tragedy." John Foster Dulles, the Republican expert on foreign affairs and now a senator from New York, agreed with Vandenberg and warned Acheson that the administration might destroy bipartisan cooperation on foreign policy issues should it push for passage of the bill in its current form. Angered and embarrassed by such criticisms, Acheson, who had only glanced at the bill, vented his wrath on his subordinates. "Even a child," Acheson sarcastically told his staff, "would have picked up the weakness in the . . . legislation."[57]

Truman and Acheson acted quickly to accommodate their critics. Both realized that compromise was essential to the approval of an arms bill; both were anxious about the effects on European morale of a lengthy delay in implementing the MAP. The revised legislation, which Truman sent to Congress on 5 August, was far more restrictive in its grant of executive power. It empowered the president to provide military assistance only to specific countries in specific amounts: $1,160.9

million for the North Atlantic countries; $211.4 million for Greece and Turkey; and $27.6 million for Iran, Korea, and the Philippines. Despite sweeping changes in the language of the legislation, the only major revisions in the MAP were elimination of the emergency fund and of aid to Austria. And even though it omitted the contingency fund and limited the scope of the president's authority to furnish military assistance, the revised bill empowered the chief executive to sell military equipment to any nation "which has joined with the United States in a collective defense and regional arrangement." Vandenberg nevertheless found that the State Department had "totally surrendered on eighty per cent of my criticisms" and pronounced the new bill "really pretty good."[58]

Regardless of these concessions, the administration still faced an uphill fight. Under pressure from Republican conservatives who opposed heavy spending on foreign assistance, Vandenberg and Dulles asked for further modifications in the administration's plans. Fearful that the MAP would encourage the uncoordinated expansion of national armies rather than the integrated defense of Europe, they urged the administration to scale down its request to an interim program—one that met only the most urgent needs—until the North Atlantic Council could adopt detailed strategic plans. Acheson tried to explain to the senators that he was proposing precisely the sort of program that they demanded: an interim effort aimed only at arming forces already in existence and that would contribute to any conceivable plan for the defense of Europe. But when Secretary Johnson disclosed that deliveries of military supplies under the proposed MAP would stretch out over two years, critics dug in their heels. Stubbornly, they demanded closer coordination between the MAP and the North Atlantic defense machinery and restriction of authorization to only those funds that could be spent during the current fiscal year.[59]

Once again Truman and Acheson yielded to congressional pressure. Administration officials recognized the need for further compromise when the House passed the arms legislation on 15 August 1949 after slashing assistance for the North Atlantic allies by one-half. Rather than fighting for the full amount in the Senate—a futile endeavor—the State Department formed an informal alliance with Vandenberg and Dulles. The two senators introduced a series of amendments aimed at insuring that the MAP would be "only an interim program, to be geared into the integrating processes of the

North Atlantic Treaty at the earliest practical date." Following their lead, the Senate on 15 September trimmed the authorization for the North Atlantic countries to $1 billion, half of which could be used without restriction and half of which could be obligated during the current fiscal year, under contracts for the purchase of military supplies, but not actually spent until fiscal year 1951. In addition, the upper chamber reserved all but $100 million of this assistance until the president approved allied defense plans for "an integrated defense of the North Atlantic area."[60] FACC planners accepted these modifications with little remorse since, as Vandenberg and Dulles noted, they would not "delay by a day, or substantially reduce in scope, the present program." More reluctantly, the House accepted these Senate terms in the final version of the bill, but only after Truman made the shocking announcement that the Soviets had exploded their first atomic device.[61]

A far more acrimonious dispute arose over the omission of China from the MAP. The vehemence of these complaints surprised State Department officials. Only a few months earlier, Acheson had parried the efforts of Senator Pat McCarran (D-Nev.), who proposed a new China aid bill of $1.5 billion. Acheson hoped that the release on 5 August of a lengthy official explanation of administration policy, complete with enormous documentary appendixes, would further strengthen the administration's case that additional military aid to the nearly defeated Nationalist armies of Chiang Kai-shek would be useless. "Nothing that this country did or could have done within the reasonable limits of its capabilities" would have saved Chiang, Acheson declared in the introduction to the China White Paper. The Nationalist defeat "was the product of internal Chinese forces, forces which this country tried to influence but could not." Yet Chiang's congressional supporters found in the White Paper evidence that confirmed their antithetical interpretations of Truman's China policy. Senator H. Alexander Smith, for example, thought that the report proved that the United States had "let down" Chiang.[62]

Led by Senator William F. Knowland (R-Calif.) and Representative Walter H. Judd (R-Minn.), a group of legislators clamored for military aid to the Nationalists. Judd turned the hearings on the MAP in the Foreign Affairs Committee into an inquest into the death of the Nationalist government in China, one in which he sought to demonstrate, at the very least, that the Truman administration was guilty of manslaughter. In the Senate, Knowland, an unyielding foe of the administration's Europe-first strategy, pressed for approval of $175 million in military assistance for the Nationalists. While Acheson publicly opposed this demand, he privately told Truman on 18 August that he would not object to the establishment of a confidential fund of $100 million for use in Asia. Representative John M. Vorys (R-Ohio), an ardent supporter of the Nationalist Chinese, condemned such an account as an "anything you please proposition" and urged restrictions on the president's discretion. But both houses ultimately approved an unvouchered fund of $75 million, which the president could expend in the "general area" of China. Such flexibility appealed to many legislators because it would enable the president to furnish covert aid to a variety of anti-Communist forces in China. In any event, none of the money went for that purpose. Instead, Truman used most of the confidential fund for the first direct military assistance to halt communism in Indochina. Ironically, a Congress suspicious of broad executive power to arm foreign nations granted the president exceptional authority to pursue military containment in Southeast Asia.[63]

Truman, then, had good reason to be pleased on 6 October 1949 when he signed the Mutual Defense Assistance Act. Congress had not rubber-stamped his military aid proposals, but neither had it forced sweeping changes. In spite of the rumblings of fiscal conversations, Congress appropriated $1.314 billion, almost the entire sum Truman requested. Despite complaints about excessive executive power, Truman secured wide latitude to distribute arms in East Asia without any accounting to Congress. The Dulles-Vandenberg amendments required of the administration no more than it originally intended: the arming of European forces that could contribute to any possible NATO defense plan.[64]

Still, perhaps the administration's most significant victory was one that few, if any, contemporary observers recognized. Regardless of its critical reviews of the MAP, Congress did not probe deeply into some of the larger issues that the program suggested. Legislators argued about how much military aid to extend and how to apply it most effectively, but almost no one inquired about how to evaluate the effectiveness or ultimately to control an armaments program that aimed more at psychological than military goals. At a time when military assistance was still a secondary and even somewhat novel instrument of national policy, Congress demanded from the Truman administration only a superficial justification of its preference for large-scale arms aid to accomplish its foreign goals. The Truman administration, in short, secured passage of a billion-dollar arms bill, one that was admittedly the first of several annual installments, without ever having to explain how the provision of armaments would raise foreign morale or how long the United States would have to keep furnishing such help to sustain the will to resist communism.[65]

Epilogue

I think that one of the great problems is . . . can we ever stop once we start[?]
—John O. Bell, Assistant Director, Mutual Defense Assistance Program,
3 December 1949

In the last half of 1949, there was a good deal of confusion and uncertainty within the Truman administration about the future of the Military Assistance Program. Top policymakers knew that the United States was only beginning to strengthen the defenses of Western Europe and build up the military establishments and internal security forces in Turkey, Iran, and elsewhere, but they were unsure about the magnitude and duration of American assistance. Appearing before the Senate Foreign Relations Committee, Secretary of Defense Louis Johnson predicted that the MAP would last four or five years and require progressively smaller appropriations. At almost the same time, Frank Pace, Jr., the director of the Bureau of the Budget, asserted that the president had approved the MAP "as a 'one-shot' operation."[1]

These conflicting assessments came before the National Security Council in mid-1949 when Truman ordered a review of national security expenditures in anticipation of "serious fiscal and economic problem[s]" during the coming year. Hoping to minimize a projected budget deficit, Pace thought the next budget should contain only $200,000 for the MAP and a host of smaller foreign aid programs. The State Department objected vehemently. So did the Joint Chiefs of Staff, who worried that such a drastic cut would sow doubts about American leadership and turn the North Atlantic allies into military liabilities. The NSC ultimately recommended, and Truman finally decided to seek, a new annual appropriation of between $1 billion and $1.5 billion for the MAP in order to "bolster the psychological attitudes and morale of our allies and make them willing to strive more energetically toward the objectives we deem essential." The logic that justified the creation of the MAP in 1949 supported its continuation in 1950 at the same level of expenditures.[2]

Planning for long-term arms aid caused even greater problems. In August 1949 the Joint Munitions Allocation Committee (JMAC) outlined a long-range military assistance program that would enable the United States and its allies to defend Western Europe and eventually destroy the "will and capacity" of the Soviet Union to resist should war occur in 1957. To accomplish these goals, the committee recommended an enormous sum, $21 billion, to be spent during the next eight years to assist fifty countries. Beyond these preliminary estimates, which they conceded were "essentially speculative," the JMAC planners made no further progress. The Joint Chiefs tabled the extended plan in December 1949, although they did agree that the overall military goal of the MAP should be to improve the ability of the United States and its allies to achieve their war aims against the Soviet Union. Rather than trying to develop a detailed plan to achieve this goal, the Joint Chiefs instead shifted their focus to preparing a military assistance program for the coming fiscal year.[3]

Even less clearly defined was the long-term arms aid program proposed in NSC 68. This famous reassessment of national security policy, produced by a joint State-Defense task force in early 1950, proposed drastic countermeasures to deal with a Soviet Union bent on world domination. Using incendiary language, the authors of NSC 68 depicted the Soviet Union as a "slave society" whose leaders required "the dynamic extension of their authority" to achieve their "fundamental design." Having exploded their first atomic device in 1949, the Soviets would reach atomic parity with the United States in 1954, at which time they would be prepared to risk war. The United States would have "no better choice" in meeting this threat "than to capitulate or precipitate global war," unless it undertook "a more rapid build-up of political, economic, and military strength and thereby of confidence in the free world than is now contemplated." Arms aid was an essential component of this mobilization, not only because it would help deter and, ultimately, defeat Soviet aggression but also because of its "psychological impact—the revival of confidence and hope in the future." Although NSC 68 provided no estimate of the cost of such a military aid program, or even a listing of potential recipients, it clearly called for a vast expansion of American arms transfers, perhaps amounting to as much as $25 billion over the next several years. Unwilling as yet to sanction such a drastic change in national security policy, Truman temporarily deferred any action on NSC 68 until he received further information about the probable costs of the proposed programs.[4]

Even long-range NATO defense plans remained unformulated, unrealistic, or unclear and the American contribution to them unspecified or uncertain. Some progress toward a common defense did occur during late 1949, when the North Atlantic Defense Committee approved a strategic concept that called for the United States, in the event of war, to carry out strategic bombing missions and to share with Great Britain the task of securing the Atlantic sea lanes, while the European members of the alliance provided the bulk of the ground forces. Although this strategic concept satisfied the requirement in the MDAA for integrated defense planning, it left undecided vital matters about how to establish the necessary forces. More detailed was the NATO Medium Term Defense Plan for a war in 1954. But, because of a lack of critical information from the member countries about military production and manpower, there was no way of knowing in early 1950, as Secretary of State Dean Acheson privately complained, whether the plan was "practicable of accomplishment or represents wishful thinking." Any realistic plan for the defense of Western Europe, American experts estimated, would require $30 billion of spending on armaments beyond current budgetary levels during the next five years. But during the spring of 1950, the Truman administration did not press NATO committees to consider how this spending might be apportioned—between American arms aid or additional European military spending—for fear that the sum might seem so vast that mere discussion of the issue would undermine the confidence in the future that the Truman administration had so carefully cultivated during the previous year. Instead, the Truman administration elaborately publicized the first shipments of MAP materiel to Europe and carefully avoided any mention that these were token amounts and that deliveries would stretch out over two years. At the same time, the administration sought an additional grant of $1 billion in fiscal year 1951 for military assistance to NATO even though, once again, the planning that underlay this request was not truly integrated but simply the consolidation of national efforts.[5]

So much did national security officials take as a matter of faith that American arms aid fostered foreign confidence and deterred aggression that they were willing to provide another annual installment without settling the most vital issues about the program's ultimate objectives. After leaving the government, Acheson conceded that the administration's thinking "really went in a circle." He and his colleagues promised Congress that American aid would contribute to an integrated defense of the North Atlantic "at a considerable overall saving" and "at a cost which the Europeans could support in time, without aid from the United States." But "that all depended on what was going to be set up," Acheson reflected, and "of course left the thing vague."[6]

A major reason for these difficulties in formulating a long-term program of arms aid that could strengthen Western defenses was that the Truman administration had far greater experience with using military assistance as a political and psychological instrument. Although the first military aid programs clearly had military purposes—the defeat of the guerrillas in Greece, the modernization of the Turkish armed forces, the promotion of a collective defense of Western Europe—they had overriding political objectives, such as cultivating goodwill overseas, raising foreign morale, and stiffening the will to resist communism. Even projects that the service departments sponsored, such as the Western Hemisphere Defense Program, aimed fundamentally at political ends. Not only did government officials believe that military assistance would strengthen the fiber of the recipients, but also they hoped that it would reassure foreign nations of American determination to contain Soviet expansion, if necessary, with stronger measures. In short, building foreign confidence by strengthening foreign military establishments was the Truman administration's primary concern during the late 1940s.

Because of this preoccupation with the morale of the recipients, the giving of military aid was more important than the specific purposes to which the aid was put. The extension of arms assistance was a symbolic act; it required frequent repetition, lest the cessation of aid destroy the foreign confidence that the United States had so sedulously tried to nurture. During Senate hearings in 1949, Kenneth S. Wherry (R-Nebr.) declared that once the United States began to furnish arms aid it would be "morally bound to continue those appropriations; and if we cut them off next year . . . my opinion is that we would be worse off, as far as the morale of those forces are [sic] concerned, if we did not continue it than if we had never started." Even though Wherry was a staunch foe of the MAP, administration officials shared his reasoning. During planning conferences in late 1949 for the continuation of the MAP, State Department analysts asserted that it would be more "dangerous" to request smaller appropriations in the coming year than in the current one because any reduction would indicate a "weakening" of American interest in the North Atlantic alliance. Anxieties about foreign resolve and American reliability thus not only inspired the MAP but also defined objectives that were unmeasurable, open-ended, and quite possibly unattainable.[7]

The expansive justification for arms aid that emerged during the late 1940s helps explain the rapid growth of the MAP. Responding to administration warnings about the dangers of reduced arms aid expenditures, Congress provided an additional appropriation for the MAP in fiscal year 1951 of $1.222 billion. An enormous increase in military aid followed the outbreak of the Korean War. Among the first casualties of the North Korean invasion were the budgetary restraints that Truman had imposed on national security spending and that served as the principal barrier to a massive increase in arms aid. Truman approved a revised version of NSC 68 on 29 September 1950, only days after he had secured from Congress a $4 billion supplemental appropriation for the MAP. Apprehensive that the North Korean attack was the prelude to further Communist military action, the Truman administration considered these funds necessary to accelerate the equipping of NATO forces as well as to fortify containment efforts in East Asia. At any rate, because the Pentagon gave priority to equipping American troops, little additional equipment actually reached the NATO countries even as late as the end of 1951.[8] Consequently, the main effect of the supplemental appropriation was to calm European anxieties about NATO defenses and warn the Soviets of American resolve. The concerns about foreign morale and American resolve and the growth of the MAP were inseparable.[9]

In the late 1940s some American officials recognized that the impetus behind the growth of the MAP would be difficult to control. Paul G. Hoffman, the Economic Cooperation administrator, wondered whether the MAP was "the beginning of an enormously costly program that will go first to Europe and then perhaps to Asia and then to South American [sic] and where does it stop?" Likewise, John O. Bell, assistant director of the MAP, averred that "if we indulge in either starting or continuing programs without having pretty clearly in mind where we want to stop and when we want to stop and what we are trying to do, then we can very easily get into a large series of ratholes which are both costly and dangerous." Despite these prophetic warnings, the Truman administration did not clearly define its goals or establish criteria for gauging the effectiveness of military aid. Programs devoted primarily to psychological and political purposes—altering the perceptions of adversaries and the will of allies—had no inherent limits. "Can we ever stop once we start[?]" Bell wondered in 1949. The Truman administration never answered that question, and because it did not it left as a legacy a momentum for arms aid that its successors could not resist.[10]

Notes

ABBREVIATIONS

AG	Records, Adjutant General's Office, National Archives
ASA	Records, Assistant Secretary of the Army, National Archives
Asst. SecDef FMA	Records, Assistant to the Secretary of Defense for Foreign Military Assistance, National Archives
Budget	Records, Bureau of the Budget, National Archives
C-3	Minutes, Meetings of the Committee of Three, National Archives
CMH	Center of Military History, Washington, D.C.
C/S	Records, Office of the Chief of Staff, War Department General and Special Staffs, National Archives
Compilation Book	"Compilation of Studies and Policies Pertaining to Countries Under Consideration for Military Assistance," [January 1949], file 092 Top Secret (1/8), G-3.
DOHP	John Foster Dulles Oral History Project, Seeley G. Mudd Library
DSB	*Department of State Bulletin*
EUR	Records, Office of European Affairs, Department of State, National Archives
ExecSecretariat	Records, Secretary's Daily Meetings, Department of State, National Archives
FACC-MAP	FACC and MAP Documents, Assistant Secretary of Defense (International Security Affairs), National Archives
FRUS	*Foreign Relations of the United States*
G-3	Records, Deputy Chief of the United States Army, G-3, National Archives
G-4	Records, Assistant Chief of the United States Army, G-4, National Archives
ISA	Records, Assistant Secretary of State for International Security Affairs, National Archives
JCS	Records, United States Joint Chiefs of Staff, National Archives
OPD	Records, Operations Division, War Department General and Special Staffs, National Archives

PCA	Records, Policy Committee on Arms and Armaments, National Archives
P&O	Records, Plans and Operations Division, United States Army Staff, National Archives
PP	*Public Papers of the Presidents: Harry S. Truman*
PPS	Records, Policy Planning Staff, Department of State, National Archives
PSF	President's Secretary's File, Truman Library
S/A (Gray-Pace)	Records, Secretary of the Army, Gordon Gray and Frank Pace, Jr., National Archives
S/A (Royall)	Records, Secretary of the Army, Kenneth C. Royall, National Archives
S/D	Records, Office of the Secretary of Defense, National Archives
SecNavy	Forrestal Papers, General Records of the Department of the Navy, National Archives
State	General Records, Department of State, National Archives
SWNCC	Records, State-Army-Navy-Air Force Coordinating Committee, National Archives
WHCF	Confidential File, White House Central Files, Truman Library

INTRODUCTION

1. *Report of the Secretary of Defense,* 92–99.
2. JCS 2032/3, 6 August 1949, file JCS Papers, G-3.
3. Pach, "Military Assistance and American Foreign Policy," 137–38; Agency for International Development, *U.S. Overseas Loans and Grants,* 4; *Congressional Quarterly Almanac* 43: 469, 477.
4. Kemp, "Dilemmas of the Arms Traffic"; Gelb, "Arms Sales"; Farley, Kaplan, and Lewis, *Arms Across the Sea,* 34–37; *Washington Post,* 20 April 1977.
5. Transcript, Princeton Seminars, 10 October 1953, reel 1, track 1, p. 4, Acheson Papers, Truman Library.

CHAPTER 1

1. Memorandum, Shephard to Almond, 30 May 1946, folder C46, series 39.1, Budget.
2. DeConde, *Encyclopedia of American Foreign Policy,* 2:372; Atwater, *American Regulation of Arms Exports,* 174–75; Conn and Fairchild, *The Framework of Hemisphere Defense,* 208–9; Harkavy, *The Arms Trade,* 146–47; Kemp, "The Arms Transfer Phenomenon," 15–25; Huston, *The Sinews of War,* 394–97; Field, *America and the Mediterranean World,* 311–13. For a discussion of the legal bases for the transfer of military equipment to foreign nations, see memorandum, Leva to Forrestal, 16 September 1948, file CCS 092 (8-22-46) sec. 14, JCS.
3. Hermes, "Survey of the Development of the Role of the U.S. Army Military Adviser"; Wright, *United States Policy Toward Egypt,* 72–83; Field, *America and the Mediterranean World,* 389–91; Sawyer, *Military Advisors in Korea,* 4.
4. 41 Stat. 1056; 44 Stat. 565.

5. Atwater, *American Regulation of Arms Exports*, 37–115, 157–68; Lieuwen, *Arms and Politics in Latin America*, 33, 153; R. Smith, *The United States and Revolutionary Nationalism in Mexico*, 224; Munro, *The United States and the Caribbean Republics*, 163, 219, 292; DeConde, *Herbert Hoover's Latin American Policy*, 52–53; Tulchin, *The Aftermath of War*; Millett, *Semper Fidelis*, 178–211, 236–63.

6. Quoted in Herring, *Aid to Russia*, 3.

7. Reynolds, *The Creation of the Anglo-American Alliance*, 108–13; Dallek, *Franklin D. Roosevelt and American Foreign Policy*, 226–32; Pogue, *George C. Marshall: Ordeal and Hope*, 46–52; Coakley and Leighton, *Global Logistics and Strategy*, 30–36.

8. 54 Stat. 396. The legislation bore the name of Senator Key Pittman, Democrat of Nevada, Chairman of the Foreign Relations Committee.

9. Gellman, *Good Neighbor Diplomacy*, 131–32; Kimball, *The Most Unsordid Act*, 52–53; Divine, *The Reluctant Belligerent*, 90.

10. 55 Stat. 31.

11. Quotations from *Complete Presidential Press Conferences of Franklin D. Roosevelt*, 16:354; Rosenman, *The Public Papers and Addresses of Franklin D. Roosevelt*, 9:643; Kimball, *The Most Unsordid Act*, 53, 91–133; Dallek, *Franklin D. Roosevelt and American Foreign Policy*, 252–60; Martel, *Lend-Lease, Loans, and the Coming of the Cold War*, 1–6; Coakley and Leighton, *Global Logistics and Strategy*, 816; Reynolds, *The Creation of the Anglo-American Alliance*, 145–61, 166–68; Brown and Opie, *American Foreign Assistance*, 544; Coakley, "Roosevelt and Lend-Lease."

12. See Stettinius, *Lend-Lease: Weapon for Victory*.

13. Memorandum, Matthews to Dunn, 23 June 1944, folder International Organization for Security and Peace, EUR; memorandum for record by Gilmour, 8 May 1945, file 400 Top Secret (7), OPD.

14. Coakley and Leighton, *Global Logistics and Strategy*, 818–19; Vigneras, *Rearming the French*, 334–36, 362–63; Department of Commerce, *Foreign Aid by the United States Government*, 86–88.

15. "Lend-Lease as of September 30, 1945," 1299.

16. Baram, *The Department of State in the Middle East*, 204–14, 223–38; A. Miller, *Search for Security*, 67–71, 122–49; Stoff, *Oil, War, and American Security*, 46–61, 70–80; Gormly, "Keeping the Door Open in Saudi Arabia," 189–205; Coakley and Leighton, *Global Logistics and Strategy*, 644–52; "Lend-Lease as of September 30, 1945," 283–89; letters, Hull to Leahy, 25 May 1943; Leahy to Hull, 3 June 1943; Hayter to Alling, 4 December 1943; Alling to Hayter, 15 December 1943; and Hayter to Alling, 22 December 1943; all in *FRUS: 1943*, 4:1–4, 915–16, 917–18, 920; memorandum, Stettinius to Roosevelt, 22 December 1944, *FRUS: 1944*, 5:757–58; memorandum, Byrnes to Truman, 31 January 1946, *FRUS: 1945*, 8:999–1000.

17. Letter, Leahy to Hull, 30 December 1943, *FRUS: 1944*, 7:87–92. See below, chap. 2.

18. JCS 771/18, 5 September 1945, folder Gen. Marshall-Col. Byroade Dec. 1945, JCS-SWNCC Papers, Marshall Mission; memorandum, Crowley to Truman, 6 July 1945, 800.24/7-645, State.

19. Herring, *Aid to Russia*, 155–56, 181–236 (quotation from 192–93); Paterson, *Soviet-American Confrontation*, 159; Donovan, *Conflict and Crisis*, 53–54; Gaddis, *The United States and the Origins of the Cold War*, 254; Martel, *Lend-Lease, Loans, and the Coming of the Cold War*, 7–24; Hathaway, *Ambiguous Partnership*, 142–48, 182–85.

20. Quotation from memorandum for Roosevelt, 28 December 1944, encl. to SWNCC 17/1, 10 March 1945, file SWNCC 17, SWNCC; SWNCC 4/10, 7 July 1945, *FRUS: 1945*, 9:251–54.

21. NSC 14/1, 1 July 1948, *FRUS: 1948*, 1: pt. 2, 586.

22. Quotation from memorandum, JCS to Hull, 11 October 1944, encl. to SWNCC 17, 5 February 1945, folder SWNCC 17, SWNCC; CCS 636, 1 August 1944; CCS 653, 22 August 1944; JCS 1039, 8 September 1944; JCS 1039/1, 28 September 1944; and CCS 653/1, 10 September 1944, all in file CCS 400 (7-30-44), JCS; Coakley and Leighton, *Global Logistics and Strategy*, 709–12.

23. Quotation from memorandum, Stettinius to Roosevelt, 28 December 1944, 851.24/1-345, State; memorandum, Grew to Roosevelt, 21 March 1945, 851.24/1-845, State; Coakley and Leighton, *Global Logistics and Strategy*, 712–15.

24. Brief accounts of demobilization can be found in Sparrow, "Demobilization of the United States Army after World War II"; and Coakley et al., "Resumé of Army Roll-Up Following World War II."

25. Memorandum, Crowley to Truman, 6 July 1945, 800.24/7-645, State; memorandum concerning S. 1975, n.d., 800.24/5-645, State; Gaddis, *The United States and the Origins of the Cold War*, 215–19.

26. See Sherry, *Preparing for the Next War*, chap. 1; Hewes, *From Root to McNamara*, 131–37.

27. For State Department planning, see Notter, *Postwar Foreign Policy Preparation*. For Leahy's views, see minutes, 177th meeting of the Combined Chiefs of Staff, 29 September 1944, file CCS 400 (7-30-44), JCS. For the creation of the SWNCC, see letter, Stettinius to Forrestal, 29 November 1944; and letter, Stimson and Forrestal to Stettinius, 1 December 1944, both in *FRUS: 1944*, 1:1466–68; Etzold, "American Organization for National Security," 1–6.

28. Gellman, *Good Neighbor Diplomacy*, 140–41.

29. Wolk, *Planning and Organizing the Postwar Air Force*, 60–61, 238–39; Sherry, *Preparing for the Next War*, 204–5; Goldberg, *A History of the United States Air Force*, 29; Mason, *The United States Air Force*, 74–75; P. Smith, *The Air Force Plans for Peace*, 104–6.

30. For detailed discussions of proposed air assistance to Latin America and China, see below, chaps. 2 and 3, respectively.

31. Quotations from memorandum, Lovett to McCloy, 16 January 1945; and memorandum, McCarthy to McCloy, 3 January 1945, both in folder SWNCC 17, SWNCC.

32. Converse, "United States Plans for a Postwar Overseas Military Base System," 80–97; House Committee on International Relations, *Selected Executive Session Hearings*, 7:11–23; Rogow, *James Forrestal*, 175–78; Gellman, *Good Neighbor Diplomacy*, 140–41.

33. Quotations from memorandum SWN-4096, JCS to Byrnes, 29 March 1946, *FRUS: 1946*, 1:1166; Sherry, *Preparing for the Next War*, 234–36.

34. Quotations from JPS 633/4, 18 July 1945; JCS 1496/2, 17 September 1945; and JCS 1518, 19 September 1945, all in file CCS 381 (5-13-45) sec. 1, JCS; Sherry, *Preparing for the Next War*, 198–205.

35. Quotations from JCS 1518, 19 September 1945; and Harbutt, *The Iron Curtain*, 153–54; JIC 329, 3 November 1945, file ABC 336 Russia (19 Aug 43), P&O; Poole, "From Conciliation to Containment," 12–15; Stoler, "From Continentalism to Globalism," 312–21; Millis, *The Forrestal Diaries*, 95–96; Gormly, *The Collapse of the Grand Alliance*, 39–54.

36. JCS 1496/2, 17 September 1945, file CCS 381 (5-13-45) sec. 1, JCS.

37. JCS 1518, 19 September 1945, file CCS 381 (5-13-45) sec. 1, JCS.

38. House Committee on International Relations, *Selected Executive Session Hearings*, 7:12–13. See also memorandum SM-5233, JCS to SWNCC, 12 March 1946, folder SWNCC 276, SWNCC.

39. Quotation from JPS 633/4, 18 July 1945, file CCS 381 (5-13-45) sec. 1, JCS; Leffler, "The American Conception of National Security," 350–51.

40. Minutes of the 167th meeting of the Secretary of State's Staff Committee, 13 November 1945; memorandum SC-169b by Secretary's Staff Committee, 16 November 1945; and SWNCC 282, 27 March 1946, all in *FRUS: 1946*, 1:1118–28, 1160–65; O'Brien, "National Security and the New Warfare," 50–51.

41. Quotation from "Special Information for the President," 13 April 1945, folder Secretary of State Edward R. Stettinius, Subject File, PSF; notes for conference with the president, 3 July 1945, folder Foreign—Memos for the President, 1945–1949, Subject File, PSF; memorandum, Hickerson to SWNCC, 29 November 1945, 851.24/10-1545, State; letter, Byrnes to Patterson, 10 December 1945, 851.24/11-2745, State; memorandum, McCabe to Clayton, 7 December 1945, 851.24/12-745, State; aide-memoire to the French Embassy, 20 December 1945, 851.24/12-2045, State; memorandum, Elliott to Brown, 31 March 1949, 851.24/3-1949, State; memorandum, Cleveland to Cummins, 2 July 1946, encl. to PCA M-6, 3 July 1946; and PCA S-6, 3 July 1946, both in PCA; *DSB* 21 (26 September 1949): 48; Gimbel, *The Origins of the Marshall Plan*, 35–38.

42. Quotations from Messer, "Paths Not Taken," 304, 309; DeSantis, *The Diplomacy of Silence*, 155–69; Harbutt, *The Iron Curtain*, 154–55; Isaacson and Thomas, *The Wise Men*, 338–40.

43. Chern, *Dilemma in China*, 194–95.

44. Memorandum, Lincoln to Joint Staff Planners, 19 October 1945, file 400.3295, OPD.

45. Memorandum SWN-3276, Secretary of SWNCC to SWNCC, 3 October 1945, folder SWNCC 202, SWNCC; JCS 1448/1, 31 August 1945, folder Gen. Marshall-Col. Byroade Dec. 1945, JCS-SWNCC Papers, Marshall Mission.

46. JPS 765/1, 11 December 1945, file CCS 400.3 (10-20-45), JCS.

47. In a related action, the SWNCC recommended that the State Department use surplus property as a means of acquiring overseas bases and sites for legations. See SWNCC 179/1, 10 December 1945, folder SWNCC 179, SWNCC.

48. SWNCC 202/1, 24 January 1946, folder SWNCC 202, SWNCC.

49. 58 Stat. 765.

50. SWNCC 202/1, 24 January 1946, folder SWNCC 202, SWNCC.

51. Memorandum by Ludlow, 12 February 1946, ibid.; memorandum, Blaisdell to Matthews, 28 January 1946, 800.24/1-2846, State.

52. On the disposal of surplus property, see memorandum, Hoopes to Leva, 3 December 1948, file CD 19-2-10, S/D; memorandum, Lutes to Lemnitzer, 8 June 1949, file MISC 400.703 (Surplus Property), CMH.

53. SWNCC 202/2, 21 March 1946, *FRUS: 1946*, 1:1145–60.

54. SC/R-184, 5 February 1946, ibid., 1141–42.

55. PCA M-4, 19 June 1946; and PCA M-6, 3 July 1946, both in PCA; letter, Clayton to Byrnes, 12 September 1946, *FRUS: 1946*, 7:210.

56. Messer, *The End of an Alliance*, 161–81; Harbutt, *The Iron Curtain*, 159–82; Thomas, *Armed Truce*, 481–86.

57. SWNCC 202/2 stated that while the administration expected that Sweden would purchase military equipment primarily from Great Britain, favor-

able consideration should be given to specific requests for a limited number of aircraft.

58. Telegram no. 428, Johnson to Byrnes, 6 March 1946, 858.24/3-646, State; telegram no. 555, Byrnes to Johnson, 20 March 1946, 858.24/3-646, State; memorandum, Hickerson to Acheson, 30 April 1946, 858.24/3-1646, State; note, State Department to Counselor, Swedish Legation, 10 May 1946, 858.24/3-1346, State; memorandum, Acheson to Hickerson, n.d., FW 858.24/3-1346, State; memorandum, Cumming to Hickerson, 18 April 1946, 858.24/3-1346, State; telegram no. 1592, Acheson to Ravndal, 9 October 1946, 858.24/5-646, State; memorandum of conversation by Acheson, 13 August 1946, 858.24/8-1346, State; memorandum, Cumming to Hickerson, 16 August 1946, 858.24/8-1346, State; memorandum, Acheson to Clayton, 28 September 1946, FW 858.24/9-1646, State; telegram no. 5469, Acheson to Jacobs, 11 October 1946, 858.24/10-1146, State; PCA M-10, 5 August 1946; and PCA M-17, 23 September 1946, both in PCA.

59. Quotation from House Committee on International Affairs, *Selected Executive Session Hearings* 7:12, 24–31; Hess, *The United States' Emergence as a Southeast Asian Power,* 217–28, 244–50; Kerkvliet, *The Huk Rebellion,* 110–55; Shalom, *The United States and the Philippines,* 14–32; Schirmer and Shalom, *The Philippines Reader,* 96–100.

60. Quotations from SWNCC 201, 2 October 1945, folder SWNCC 201, SWNCC; and *Congressional Record* 92: 10336; letter, Murray to Henderson, 9 October 1945, 891.20 Missions/10-945, State; memorandum, "Proposed Amendments to Legislation," 21 November 1945, folder MAG—Agreement, Marshall Mission.

CHAPTER 2

1. Memorandum by Dreier, 13 March 1945, 810.24/3-1445, State.

2. Memorandum SM-5062, McFarland to SWNCC, 21 February 1946, file CCS 092 United States (12-21-45) sec. 1, JCS.

3. SWNCC 4/10, 7 July 1945, *FRUS: 1945,* 9:251–52.

4. The best study of United States policies toward Latin America prior to and during World War II is Gellman, *Good Neighbor Diplomacy.* See also Fagg, *Latin America,* 795–99; Connell-Smith, *The Inter-American System,* 110–24; Langer and Gleason, *The Challenge to Isolation,* 129–36, 272–80, 607–37, 688–702; Langer and Gleason, *The Undeclared War,* 147–69, 593–624; Davis, Finan, and Peck, *Latin American Diplomatic History,* 222–42; Mecham, *The United States and Inter-American Security;* Dallek, *Franklin D. Roosevelt and American Foreign Policy,* 175–77, 233–36; Child, *Unequal Alliance,* 16–62.

5. On German penetration and Roosevelt's reaction, see Frye, *Nazi Germany and the American Hemisphere;* Friedlander, *Prelude to Downfall,* 3–30, 105–12; 225–28; Hilton, *Hitler's Secret War in South America,* 12–50; Reynolds, *The Creation of the Anglo-American Alliance,* 40–42; Grow, *The Good Neighbor Policy and Authoritarianism in Paraguay,* 25–41. On propaganda and cultural diplomacy, see Ninkovich, *The Diplomacy of Ideas,* 24–49; Haines, "Under the Eagle's Wing," 373–88. On economic and trade relations, see McCann, *The Brazilian-American Alliance,* 148–75. On the inter-American conferences, see *The Memoirs of Cordell Hull,* 601–11, 688–92, 821–29, 1143–50.

6. Manuscript prepared by American Theater Section, OPD, "History of Latin American Military Cooperation in the War Effort," [September 1944], file 336 Latin America (42), OPD; Lieuwen, *Arms and Politics in Latin America,* 190–91; Conn and Fairchild, *The Framework of Hemisphere Defense,* 173–74, 184–85; Haglund, *Latin America and the Transformation of U.S. Strategic Thought,* 146–222.

7. Conn and Fairchild, *The Framework of Hemisphere Defense,* 178–79.

8. Ibid., 207–37; Pogue, *George C. Marshall: Ordeal and Hope,* 53–54; Stimson Diaries, 32:57–58 (reel 6), Yale University Library; McCann, *The Brazilian-American Alliance,* 204–9.

9. Quotation from "Statement of War Department Policy as Regards Supply of Lend Lease Materials to Latin America," 6 August 1943, file 400.3295 (26), OPD; Hilton, "The United States, Brazil, and the Cold War," 599–601. By the end of the war, the United States furnished $492.5 million of military and naval supplies to Latin America, about 1 percent of total lend-lease expenditures. Because of its failure to cooperate with the United States in measures of hemispheric defense, Argentina was the only Latin American nation that did not receive lend-lease arms. See Child, *Unequal Alliance,* 48.

10. Lieuwen, *Arms and Politics in Latin America,* 192–95; Furniss, "American Wartime Objectives in Latin America," 260–71; Estep, *United States Military Aid to Latin America,* 19; McCann, "Brazil, the United States, and World War II," 59–76; Gellman, *Good Neighbor Diplomacy,* 136–38.

11. Quotations from "Statement of War Department Policy as Regards Supply of Lend Lease Materials to Latin America," 6 August 1943, file 400.3295 (26), OPD; and "Report by the Joint Army and Navy Advisory Board on American Republics," n.d., *FRUS: 1944,* 7:87–92.

12. Quotation from JCS 629/7, 27 August 1944, file CCS 400.3295 (12-16-43) sec. 2, JCS; letter, Leahy to Hull, 30 December 1943; letter, Stettinius to Leahy, 29 February 1944; "Statement of Policy . . . Concerning the Supplying of Lend-Lease Materials to the American Republics," 24 June 1944; and memorandum by McGurk, 4 August 1944, all in *FRUS: 1944,* 7:87, 93–96, 97–99; transcript, Hertford oral history, 12–13, Truman Library.

13. Quotation from memorandum by Chalmers, 29 February 1944, 810.248/91, State; memorandum, Johnson to Bonsal, 10 March 1944, 810.248/92, State; letter, Hull to Forrestal, 17 August 1944; and memorandum, Hull to Roosevelt, 28 August 1944, both in *FRUS: 1944,* 7:101–2; memorandum by Dreier, 6 September 1944, 810.24/9-644, State; memorandum, Dreier to Lockwood, 2 January 1945, 810.24/1-1145, State; memorandum, Leahy to Stimson and Forrestal, 5 September 1944; SWNCC 4, 9 January 1945; SWNCC 4/1, 19 January 1945; SWNCC 4/3, 4 April 1945; and SWNCC 4/4, 16 April 1945, all in file CCS 400.3295 (12-16-43) sec. 2, JCS; memorandum, Johnson to Matthews, 18 April 1945, 810.24/4-1845, State; Stamey, "The Origin of the United States Military Assistance Program," 152–53. See also *FRUS: 1944,* 7:1504–14.

14. Summary sheet, Hull to Marshall and Stimson, 2 November 1944, file 336 Latin America (26), OPD.

15. Quotation from memorandum, Braden to Johnson, 4 August 1944, *FRUS: 1944,* 7:111–12; letter, Hull to Leahy, 24 August 1944; letter, Stimson and Forrestal to Hull, 20 September 1944; memorandum, Armour to Hull, 5 October 1944; memorandum, Stettinius to Roosevelt, 1 November 1944; memorandum by Armour, 3 November 1944; and memorandum and annex,

Armour to Stettinius, 7 December 1944; all in ibid., 7:113–15, 121–23, 126–30; memorandum, Spears to Horne, 28 August 1944; summary sheet, Handy to Marshall and Stimson, 16 September 1944; memorandum for record by Edwards, 3 November 1944; and memorandum of conference by Edwards, 28 November 1944, all in file 336 Latin America (26), OPD.

16. Quotations from letter, Brett to Handy, 28 October 1944, file 336 Latin America (26/20), OPD; and Caribbean Defense Command, "Bi-Lateral Staff Conversations," 102; memorandum, McGurk to Rockefeller, 14 December 1944, 810.20 Missions/12-844, State; despatch no. 291, Briggs to Hull, 5 September 1944, *FRUS: 1944*, 7:1021–25; Stimson Diaries, 51:193–94 (reel 9), Yale University Library; Tillapaugh, "From War to Cold War," 282.

17. Quotation from memorandum by Edwards, 13 November 1944, file 336 Latin America; summary sheet, Smith to OPD, 14 September 1944; and memorandum for record by OPD officer (unsigned), 30 October 1944, both in ibid.; memorandum of conversation by Johnson, 11 August 1944, 810.248/8-1144, State; memorandum of conversation by Johnson, 30 November 1944, 810.20 Missions/11-3044, State; Stamey, "Military Assistance Program," 147–48.

18. Quotation from memorandum, Handy to the Assistant Secretary of War, 10 January 1945, file 336 Latin America, OPD; memorandum, Walsh to Handy, 26 December 1944, 810.248/12-2844, State; memorandum, Edwards to Stimson and Forrestal, 6 February 1945, file 336 Latin America (89), OPD; Stamey, "Military Assistance Program," 150.

19. Quotations from letter, Brett to Handy, 28 October 1944, file 336 Latin America (26/20), OPD; and minutes, meeting of Committee of Three, 11 December 1945, C-3; memorandum, Walsh to Rockefeller, 26 December 1944, 810.248/12-2844, State; memorandum, Handy to Assistant Secretary of War, 10 January 1945, file 336 Latin America, OPD; Caribbean Defense Command, "Bi-Lateral Staff Conversations," app. 2.

20. JCS 1496/2, 17 September 1945, file CCS 381 (5-13-45) sec. 1, JCS; memorandum of conversation by Johnson, 11 August 1944, 810.248/8-1144, State; Stimson Diaries, 49:2 (reel 9), Yale University Library; P. Smith, *The Air Force Plans for Peace*, 105–6; Green, *The Containment of Latin America*, 180–81, 260.

21. Quotation from letter, Stimson to Hull, 20 September 1944, *FRUS: 1944*, 7:120–21; JCS 629/13, 15 October 1945, file CCS 400.3295 (12-16-43) sec. 3, JCS; "Instructions for Staff Conversations with Military and Naval Representatives of the Other American Republics," n.d., *FRUS: 1944*, 7:106–11; Sherry, *Preparing for the Next War*, vii–ix, 191–232.

22. Memorandum, Vincent to Grew, 23 October 1944, 810.24/10-2344, State. On the broader problem of regional security in Latin America, see Tillapaugh, "Closed Hemisphere and Open World?" 25–42.

23. Quotation from memorandum by Dreier, "Comments on Military and Naval Objectives in the Other American Republics," 13 March 1945, 810.24/3-1445, State; memoranda, Strong to Stimson, 5 January 1945 and 22 January 1945, both in file 400.3295 (37), OPD; despatch no. 589, Briggs to Stettinius, 20 December 1944, *FRUS: 1944*, 7:131–33.

24. Memorandum of conversation by Bohan, 29 January 1945, *FRUS: 1945*, 9:72–73; Rabe, *Eisenhower and Latin America*, 16–18; Rabe, "The Elusive Conference," 280–84; Gellman, *Good Neighbor Diplomacy*, 202.

25. Rabe, *Eisenhower and Latin America*, 16; Hilton, "The United States,

Brazil, and the Cold War," 599–605; Bohlin, "United States-Latin American Relations," 30–31.

26. SWNCC 4/10, 7 July 1945, *FRUS: 1945*, 9:251–54.

27. Caribbean Defense Command, "Bi-Lateral Staff Conversations," 63, 112–13; memorandum, Wooten to Hull, 5 August 1945, file 400.3295 (38), OPD; despatch no. 2186, Berle to Byrnes, 26 July 1945, *FRUS: 1945*, 9:600–606.

28. Quotation from JCS 629/13, 15 October 1945, file CCS 400.3295 (12-16-43) sec. 3, JCS; "Brief of Western Hemisphere Defense Program," 12 November 1946, folder Miscellaneous Papers, Western Hemisphere Defense Program, Lend-Lease, etc., G-4.

29. Quotations from JCS 629/14, 30 October 1945; and JCS 629/16, 10 November 1945, both in file CCS 400.3295 (12-16-43) sec. 3, JCS; Gellman, *Good Neighbor Diplomacy*, 129–30, 139–40. Because of King's objections, the Joint Chiefs agreed to reconsider the program of naval assistance and to approve the programs of army and air force assistance for planning purposes only.

30. Quotation from Forrestal Diaries, 14 November 1945, 621, Naval History Division; memorandum, Edwards to Forrestal, [November 1945], ibid., 639; minutes, meeting of the Committee of Three, 20 November 1945, C-3; memorandum, Hull to Marshall, 20 November 1945, file 336 Latin America, OPD; memorandum, Dreier to Briggs, Butler, and Bràden, 15 December 1945, 810.24/12-1345, State.

31. Letter, Stimson to Byrnes, 4 September 1945; memorandum, Vittrup to Briggs, 30 October 1945; and memorandum for record by Shaw, 30 October 1945, all in file 336 Latin America (89), OPD.

32. Braden was appointed assistant secretary on 25 August 1945 and formally took up his duties two months later; Briggs was named director of ARA on 22 October 1945. *Register of the Department of State*, 1946, 152, 155.

33. Quotations from memorandum, Spaeth to Braden, 9 November 1945, 800.24/11-945, State; and memorandum for the Secretary's Staff Committee, "International Embargo on the Export of Armaments," 3 November 1945, FW 810.24/11-645, State; memorandum, Jarvis to Morgan, 8 October 1945, 810.20 Defense/10-845, State; memorandum, Bell to Jarvis, Latchford, and Morgan, 18 October 1945, 810.20 Defense/10-1845, State; memorandum, Jarvis to Morgan, Latchford, and Bell, n.d., FW 810.20 Defense/10-1845, State; memorandum, Cochran to Erwin, 31 October 1945, 800.24/10-3145, State; memorandum, Barber to Briggs and Braden, 18 October 1945, 810.24/10-1845, State; memorandum, Barber to Braden, 28 November 1945, 800.24/11-2845, State; *New York Times*, 30 October 1945.

34. Quotation from letter, Patterson to Byrnes, 7 December 1945, *FRUS: 1945*, 9:258–59; minutes, meeting of the Committee of Three, 11 December 1945, C-3; memorandum, Wooten to Hull, 5 August 1945, file 400.3295 (38), OPD; Caribbean Defense Command, "Bi-Lateral Staff Conversations," 112–13, 130, 137, 138.

35. Memorandum of meeting by Dreier, 22 January 1946, *FRUS: 1946*, 11:91.

36. The State Department excepted Brazil and Mexico because of special commitments made to these nations during World War II. See memorandum, Chalmers to Braden, 5 January 1946, 810.20 Defense/1-546, State. The department's restriction on the provision of bomber aircraft applied specifically to the B-25s and the AT-11s—advanced training planes used in the instruction of bomber pilots—scheduled for transfer in the interim program.

37. Quotation from letter, Acheson to Royall, 4 January 1946, *FRUS: 1946*,

11:86–87; memorandum, Briggs to Acheson, 19 December 1945, 810.24/ 12-1945, State; letter, Acheson to Patterson, 19 December 1945; and telegram no. 2618, Acheson to Harriman, 21 December 1945, both in *FRUS: 1945*, 9:261–63.

38. Letter, Royall to Byrnes, 31 December 1945, *FRUS: 1945*, 9:263–64; letters, Royall to Acheson, 6 January 1946, and Braden to Royall, 9 January 1946, both in *FRUS: 1946*, 11:87–89; memorandum, Briggs to Acheson, 18 January 1946, 810.24/1-1846, State; Arnold, *Global Mission*, 601–6.

39. The navy submitted its interim program to the State Department on 30 March 1946, and Byrnes approved the allocations on 9 April, with the exception that no vessels should be offered for the time being to Argentina, the Dominican Republic, Haiti, Nicaragua, and Cuba. Memorandum, Hidalgo to Forrestal, 29 March 1946, file 81-1-27, SecNavy; letters, Acheson to Forrestal, 9 April and 1 July 1946, both in *FRUS: 1946*, 11:97–98.

40. Quotation from Forrestal Diaries, 2 April 1946, 954–57, Naval History Division; memorandum by Sullivan, [probably February 1946], folder SWNCC 246, ASA; minutes, meetings of the Committee of Three, 11 December 1945 and 24 January 1946, C-3.

41. Memorandum SM-5062, McFarland to SWNCC, 21 February 1946, file CCS 092 United States (12-21-45) sec. 1, JCS.

42. Quotation from memorandum, Hertford to Eisenhower, 22 April 1946, file 091 Latin America (1946), C/S; letter, Eisenhower to Acheson, 2 February 1946, in Galambos, *The Papers of Dwight D. Eisenhower*, 7:821–23.

43. Quotation from Intelligence Research Project no. 1713, "Soviet-Communist Penetration in Latin America," 24 March 1945, Military Intelligence Service, War Department General Staff, file 336 sec. 2, OPD; letter, Patterson to Byrnes, 4 October 1945, file 091 Latin America Top Secret (1945), C/S; memorandum prepared in the State Department, "Foreign Policy of the United States," 1 December 1945, file CCS 092 United States (12-21-45) sec. 1, JCS; Berle and Jacobs, *Navigating the Rapids*, 533–34.

44. Caribbean Defense Command, "Bi-Lateral Staff Conversations," 104; telegram no. 10694, Byrnes to Winant, 10 December 1945, *FRUS: 1945*, 9:260; telegrams, no. 66, Bowers to Byrnes, 16 January 1946, no. 68, Bowers to Byrnes, 17 January 1946, and no. 710, Byrnes to Acheson, 21 January 1946, all in *FRUS: 1946*, 11:561–63.

45. Memorandum, Hickerson to Dunn, 11 December 1945, 810.20 Defense/12-1145, State; minutes, meetings of the Committee of Three, 11 December 1945 and 24 January 1946, C-3; telegram no. 13285, Winant to Byrnes, 19 December 1945; and aide-memoire, State Department to the British Embassy, 15 November 1945, both in *FRUS: 1945*, 9:260–61, 555–57; memorandum, Bevin to Byrnes, 14 January 1946, 810.20 Defense/1-1446, State.

46. Quotation from letter, Braddock to Pawley, 27 December 1946, 810.24/12-2746, State; memorandum, Briggs to Acheson, 18 April 1946, 800.24/4-1846, State.

47. *PP: 1946*, 233–35; memorandum, Elliott to Johnson, 8 August 1946, *FRUS: 1946*, 11:296; memorandum, Smith to Brynes, 2 May 1946, 810.20 Defense/5-246, State; memorandum, Warren to Acheson and others, 30 July 1945, 810.20 Defense/7-3045, State; memorandum of meeting by Warren, 6 August 1945, 810.20 Defense/8-645, State; memorandum, Briggs to Butler, 13 February 1946, 810.20 Defense/2-1346, State; minutes, meetings of SWNCC, 7 February 1946, 14 February 1946, and 18 April 1946, file SWNCC—Agenda

and Minutes of Meetings, SWNCC; memorandum SM-4674, McFarland to SWNCC, 8 January 1946, file CCS 092 (1-18-45) sec. 1, JCS; memorandum, Lincoln to Petersen, 6 February 1946; memorandum SWN-3867, 13 February 1946; memorandum for record, meeting of the Latin American Subcommittee of SWNCC, 14 February 1946; SWNCC 246/2, 22 March 1946; and SWN-4204, 26 April 1946, all in folder SWNCC 246, ASA.

48. Duggan, *The Americas*, 186–89.

49. Quotation from memorandum, Dreier to Briggs, 8 July 1946, 810.20 Defense/7-846, State; House Committee on Foreign Affairs, *Inter-American Military Cooperation Act*, 1946; memorandum, Elliott to Johnson, 8 August 1946, *FRUS: 1946*, 11:296; memorandum, Norstad to Ordway, 27 August 1946, file 091 Latin America, P&O; PCA M-8, 19 July 1946; and PCA M-11, 10 August 1946, both in PCA.

50. Quotation from memorandum, Braden to Byrnes, 16 December 1946, *FRUS: 1946*, 11:108–10; minutes, meeting of the Committee of Three, 28 August 1946, C-3; letters, Forrestal to Byrnes, 12 November 1946, and Patterson to Byrnes, 5 December 1946, both in file 091 Latin America, P&O; memorandum, Braden to Acheson, 9 December 1946, 810.20 Defense/12-946, State; letter, Braddock to Pawley, 27 December 1946, 810.24/12-2746, State.

51. Minutes, meeting of the Committee of Three, 18 December 1946, C-3.

52. Ibid.

53. Letter, Patterson to Byrnes, 18 December 1946, file 091 Latin America (16/7), P&O.

54. On this point, see E. May, "The 'Bureaucratic Politics' Approach," 150–54.

55. Senate Committee on Foreign Relations, *Executive Sessions*, 1:11.

56. Quotation from letter, Patterson to Marshall, 24 January 1947, file 092 Top Secret (23/3) P&O; letter, Patterson to Byrnes, 18 December 1946; and letter, Marshall to Patterson, 7 February 1947, both in file 091 Latin America, P&O; memorandum, Acheson to Marshall, 7 February 1947, 810.20 Defense/2-747, State.

57. Memorandum, Hickerson to Dunn, 11 December 1945, 810.20 Defense/12-1145, State.

58. Memorandum, Maxwell to Commanding General, Army Air Forces and Commanding General, Army Service Forces, 1 March 1946, file 091 Latin America (26 Feb. 46), C/S; disposition forms, Lutes to Norstad, 20 December 1946; Ordway to Lutes, 30 December 1946; Osborne to P&O, 13 January 1947; and memorandum, Lincoln to Petersen, 7 April 1947, all in file 091 Latin America, P&O; memorandum by Dreier, 22 November 1946, *FRUS: 1946*, 9:106–7; letter, Forrestal to Truman, 19 December 1946, folder Navy—1946, WHCF.

59. Memorandum, Braden to Byrnes, 16 December 1946, *FRUS: 1946*, 11:108–10; letter, Forrestal to Marshall, 26 February 1947, file 81-1-27, SecNavy; letter, Patterson to Byrnes, 2 January 1947, file 092 Top Secret (23/3), P&O; disposition form, Lutes to P&O, 26 December 1946, file 091 Latin America, P&O; memorandum, Braden to Marshall, 22 January 1947, FW 810.20 Defense/1-2247, State. In his memoirs, Braden stated that he repeatedly asked the services about the costs of the standardization program before he finally received an estimate for accessory equipment, which amounted to $1,066,000,000 over ten years. I have not been able to find either in War or State Department records any State Department inquiry about the costs of standardization before Byrnes

raised the issue at the meeting of the Committee of Three on 19 December 1946. Patterson furnished an estimate on 2 January 1947. Braden was probably referring to this statement of costs in his memoirs, but the figures he cited do not correspond exactly to any of the estimates that I have seen. Braden, *Diplomats and Demagogues*, 365–66.

60. Letter, Acheson to Patterson, 19 March 1947, *FRUS: 1947*, 8:105–6; "Interim Report on Financial Aspects of Participation by Latin American Countries in the Inter-American Arms Program Under H.R. 6326," file 092.2 (25 July 1946) Inter-American Military Cooperation Act, AG; Quirós, "United States Reactions to the Costa Rican Counter-Revolution," 13.

61. Quotations from letter, Patterson to Acheson, 27 March 1947, *FRUS: 1947*, 8:106–9; summary sheet, Norstad to Patterson, 25 March 1947; and chit by Eisenhower, n.d., both in file 092.2 (25 July 1946) Inter-American Military Cooperation Act, AG. For Forrestal's reaction to the State Department's report, see his letter to Acheson, 31 March 1947, ibid., 109–10.

62. *PP: 1947*, 178–79.

63. SWNCC 360/1, encl. B, 12 May 1947, *FRUS: 1947*, 1:743.

64. ORE 16, 10 April 1947, folder Central Intelligence Reports—ORE, 1947—No. 15-39, Intelligence File, PSF. The State Department Intelligence Organization dissented from ORE 16 because it exaggerated the immediate Soviet danger in Latin America.

65. Quoted in Fairchild, "The US Army and the Military Assistance Program," chap. 2, p. 5.

66. Letter, Patterson to Acheson, 27 March 1947, *FRUS: 1947*, 8:108. See also Kaplan, "U.S. Arms Transfers to Latin America," 407–12.

67. Cable WOC 19, Chamberlin to Norstad, 27 March 1947, file 091 Latin America, P&O.

68. Quotations from handwritten note by Truman, n.d., folder General File—A, PSF; memorandum for the president, 26 March 1947, ibid.; and memorandum, Ridgway, Jones, and Weyland to Secretary, Presidential Staff, Charged with Legislation, 30 March 1947, folder Inter-American Military Cooperation Act, WHCF.

69. For a different analysis, see Rabe, "Inter-American Military Cooperation," 140; Tillapaugh, "From War to Cold War," 290.

70. Quotations from memorandum, Ordway to Norstad, 10 April 1947, file 091 Latin America (16/16), P&O; memorandum, Ordway to Norstad, 8 April 1947, ibid.; minutes, meeting of the Committee of Three, 2 April 1947, C-3; memorandum, Braden to Acheson, 4 April 1947, 810.20 Defense/4-447, State; memorandum, Braden to Acheson, 28 April 1947, 810.24/4-2847, State; Braden *Diplomats and Demagogues*, 367; minutes, meeting of the Secretaries of State, War, and Navy, 23 April 1947, file 334 Committee of Three, SWNCC; memorandum, Allen to Acheson, 21 April 1947; FW 810.20 Defense/4-447, State; minutes, meeting of the Secretaries of State, War, and Navy, 1 May 1947, *FRUS: 1947*, 8:113–15; Fairchild, "The US Army and the Military Assistance Program," chap. 2, p. 6.

71. Hull quoted in E. May, "The 'Bureaucratic Politics' Approach," 132; Woods, *The Roosevelt Foreign-Policy Establishment*, 8–10.

72. Telegram, Byrnes to Diplomatic Representatives in the American Republics, 14 November 1945, *FRUS: 1945*, 9:167–68; S. Spector, "United States Attempts at Regional Security," 142–59; Acheson, *Present at the Creation*,

187–90; telegram no. 2066, Braden to Byrnes, 4 September 1945, *FRUS: 1945,* 9:406–8; Woods, *The Roosevelt Foreign-Policy Establishment,* 205–6.

73. Braden quoted in Wood, *The Dismantling of the Good Neighbor Policy,* 111; Stiller, *George S. Messersmith,* 231; Gellman, *Roosevelt and Batista,* 198–220.

74. Braden, *Diplomats and Demagogues,* 316–38; memorandum by Acheson, 29 September 1945, *FRUS: 1945,* 9:159; Trask, "The Impact of the Cold War on United States-Latin American Relations," 274–77; "Consultation Among the American Republics with Respect to the Argentine Situation," n.d., folder Argentina (2), Subject File—Foreign Affairs, PSF; memoranda, Acheson to Truman, 12 July 1946, and Truman to Acheson, 22 July 1946, both in *FRUS: 1946,* 11:270–78, 282; *PP: 1946,* 257; *New York Times,* 23 October 1946.

75. Letters, Messersmith to Byrnes, 15 June 1946, and Messersmith to Truman, 16 August 1946, both in folder Argentina (2), Subject File—Foreign Affairs, PSF; letters, Messersmith to Byrnes, 12 October 1946 and 15 October 1946; Messersmith to Acheson, 16 October 1946; and Messersmith to Truman, 16 October 1946 and 23 October 1946, all in folder Argentina (3), ibid.; memorandum, Armour to Marshall, 17 July 1947, file 123 Messersmith, George S., State. On the Braden-Messersmith conflict, see Braden *Diplomats and Demagogues,* 358–64; Peterson, *Argentina and the United States,* 450–58; Tillapaugh, "From War to Cold War," 261–63; E. May, "The 'Bureaucratic Politics' Approach," 153–55; Trask, "Spruille Braden versus George Messersmith," 69–95; Stiller, *George S. Messersmith,* 228–63.

76. Quotation from letter, Vandenberg to Gilmore, 25 February 1947, folder correspondence—February 1947, Vandenberg Papers, Bentley Historical Library; Connally, *My Name is Tom Connally,* 319; Welles, *Where Are We Heading?,* 182–241; J. Campbell, *The United States in World Affairs, 1947–1948,* 106–8.

77. Quotation from memorandum, Eisenhower to JCS, 18 February 1946, in Galambos, *The Papers of Dwight D. Eisenhower,* 7:877; Forrestal Diaries, 7 February 1947, 1470, Naval History Division; SWNCC 360/1, encl. B, 12 May 1947, *FRUS: 1947,* 1:742–44; memorandum, Trueblood to Briggs and Braden, 13 November 1946, 810.20 Defense/11-1346, State; Hertford oral history, 40–42, Truman Library.

78. Letter, Vandenberg to Howard, 12 October 1945, folder Correspondence, October 1945, Vandenberg Papers, Bentley Historical Library.

79. Quotation from SWNCC 360/1, encl. B, 12 May 1947, *FRUS: 1947,* 1:743; Welles, *Where Are We Heading?,* 239–40; Hertford oral history, 40, Truman Library. See also despatch no. 1874, 21 February 1947, Messersmith to Marshall, file ABC 400.3295 (15 March 44), sec. 1C, P&O.

80. Memorandum, Dreier to Byrnes, 14 January 1946, 810.20 Defense/1-1446, State; aide-memoire from the British embassy to the Department of State, 16 July 1946; and aide-memoire from the Department of State to the British embassy, 26 August 1946, both in *FRUS: 1946,* 11:278–79, 307–9; memorandum of conversation and annex by Acheson, 27 January 1947; and letter, Inverchapel to Marshall, 21 May 1947, both in *FRUS: 1947,* 8:171–72, 224–25.

81. Forrestal Diaries, 7 February 1947, 1470, Naval History Division.

82. Quotation from notes on Cabinet meeting, 7 February 1947, folder Cabinet Meetings, Jan. 3–Dec. 19, 1947, Connelly Files; memorandum, Braden to Marshall, 4 February 1947, *FRUS: 1947,* 8:218–19.

83. Memorandum, Braden to Acheson, 10 February 1947; and telegram no.

252, Acheson to Messersmith, 2 April 1947, both in *FRUS: 1947*, 8:176–78, 186–87; Senate Committee on Foreign Relations, *Executive Sessions*, 1:11.

84. Quotation from memorandum of conversation by Acheson, 27 January 1947, *FRUS: 1947*, 8:171; memorandum by Briggs, 20 May 1947; and letter, Inverchapel to Marshall, 21 May 1947, both in ibid., 221–25; memoranda, Marshall to Bevin, 17 May 1947, and Acheson to Truman, 19 May 1947, both in folder Argentina (3), Subject File—Foreign Affairs, PSF.

85. Braden, *Diplomats and Demagogues*, 369–70. The White House announced that Messersmith had resigned, but the president actually had fired him. On 6 June, Messersmith cabled to Marshall, "As I have not submitted any resignation to the President, has my 'resignation' been accepted by him?" Telegram no. 687, file 123 Messersmith, George S., State.

86. *PP: 1947*, 261; minutes, meeting of the Committee of Three, 19 June 1947, C-3; memorandum, Marshall to Truman, 26 June 1947, *FRUS: 1947*, 8:225–26; memoranda, Crain to Hilldring, 14 July 1947, and Hilldring to Lovett, 4 August 1947, both in folder Policy Committee on Arms and Armaments (2), ISA; PCA M-53, 25 July 1947, PCA; Forrestal Diaries, 27 June 1947, 1696, Naval History Division.

87. Telegram no. 147, Marshall to Embassy in Dominican Republic, 1 August 1947; memorandum and annexes by Sohm, 4 August 1947; letter, Lovett to Royall, 22 August 1947; and memorandum by Dreier, 4 November 1947, all in *FRUS: 1947*, 8:116–21, 125–27, 648; PCA M-52, 18 July 1947; PCA M-54, 1 August 1947; and PCA S-69, 14 November 1947, all in PCA; summary of meeting between representatives of State, War, and Navy, 11 September 1947, folder Rearmament Subcommittee of SWNCC (1), ISA; *Register of the Department of State*, 1948, 136, 312.

88. House Committee on Foreign Affairs, *Inter-American Military Cooperation Act*, 1947, 7.

89. Letter, Acheson to Patterson, 5 March 1947, *FRUS: 1947*, 5:94–95; SWNCC 360, 21 April 1947, *FRUS: 1947*, 3:204–19; SWNCC 360, 21 April 1947, *FRUS: 1947*, 1:725–33.

90. "Appreciation of Foreseeable Foreign Needs for U.S. Military Assistance During the Next Three to Five Years," report by the Rearmament Subcommittee of the SWNCC to the Special Ad Hoc Committee, 10 July 1947, folder Foreseeable Military Assistance to Foreign Nations for Next 3–5 Years, ISA.

91. PCA M-37, 7 March 1947; SWNCC 360/1, encl. B, 12 May 1947; and PCA S-49, 20 June 1947, all in *FRUS: 1947*, 1:722–24, 734–50, 759–60; memorandum, Eisenhower to JCS, 10 May 1947, in Galambos, *Papers of Dwight D. Eisenhower* 8:1700–1703.

92. Quotation from memorandum, Sandifer to Marshall, 10 June 1947, 810.20 Defense/6-1047, State; memorandum, Ordway to Norstad, 11 June 1947, file 091 Latin America, P&O.

93. *PP: 1947*, 255–57; memorandum, Webb to Marshall, 20 May 1947, 810.20 Defense/5-2047, State; memorandum and encl., Ridgway, Jones, and Weyland to Secretary, Presidential Staff, Charged with Legislation, 9 June 1947, folder Inter-American Military Cooperation Act, WHCF; memoranda, Lincoln to Norstad, 11 June 1947, and Franklin to Ordway, 13 June 1947, both in file 091 Latin America, P&O; memorandum, Sandifer to Marshall, 19 June 1947, 810.20 Defense/6-1947, State; Stueck, *The Road to Confrontation*, 81–82; Hinson, "Plans of the United States for Postwar Military Assistance to Latin America," 277–82; J. Campbell, *The United States in World Affairs, 1947–1948*, 110.

94. Pogue, *George C. Marshall: Statesman*, 388–93. On the *bogotazo*, see Braun, *The Assassination of Gaitán.*

95. Letter, Marshall to Eaton, 26 May 1948; and memorandum, Armour to Marshall, 4 June 1948, both in *FRUS: 1948*, 9:213–15; memorandum, Woodward to Tewksbury, 20 April 1948, 810.20 Defense/4-2048, State; memorandum, Bohlen to Woodward, 29 April 1948; 810.20 Defense/4-2948, State; memorandum of meeting by Woodward, 4 May 1948, 810.20 Defense/5-448, State; memorandum of telephone conversation between Ruffner and Muir, 24 May 1948, file 091 Latin America, P&O; memorandum, Dreier to Daniels, 2 June 1948, 810.20 Defense/6-248, State.

96. For a detailed discussion of the implementation of the interim program, see Fairchild, "The US Army and the Military Assistance Program," chap. 2, pp. 6–19; and Pilgert, "The History of Foreign Surplus Property Disposal, 1945–1949," 2: pt. 10, 23–37, 46–58, 89–99. For reports on the status of the interim program, see memorandum, Braden to Clayton, 18 June 1946, 810.24/6-1846, State; memorandum, McCabe to Clayton, 21 June 1946, 810.24/6-2146, State; letter, Forrestal to Truman, 19 December 1946, folder Navy—1946, WHCF; memorandum of conversation by Hickerson, 18 February 1947, folder memoranda of conversation, 1947–48, EUR; letter, Patterson to Truman, 3 March 1947, folder War Department (4), WHCF; memorandum, Kingman to Dreier, 27 May 1947, 810.24/5-2747, State; memorandum, Carney to Forrestal and Nimitz, 16 June 1947, folder Navy—1946, WHCF; memorandum, Spencer to Daniels, 7 October 1948, 810.24/10-748, State; *DSB* 21 (26 September 1949): 480–81.

97. Cable, Crittenberger to Wedemeyer, 15 December 1947; memorandum, Ordway to Dreier, 28 January 1948; summary sheet, Wedemeyer to Eisenhower, 3 May 1948; memorandum, Freeman to Swett, 27 May 1948, all in file 091 Argentina, P&O; memorandum, Royall to Sosa Molina, 4 June 1948, *FRUS: 1948*, 9:322; memorandum, Royall to Truman, 3 June 1948, file 400 (22 July 1949), S/A (Gray-Pace); memorandum, "Military Assistance for Argentina Under the Act of June 15, 1940," n.d., unsigned, folder "Miss Thiel's file," Lend-Lease Records, 1945–1953, G-4.

98. Despatch, Marshall to Diplomatic Representatives in the American Republics, 30 July 1948, *FRUS: 1948*, 9:218–20; memorandum, Maddocks to Daniels, 28 June 1948, file 400 Latin America (1 June 1948), S/A (Royall).

99. Eisenhower to JCS, 10 May 1947, in Galambos, *The Papers of Dwight D. Eisenhower* 8:1700–1703.

CHAPTER 3

1. Memorandum, Vincent to Byrnes, 12 November 1945, *FRUS: 1945*, 7:615.

2. Quoted in Dallek, *Franklin D. Roosevelt and American Foreign Policy*, 355.

3. Schaller, *The U.S. Crusade in China*, 96–99. Other useful accounts of wartime Sino-American relations are: Dallek, *Franklin D. Roosevelt and American Foreign Policy*, 328–31, 354–58, 382–92, 397–99, 485–502; Thorne, *Allies of a Kind*, especially chaps. 6, 12, 19, and 26; Tsou, *America's Failure in China*; Feis, *The China Tangle*; Tuchman, *Stilwell and the American Experience in China*; and Varg, *The Closing of the Door.*

4. Romanus and Sunderland, *Stilwell's Mission to China*, 153–57; Romanus

and Sunderland, *Stilwell's Command Problems*, 3–5; Coakley and Leighton, *Global Logistics and Strategy*, 532–35.

5. Sunderland, "The Secret Embargo," 75–80; Davies, *Dragon by the Tail*, 289–90; Ringwalt oral history, Truman Library.

6. Tuchman, *Stilwell and the American Experience in China*, 264–66, 304–7, 314–16; Liu, *A Military History of Modern China*, 143–52; Romanus and Sunderland, *Stilwell's Mission to China*, 33–37; memorandum, Davies to Gauss, 9 March 1943, *FRUS: 1943, China*, 25–29; Sheridan, *China in Disintegration*, 183–206, 209–13.

7. Chennault, *Way of a Fighter*, 212–16, 222–24; Dallek, *Franklin D. Roosevelt and American Foreign Policy*, 383–88; Romanus and Sunderland, *Stilwell's Mission to China*, 277–83; Coakley and Leighton, *Global Logistics and Strategy*, 727; Sherry, *The Rise of American Air Power*, 159–60.

8. Stilwell quoted in Tuchman, *Stilwell and the American Experience in China*, 394; Romanus and Sunderland, *Stilwell's Mission to China*, 384–85; Romanus and Sunderland, *Stilwell's Command Problems*, 49–82; Matloff, *Strategic Planning for Coalition Warfare*, 326, 373; Coakley and Leighton, *Global Logistics and Strategy*, 730–31.

9. Quoted in Thorne, *Allies of a Kind*, 427.

10. Romanus and Sunderland, *Stilwell's Command Problems*, 316–28; 379–84 (quotation from 384); Elsey, *Roosevelt and China*, 34–41; R. Spector, *Eagle Against the Sun*, 364–67.

11. Quotation from Stimson Diaries, 3 October 1944, 48:114 (reel 9), Yale University Library; Romanus and Sunderland, *Stilwell's Command Problems*, 413–42; Tuchman, *Stilwell and the American Experience in China*, 470–502; Dallek, *Franklin D. Roosevelt and American Foreign Policy*, 491–99.

12. Campbell and Herring, *The Diaries of Edward R. Stettinius, Jr.*, 210.

13. Dallek, *Franklin D. Roosevelt and American Foreign Policy*, 499–502, 535–36; Schaller, *The U.S. Crusade in China*, 177–80.

14. Memorandum by Davies, "Will the Communists Take Over China?," 7 November 1944; memorandum by Davies, "American-Chinese Relations During the Next Six Months," 15 November 1944; memorandum by Service, 10 October 1944, all in *FRUS: 1944*, 6:670–71, 695–97, 708–11; Service, *The Amerasia Papers*, 136 ff.; Davies, *Dragon by the Tail*, 361–64, 370–72; U.S. Department of State, *United States Relations with China*, 564–76.

15. Unnumbered telegram, Hurley to Stettinius, 24 December 1944, *FRUS: 1944*, 6:745–49; telegram no. 141500 NCR 6810, Hurley to Roosevelt, 14 January 1945, *FRUS: 1945*, 7:172–77; Buhite, *Patrick J. Hurley and American Foreign Policy*, 162–87; Service, *The Amerasia Papers*, 100–114; Davies, *Dragon by the Tail*, 383–84; Schaller, *The U.S. Crusade in China*, 202–7; Ringwalt oral history, Truman Library.

16. Quotation from memorandum, Vincent to Grew, 29 January 1945; minutes, meeting of the Committee of Three, 16 January 1945, both in *FRUS: 1945*, 7:34, 37–39.

17. Memorandum by Vincent, 1 March 1945, ibid., 247–49; G. May, *China Scapegoat*, 122–24.

18. The full text of the embassy despatch is in Service, *Amerasia Papers*, 109–12; memorandum, Grew to Roosevelt, 2 March 1945, *FRUS: 1945*, 7:254.

19. Dallek, *Franklin D. Roosevelt and American Foreign Policy*, 516–18, 523; Buhite, *Patrick J. Hurley and American Foreign Policy*, 187–94; G. May, *China Scapegoat*, 125–28; Kahn, *The China Hands*, 150–60.

20. In February 1945 the War Department approved an interim program of assistance to the Chinese air force. It was to be completed in May 1946 and aimed at the establishment of four-and-one-half air groups consisting of 199 aircraft. In 1943 the War Department approved the creation of a Chinese-American Composite Wing, comprising one bomber and two fighter groups, as part of Chennault's Fourteenth Air Force. Letter, Chennault to Wedemeyer, 17 February 1945; and memorandum, adjutant general to Wedemeyer, 26 February 1945, both in file 336.2 Top Secret sec. 1, OPD; Craven and Cate, *The Army Air Forces in World War II*, 4:438–41, 529–36.

21. SWNCC 83/D, 3 April 1945, file CCS 452 (4-3-45) sec. 1, JCS.

22. Quotation from ibid.; P. Smith, *The Air Force Plans for Peace*, 105–6. Wedemeyer also pointed out the beneficial effects of such assistance on the American aircraft industry. See his letter to Marshall, 24 January 1945, file 336.2 Top Secret sec. 1, OPD.

23. "Memorandum Concerning United States Post-War Military Policies with Respect to China," by the State Department, 3 April 1945; and memorandum, Matthews to Stettinius, 29 May 1945, both in *FRUS: 1945*, 7:74–79, 116–17; JCS 1330, 27 April 1945; and JCS 1330/1, 5 May 1945, both in file CCS 452 China (4-3-45) sec. 1, JCS.

24. By V-J Day, approximately one-third of the equipment under the thirty-nine-division program had been delivered to Chinese forces. JCS 1330/3, 27 September 1945, file CCS 452 China (4-3-45) sec. 1, JCS.

25. "The China Theater," report by Wedemeyer to Eisenhower, February 1946, folder 228.03 Permanent, Geog V. China 319.1, Wedemeyer, A. C. LTG, CMH.

26. Memorandum and encl., Grew to Truman, 27 April 1945, folder Secretary of State Edward R. Stettinius, Subject File—Foreign Affairs, PSF.

27. Directive, Truman to MacArthur, 15 August 1945; unnumbered telegram, Wedemeyer to Marshall, 19 August 1945; and telegram no. 1514, Hurley to Byrnes, 4 September 1945, all in *FRUS: 1945*, 7:530–34, 549–50; memorandum SM-2964, JCS to SWNCC, 21 August 1945, file 336 Top Secret (133/17), OPD.

28. "History of the China Theater," chap. 15, 1–60.

29. Gallicchio, *The Cold War Begins in Asia*, 95–100.

30. Telegram no. WARX 47513, JCS to Wedemeyer, 10 August 1945, *FRUS: 1945*, 7:527–28; Gallicchio, *The Cold War Begins in Asia*, 82–83, 100; Feis, *The China Tangle*, 362–67; Schaller, *The U.S. Crusade in China*, 263–74; Rose, *Roots of Tragedy*, 154–55; "United States Government Economic, Financial, and Military Aid to China Since 1937," folder K14-1, series 47.3, Budget; memorandum and encl., Truman to Pepper, 1 February 1946, folder P(1), General File, PSF.

31. Quotation from telegram no. 1330, Hurley to Byrnes, 11 August 1945; letter and encl., Forrestal to Byrnes, 27 August 1945; and telegram no. 1505, Hurley to Byrnes, 2 September 1945, all in *FRUS: 1945*, 7:529–30, 538–39, 546–47; memoranda, Soong to Truman, 30 August 1945, folder Foreign—China, 1945, Subject File—Foreign Affairs, PSF.

32. "History of the China Theater," chap. 17.

33. Memorandum, Leahy to Truman, 5 September 1945, folder Foreign—China, 1945, Subject file—Foreign Affairs, PSF.

34. Memorandum, Forrestal to Truman, 24 August 1945, folder Navy, 1945, WHCF.

35. Quotation from telegram CFB 6817, Wedemeyer to War Department,

3 September 1945, encl. to JCS 1330/2, 11 September 1945, file CCS 452 China (4-3-45) sec. 1, JCS; memorandum, Vandenberg to Arnold, [approx. 20 August 1945], file CCS 452 China (4-3-45) sec. 2, JCS; memorandum for Marshall, 30 August 1945; and memorandum, Eaker to Marshall, 30 August 1945, both in file 336.2 Top Secret (24/6), OPD.

36. While there was no record of Roosevelt's ninety-division pledge in the files of any government agency, Harry Hopkins, an assistant to the former president, confirmed that Roosevelt had made such a statement to Chiang. He told White House officials in September 1945 that "if the Chinese were now trying to hold the U.S. to President Roosevelt's verbal agreement at Cairo, President Truman should reply that he could find no record of it." Truman accepted this advice. See memorandum, Elsey to Vardaman, 3 September 1945, folder Foreign—China, 1945, Subject File—Foreign Affairs, PSF; memorandum, Hull to Truman, 3 September 1945, ibid.; memorandum of conversation by Acheson, 7 September 1945, FRUS: 1945, 7:551-52.

37. Quotation from memorandum and encl., Acheson to Truman, 13 September 1945, FRUS: 1945, 7:559-62; SWNCC 83/2/D, 4 September 1945, file CCS 452 China (4-3-45) sec. 1, JCS.

38. Minutes of the 221st meeting of the Joint Staff Planners, 10 October 1945; and JCS 1330/7, 15 October 1945, both in file CCS 452 China (4-3-45) sec. 2, JCS; unnumbered telegram Wedemeyer to Marshall, 19 August 1945, FRUS: 1945, 7:531-34; Varg, The Closing of the Door, 217-19; Stueck, The Road to Confrontation, 28-29.

39. JCS 1330/9, 22 October 1945, folder Gen. Marshall-Col. Byroade Dec. 1945, JCS-SWNCC Papers, Marshall Mission; JCS 1330/10, 22 October 1945, FRUS: 1945, 7:590-98. For a detailed description of the proposed advisory group, see JCS 1330/15, 22 November 1945, folder Gen. Marshall-Col. Byroade Dec. 1945, JCS-SWNCC Papers, Marshall Mission.

40. Memorandum, Vincent to Byrnes, 12 November 1945, FRUS: 1945, 7:614-17.

41. Telegram no. 23, Meyer to Byrnes, 30 October 1945; telegram no. 1920, Robertson to Byrnes, 4 November 1945; and telegram no. CFB 13529, Wedemeyer to Marshall, 5 November 1945, all in ibid., 599, 601-2, 603-5; Schaller, The United States and China in the Twentieth Century, 109-12; "History of the China Theater," 61-67, 123-32.

42. Minutes, meeting of the Secretaries of State, War, and Navy, 6 November 1945, FRUS: 1945, 7:606-7.

43. Ferrell, Off the Record, 74.

44. Telegram no. CFBX 13955, Wedemeyer to Marshall, 9 November 1945; and telegram no. CLO 672, Wedemeyer to Marshall, 14 November 1945, both in FRUS: 1945, 7:611-13, 627-28; SWNCC 224/D, 16 November 1945, file SWNCC 224 series, SWNCC; "History of the China Theater," 65.

45. Quotation from telegram no. 84904, Eisenhower to Wedemeyer, 19 November 1945, FRUS: 1945, 7:644-45; Millis, The Forrestal Diaries, 108-9.

46. Minutes, 222d meeting of the Joint Staff Planners, 17 October 1945, file CCS 452 China (4-3-45) sec. 2, JCS.

47. Stueck, "The Marshall and Wedemeyer Missions," 93-96.

48. Wedemeyer's reports quoted in the previous three paragraphs are in telegram no. CFBX 15120, Wedemeyer to Eisenhower, 20 November 1945; telegram no. CFB 15452, Wedemeyer to Eisenhower, 23 November 1945; and

telegram no. CFBX 15676, Wedemeyer to Eisenhower, 26 November 1945, all in *FRUS: 1945,* 7:650–60, 662–65, 679–84; Wedemeyer, *Wedemeyer Reports!,* 344–51.

49. The memorandum was prepared in the Strategy and Policy Group of the War Department Operations Division and revised to fit McCloy's views. See memorandum for record by Lincoln, 24 November 1945; and memorandum for record by Dupuy, 25 November 1945, both in folder Gen. Marshall-Col. Byroade Dec. 1945, JCS-SWNCC Papers, Marshall Mission.

50. Memorandum, Patterson and Forrestal to Byrnes, 26 November 1945, *FRUS: 1945,* 7:670–78.

51. Memorandum by Vincent, 19 November 1945, ibid., 639–43; Acheson, *Present at the Creation,* 139–40; G. May, *China Scapegoat,* 135–38.

52. Minutes, meeting of the Secretaries of State, War, and Navy, 27 November 1945, *FRUS: 1945,* 7:684–86; minutes, meeting of the Committee of Three, 20 November 1945, C-3; Acheson, *Present at the Creation,* 140; Feis, *The China Tangle,* 404–5; G. May, *China Scapegoat,* 138–39; Schaller, *The U.S. Crusade in China,* 286–87.

53. Quotation from J. Blum, *The Price of Vision,* 519; Millis, *The Forrestal Diaries,* 113; Buhite, *Patrick J. Hurley and American Foreign Policy,* 260–72; Byrnes, *All in One Lifetime,* 328–29; letter, Hurley to Truman, 26 November 1945, *FRUS: 1945,* 7:722–26. Hurley, who was nothing if not erratic, told Presidential Press Secretary Charles G. Ross on 9 January 1946 that his resignation had no political implications whatsoever and that he was eager to serve Truman in any way possible. See memorandum, Ross to Truman, 9 January 1946, folder "Hf-Hz," General File, PSF.

54. J. Blum, *The Price of Vision,* 520. For a discussion of American anxieties over Soviet intentions in China, see Levine, "A New Look at American Mediation in the Chinese Civil War," 349–75.

55. Memorandum by Vincent, n.d.; memorandum, Marshall to Leahy, 30 November 1945; memorandum prepared in the State Department, "U.S. Policy Towards China," 8 December 1945; and memorandum, Hull to Marshall, 8 December 1945, all in *FRUS: 1945,* 7:745–51, 754–59; Acheson, *Present at the Creation,* 142.

56. Quotations from memorandum of conversation by Marshall, 11 December 1945; memorandum of conversation by Hull, 10 December 1945; and memorandum of conversation by Marshall, 14 December 1945, all in *FRUS: 1945,* 7:761–63, 767–69, 770; memorandum, Leahy to Truman, 11 December 1945, folder Foreign—China, 1945, Subject File—Foreign Affairs, PSF; memorandum, Truman to Patterson and Forrestal, n.d., in compilation book for General Wedemeyer, file 091 China Top Secret, P&O; Cohen, *America's Response to China,* 184–86; Chern, *Dilemma in China,* 190–91.

57. Memorandum, Truman to Wallace, 25 January 1946, folder Foreign—China, 1946, Subject File—Foreign Affairs, PSF.

58. Memorandum, Vincent to Byrnes, 9 December 1945, *FRUS: 1945,* 7:759–60; memorandum, Ariyoshi to Wedemeyer, 27 November 1945, folder Yenan Observer Group, Marshall Mission; Acheson, *Present at the Creation,* 140–42; G. May, *China Scapegoat,* 142.

59. For Marshall's negotiations, see Pogue, *George C. Marshall: Statesman,* 37–143; Varg, *The Closing of the Door,* 238–52; Melby, *The Mandate of Heaven,* 69–82, 91–98; Marshall, *Marshall's Mission to China,* 1:6–49.

60. Quotation from memorandum, Shepley to Truman, 28 February 1946,

folder Foreign—China, 1946, Subject File—Foreign Affairs, PSF; telegram CFBX 25549, Wedemeyer to War Department, 13 March 1946, folder Ground Forces, Marshall Mission.

61. Memorandum OSE 418, Caughey to Fischer, 4 September 1946, folder U.S. Assistance to China, Marshall Mission.

62. The thirty-nine-division program existed after World War II only for bookkeeping purposes. Under this program, supplies were issued to the Nationalist forces on the basis of operational necessity. No attempt was made to equip thirty-nine specific divisions, even though the Nationalist forces received the equivalent in equipment. Memorandum for the Joint Chiefs of Staff, n.d., folder MAG—Miscellaneous, Marshall Mission.

63. American officials did not know the total amount of equipment in the West China stockpiles, although the amount was considerable. The ammunition involved in this sale, for example, was sufficient to supply thirty-nine divisions for 120 days of combat. See telegram no. CFBX 19018, Wedemeyer to War Department, 4 January 1946, file CCS 452 China (4-3-45) sec. 4, JCS.

64. Quotations from Forrestal Diaries, 14 July 1946, 1152, Naval History Division; and notes on Cabinet meeting, 2 August 1946, folder Cabinet Meetings, 1946, Connelly Files; notes by Patterson on Cabinet meeting, 2 August 1946, folder Basic (Policy), Marshall Mission; J. Blum, *The Price of Vision*, 608–9. Patterson and Truman expressed approval of Acheson's views.

65. Memorandum for Petersen, 3 January 1946, folder SWNCC 83/14—Part 2, SWNCC; telegram no. 170200Z, Lincoln to Hull, 17 January 1946; and telegram no. CFBX 25154, Wedemeyer to Eisenhower, 8 March 1946, both in folder Army Advisory Group, Marshall Mission.

66. SWNCC 83/16, 5 January 1946, *FRUS: 1946*, 10:810–11. See also memorandum, Vincent to Acheson, 8 April 1946, ibid., 825–27.

67. Wedemeyer reported to the War Department that Chiang had told him confidently that the Soviet Union and Great Britain had offered to establish military advisory groups in China. Telegram no. 20766, Wedemeyer to Eisenhower, 21 January 1946, ibid., 811–16.

68. Because of the failure of Congress to enact necessary legislation and because of intramural service disputes, a joint military advisory group was not established in China until 1 November 1948. In the meantime separate army, navy, and army air force (and, later, air force) groups rendered advice to the Nationalists. See memorandum, Bolté to Bradley, 10 August 1949, file 091 China Top Secret, G-3.

69. SWNCC 83/17, 13 February 1946; memorandum, Vincent to Byrnes, 19 February 1946; and memorandum and annex, Byrnes to Truman, 21 February 1946, all in *FRUS: 1946*, 10:817–20, 820–23; telegram no. WAR 93194, Eisenhower to Marshall, 16 January 1946, in Galambos, *The Papers of Dwight D. Eisenhower*, 7:762–64.

70. Minutes of the 222d meeting of the Joint Staff Planners, 17 October 1945, file CCS 452 China (4-3-45) sec. 2, JCS; memorandum of conversation by Sweeney, 25 November 1947, 893.24/11-2547, State.

71. Memorandum, Arnold to Truman, 29 November 1945, General Marshall Personal China File, Marshall Mission; memorandum, Marshall to Wedemeyer, 9 January 1946; and memorandum, McConnell to Marshall, 26 October 1946, both in folder Chinese Air Force, ibid.; memorandum, Byrnes to Patterson, 12 February 1946, *FRUS: 1946*, 10:769–70.

72. Memorandum, Trezise to Ringwalt, 22 January 1947, 893.24/1-2247,

State; "United States Government Economic, Financial, and Military Aid to China Since 1937," 9 March 1950, folder K14-1, series 47.3, Budget; memorandum, Bissell to Lincoln, 12 October 1945, file 336 Top Secret (219), OPD; Chassin, *The Communist Conquest of China*, 43–52; Khrushchev, *Khrushchev Remembers*, 238; memorandum, Wilbur to Rice, 19 March 1947, 893.24/3-1947, State; Forrestal Diaries, 9 July 1946, 1133–35, Naval History Division.

73. Quotation from Forrestal Diaries, 9 July 1946, 1133–35, Naval History Division; memorandum, Shepley to Truman, 28 February 1946, folder Foreign—China, 1946, Subject File—Foreign Affairs, PSF; Melby, *The Mandate of Heaven*, 108–34; G. May, *China Scapegoat*, 144; U.S. Department of State, *United States Relations with China*, 214.

74. Quotation from telegram no. 995, Marshall to Truman, 26 June 1946, *FRUS: 1946*, 9:1201–3; minutes, meeting between Marshall and Chou, 30 May 1946; meeting between Marshall and Chou, 3 June 1946; and meeting between Marshall and Chou, 21 June 1946; all in ibid., 925–26, 952–63, 1132–33.

75. Memorandum OSE 418, Caughey to Fischer, 4 September 1946, folder U.S. Assistance to China, Marshall Mission.

76. Telegram no. 1164, Marshall to Carter, 22 July 1946; telegram no. 95280, Carter to Marshall, 23 July 1946; and telegram no. 1173, Marshall to Carter, 24 July 1946, all in *FRUS: 1946*, 10:753, 754–55; House Committee on International Relations, *Selected Executive Session Hearings*, 7:109–51.

77. Telegram no. 95249, Carter to Marshall, 23 July 1946; telegram no. 1181, Marshall to Carter, 26 July 1946; letter, Acheson to Littlejohn, 6 August 1946; and letter, Acheson to Littlejohn, 20 August 1946, all in *FRUS: 1946*, 10:753–54, 755–57; Marshall, *Marshall's Mission to China*, 1:394–403.

78. Quotations from letter, Truman to Koo, 10 August 1946, *FRUS: 1946*, 10:3; and U.S. Department of State, *United States Relations with China*, 688; G. May, *China Scapegoat*, 151–52; Stueck, *The Road to Confrontation*, 29.

79. Quotation from telegram no. 86246, Carter to Marshall, 23 November 1946, *FRUS: 1946*, 10:559; telegram no. 1891, Marshall to Truman, 28 December 1946, ibid., 661–65; Iriye, *The Cold War in Asia*, 142–47; Borg and Heinrichs, *Uncertain Years*, 3–12, 282–83.

80. Truman quoted in J. Blum, *The Price of Vision*, 520; Gaddis, *The Long Peace*, 77–79.

CHAPTER 4

1. *PP: 1947*, 178–79.

2. Telegram no. 4122, Acheson to Byrnes, 15 August 1946, *FRUS: 1946*, 7:841.

3. Memorandum by Henderson, 21 October 1946, ibid., 894.

4. Report by the Coordinating Committee of the Department of State, 2 May 1945; and memorandum and encl., Acheson to Byrnes, 9 October 1945; both in *FRUS: 1945*, 8:34–39, 43–48; Baram, *The Department of State in the Middle East*, 53–61, 106–15; Lenczowski, *The Middle East in World Affairs*, 689–93. For the evolution of wartime oil policy, see Painter, *Oil and the American Century*, 1–95; also, Feis, *Seen from E. A.*, 93–190.

5. Memorandum and annexes, Henderson to Byrnes, 13 November 1945, *FRUS: 1945*, 8:11–18.

6. The Soviet-Turkish Treaty of Friendship and Neutrality of 17 December 1925 was to expire on 7 November 1945 following its denunciation by the Soviet Union on 19 March 1945. Telegrams nos. 835 and 853, Harriman to Stettinius, 19 March and 21 March 1945, both in ibid., 1219–20, 1221–23.

7. Quotation from telegram no. 916, Wilson to Grew, 5 July 1945, *FRUS: The Conference of Berlin, 1945,* 1:1041–42; telegrams no. 817, Wilson to Grew, 18 June 1945; no. 844, Wilson to Grew, 22 June 1945; and no. 893, Wilson to Grew, 2 July 1945, all in ibid., 1020–22, 1024–26, 1033–34; telegram no. 1252, Wilson to Byrnes, 25 September 1945; telegram no. 3488, Kennan to Byrnes, 8 October 1945; and telegram no. 3547, Harriman to Byrnes, all in *FRUS: 1945,* 8:1248–49, 1252–53; Forrestal Diaries, 17 July 1945, 401, Naval History Division; SM-2610, 17 July 1945, *FRUS: The Conference of Berlin, 1945,* 2:1420–22.

8. The Montreux Convention was signed on 20 July 1936 by Bulgaria, France, Great Britain, Greece, Japan, Rumania, Turkey, the Soviet Union, and Yugoslavia. The United States was not a party to the agreement. For a thorough discussion of the Montreux Convention, see Howard, *Turkey, the Straits, and U.S. Policy,* 130–60.

9. Telegram no. 1049, Byrnes to Wilson, 30 October 1945, *FRUS: 1945,* 8:1265–66; "Memorandum Regarding the Montreux Convention," 30 June 1945; and memorandum, Allen to Dunn, 15 July 1945, both in *FRUS: The Conference of Berlin, 1945,* 1:1013–15, 1053–54; State Department minutes, Seventh Plenary Session, 23 July 1945; and "Protocol of the Proceedings of the Berlin Conference," 1 August 1945, both in *FRUS: The Conference of Berlin, 1945,* 2:301–5, 1496–97; Alvarez, *Bureaucracy and Cold War Diplomacy,* 54–66. Under the Montreux Convention warships of the Black Sea powers could pass the straits in time of peace. But during wartime Turkey had the right, under certain conditions, to deny passage to warships.

10. State Department memorandum, "The Problem of the Turkish Straits," 19 December 1945, *FRUS: 1946,* 7:801–4; telegram no. 1412, Wilson to Byrnes, 3 November 1945, *FRUS: 1945,* 8:1271–73. On Soviet propaganda, see telegram no. 3228, Harriman to Byrnes, 10 September 1945; and telegram no. 1604, Wilson to Byrnes, 22 December 1945, both in ibid, 1245–46, 1285–86; telegram no. 73, Wilson to Byrnes, 15 January 1946; telegram no. 161, Wilson to Byrnes, 2 February 1946; and telegram no. 195, Wilson to Byrnes, 13 February 1946, all in *FRUS: 1946,* 7:808–9, 813–14, 815–16. On the troop movements, see telegram no. 1371, Wilson to Byrnes, 27 October 1945; and telegram no. 1399, Wilson to Byrnes, 1 November 1945, both in *FRUS: 1945,* 8:1260–62, 1268.

11. Memorandum and encl., Henderson to Byrnes, 5 January 1946, 711.61/1-546, State; Kuniholm, *The Origins of the Cold War in the Near East,* 298–302.

12. Quotations from Rubin, *The Great Powers in the Middle East,* 83–84; and memorandum, Henderson to Byrnes, 23 August 1945, *FRUS: 1945,* 8:399–400; Lenczowski, *Russia and the West in Iran,* 263–76; Motter, *The Persian Corridor,* 240–41; Rubin, *Paved With Good Intentions,* 19–28; Mark, "Allied Relations in Iran, 1941–1947," 51–63.

13. Hess, "The Iranian Crisis," 126, 129–30.

14. Telegram no. 768, Murray to Byrnes, 25 September 1945; memorandum of conversation by Henderson, 20 November 1945; memorandum, Henderson to Byrnes, 28 November 1945; telegram no. 1134, Murray to Byrnes, 15 December 1945; letter, Minor to Henderson, 17 December 1945; telegram no. 4262, Harriman to Acheson, 23 December 1945; and telegram no. 4311, Har-

riman to Byrnes, 28 December 1945, all in *FRUS: 1945*, 8:417–19, 435, 461–62, 496–97, 501, 510–511, 517–19; Byrnes, *Speaking Frankly*, 118–121; Kuniholm, *The Origins of the Cold War in the Near East*, 274–79.

15. Memorandum by Henderson, [approx. 28 December 1945], *FRUS: 1946*, 7:1–6; DeSantis, *The Diplomacy of Silence*, 198–201.

16. Vandenberg, *The Private Papers of Senator Vandenberg*, 233.

17. Quoted in Messer, *The End of an Alliance*, 165–67, 262.

18. Gaddis, *The United States and the Origins of the Cold War*, 282–96.

19. Diary, 17 December 1945, Ayers Papers, Truman Library; Truman, *Memoirs*, 1:551–52; Ferrell, *Off the Record*, 53.

20. Messer, *The End of an Alliance*, 156–65; diary, 27 February 1946, Ayers Papers, Truman Library.

21. Telegram no. 40, Rossow to Byrnes, 5 March 1946, *FRUS: 1946*, 7:340. See also telegrams nos. 41 and 42, Rossow to Byrnes, 6 March 1946 and 7 March 1946, both in ibid., 342–43, 344–45.

22. Ibid., 347.

23. Byrnes, *Speaking Frankly*, 304; Hess, "The Iranian Crisis," 132–42; Gaddis, *The United States and the Origins of the Cold War*, 309–12; Allen, "Mission to Iran," 8–12, Allen Papers, Truman Library. For a detailed account of the confrontation over Iran, see Harbutt, *The Iron Curtain*, 217–66.

24. JCS 1641/3, 13 March 1946, file CCS 092 USSR (3-27-45) sec. 6, JCS. See also JCS 1641/1, 10 March 1946, ibid.

25. Schnabel, *The Joint Chiefs of Staff and National Policy*, 1:158–60; Rosenberg, "The U.S. Navy and the Problem of Oil in a Future War," 54–55; Herken, *The Winning Weapon*, 219–24; memorandum, Lincoln to Hull, 12 March 1946, file 350.05 Top Secret (State Dept. Red File), P&O; JPS 789, 2 March 1946; and JWPC 432/2, 27 April 1946, all in file CCS 381 USSR (3-2-46) sec. 1, JCS; JCS 1641/5, 11 April 1946, file CCS 092 USSR (3-27-45) sec. 6, JCS.

26. Forrestal wanted to send elements of the Eighth Fleet, normally based in Atlantic waters, into the Mediterranean to accompany the *Missouri*. Byrnes agreed with his proposal on 28 February, but after the start of the Iranian crisis he suggested a postponement, for fear that the dispatch of such a task force might seem a provocative act. Forrestal, however, made arrangements for two cruisers from the Eighth Fleet to join the *Missouri* on its Mediterranean cruise. See minutes, meetings of the Committee of Three, 28 February and 6 March 1946, C-3; Millis, *The Forrestal Diaries*, 141, 144–45; V. Davis, *Postwar Defense and the U.S. Navy*, 223–24; Xydis, *Greece and the Great Powers*, 156–59, 175–76; Steel, *Walter Lippmann and the American Century*, 427–28.

27. FPI 30, memorandum by SWNC Subcommittee on Foreign Policy Information, "Public Information Program on United States Aid to Greece," 4 March 1947, file CCS 092 (8-22-46) sec. 1, JCS; letter, Diamantopoulos to Taylor, 20 August 1945, *FRUS: 1945*, 8:233–34.

28. A leading student of the Second Round (December 1944–February 1945) of the Greek civil war has written, "Whatever their motives and deeds, the Greek Communists were truly their own agents and not Moscow's. Nevertheless, it must be recognized that had they perchance succeeded in seizing power once the battle started, it is difficult to see how they could have avoided becoming Stalin's helpless wards." Iatrides, *Revolt in Athens*, 279.

29. For Churchill, see Campbell and Herring, *The Diaries of Edward R. Stettinius, Jr.*, 231–32. For discussions of Greece during World War II and immediately afterward, see Iatrides, *Revolt in Athens*; and McNeill, *The Meta-*

morphosis of Greece, 65–79. For background on the Greek armed forces, see Gardner, "Civil War in Greece."

30. Telegrams B and C, Jackson to Lehman, 28 October 1945 and 27 October 1945; telegrams nos. 4015 and 4042, Kirk to Byrnes, 2 November 1945 and 4 November 1945, and telegram no. 1136, Byrnes to MacVeagh, 2 November 1945, all in *FRUS: 1945,* 8:247–55.

31. Memorandum, Henderson to Byrnes, 10 November 1945; memorandum, Byrnes to Truman, 10 November 1945, both in ibid., 263–67, *DSB* 14 (20 January 1946): 79; Paterson, *Soviet-American Confrontation,* 183–85.

32. Memorandum, Acheson to Truman, 7 August 1946; and telegram no. 1002, Acheson to MacVeagh, 14 August 1946, both in *FRUS: 1946,* 7:187–88, 190–91.

33. Quotation from despatch no. 2002, MacVeagh to Byrnes, 15 December 1945, *FRUS: 1945,* 8:284; telegram no. 64, MacVeagh to Byrnes, 11 January 1946; and despatch no. 2100, MacVeagh to Byrnes, 19 January 1946, both in *FRUS: 1946,* 7:91–92, 97–99; Iatrides, *Ambassador MacVeagh Reports,* 685–98.

34. The Export-Import Bank loan to Greece was approved in January 1946, the surplus property credit in May 1946. Between October 1944 and June 1947 Greece also received from the United Nations Relief and Rehabilitation Administration $416 million in aid, $312 million of which was contributed by the United States. Turkey received two Eximbank loans, one for $3.060 million in September 1945 and another for $25 million in July 1946. The surplus property credit of $10 million for Turkey was approved in May 1946. See Paterson, *Soviet-American Confrontation,* 185, 187, 191; U.S. Department of State, *U.S. Foreign Assistance,* 43, 45, 53; "Foreign Aid to Greece," 1 April 1950, folder Appointment—Ambassador to Greece, Grady Papers, Truman Library. On Iran's effort to secure American aid after World War II, see Ramazani, *Iran's Foreign Policy,* 154–59.

35. Memorandum, Acheson to Byrnes, 9 October 1945, *FRUS: 1945,* 8:43–48; memorandum, Henderson to Acheson, 4 June 1946; and memorandum, Luthringer to Henderson, 20 June 1946, both in *FRUS: 1946,* 7:7–9, 10–14.

36. Quotation from telegram no. 220, Hull to Dreyfus, 21 August 1942, *FRUS: 1942,* 4:247–48; letter, Stimson to Hull, 23 June 1944; and telegram no. 497, Stettinius to Ford, 14 August 1944, both in *FRUS: 1944,* 5:412–13, 425–26; letter, Byrnes to Patterson, 17 October 1945, *FRUS: 1945,* 8:534–36; letter, Handy to Ridley, 24 September 1942; memorandum, Ridley to Hull, 8 November 1944; and memorandum for Smith, 19 May 1945, all in folder Ridley Mission, file 091 Iran Top Secret, P&O; Motter, *The Persian Corridor,* 461–80.

37. SC/R-184, 5 February 1946; and SWNCC 202/2, 21 March 1946, both in *FRUS: 1946,* 1:1141–42, 1145–60; telegram no. 318, Murray to Byrnes, 12 March 1946, 891.24/3-1246, State; memorandum, Ludlow to Exton, 19 March 1946, 891.24/3-1246, State; telegram no. 236, Byrnes to Murray, 22 March 1946, *FRUS: 1946,* 7:372–73; memorandum no. 864/110, Turkish chargé to Acheson, 5 July 1946, 867.24/7-546, State; memorandum, Acheson to Turkish chargé, 6 August 1946, 867.24/7-546, State; airgram no. A-207, Wilson to Byrnes, 11 September 1946, 867.24/9-1146, State.

38. Quotation from telegram no. 856, Wilson to Byrnes, 12 August 1946; memorandum, Orekhov to Acheson, 7 August 1946; telegram no. 853, Wilson to Byrnes, 10 August 1946, all in *FRUS: 1946,* 7:827–29, 834–35, 836–38; Leffler, "Strategy, Diplomacy, and the Cold War," 810–11.

39. Memorandum by the Joint Chiefs of Staff to Patterson and Forrestal, 23 August 1946, *FRUS: 1946*, 7:857.

40. Millis, *The Forrestal Diaries*, 191; Forrestal Diaries, 14 August 1946, 1201–3, Naval History Division; memorandum, Jones to Henderson, 9 August 1946, *FRUS: 1946*, 7:830–33.

41. Telegram no. 4122, Acheson to Byrnes, *FRUS: 1946*, 7:840–42.

42. Quotations from ibid. Acheson wrote about an incident that took place during this meeting as follows: "General Eisenhower asked me in a whisper whether I had made it sufficiently clear that the course we had recommended could lead to war. Before I could answer, the President asked whether the General had anything to add. I repeated his question to me." Truman then delivered, according to Acheson's account, a lecture about the strategic implications of the Near East, which left no doubt that he understood the consequences of the recommendations. While someone may have whispered that question to Acheson, it could not have been Eisenhower, who was in Mexico City that afternoon and did not return to Washington until four days later. General Thomas T. Handy, the deputy chief of staff, represented the army at the meeting. Eisenhower, however, clearly did not share the view that the United States should use force to defend the Dardanelles. He met with Admiral Chester W. Nimitz, the chief of naval operations, and Forrestal on 21 August, and according to the latter's account: "Much to Nimitz's surprise and my own, he [Eisenhower] added . . . that neither could he conceive Russian occupation of a part of the Dardanelles area being an occasion for war." Forrestal curtly dismissed Eisenhower's views as an example of "the Army's inability to grasp the importance of control of the seas and their lack of appreciation of strategy in the broadest geographic terms." See Acheson, *Present at the Creation*, 195–96; memorandum, Handy to Eisenhower, 15 August 1946, file 092 Top Secret (76/5), P&O; Galambos, *The Papers of Dwight D. Eisenhower*, 9:2345; Forrestal Diaries, 21 August 1946, 1217–18, Naval History Division. An account of the Eisenhower incident similar to Acheson's also appears in J. Jones, *The Fifteen Weeks*, 63–64.

43. Quotations from telegram no. 4122, Acheson to Byrnes, 15 August 1946, *FRUS: 1946*, 7:840–42; and Millis, *The Forrestal Diaries*, 192; minute by Elsey, 12 July 1946, folder 1 (Foreign Relations-Russia), Elsey Papers, Truman Library.

44. Quotation from memorandum, Vandenberg to Truman, 24 August 1946, folder Central Intelligence—memoranda, 1945–1948, Intelligence File, PSF; CIG Special Study No. 4, 18 September 1946, folder Central Intelligence Reports—CIG, Intelligence File, PSF; minutes, meeting of the Secretaries of State, War, and Navy, 2 October 1946, 767.68119/10-246, State; telegram no. 589, Acheson to Wilson, 16 August 1946; memorandum, Acheson to Orekhov, 19 August 1946; telegram no. 912, Wilson to Byrnes, 22 August 1946; telegram no. 1035, Bursley to Byrnes, 26 September 1946; telegram no. 1785, Acheson to Smith, 8 October 1946; and despatch no. 1187, Wilson to Byrnes, 19 October 1946, all in *FRUS: 1946*, 7:843–44, 847–48, 852–55, 860–66, 874–75, 879–93; Howard, *Turkey, the Straits, and U.S. Policy*, 244–60.

45. On 7 September, the navy obtained the State Department's permission to station indefinitely the carrier *Franklin D. Roosevelt* in Mediterranean waters. On 30 September, Forrestal announced that the navy would maintain a permanent force in the Mediterranean. Millis, *The Forrestal Diaries*, 211; memorandum of conversation by Riddleberger, 7 September 1946, folder Memoranda of

Conversation 1946–1947, EUR; Albion and Connery, *Forrestal and the Navy,* 187–88.

46. Memorandum, JCS to Patterson and Forrestal, 23 August 1946, *FRUS: 1946,* 7:857–58. For a different interpretation, which stresses the strategic imperative behind American military assistance to Turkey, see Leffler, "Strategy, Diplomacy, and the Cold War," 812–15.

47. Quotations from letter, Clayton to Byrnes, 12 September 1946, *FRUS: 1946,* 7:209–13; minutes, meeting of the Committee of Three, 11 September 1946, C-3.

48. Telegram no. 4787, Byrnes to Clayton, 24 September 1946, *FRUS: 1946,* 7:223–24.

49. Telegram no. 5007, Byrnes to Acheson, 5 October 1946, 740.00119 Council/10-546, State; letter, Patterson to Clayton, 12 September 1946, file 091 Turkey (12 Sept. 46), C/S; Millis, *The Forrestal Diaries,* 192; memorandum, JCS to Patterson and Forrestal, 23 August 1946; and memorandum by the British Embassy in Greece to the American Embassy in Greece, 5 November 1946, both in *FRUS: 1946,* 7:857–58, 913–15; E. May, *"Lessons" of the Past,* 41–42.

50. Clifford based his report, in part, on memoranda on Soviet-American relations that he solicited from the State, War, and Navy Departments and from the president's senior foreign policy advisers. Clifford's principal assistant, George M. Elsey, conceived of the report as a "great all-inclusive evaluation + definition of policy." Minute by Elsey, 19 July 1946, folder 1 (Foreign Relations—Russia), Clifford Papers, Truman Library. For background on the Clifford report, see Yergin, *Shattered Peace,* 241–45; Donovan, *Conflict and Crisis,* 221–22.

51. The Clifford memorandum is reprinted in Krock, *Memoirs,* 419–82. (Quotations from 477, 479).

52. Gaddis, *The United States and the Origins of the Cold War,* 284. See also Powers, "Who Fathered Containment?," 526–43; McLellan, "Who Fathered Containment?," 205–26.

53. At a meeting of the Committee of Three on 25 September, Forrestal and Patterson endorsed a new State Department arms policy that permitted transfers of military equipment to nations whose independence and territorial integrity were important to the security of the United States. Byrnes gave his consent five days later. State Department officials prepared a memorandum for Truman asking his approval of the policy as well, but there is no indication on the copy in the State Department records whether the memorandum was actually presented to the president, and if it was, whether he consented. But on 28 October, Byrnes and his advisers apparently changed their minds and decided to amend SC/R-184 to provide the secretary of state with new authority to make exceptional arms transfers. The department's decision not to adopt a new general arms policy at that time may have been made because the Policy Committee on Arms and Armaments had been preparing a new statement of policy since July and planned to submit its recommendations shortly. Minutes, meeting of the Committee of Three, 25 September 1946, C-3; Forrestal Diaries, 25 September 1945, 1274–75, Naval History Division; telegram no. 4906, Byrnes to Clayton, 30 September 1946, 740.00119 Council/9-3046, State; memorandum for the president, 8 October 1946, 800.24/10-846, State.

54. Quotation from memorandum, Hilldring to Acheson, 29 October 1946, *FRUS: 1946,* 7:255; telegram no. 5007, Byrnes to Acheson, 5 October 1946, 740.00119 Council/10-546, State; minutes, meeting of the Committee of Three, 6 November 1946, C-3.

55. Policy and Information Statement Prepared in the Department of State, 15 July 1946; and telegram no. 1293, Allen to Byrnes, 30 September 1946, both in *FRUS: 1946*, 7:507–9, 518–20; Pfau, "Containment in Iran," 359–72; PCA M-15, 9 September 1946, PCA.

56. Memorandum, Henderson to Acheson, 8 October 1946, *FRUS: 1946*, 7:523–25.

57. Memorandum, SWNCC to Hilldring, 12 October 1946, ibid., 529–32.

58. Quotations from telegram no. 1400, Allen to Byrnes, 22 October 1946; and memorandum, Henderson to Acheson, 18 October 1946, both in ibid., 539–40, 533–35; Allen, "Mission to Iran," 37–39, 109–25, Allen Papers, Truman Library; letter, Ala to Henderson, 15 October 1946, FW 891.51/10-1546, State; telegram no. 1447, Allen to Byrnes, 8 November 1946, FW 891.51/11-846, State; and telegram no. 948, Acheson to Allen, 14 November 1946, 891.51/11-846, State.

59. Memorandum, Hilldring to Acheson, 29 October, 1946; telegram no. 976, Acheson to Allen, 22 November 1946; and telegram no. 263, Sutton to Byrnes, 12 December 1946, all in *FRUS: 1946*, 7:255, 546–47, 561–62; Hess, "The Iranian Crisis," 143–44; Pfau, "Containment in Iran," 369–72; Kuniholm, *The Origins of the Cold War in the Near East*, 383–95; Allen, "Mission to Iran," 51–65, Allen Papers, Truman Library.

60. The American advisory mission took no part in the occupation of Azerbaijan. See letter, Grow to Stokes, 10 June 1946, folder M/G R. W. Grow—Iran, Fairchild Working Papers, Center of Military History.

61. Quotations from memorandum and annex by Henderson, 21 October 1946; and letter, Acheson to Wilson, 8 November 1946, both in *FRUS: 1946*, 7:893–97, 916–17; Leffler, "Strategy, Diplomacy, and the Cold War," 814–16.

62. Memorandum to Henderson, [approx. 20 November 1946], file 337 Top Secret (1), P&O; memorandum of conversation in Henderson's office, 18 November 1946, 867.20/11-1846, State; minutes, meetings of the Committee of Three, 6 November 1946 and 13 November 1946, C-3; telegram no. 1180, Wilson to Byrnes, 10 November 1946; and letter, Henderson to Wilson, 12 November 1946, both in *FRUS: 1946*, 7:917–19.

63. Letters, Wilson to Acheson, 7 December 1946; and Wilson to Henderson, 7 December 1946, both in *FRUS: 1946*, 7:920–22; telegram no. 15, Byrnes to Wilson, 10 January 1947; and telegram no. 38, Wilson to Byrnes, 17 January 1947, both in *FRUS: 1947*, 5:3–4, 7–8; telegram no. 27, Byrnes to Wilson, 20 January 1947, 868.24/1-2047, State. In the meantime, Turkey continued to submit requests for military aid. See, for example, despatch no. 70/14, Wilson to Acheson, 16 January 1947, 867.24/1-1647, State.

64. Quotation from Alexander, *The Prelude to the Truman Doctrine*, 205–24; telegram no. 1384, MacVeagh to Byrnes, 11 October 1986, *FRUS: 1946*, 7:233–35; telegram no. 1500, MacVeagh to Byrnes, 2 November 1946, 868.00/11-246, State; ORE 6/1, 7 February 1947, folder Central Intelligence Reports, ORE—1947, Nos. 1-14, Intelligence File, PSF.

65. Djilas, *Conversations with Stalin*, 181–83. The best account of the beginning of the Third Round of the Greek civil war is in Woodhouse, *The Struggle for Greece*, 169–202. See also O'Ballance, *The Greek Civil War*, 121–35.

66. Memorandum by McCormack, 6 September 1946, file 092 Top Secret, P&O. See also memorandum, War Department Intelligence Division to Eisenhower, 29 August 1946, file 091 Greece (29 August 1946), C/S; and memorandum, Bonesteel to Lincoln, 6 December 1946, 868.00/12-646, State.

67. Telegram no. 1307, MacVeagh to Byrnes, 30 September 1946, *FRUS: 1946*, 7:227.

68. Memorandum prepared in NEA, 21 October 1946, ibid., 240–45. This NEA memorandum was a revised version of McCormack's memorandum.

69. Woodhouse, *The Struggle for Greece*, 185–87; telegram no. 1659, MacVeagh to Byrnes, 30 November 1946, 868.00/11-3046, State.

70. Xydis, *Greece and the Great Powers*, 434; memorandum, Chamberlin to Norstad, 13 December 1946, file 400 Top Secret (39), P&O; telegram no. 1721, MacVeagh to Byrnes, 16 December 1946, *FRUS: 1946*, 7:282–83; memorandum, Byrnes to Truman, 20 December 1946, 868.00/12-2046, State; telegram no. 10186, Gallman to Byrnes, 20 December 1946, 868.24/12-2046, State.

71. Telegram no. 6, MacVeagh to Byrnes, 3 January 1947, 868.24/1-347, State; memorandum, Norstad to Chamberlin, 17 December 1946, file 400 Top Secret (39), P&O; briefing paper, Sparrow to Eisenhower, 13 January 1947, file 092 Top Secret, P&O; memorandum, Bastion to State Department, 24 February 1947, file 400 Top Secret, P&O.

72. Memorandum, Jernegan to Henderson, 30 December 1946, 868.24/12-3046, State; PCA M-34, 7 February 1947, and enclosed memoranda, Henderson to Acheson, 4 February 1947, and Crain to Baxter, 5 February 1947, PCA.

73. Telegram no. 237, MacVeagh to Marshall, 19 February 1947, *FRUS: 1947*, 5:27–28; memorandum, Henderson to Acheson, 20 February 1947, 868.00/2-2047, State; Xydis, *Greece and the Great Powers*, 432–36, 472–74.

74. Letter, Porter to Clayton, 17 February 1947; and telegram no. 232, Porter to Marshall, 19 February 1947, both in *FRUS: 1947*, 5:17–22, 26.

75. Telegram no. 227, Ethridge to Marshall, 17 February 1947, ibid., 24.

76. Telegram no. 243, MacVeagh to Marshall, 20 February 1947, ibid., 28.

77. Memorandum, Acheson to Marshall, 21 February 1947, ibid., 29–31; J. Jones, *The Fifteen Weeks*, 131; Acheson, *Present at the Creation*, 217.

78. Aide-memoires, British embassy to the State Department, both 21 February 1947, *FRUS: 1947*, 5:32–37.

79. Senate Committee on Foreign Relations, *Legislative Origins of the Truman Doctrine*, 3–4; Xydis, *Greece and the Great Powers*, 243, 317, 332, 351; telegrams nos. 684 and 1130, Gallman to Marshall, 31 January 1947 and 19 February 1947, both in *FRUS: 1947*, 5:13–14, 26–27; Dalton, *High Tide and After*, 206–7; Watt, "Withdrawal from Greece," 103–25; Byrnes, *Speaking Frankly*, 300; Henderson oral history, 80, Truman Library; Alexander, *The Prelude to the Truman Doctrine*, 240–44; Wittner, *American Intervention in Greece*, 64–66; Louis, *The British Empire in the Middle East*, 91–102.

80. Quotation from Henderson oral history, 80, Truman Library; "Memorandum [by Henderson] Regarding Proposals Contained in British notes of February 24 Relating to Greece and Turkey," n.d., FW 868.00/2-2447, State; Acheson, *Present at the Creation*, 217–19; minutes, meeting of the Secretaries of State, War, and Navy, 25 February 1947; and memorandum and annex, Marshall to Truman, 26 February 1947, both in *FRUS: 1947*, 5:56–60.

81. Quotation from Acheson, *Present at the Creation*, 218; minutes, first meeting of the Special Committee to Study Assistance to Greece and Turkey, 24 February 1947, *FRUS: 1947*, 5:45–47; Henderson oral history, 80–82, Truman Library.

82. Quotation from minutes, first meeting of the Special Committee to

Study Assistance to Greece and Turkey, 24 February 1947, *FRUS: 1947,* 5:45–47; J. Jones, *The Fifteen Weeks,* 130; Kennan, *Memoirs,* 313–14.

83. Quotations from unnumbered telegram, Porter to Truman, 3 March 1947, folder Correspondence and Memoranda, 1946–47, Porter Papers, Truman Library; and letter, MacVeagh to Acheson, 6 March 1947, 868.00/3-647, State.

84. Summary sheet, Chamberlin to Eisenhower, 24 February 1947, file 091 Greece (24 February 1947), C/S; memorandum, Lincoln to Patterson, 26 February 1947, file 092 Top Secret, sec. 6A, P&O; memorandum, Arnold to Eisenhower, 6 March 1947, file 091 Greece Top Secret, P&O.

85. Quotation from FPI 30, "Public Information Program on United States Aid to Greece," by SWNC Subcommittee on Foreign Policy Information, file CCS 092 (8-22-46) sec. 1, JCS; memorandum, Lincoln to Patterson, 26 February 1947, file 096 Top Secret, sec. 6A, P&O; House Committee on International Relations, *Selected Executive Session Hearings,* 6:349.

86. Kennan, *Memoirs,* 316–17.

87. Memorandum, Kennan to Acheson, 6 March 1947, 868.00/3-647, State, J. Jones, *The Fifteen Weeks,* 154–55; minutes, meeting of the Secretaries of State, War, and Navy, 12 March 1947, *FRUS: 1947,* 5:109–10.

88. Memorandum, JCS to Patterson and Forrestal, 13 March 1947, *FRUS: 1947,* 5:110–14.

89. Memorandum, Henderson to Acheson, n.d., ibid., 52. On Congress, economy in government, and foreign aid, see Gaddis, *The United States and the Origins of the Cold War,* 341–46; Freeland, *The Truman Doctrine,* 75–81; J. Jones, *The Fifteen Weeks,* 90–91; Hartmann, *Truman and the 80th Congress,* 11.

90. Quotations from Acheson, *Present at the Creation,* 219; memorandum and annex, Marshall to Truman, 27 February 1947, *FRUS: 1947,* 5:60–62. The best account of the White House meeting is in J. Jones, *The Fifteen Weeks,* 138–42. Jones's knowledge of that meeting came primarily from conversations with Acheson. See "JMJ Notes on Acheson's Presentation to Dep't Working Group," 28 February 1947, folder Truman Doctrine—Important, Relevant Papers, Jones Papers; and memorandum for file, 12 March 1947, folder Drafts of Truman Doctrine, Jones Papers, Truman Library.

91. Minutes, meeting of the SWNC Subcommittee on Foreign Policy Information, 28 February 1947, folder Truman Doctrine—Important, Relevant Papers, Jones Papers, Truman Library.

92. FPI 30, "Public Information Program on United States Aid to Greece," by SWNC Subcommittee on Foreign Policy Information, 4 March 1947, file CCS 092 (8-22-46) sec. 1, JCS.

93. Notes on Cabinet Meeting, 7 March 1947, folder Cabinet Meetings: Jan. 3–Dec. 19, 1947, set 2, Connelly Files; J. Jones, *The Fifteen Weeks,* 152–53. For accounts of the drafting of the president's message to Congress, see ibid., 148–70; and Iselin, "The Truman Doctrine," chap. 11.

94. Minutes, meeting of SWNC Subcommittee on Foreign Policy Information, 28 February 1947, folder Truman Doctrine—Important, Relevant Papers, Jones Papers, Truman Library. A poll conducted at the end of March 1947 did reveal some opposition to the extension of military aid to Greece and Turkey. Among those who raised objections to the administration's proposals, opposition to military aid was the fifth most frequently expressed criticism. Other objections included the failure to act through a multilateral organization (mentioned by 14.8 percent of the respondents); the establishment of a precedent

for endless foreign aid (12.6 percent); the possibility of aid increasing chances of war (11.7 percent); the belief that domestic needs were more important (10.4 percent); and a dislike of military aid (9.6 percent). Overall, 51.0 percent of the respondents expressed some objection to the president's proposals; 62.3 percent expressed full or qualified support; and 24.2 percent expressed complete or qualified opposition. Roper, "A Study of What People Say in Describing their Reactions toward the Truman Proposal for Aid to Greece and Turkey," April 1947, folder State Department Correspondence, 1946–47, WHCF.

95. Quotations from *PP: 1947,* 176–80; "Foreign Aid to Greece," April 1950, folder Appointment—Ambassador to Greece, Grady Papers, Truman Library. See also Brown and Opie, *American Foreign Assistance,* 129.

96. Quotation from subannex to memorandum, Howard to Acheson, 4 March 1947, *FRUS: 1947,* 5:85; J. Jones, *The Fifteen Weeks,* 158–59; minutes, meeting of the Rearmament Subcommittee of SWNCC, 5 March 1947; and memorandum for record by Sparrow, 6 March 1947, both in folder Rearmament Subcommittee of SWNCC #1, ISA; memorandum and encl., Acheson to Truman, 6 March 1947, folder Foreign Aid—Truman Doctrine (Greece-Turkey), Elsey Papers, Truman Library. For the text of the bill that the administration submitted to Congress, see House Committee on International Relations, *Selected Executive Sessions Hearings,* 6:417–18.

97. Quotations from Kennan, *Memoirs,* 320; "The President's Message to Congress on the Greek Situation, Revised Draft 3/6/47," encl. to memorandum, Kennan to Acheson, 6 March 1947, 868.00/3-647, State.

98. Bohlen, *Witness to History,* 261; Pogue, *George C. Marshall: Statesman,* 165.

99. Memorandum, Elsey to Clifford, 8 March 1947, folder Truman Doctrine Speech 3/12/47, Elsey Papers, Truman Library.

100. *PP: 1947,* 176–80; minutes by Elsey, n.d., folder Truman Doctrine Speech 3/12/47, Elsey Papers, Truman Library; Truman, *Memoirs,* 2:105.

101. Excerpts from telephone conversation between Vinson and Forrestal, 13 March 1947, speech file, folder speech to Congress on Greece, 3/12/47, Clifford Files, Truman Library.

102. Senate Committee on Foreign Relations, *Legislative Origins of the Truman Doctrine,* 128. See also Vandenberg, *The Private Papers of Senator Vandenberg,* 342–43.

103. Hartmann, *Truman and the 80th Congress,* 64; J. Campbell, *The United States in World Affairs, 1947–1948,* 34–48; House Subcommittee on Appropriations, *Supplemental Appropriation Bill for 1948,* 1105–386; Henderson, "Congressman John Taber of New York," 331–33. The Senate approved the Greek-Turkish Aid bill on 22 April by a margin of 67 to 23, the House on 9 May by a tally of 287 to 107.

104. Senate Committee on Foreign Relations, *Legislative Origins of the Truman Doctrine,* 10.

105. House Committee on International Relations, *Selected Executive Session Hearings,* 6:403–10.

106. Senate Committee on Foreign Relations, *Legislative Origins of the Truman Doctrine,* 54, 95.

107. Ibid., 128.

108. Quotations from 61 Stat. 572; Acheson, *Present at the Creation,* 224; and memorandum, "Public Opinion Survey of Reactions to President Truman's Proposal Regarding Greece and Turkey," [April 1947], State Dept. Correspondence, 1946–47, WHCF; Roper, "A Study of What People Say in Describ-

ing Their Reactions Toward the Truman Proposal for Aid to Greece and Turkey," April 1947, ibid.; Senate Committee on Foreign Relations, *Legislative Origins of the Truman Doctrine*, 13–17, 101–17; Wittner, *American Intervention in Greece*, 90–92.

109. Senate Committee on Foreign Relations, *Assistance to Greece and Turkey*, 1947, 7.

110. Senate Committee on Foreign Relations, *Legislative Origins of the Truman Doctrine*, 17.

111. Quotation from Senate Committee on Foreign Relations, *Assistance to Greece and Turkey*, 31; Freeland, *The Truman Doctrine*, 102–14; Gaddis, "Was the Truman Doctrine a Real Turning Point?" 390–91.

112. Quotation from memorandum, Marshall to Truman, 26 February 1947, *FRUS: 1947*, 5:58; memorandum, Henderson to Acheson, n.d.; minutes, meeting of the Secretaries of State, War, and Navy, 26 February 1947; memorandum, Crain to Jernegan, 4 March 1947; and letter, Acheson to Patterson, 5 March 1947, all in ibid., 47–48, 56–57, 81–84, 94–95; J. Jones, *The Fifteen Weeks*, 137–38.

113. For the genesis of SWNCC 202/2, "Policy Concerning Provision of United States Government Military Supplies for Post-War Armed Forces of Foreign Nations," 21 March 1946, and SC/R-184, "Policy of the [State] Department Regarding Disposal to Foreign Governments of Military-Type Surplus Equipment," 5 February 1946, see above, chap. 1.

114. Quotation from PCA M-1, 3 June 1946; PCA M-6, 3 July 1946; PCA M-15, 9 September 1946; PCA M-27, 13 December 1946; and PCA M-28, 20 December 1946, all in PCA; minutes of the 206th Meeting of the Secretary's Staff Committee, 20 December 1946; and SC-208, memorandum by the Secretary's Staff Committee, 20 December 1946, both in *FRUS: 1946*, 1:1185–96.

115. At the request of the State Department's Office of Far Eastern Affairs, SWNCC 202/4 contained no reference to the approved programs of military aid to China. These programs had been suspended in August 1946 at the request of General George C. Marshall and would be resumed only with the approval of the secretary of state. Minutes, 206th Meeting of the Secretary's Staff Committee, 20 December 1946, *FRUS: 1946*, 1:1185–88; PCA M-27, 13 December 1946, PCA.

116. Quotations from SWNCC 202/4, 8 January 1947, folder SWNCC 202, SWNCC; memorandum, Cummins to Crain, 11 February 1947, folder Rearmament Subcommittee of SWNCC #1, ISA; and United Nations General Assembly Resolution, 14 December 1946, *FRUS: 1946*, 1:1100.

117. Memorandum, Wooten to Connelly, 21 January 1947, folder Rearmament Committee of SWNCC #1, ISA; PCA D-13b, 25 February 1947, PCA.

118. Memorandum, Mosely to Raynor, 22 March 1946, FW 800.24 FLC/3-2246, State; memorandum of conversation by Exton, 29 March 1946, 800.24 FLC/3-2946, State; letter, Patterson to Byrnes, 1 July 1946; and memorandum for record by Twitchell, 14 August 1946, both in folder ABC 400.3295 (15 March 1944), sec. 1C, OPD.

119. Under the terms of the Surplus Property Act, the War Department could not be reimbursed for these expenses. Funds received from foreign governments for these services were deposited in the Treasury as miscellaneous receipts and not credited to departmental appropriations. See Department of the Army presentation to JCS committee, "Military Assistance to Foreign Powers," 3 September 1948, file 320, sec. 3A, pt. 1, P&O.

120. Quotation from SWNCC 202/5/D, 8 January 1947, folder SWNCC 202,

SWNCC; summary sheet, Norstad to Patterson and Eisenhower, 20 December 1946; memorandum, Lincoln to Petersen, 20 December 1946; summary sheet, Norstad to Patterson and Eisenhower, 23 December 1946; letter, Littlejohn to Patterson, 16 January 1947, and letter, Acheson to Patterson, 21 January 1947, all in file 400 Top Secret, sec. 2, P&O.

121. PCA D-13b, 25 February 1947, folder Rearmament Subcommittee of SWNCC #1, ISA. On the military's penchant for formulaic policies, see Betts, *Soldiers, Statesmen, and Cold War Crises,* 157.

122. Memorandum, Elliott to Crain, 13 February 1947, folder Rearmament Subcommittee of SWNCC #1, ISA. On 13 February, the Security Council passed a resolution that instructed the Commission on Conventional Armaments to submit recommendations for the reduction of armaments and armed forces and for effective safeguards to insure international compliance with any such reduction. In the debate on that resolution, American representatives emphasized that conditions of international security would have to prevail before there could be any meaningful limitations on armaments and armed forces. See *FRUS: 1947,* 1:327–415.

123. Quotation from memorandum, Cummins to Crain, 11 February 1947; memorandum, Dreier to Crain, 5 February 1947; report by the Rearmament Subcommittee of SWNCC, 26 February 1947; minutes of the Meeting of the Rearmament Subcommittee of SWNCC, 5 March 1947; and memorandum, Crain to Sparrow, 19 March 1947, all in folder Rearmament Subcommittee of SWNCC #1, ISA.

124. Quotations from letter, Acheson to Patterson, 5 March 1947, *FRUS: 1947,* 5:94–95; and J. Jones, *The Fifteen Weeks,* 200, 201; memorandum by Hilldring, 17 March 1947, *FRUS: 1947,* 3:198–99; SWN-5231, 18 March 1947, folder SWNCC 382, SWNCC; B. Smith, *The Shadow Warriors,* 134; Gimbel, *The Origins of the Marshall Plan,* 9.

125. Quotations from SWNCC 360, 21 April 1947, *FRUS: 1947,* 3:204, 219; SWNCC Memorandum for Information No. 78, "Appreciation of Foreseeable Foreign Needs for U.S. Military Assistance Through Fiscal Year 1948," 22 April 1947, file 334 Rearmament Committee, SWNCC.

126. Quotations from SWNCC 360, 21 April 1947, *FRUS: 1947,* 3:217; Paterson, *Soviet-American Confrontation,* 208–9; McLellan, *Dean Acheson,* 126.

127. SWNCC 360, 21 April 1947, *FRUS: 1947,* 1:725–26.

128. Quotations from SWNCC 360, 21 April 1947, ibid., 3:208.

129. Memorandum, Eisenhower to JCS, 10 May 1947, in Galambos, *The Papers of Dwight D. Eisenhower,* 8:1701; cable WOC 19, Chamberlin to Bonesteel, 27 March 1947, file 091 Latin America, P&O. See also letter, Patterson to Marshall, 11 March 1947, *FRUS: 1947,* 5:105–7.

130. The SWNCC Committee assessed Soviet intentions in the seven countries that might require emergency assistance as follows: domination of Greece, Turkey, Iran, and Austria; establishment of a Communist government in Italy, which was tantamount to Soviet control; predominant influence over all of Korea; neutralization of France; and strengthening of the French Communist party as the basis for a pro-Soviet regime. SWNCC 360, annexes C, D, and E to app. A, 23 July 1947, file SWNCC 360-360/2, pt. 1, SWNCC. Also SWNCC 360, 21 April 1947, *FRUS: 1947,* 1:725–33.

131. *FRUS: 1947,* 1:726, 732–33.

132. The Joint Chiefs listed the following priorities for assistance based on urgency of need and importance to American security: 1. Great Britain;

2. France; 3. Germany; 4. Italy; 5. Greece; 6. Turkey; 7. Austria; 8. Japan; 9. Belgium; 10. Netherlands; 11. Latin America; 12. Spain; 13. Korea; 14. China; 15. the Philippines; 16. Canada.

133. SWNCC 360/1, 12 May 1947, *FRUS: 1947*, 1:734–50.

134. Eisenhower quoted in Kolodziej, *The Uncommon Defense and Congress,* 56–65; *PP: 1947*, 55–68.

135. Quotation from disposition form, Lutes to Norstad, 3 May 1947, file 092 Top Secret, P&O; summary sheet, Hall to Norstad, 19 May 1947, file 400 (19 May 47), C/S; memorandum, Norstad to Lutes, 7 May 1947, file 400 Top Secret, P&O.

136. Nations that "might" need arms aid were Iraq, Egypt, Afghanistan, India, Burma, the Netherlands East Indies, Thailand, and Palestine.

137. "Appreciation of Foreseeable Needs for U.S. Military Assistance during the Next Three to Five Years," report by the Rearmament Subcommittee of SWNCC to Special *Ad Hoc* Committee, 10 July 1947, folder Foreseeable Military Assistance to Foreign Nations for Next 3–5 Years, ISA.

138. Quotation from State Department Press Release, 4 June 1947, *FRUS: 1947*, 3:237; Gaddis, "Was the Truman Doctrine a Real Turning Point?," 390–91. On the origins of the Marshall Plan, see three articles by Hogan: "The Search for a Creative Peace," 267–85; "Paths to Plenty," 337–66; and "American Marshall Planners," 44–72; also, Gimbel, *The Origins of the Marshall Plan;* and Arkes, *Bureaucracy, the Marshall Plan, and the National Interest.*

139. SWNCC 382, 5 August 1947 file SWNCC 382 series, SWNCC.

140. Quotations from report by Rearmament Subcommittee for Special *Ad Hoc* Committee, 10 July 1947, folder Foreseeable Military Assistance to Foreign Nations for Next 3–5 Years, ISA; summary sheet, Norstad to SS&P, 7 May 1947, file 400 Top Secret (39), P&O; summary sheet, Norstad to Eisenhower, 9 June 1947; and memorandum for record, 18 June 1947, both in ibid.; memorandum for record by Sibley, 6 June 1947; and memorandum, Lutes to Eisenhower, 1 August 1947, both in file 400 (154), P&O.

141. SWNCC 360/2, 30 June 1947, file SWNCC 360-360/2, Pt. 1, SWNCC; SWN-5602, 30 July 1947, file SWNCC 382 series, SWNCC; SANA 5827, 19 November 1947, ibid.

142. Quotation from SWNCC 202/4, 8 January 1947, folder SWNCC 202, SWNCC; Wittner, *American Intervention in Greece,* 231.

CHAPTER 5

1. Memorandum, Sparrow to Wedemeyer, 31 October 1947, file 337 Top Secret, P&O.

2. NSC 14/1, 1 July 1948, *FRUS: 1948*, 1: pt. 2, 587.

3. See, for example, staff study no. 3736 by the War Department Intelligence Division, 15 May 1947, file 350.05 Top Secret, P&O; speech by Kennan, "Problems of U.S. Foreign Policy After Moscow," 6 May 1947, folder speeches, articles, and lectures, unpublished—1947, April to May, Kennan Papers, Mudd Library; minutes, 46th meeting of the Policy Planning Staff, 21 August 1947, PPS.

4. Memorandum by the Advisory Steering Committee, 29 September 1947, *FRUS: 1947*, 3:475.

5. CIA 1, 26 September 1947, Intelligence File, PSF.

6. PPS 6, 14 August 1947, *FRUS: 1947*, 3:361; Ulam, *Expansion and Coexistence*, 459–61; Paterson, *On Every Front*, 59–62. For background information on the European Recovery Program, see especially Hogan, *The Marshall Plan*; also, Wilson, *The Marshall Plan, 1947–1951*; Arkes, *Bureaucracy, the Marshall Plan, and the National Interest*; and Price, *The Marshall Plan and Its Meaning*.

7. Memorandum and annex, Bohlen to Lovett, 2 September 1947, *FRUS: 1947*, 1:761–65.

8. PPS 13, 6 November 1947, ibid., 770–71; Millis, *The Forrestal Diaries*, 340–42.

9. Yergin, *Shattered Peace*, 328.

10. Vandenberg, *The Private Papers of Senator Vandenberg*, 378; letter, Vandenberg to Zimmerman, 9 December 1947, folder correspondence, Nov.–Dec. 1947, Vandenberg Papers, Bentley Historical Library.

11. 91 Stat. 934.

12. *PP: 1947*, 515–29; Freeland, *The Truman Doctrine*, 187–200; Hartmann, *Truman and the 80th Congress*, 116–20.

13. CIA 2, 14 November 1947; and CIA 3, 17 December 1947, both in CIA Collection, Modern Military Branch, NA; memorandum, Hillenkoetter to Truman, 7 November 1947, folder Central Intelligence Memoranda, 1945–48, Intelligence File, PSF; ORE 64, 31 December 1947, folder Central Intelligence Reports—ORE—1947, ibid.; PPS/13, 6 November 1947, *FRUS: 1947*, 1:771.

14. Quotation from memorandum, Livesay to Griswold, 21 August 1947, file 091 Greece Top Secret, P&O; Amen, *American Foreign Policy in Greece*, 130–44; Wittner, *American Intervention in Greece*, 223–31.

15. Quotations from memorandum, MacVeagh to Henderson, n.d.; and report by Chamberlin to Eisenhower, 20 October 1947, both in *FRUS: 1947*, 5:375–77, 385–86; and report, Chamberlin to Eisenhower, 20 October 1947, file 091 Greece Top Secret, P&O; telegram no. Amag 222, Griswold to Marshall, 15 September 1947; and memorandum, Souers to National Security Council, 30 October 1947, both in *FRUS: 1947*, 5:337–40, 391–93; Wittner, *American Intervention in Greece*, 233–34.

16. Memorandum for record by Arnold, 13 November 1947, file 091 Greece Top Secret, P&O; Wittner, *American Intervention in Greece*, 234–35; H. Jones, *"A New Kind of War,"* 107–8.

17. Quotations from memorandum, Henderson to Lovett, 15 October 1947, *FRUS: 1947*, 5:368–70; handwritten note by Truman on memorandum by Leahy, 18 July 1847, Leahy Files, no. 123, JCS; and ORE 51, 20 October 1947, folder Intelligence Reports—ORE—1947, Intelligence File, PSF; memorandum, Livesay to Griswold, 21 August 1947, file 091 Greece Top Secret, P&O.

18. Quotations from NSC 5, 6 January 1948; and memorandum, Henderson to Marshall, 9 January 1948, both in *FRUS: 1948*, 4:2–7, 9–14; PPS 8, 18 September 1947, PPS; and JCS 1826/8, 1 April 1948, file 091 Greece Top Secret (13), P&O; JCS 1798/1, 15 October 1947, file JCS Papers, P&O; ORE 69, 9 February 1948; and ORE 10-48, 5 April 1948, both in folder Intelligence Reports—ORE—1948, Intelligence File, PSF; minutes of the meeting of the National Security Council, 12 February 1948, folder NSC Meeting No. 6, Subject File, NSC-Meetings, PSF; NSC 5/2, 12 February 1948; and NSC 5/3, 25 May 1948, both in *FRUS: 1948*, 4:46–51, 93–95.

19. For background on the economic situation in Italy, see SWNCC 360, 23 July 1947, folder SWNCC 360-360/2, pt. 1, SWNCC; despatch no. 677, Dunn to

Marshall, 7 May 1947, *FRUS: 1947*, 3:897–901; minutes, 18th meeting of the Policy Planning Staff, 13 June 1947, PPS; J. Miller, *The United States and Italy,* 205–10.

20. Memorandum of conversation by Marshall, 16 May 1947; memorandum of conversation by Matthews, 20 May 1947; telegram no. 726, Marshall to Dunn, 20 May 1947; and telegram no. 1322, Dunn to Marshall, 28 May 1947, all in *FRUS: 1947*, 3:904–10, 911–13; Kolko and Kolko, *The Limits of Power,* 348.

21. Memorandum by the Policy Planning Staff, 24 September 1947, *FRUS: 1947*, 3:977.

22. Quotation from telegram FX 75414, Morgan to Combined Chiefs of Staff, 8 March 1947, ibid., 872–73; SANACC 390, 23 December 1947, folder SANACC 390, SWNCC; memorandum, Timberman to Wedemeyer, 26 January 1948, file 091 Top Secret, P&O.

23. Quotation from telegram no. 1634, Dunn to Marshall, 19 June 1947; telegram no. 726, Marshall to Dunn, 20 May 1947; and letter, Taff to Del Vecchio, 21 July 1947, all in *FRUS: 1947*, 3:909–10, 926, 939–41.

24. Quotation from letter, Marshall to Patterson, 1 July 1947; and letter, Petersen to Marshall, 30 July 1947, both in folder 400 Italy (7-30-47), Projects File, S/A (Royall); letter, Patterson to Marshall, 23 June 1947; telegram no. WARX 81070, Norstad to Lee, 27 June 1947; and telegram no. 2718, Dunn to Marshall, 11 September 1947, all in *FRUS: 1947*, 3:927–28, 929–30, 967–69; Kolodziej, *The Uncommon Defense and Congress,* 56–61.

25. Special Evaluation no. 20 by the Central Intelligence Group, 16 September 1947, file 091 Italy Top Secret (1), P&O.

26. Quotation from memorandum, Norstad to Eisenhower, 18 September 1947, file 091 Italy (18 Sept. 47), C/S; memorandum for record by Sparrow, 24 September 1947, file 091 Italy Top Secret, P&O.

27. Quotations from report by United States Army Survey Group to Italy, 13 October 1947 (emphasis in original); letter, Sparrow to Verbeck, 3 October 1947; and memorandum, ASGI to record, 8 October 1947, all in file 091 Italy Top Secret, P&O; telegram no. 3185, 10 October 1947, *FRUS: 1947*, 3:989–91. On the Venezia Giulia dispute, see Rabel, "Prologue to Containment," and J. Miller, *The United States and Italy,* 162–66, 198–200.

28. NSC 1, 15 October 1947, file 091 Italy Top Secret, P&O.

29. JCS 1808/1, 23 October 1947; and JCS 1808/2, 29 October 1947, both in file CCS 092 Italy (10-2-47) sec. 2, JCS; memorandum, Timberman to Wedemeyer, 26 January 1948, file 091 Italy Top Secret, P&O; NSC 1/1, 14 November 1947, *FRUS: 1948*, 3:724–26; Condit, *The Joint Chiefs of Staff,* 2:64–68.

30. Quotations from telegram no. 3957, Dunn to Marshall, 7 December 1947; and NSC 1/1, 14 November 1947; memorandum, Reber to Lovett, 28 November 1947; and telegram no. 3918, Dunn to Marshall, 5 December 1947, all in *FRUS: 1948*, 3:724–26, 727–29, 736–37, 738–39; memorandum, Eisenhower to Forrestal, 9 December 1947, file 400 Italy (12/9/47), S/A (Royall); Forrestal Diaries, 9 December 1947, 1969, Naval History Division; J. Miller, *The United States and Italy,* 240–41.

31. Telegram no. Telmar 70, Lovett to Marshall, 11 December 1947; and telegram no. Martel 71, Marshall to Lovett, 12 December 1947, both in *FRUS: 1948*, 3:746, 748–49; J. Miller, *The United States and Italy,* 236–39.

32. The CIA's director, Admiral Roscoe H. Hillenkoetter, however, told Forrestal that he doubted that the Communists would risk a coup d'état. Forrestal Diaries, 9 December 1947, 1970, Naval History Division.

33. Quotations from CIA 3, 17 December 1947, CIA Collection, Modern Military Branch, NA; and telegram no. 3957, Dunn to Marshall, 7 December 1947, *FRUS: 1948*, 3:738–39; telegram no. 3918, Dunn to Marshall, 5 December 1947, ibid., 736–37; memorandum, Chamberlin to Eisenhower, 2 December 1947; and memorandum, Chamberlin to Eisenhower, 4 December 1947, both in file 350.05 Top Secret, P&O.

34. Memorandum for record by Schuyler, 9 December 1947, file 091 Italy Top Secret, P&O.

35. Memorandum, Wedemeyer to Royall, 10 December 1947, file 400 Italy (12-10-47), S/A (Royall); memorandum for record by Sparrow, 11 December 1947; and memorandum, Royall to Souers, 17 December 1947, both in file 091 Italy Top Secret, P&O; memorandum, Souers to SANACC, 18 December 1947, file SANACC 390, SWNCC; memorandum, Forrestal to Marshall, 11 December 1947; and memorandum, Wedemeyer to Marshall, 13 December 1947, both in *FRUS: 1948*, 3:743–44, 749–50.

36. Quotations from telegram no. 261, Dunn to Marshall, 20 January 1948; and telegram no. 473, Dunn to Marshall, 4 February 1948, both in *FRUS: 1948*, 3:757, 764; memorandum, Reber to Lovett, 16 December 1947; and telegram no. 4181, Dunn to Marshall, 27 December 1947, both in ibid., 750–51, 754; memorandum, Reber to Arnold, 18 December 1948, file 091 Italy Top Secret (1/11), P&O.

37. SANACC 390/1, 16 January 1948; and memorandum, Souers to Truman, 12 February 1948, both in *FRUS: 1948*, 3:757–62, 769–70; letter and attachments, Stilwell to Byroade, 25 February 1948, 865.24/2-2548, State.

38. In 1940 President Franklin D. Roosevelt invoked his "plenary powers as Commander in Chief and as the head of the state in its relations with foreign governments" to authorize the transfer of destroyers and other military equipment to Great Britain in return for rights to establish military and naval bases. While the justification for the destroyer-bases deal was similar to the one for the transfer of armaments to Italy, it was more circumscribed. Roosevelt relied on an opinion of his attorney general that predicated his action on statutory law as interpreted by the Supreme Court, "rather than solely on the Constitution." Truman invoked plenary powers in the absence of specific legislative authority. Memorandum, Leva to Forrestal, 16 September 1948, file CCS 092 (8-22-46) sec. 14, JCS.

39. Telegram no. 461, Marshall to Dunn, 19 February 1948; and letter, Truman to Forrestal, 10 March 1948, both in *FRUS: 1948*, 3:771–72, 781; J. Miller, "Taking Off the Gloves," 48; memorandum, Marshall to Truman, n.d., folder Foreign—Italy, Subject File—Foreign Affairs, PSF; minutes of the meeting of the National Security Council, 11 March 1948, folder NSC Meeting No. 7, Subject File, NSC-Meetings, PSF.

40. NSC 1/2, 10 February 1948; NSC 1/3, 8 March 1948; and telegram no. 1062, Dunn to Marshall, 12 March 1948, all in *FRUS: 1948*, 3:765–69, 775–79, 784; J. Miller, *The United States and Italy,* 243–49.

41. Memorandum, Cook to Eisenhower, 20 February 1948, file 091 Italy (20 Feb. 48), C/S; memorandum, Timberman to Royall, 10 March 1948, file 400 Italy (3-10-48), Projects File, S/A (Royall); memorandum by Ware, 28 April 1948, file 091 Italy Top Secret, P&O; telegram no. 677, Marshall to Dunn, 12 March 1948; telegram no. 680, Marshall to Dunn, 13 March 1948; telegram no. 1195, Dunn to Marshall, 18 March 1948; telegram no. 1347, Dunn to Marshall, 26 March 1948; and telegram no. 1558, Dunn to Marshall, 6 April 1948, all in *FRUS: 1948*,

3:784–88, 789–90; memorandum, Marshall to Truman, 5 March 1948, 840.50 Recovery/3-548, State.

42. CIA memorandum ORE 47/1, 16 February 1948, file 091 Italy Top Secret (FW 5), P&O; NSC 1/2, 10 February 1948; and letter, Lovett to Forrestal, 17 February 1948, both in *FRUS: 1948*, 3:765–70.

43. Memorandum for record by Parker, 9 January 1948, file 092 Top Secret, P&O; report by Department of the Army *Ad Hoc* Committee, [approx. 1 April 1948], folder 400 Jan.–Dec. 1948, Projects File, S/A (Royall).

44. Transcript, Achilles oral history, 10, Truman Library. See also Reid, *Time of Fear and Hope*, 36.

45. The Treaty of Alliance and Mutual Assistance between the United Kingdom and France, signed at Dunkirk on 4 March 1947 and ratified on the following 8 September, obligated the two contracting parties to "collaborate in measures of mutual assistance in the event of any renewal of German aggression" for a period of fifty years. Carlyle, *Documents on International Relations*, 194–97.

46. Quotations from *Parliamentary Debates* (Commons) 5th ser., 446 (1947–48): 402, 407–8; British memorandum of conversation, n.d., *FRUS: 1947*, 2:815–17; Gladwyn, *The Memoirs of Lord Gladwyn*, 209–11.

47. Quotations from memorandum, Hickerson to Marshall, 19 January 1948, *FRUS: 1948*, 3:6–7; and transcript, Achilles oral history, 8 9, Truman Library; transcript, Achilles oral history, 3–4, DOHP; transcript, Hickerson oral history, 506, DOHP; memorandum of conversation by Hickerson, 21 January 1948, *FRUS: 1948*, 3:9–12. For Dulles's views on the crisis in Europe, see notes by Dulles, 8 January 1948; and draft statement, 12 January 1948, both in folder European Recovery, Dulles Papers, Mudd Library.

48. Memorandum, Kennan to Marshall, 20 January 1948, *FRUS: 1948*, 3:7–8.

49. Kennan, *Memoirs*, 408.

50. Transcript, Achilles oral history, 11, Truman Library; Reid, *Time of Fear and Hope*, 37.

51. Memorandum by Achilles, 20 January 1948, 840.00/1-2048, State.

52. Kennan, *Memoirs*, 408–9.

53. Remarks by Kennan, "Preparedness as Part of Foreign Relations," Washington, D.C., 8 January 1948, folder Jan.–Apr. 1948, Kennan Papers, Mudd Library.

54. Quotations from memorandum of conversation by Hickerson, 7 February 1948, *FRUS: 1948*, 3:21–23; letter, Marshall to Inverchapel, 20 January 1948; letter, Lovett to Inverchapel, 2 February 1948; and letter, Inverchapel to Lovett, 6 February 1948, all in ibid., 8–9, 17–18, 19–20.

55. PPS/13, 6 November 1947, *FRUS: 1947*, 1:773.

56. Quotation from M. Truman, *Harry S. Truman*, 359; Yergin, *Shattered Peace*, 343–50; Ulam, *Expansion and Coexistence*, 421–22. See also Adler and Patterson, "Red Fascism," 1046–64; and note, Elsey to Clifford, n.d., Speech File—3/17/48, Elsey Papers, Truman Library.

57. Telegram no. 88, Bay to Marshall, 19 February 1948, *FRUS: 1948*, 3:24–26; *FRUS: 1948*, 4:759–76; Kaplan, *The United States and NATO*, 62–64; Riste, "Was 1949 a Turning Point?," 130–41.

58. Quotation from telegram no. 107, Marshall to Embassy in Norway, 12 March 1948; and aide-memoire, British Embassy to State Department, 11 March 1948, both in *FRUS: 1948*, 3:46–48, 51–52; letter, Embassy in London to

Hickerson, 13 March 1948, 840.00/3-1348, State; Henrikson, "The Creation of the North Atlantic Alliance," 11–12; Folly, "Breaking the Vicious Circle," 67–68.

59. Carlyle, *Documents on International Relations*, 227.

60. *PP: 1948*, 184.

61. Quotation from minutes, second meeting of the United States–United Kingdom–Canada Security Conversations, 23 March 1948, *FRUS: 1948*, 3:65; telegram no. 1110, Caffery to Marshall, 2 March 1948, ibid., 34–35; letter, Bidault to Marshall, 4 March 1948, 840.20/3-448, State; Wiebes and Zeeman, "The Pentagon Negotiations." The French did not participate in the Pentagon talks ostensibly because the United States considered them security risks, but perhaps also, as Wiebes and Zeeman point out, because they had been uncooperative in previous negotiations over Germany.

62. J. Smith, *The Papers of Lucius D. Clay*, 2:568–69. Clay's telegram may have been sent primarily to help the services secure increased defense appropriations from Congress.

63. Memorandum, Irwin to Bradley, 4 January 1949, file 381 Top Secret, C/S.

64. Quotations from CIA Special Evaluation No. 27, 16 March 1948, file 350.05 Top Secret (82), P&O; and ORE 22-48, 2 April 1948, file CD 12-1-26, S/D; memorandum, Chamberlin to Bradley, 14 March 1948, file 381, C/S; memorandum, Hickerson to Marshall, 8 March 1948, *FRUS: 1948*, 3:40–42; memorandum, Blum to Forrestal, 23 December 1948, Forrestal Diaries, 2706–8, Naval History Division; Leffler, "The American Conception of National Security," 356–75.

65. This estimate did not represent any change in thinking about Soviet capabilities. For approximately two years, intelligence analysts had thought that the Soviets, in the event of war, could quickly seize Western Europe, except perhaps Iberia and part of the Middle East. See, for example, "Intelligence Estimates . . . as of 1 January 1947, 1 July 1948, and 1 July 1951," by the War Department Intelligence Service, 25 June 1946, file 350.05 Top Secret (120), P&O; and telegram no. MA-50602, U.S. military attaché, Moscow to Chamberlin, 26 June 1946, folder-Foreign Relations, Russia, 1946 Report (1), Elsey Papers, Truman Library.

66. Quotations from ORE 22-48, 2 April 1948, file CD 12-1-26, S/D; memorandum, Chamberlin to Bradley, 14 March 1948, file 381, C/S; report by the Joint Intelligence Committee, American Embassy, Moscow, 1 April 1948, *FRUS: 1948*, 1: pt. 2, 555.

67. Quotations from CIA 3-48, 10 March 1948, CIA Collection, Modern Military Branch, NA; and memorandum, Hickerson to Marshall, 8 March 1948, *FRUS: 1948*, 3:40; memorandum, P&O to Collins, 20 March 1948, file 381 Europe Top Secret (15), G-3. Canadian officials viewed the crisis in Europe much the same as American policymakers. Lester B. Pearson, the Under-Secretary of State for External Affairs, wrote to Prime Minister W. L. Mackenzie King on 12 April, "Russia's allies in Western Europe now are not so much the Communists as the forces of despair, apathy, doubt and fear." Munro and Inglis, *Mike*, 2:47.

68. Quotations from letter and encl., Caffery to Hickerson, 26 June 1948, 840.00/6-2648, State; memorandum of conversation by Achilles, 15 April 1948, 840.00/4-1548, State; memorandum of conversation by Nolting, 11 March 1948; telegram no. 230, Marvel to Marshall, 12 March 1948; minutes, first meeting of United States–United Kingdom–Canada Security Conversations, 22 March 1948; and NSC 9, 13 April 1948, all in *FRUS: 1948*, 3:43–44, 51, 59–61, 85–88;

memorandum, Wedemeyer to Bradley, 18 March 1948, file 091 France (22 Mar. 48), C/S.

69. Quotation from memorandum, P&O to Collins, 20 March 1948, file 381 Europe Top Secret (15), P&O; memorandum Byroade to Wedemeyer, 18 March 1948, file 092 Top Secret, P&O; memorandum by Denfeld, 9 March 1948, file 334 War Council (January–June 1948), S/A (Royall); memorandum, Chamberlin to Bradley, 14 March 1948, file 381, C/S. For a different analysis of the military's motivations, see Freeland, *The Truman Doctrine*, 282–85.

70. Truman quoted in Rearden, *The Formative Years*, 312.

71. Minutes, meeting of the National Security Council, 12 February 1948, folder NSC Meeting No. 6, Subject File, NSC—Meetings, PSF.

72. Millis, *The Forrestal Diaries*, 374–77.

73. Webb quoted in Rearden, *The Formative Years*, 326.

74. Ferrell, *Off the Record*, 134.

75. Quotation from "Statement by the President to the Secretary of Defense, the Secretaries of the Three Departments, and the Three Chiefs of Staff," 13 May 1948, folder Military—President's Program—Army-Navy-Air Appropriations Data, PSF; speech by Webb, "The United States in the World Today," 4 March 1948, Speech File, Webb Papers, Truman Library; Donovan, *Tumultuous Years*, 56–59. For accounts of the dispute over the supplemental appropriation, see Rearden, *The Formative Years*, 309–30; Pollard, *Economic Security and the Origins of the Cold War*, 153–56.

76. Memorandum, Forrestal to Royall, 7 March 1948, Folder R, Forrestal Papers, Mudd Library. See also memorandum, Forrestal to Gruenther, 25 March 1948, folder G, ibid.

77. This was a sore point for the army because the peculiarities of the Surplus Property Act and other legislation often prevented the army from obtaining reimbursement for rehabilitating equipment for foreign nations and preparing it for shipment overseas. See memorandum, Aurand to Royall, file 400, S/A (Royall).

78. Report by Department of the Army *Ad Hoc* Committee, [1 April 1948], file 400 (Jan.–Dec. 48), Projects file, S/A (Royall); memorandum, Wedemeyer to Royall, 26 March 1948, file 400 (3-26-48), S/A (Royall); memorandum, Royall to Forrestal, 8 April 1948, file 400 (4-8-48), S/A (Royall).

79. Quotations from House Report 1585, 20 March 1948, in House Committee on International Relations, *Selected Executive Session Hearings*, 3:177–80; JCS 1845, 10 March 1948, file CCS 092 (8-22-46) sec. 4, JCS; Title VI, n.d., folder North Atlantic Pact—Foreign Military Assistance Act of 1949, Clifford Files; FMACC D-1/1, 4 January 1950, file FMACC vol. 3, FACC-MAP.

80. Quotation from memorandum, Hickerson to Lovett, 8 March 1948, *FRUS: 1948*, 3:390–91; memorandum of conversation by Swett, 17 March 1948, 800.20/3-1748, State; memorandum, Surrey to Bonesteel, 30 March 1948, 800.24/3-2448, State. The Foreign Assistance Act of 1948 (62 Stat. 137) authorized economic assistance to Western Europe, military and economic assistance to Greece and Turkey, economic and unrestricted assistance to China, and aid to the International Children Emergency Relief Fund of the United Nations.

81. JCS 1845/1, 2 April 1948, file CCS 092 (8-22-46) sec. 11, JCS.

82. Quotation from memorandum, Hickerson to Lovett, 8 March 1948, *FRUS: 1948*, 3:390–91; memorandum, Butler to Hummelsine, 14 April 1948, 800.24/4-1448, State; memorandum, Butler to Hummelsine, 21 April 1948,

800.24/4-2148, State; minutes, 150th meeting of the Policy Planning Staff, 5 April 1948, PPS.

83. Quotation from memorandum, Leva to Forrestal, 5 May 1948, file CD 6-2-46, folder 1, S/D; memorandum, Leva to Forrestal, 4 May 1948, ibid.; *New York Times*, 30 April and 1 May 1948; minutes by Elsey, 30 April 1948; and note by Elsey, 5 May 1948, both in folder Foreign Policy—Western Union, Elsey Papers, Truman Library; notes on Cabinet meeting, 30 April 1948, folder Cabinet meetings Jan. 9–Dec. 31, 1948, set 1, Connelly Files; Millis, *The Forrestal Diaries*, 427–28; memorandum, Bohlen to Surrey, 4 May 1948, 811.20/ 5-448, State; Rearden, *The Formative Years*, 491.

84. Memorandum and encl., Leva to Clifford, 10 May 1948, folder National Military Establishment—Miscellaneous, Clifford Papers, Truman Library; memorandum, Gross to Executive Secretariat, 7 May 1948, 800.24/5-748, State; memorandum, Forrestal to Lovett, 18 May 1948, 810.20 Defense/5-1848, State; Forrestal Diaries, 11 May 1948, 2246, Naval History Division; memorandum, Lovett to Forrestal, 21 May 1948, 810.20 Defense/5-1848, State.

85. Telegram no. 204, Lovett to Marvel, 5 April 1948; memorandum of conversation by Achilles, 5 April 1948; and NSC 9, 13 April 1948, all in *FRUS: 1948*, 3:75–78, 85–88; memorandum, Roseman to Webb, 27 April 1948, ser. 47.3, folder MS-9, Budget; PPS 27/1, 2 April 1948, PPS; memorandum for the president, 21 May 1948, folder Memos for President—Meeting Discussions, 1948, PSF.

86. Hudson, "Vandenberg Reconsidered," 46–63.

87. Quotations from memorandum of conversation by Lovett, 11 April 1948; and memorandum of conversation by Lovett, 27 April 1948, both in *FRUS: 1948*, 3:82, 105; memorandum of conversation by Lovett, 18 April 1948, ibid., 92–96; memorandum of conversation by Dulles, 27 April 1948, folder Marshall, George C., Dulles Papers, Mudd Library.

88. Quotation from Senate Resolution 239 (Vandenberg Resolution), 11 June 1948, *FRUS: 1948*, 3:136; Vandenberg, *The Private Papers of Senator Vandenberg*, 399–412; *Congressional Record* 94: 7845–46.

89. Quotations from NSC 9/3, 28 June 1948, *FRUS: 1948*, 3:141; and NSC 9/4, 20 July 1948, NSC Collections, Modern Military Branch, NA; telegram no. 2765, Marshall to Embassy in the United Kingdom, 16 July 1948, *FRUS: 1948*, 3:188.

90. Quotation from memorandum, Aurand to Draper, 19 March 1948, file 092 Foreign Aid (3-19-48), ASA; memorandum, Aurand to Bradley, 19 March 1948, file 400 (154), P&O; memorandum, Aurand to Wedemeyer, 14 May 1948, file 092 Top Secret (128), P&O; memorandum, Aurand to P&O, 1 June 1948, file 092 Top Secret, P&O.

91. Memorandum Wedemeyer to Aurand, 30 April 1948, file 092 Top Secret (128), P&O; memorandum, Wedemeyer to Aurand, 30 April 1948, file 400 sec. 9, P&O.

92. Conversely, the State Department made clear to Swedish officials that they could not expect to receive American arms if they did not adhere to the prospective North Atlantic security agreement. See Matthews oral history, Truman Library; Cumming oral history, 9–10, DOHP; and Lundestad, *America, Scandinavia, and the Cold War*, 220–30.

93. Quotations from memorandum, Wedemeyer to Hickerson, 21 June 1948, file 091 Denmark Top Secret, P&O; and memorandum, Royall to Forrestal, 12 July 1948, file 091 Norway (7-12-48), Projects File, S/A (Royall); memorandum,

W. H. G. to Wedemeyer, 13 April 1948, file 091 Denmark Top Secret, P&O; memorandum, Aurand to Bradley, 18 June 1948, file 091 Norway (5 May 48), C/S; JCS 1846/2, 21 May 1948, file 091 Norway Top Secret (1), G-3.

94. The SANACC proposed that any new military assistance legislation contain the following terms: all transfers of military equipment would be without cost to the United States, except when Congress made specific appropriations; the president would have the power to determine the form and amount of any reimbursement; the National Military Establishment would have the authority to manufacture in any installations under its control or procure from commercial sources military equipment for transfer to foreign governments; and the accounts of any department or agency of the government could be reimbursed from funds received from foreign governments for providing military assistance.

95. Quotations from SWNCC 360/4, 29 December 1947; and SANACC 360/5, 27 February 1948, both in folder SANACC 360/4-SANACC 360/11, Pt. 2, SWNCC.

96. Quotation from SANACC 382/6, 18 June 1948, *FRUS: 1948,* 1: pt. 2, 579; SC/R-184, 5 February 1946, *FRUS: 1946,* 1:1141–42; SWNCC 202/4, folder SWNCC 202, SWNCC.

97. Quotation from letter, Royall to Stimson, 21 April 1948, file 092 (4-21-48), S/A (Royall); memorandum, Wedemeyer to Royall, 16 April 1948, file 091 India (16 Apr. 48), C/S.

98. NSC 14/1, 1 July 1948, *FRUS: 1948,* 1: pt. 2, 585–88.

99. Ibid.

CHAPTER 6

1. Quoted in Ferrell, *George C. Marshall,* 90.

2. *PP: 1947,* 178–79.

3. Memorandum, Vincent to Marshall, 7 February 1947; memorandum, Sprouse to Vincent, n.d., both in *FRUS: 1947,* 7:786–93; memorandum, Ringwalt to Vincent, 11 February 1947, 893.24/2-1147, State; G. May, *China Scapegoat,* 153–54.

4. Memorandum, Vincent to Marshall, 7 February 1947, *FRUS: 1947,* 7:789–93.

5. Ibid., 791.

6. Senate Committee on Foreign Relations, *Executive Sessions,* 1:10.

7. Quotations from minutes of the meeting of the Secretaries of State, War, and Navy, 12 February 1947; and letter, Patterson to Acheson, 26 February 1947, both in *FRUS: 1947,* 7:795–97, 799–803; memorandum, Carter to Marshall, 12 February 1947, ibid., 794–95.

8. Memorandum, Marshall to Vincent, 27 February 1947, ibid., 803–4; letter, Truman to Pauley, 24 February 1947, folder China, 1947, Subject File—Foreign Affairs, PSF.

9. Letter, Marshall to Patterson, 4 March 1947, *FRUS: 1947,* 7:805–9; SWNCC 83/21, 13 March 1947, folder SWNCC 83/14—, Pt. 2, SWNCC.

10. Quotation from minutes, meeting of the Secretaries of State, War, and Navy, 12 February 1947; minutes of conference concerning China, 20 February 1947, both in *FRUS: 1947,* 7:796, 946–50.

11. Notes on Cabinet meeting, 7 March 1947, folder Cabinet Meetings: Jan. 3–Dec. 19, 1947, set 2, Connelly Files.

12. SWNCC 360, 21 April 1947, folder SWNCC 360-360/2, Pt. 1, SWNCC. For State Department proposals for economic aid to China, see Stueck, *The Road to Confrontation*, 41.

13. "Report of the Special *Ad Hoc* Committee of the State-War-Navy Coordinating Committee," 21 April 1947, *FRUS: 1947*, 3:209. For the importance of credibility in shaping American policy toward China and Korea, see Stueck, *The Road to Confrontation*.

14. Quotation from Vandenberg, *The Private Papers of Senator Vandenberg*, 522–23; Ferrell, *George C. Marshall*, 90–91. Vandenberg's views were influenced by his correspondence with Claire Chennault. See Stueck, *The Road to Confrontation*, 42.

15. House Committee on Foreign Affairs, *Assistance to Greece and Turkey*, 16–18, 47–50 (quotation from 49).

16. Tsou, *America's Failure in China*, 447–50; Freeland, *The Truman Doctrine*, 109–12; Westerfield, *Foreign Policy and Party Politics*, 241–47. For Judd's background, see Stuhler, *Ten Men of Minnesota*, 169–74. For a lengthy exposition of Judd's views on American security interests in Asia, see Judd oral history, Truman Library.

17. Memorandum AXO 30, Timberman to Butterworth, 5 July 1947, folder AXO vol. 1, Marshall Mission. For similar criticisms of the Nationalist military leadership, see memorandum, Vincent to Marshall, 5 June 1947; and memorandum, Lucas to Stuart, 28 June 1947, both in *FRUS: 1947*, 7:166–67, 860–63.

18. Quotation from telegram no. 1235, Stuart to Marshall, 7 June 1947, *FRUS: 1947*, 7:173; War Department Intelligence Service, project 3766, sec. 2G, "Analysis of the Current Military Situation," 30 June 1947, file 350.05 Top Secret (FW 62), P&O; Chassin, *The Communist Conquest of China*, 114–21; *FRUS: 1947*, 7:130–217. For Chiang's hope for a speedy victory, see despatch no. 613, Stuart to Marshall, 4 April 1947; telegram no. 916, Stuart to Marshall, 28 April 1947; and memorandum, Ringwalt to Vincent, 3 June 1947, all in ibid., 91–95, 824–25, 836–37.

19. Colonel David D. Barrett, the assistant military attaché at Peiping, reported that while the Nationalists were short of American ammunition, they had adequate supplies of Japanese and Chinese munitions, as well as the necessary arsenal facilities, to sustain limited operations against the Communists indefinitely. Memorandum by Barrett, 28 April 1947, folder Navy, Wedemeyer Mission.

20. Telegram no. 698, Stuart to Marshall, 31 March 1947; memorandum AXO 9, Timberman to Butterworth, 22 April 1947; and telegram no. 916, Stuart to Marshall, 28 April 1947; all in *FRUS: 1947*, 7:811–13, 821–22, 824–25; "Status Report of American Weapons," 2 April 1947; and "Requirements for Ammunition for 39 Divisions for 180 Days," n.d., both in folder U.S. Assistance to China, Marshall Mission; War Department Intelligence Service, project 3766, section 2G, 30 June 1947, file 350.05 Top Secret (FW 62), P&O.

21. Memorandum, Ringwalt to Vincent, 2 April 1947, *FRUS: 1947*, 7:813–14; telegram no. 95249, Carter to Marshall, 23 July 1946; and memorandum, Cummins to Wang, 23 August 1946, both in *FRUS: 1946*, 10:753–54, 757.

22. PCA M-42, 18 April 1947, PCA; memorandum, Exton to Cummins, 15 February 1947, FW 893.24/2-747, State; oral message from Canadian embassy, 30 April 1947, FW 893.24/2-1147, State; telegram no. 223, Marshall to Kirk, 24 February 1947; telegram no. 397, Acheson to Kirk, 25 March 1947; telegram no.

491, Kirk to Marshall, 28 March 1947; and telegram no. 553, Kirk to Marshall, 4 April 1947, all in *FRUS: 1947*, 7:798, 810–11, 816–17.

23. Telegram no. 773, Acheson to Smith, 2 April 1947, *FRUS: 1947*, 7:814–15.

24. Kenny to Butterworth, 23 June 1947, folder U.S. Assistance to China, Marshall Mission; memorandum for information by Austin, 11 July 1947, folder Navy, Wedemeyer Mission; minutes of conference concerning China, 20 February 1947; telegram no. 1408, Smith to Acheson, 16 April 1947; and memorandum, Wooldridge to Vincent, 28 April 1947, all in *FRUS: 1947*, 7:946–50, 959–60, 962–63.

25. Memorandum, Vincent to Marshall, 23 July 1947, *FRUS: 1947*, 7:877–79; memorandum, Wedemeyer to Royall, 23 December 1947, file 400 China Top Secret (FW 59/6), P&O.

26. Quotation from memorandum of conversation by Marshall, 8 May 1947; telegram no. 1373, Smith to Acheson, 15 April 1947; memorandum, Ringwalt to Vincent, 5 May 1947; memorandum by Vincent, 26 May 1947; memorandum by Ringwalt, 28 May 1947; and memorandum of conversation by Ringwalt, 29 May 1947, all in *FRUS: 1947*, 7:819–20, 831–33, 833–35, 835–36, 1115; PCA M-47, 6 June 1947, PCA; memorandum, Vincent to Marshall, 26 May 1947, 893.24/4-347, State; memorandum, Ringwalt to Carter, 27 June 1947, 893.24/6-2747, State; *DSB* 17 (6 July 1947): 49–50; memorandum, Ringwalt to Muir, 28 May 1947, folder U.S. Assistance to China, Marshall Mission.

27. Memorandum SM-8388, 9 June 1947, *FRUS: 1947*, 7:838–48.

28. Ibid.

29. Quotation from memorandum, Vincent to Marshall, 20 June 1947, *FRUS: 1947*, 7:849; SWNCC 360/1, Encl. B, 12 May 1947, ibid., 1:744–45.

30. Memorandum, Vincent to Marshall, 20 June 1947, ibid., 7:849; G. May, *China Scapegoat*, 158–59.

31. For summaries of the military situation, see especially telegram no. 1356, Stuart to Marshall, 20 June 1947, *FRUS: 1947*, 7:192–93; War Department Intelligence Service, project 3766, sec. 2G, 30 June 1947, file 350.05 Top Secret (FW 62), P&O.

32. Millis, *The Forrestal Diaries*, 285–86.

33. Memorandum, Marshall to Lovett, 2 July 1947, *FRUS: 1947*, 7:635.

34. Telegram no. 821, Marshall to Stuart, 3 July 1947, ibid., 213.

35. War Department Intelligence Service, project 3766, sec. 2G, 16 June 1947, file 350.05 Top Secret (FW62), P&O; memorandum, Ringwalt to Vincent, 3 July 1947; and minutes, meeting of the Secretaries of State, War, and Navy, 26 June 1947, *FRUS: 1947*, 7:214–15, 850–51; Millis, *The Forrestal Diaries*, 286.

36. Quoted in Tsou, *America's Failure in China*, 460.

37. Lilienthal, *Journals*, 2:201.

38. Millis, *The Forrestal Diaries*, 285–87. See also notes on Cabinet meeting, 27 June 1947, folder Cabinet Meetings: Jan. 3–Dec. 19, 1947, set 2, Connelly Files.

39. Memorandum, Marshall to Lovett, 2 July 1947, *FRUS: 1947*, 7:635–36; Wedemeyer, *Wedemeyer Reports!*, 382–83; Judd oral history, DOHP. Judd later made the exaggerated claim that he was solely responsible for the dispatch of Wedemeyer to China.

40. Memorandum, Marshall to Truman, 8 July 1947; and directive to Wedemeyer, 9 July 1947, both in *FRUS: 1947*, 7:639–41. For a detailed study of the Wedemeyer mission, see Stueck, *The Wedemeyer Mission*.

41. Memorandum, Forrestal to Marshall, 8 July 1947, folder Wedemeyer Mission, Marshall Mission; Vandenberg quoted in G. May, *China Scapegoat*, 167.

42. Ferrell, *George C. Marshall,* 204; JCS 1721/6, 26 June 1947, file CCS 452 China (4-3-45) sec. 7 pt. 1, JCS.

43. Memorandum, Wedemeyer to Marshall, 2 July 1947; memorandum, Marshall to Truman, 8 July 1947; and directive to Wedemeyer, 9 July 1947; all in *FRUS: 1947,* 7:636–38, 639–41; E. May, *The Truman Administration and China,* 21; Stueck, *The Wedemeyer Mission,* 12.

44. Telegram no. 34, Wedemeyer to Marshall, 29 July 1947, *FRUS: 1947,* 7:682–84; Melby, *The Mandate of Heaven,* 226–30.

45. Cable, Taylor to Wedemeyer, 25 August 1947, file 091 China Top Secret (1), P&O.

46. Telegram no. 57, Wedemeyer to Marshall, 8 August 1947, *FRUS: 1947,* 7:712–15.

47. Millis, *The Forrestal Diaries,* 285; notes on Cabinet meeting, 27 June 1947, folder Cabinet meetings: Jan. 3–Dec. 19, 1947, set 2, Connelly Files; memorandum AXO 30, Timberman to Butterworth, 5 July 1947, folder AXO vol. 1, Marshall Mission; telegram no. 34, Wedemeyer to Marshall, 29 July 1947, *FRUS: 1947,* 7:682–84.

48. Melby, *The Mandate of Heaven,* 226.

49. Telegram no. 57, Wedemeyer to Marshall, 8 August 1947, *FRUS: 1947,* 7:712–15.

50. "Summary of Remarks Made by Lieutenant General Albert C. Wedemeyer Before Joint Meeting of State Council and All Ministers of the National Government," 22 August 1947, U.S. Department of State, *United States Relations with China,* 758–63.

51. Quotation from telegram no. 1789, Stuart to Marshall, 24 August 1947, *FRUS: 1947,* 7:759–61; telegram, Davis to Marshall, 2 September 1947, U.S. Department of State, *United States Relations with China,* 815–16.

52. Report, Wedemeyer to Truman, 19 September 1947, U.S. Department of State, *United States Relations with China,* 774–76, 779, 809.

53. Ibid., 808–14 (quotations from 810, 811, 814).

54. Ibid., 767; memorandum, Butterworth to Marshall, 24 September 1947; memorandum, Carter to Humelsine, 25 September 1947; memorandum, Butterworth to Lovett, 26 September 1947; memorandum, Humelsine to Lovett, 28 September 1947; and letter, Wedemeyer to Marshall, 29 September 1947, all in *FRUS: 1947,* 7:776–81; Senate Armed Services Committee, *Nomination of General of the Army George C. Marshall,* 22–23; Wedemeyer, *Wedemeyer Reports!,* 396–98; E. May, *The Truman Administration and China,* 23.

55. Telegram no. 2068, Stuart to Marshall, 14 October 1947; despatch no. 1064, Stuart to Marshall, 22 October 1947; telegram no. 2149, Stuart to Marshall, 28 October 1947; telegram no. 2169, Stuart to Marshall, 31 October 1947; and telegram no. 1332, Lovett to Stuart, 31 October 1947, all in *FRUS: 1947,* 7:325–26, 331–35, 343, 350–52.

56. Kennan, *Memoirs,* 373–74; CIA 1, 26 September 1947, Central Intelligence Reports, Intelligence File, PSF.

57. Memorandum by Bohlen, 30 August 1947, *FRUS: 1947,* 1:763–65. See above, chap. 5

58. PPS 13, 6 November 1947, *FRUS: 1947,* 1:770–77. On the Truman administration's assessment of its overseas interests, see Gaddis, *Russia, the Soviet Union, and the United States,* 184–89; and Etzold, *Aspects of Sino-American Relations Since 1784,* 102–6.

59. Memorandum by Marshall, 10 June 1948, *FRUS: 1948*, 8:90; Feaver, "The China Aid Bill of 1948," 107–9.

60. Letter, Patterson to Marshall, 23 July 1947; letter, Marshall to Royall, 28 July 1947; telegram no. 1629, Stuart to Marshall, 1 August 1947; memorandum, Ringwalt to Penfield, 7 August 1947; telegram no. 1021, Lovett to Stuart, 14 August 1947; telegram no. 1902, Stuart to Marshall, 11 September 1947; letter, Royall to Marshall, 15 October 1947; letter, Lovett to Royall, 20 October 1947; minutes, meeting of the Committee of Two, 3 November 1947; and letter, Lovett to Royall, 31 December 1947, all in *FRUS: 1947*, 7:879–82, 887–88, 896–98, 908–12, 938–39; memorandum, Carter to Marshall, 9 July 1947, envelope— "Top Secret Marshall and Stuart," Marshall Mission; letter, Saltzman to Royall, 30 September 1947; and memorandum for record by Seedlock, 7 October 1947, both in file 400 (154), P&O; memorandum, Bolté to Bradley, 10 August 1949, file 091 China Top Secret, G-3.

61. Quoted in memorandum, Bolté to Bradley, 10 August 1949, file 091 China Top Secret, G-3. See also memorandum of meeting held in the secretary's office by McWilliams, 21 October 1947; and memorandum, Schuyler to Draper, 31 October 1947, both in *FRUS: 1947*, 7:899–900, 902–4.

62. Minutes of meeting of the Committee of Two, 3 November 1947; memorandum of conversation by Butterworth, 16 December 1947; and letter, Butterworth to Whitney, 16 December 1947, all in *FRUS: 1947*, 7:908–12, 930–32; memorandum of conversation by Ringwalt, 4 November 1947, 893.24/11-447, State; memorandum, Mayo to Arnold, 21 November 1947, file 091 China Top Secret, P&O.

63. Memorandum of conversation by Rice, 22 October 1947, 893.50 Recovery/10-2247, State.

64. Memorandum, Magill and Sprouse to Butterworth, 2 February 1948, 893.24/2-248, State.

65. Quotation from memorandum of conversation by Butterworth, 13 November 1947; memorandum of conversation by Ringwalt, 10 December 1947; and memorandum of conversation by Butterworth, 16 December 1947, all in *FRUS: 1947*, 7:925–27, 930–31, 1214–17; "Extent to Which Recommendations of the Wedemeyer Report Have Been Carried Out," n.d., 893.50 Recovery/4-248, State; telegram no. 1501, Lovett to Stuart, 2 December 1947, 893.24/12-247, State.

66. Memorandum, Lucas to Norstad, 18 August 1947; memorandum, Lucas to Norstad, 8 September 1947; and memorandum for record, 19 September 1947, all in file 091 China Top Secret, P&O; letter, Lucas to Stuart, 28 June 1947; memorandum, Ringwalt to Carter, 20 August 1947; letter, Lucas to Stuart, 5 September 1947; letter, Stuart to Lucas, 6 September 1947; and memorandum, Wedemeyer to Ringwalt, 13 October 1947, all in *FRUS: 1947*, 7:860–63, 883–86, 892–93.

67. Quotation from memorandum of conversation by Butterworth, 13 November 1947; memorandum, Butterworth to Marshall, 15 October 1947; telegram no. 1302, Lovett to Stuart, 24 October 1947; and telegram no. 1436, Lovett to Stuart, 28 November 1947, all in *FRUS: 1947*, 7:895–96, 901, 923, 1214–17; memorandum for record by Seedlock, 23 October 1947, file 091 China Top Secret, P&O.

68. Melby, *The Mandate of Heaven*, 238; memorandum for record by Taylor, 16 January 1948, file 091 China Top Secret (37), P&O; telegram no. 2284, Stuart to Marshall, 22 November 1947, *FRUS: 1947*, 7:921–22.

69. Quotation from telegram no. 1436, Lovett to Stuart, 28 November 1947, *FRUS: 1947*, 7:923; memorandum, Timberman to Wedemeyer, 27 April 1948, file 091 China Top Secret (11), P&O.

70. Draft letter, Royall to Bridges, [approx. May 1948], file 091 China Top Secret (6), P&O; letter, Lucas to Stuart, 4 December 1947, file 400 Top Secret, P&O.

71. Senate Committee on Appropriations, *Third Supplemental Appropriations Bill for 1948*, 128-32.

72. Memorandum, Wedemeyer to Eisenhower and Royall, 23 January 1948, file 091 China Top Secret (10), P&O; Millis, *The Forrestal Diaries*, 383.

73. Memorandum, Wedemeyer to Royall, 28 November 1947, file 400 (12/6/47), S/A (Royall); memorandum, Wedemeyer to Royall and Eisenhower, 15 December 1947, file 091 China (12/1/47), ibid.; "List of Urgent Supplies Needed by the Chinese Air Force," FW 893.24/11-447, State; memorandum of conversation by Sweeney, 25 November 1947, 893.24/11-2547, State; memorandum, Ringwalt to Butterworth, 30 January 1948, 893.24/1-3048, State; memorandum, Ringwalt to Butterworth, 3 February 1948, 893.24/2-348, State; memorandum, Ringwalt to Butterworth, 24 March 1948, 893.24/3-2448, State; letter, Royall to Marshall, 23 January 1948; and letter and encl., Royall to Marshall, 24 February 1948, both in *FRUS: 1948*, 8:4-6, 18-22.

74. Memorandum, Schuyler to Blum, 3 January 1948, file 091 China Top Secret (6), P&O.

75. Quotation from memorandum, Forrestal to Royall, 26 February 1948, file 091 China (2/26/48), S/A (Royall); memorandum, Ohly to Byroade, 12 January 1948, file 091 China Top Secret, P&O; memorandum, Ohly to Souers, 15 January 1948, file 452 China (4-3-45) sec. 7 pt. 1, JCS.

76. NSC 6, 26 March 1948, *FRUS: 1948*, 8:44-50.

77. Telegram no. MARTEL 28, Marshall to Lovett, 7 April 1948, ibid., 52-53.

78. JCS 1721/8, 27 March 1948, file 091 China Top Secret, P&O.

79. Memorandum, Wedemeyer to Forrestal, 29 March 1948, file 091 China Top Secret (14), P&O. Wedemeyer also warned that Communist gains in East Asia would ruin American efforts to make the Japanese economy self-sufficient.

80. Memorandum, Royall to Forrestal, 22 March 1948, file 091 China, Projects Files, S/A (Royall). Royall also worried that further military aid might lead to the commitment of American troops to China. See memorandum, Royall to Forrestal, 21 February 1948, ibid.

81. House Committee on Foreign Affairs, *Emergency Foreign Aid*, 239.

82. Tsou, *America's Failure in China*, 462-70; Westerfield, *Foreign Policy and Party Politics*, 262-64; J. Campbell, *The United States In World Affairs, 1947-1948*, 197-99; Senate Committee on Foreign Relations, *Interim Aid for Europe*, 7, 43. For Judd's views, see also memorandum of conversation by Butterworth, 11 November 1947, *FRUS: 1947*, 7:917-18; memorandum, Sprouse to Butterworth, 24 December 1947, 893.24/12-2447, State; Judd oral history, 89, DOHP; Stueck, *The Road to Confrontation*, 53-56.

83. House Committee on International Relations, *Selected Executive Session Hearings*, 7:166.

84. Senate Committee on Foreign Relations, *Foreign Relief Assistance Act of 1948*, 363, 448.

85. *PP: 1948*, 144-46.

86. Quotations from Senate Committee on Foreign Relations, *Foreign Relief*

Assistance Act of 1948, 433; and memorandum, Butterworth to Thorp, 30 December 1947; memorandum, Butterworth to Lovett, 3 January 1948; memorandum by Magill, n.d.; and memorandum, Butterworth to Lovett, 21 January 1948, all in *FRUS: 1948*, 8:442–44, 445–46, 448–50, 454–57; memorandum, Magill and Sprouse to Butterworth, 2 February 1948, 893.24/2-248, State.

87. House Committee on International Relations, *Selected Executive Session Hearings*, 7:159–68.

88. Ibid.

89. Stueck, *The Road to Confrontation*, 54–58; Feaver, "The China Aid Bill of 1948," 118.

90. Telegram no. ZX 40728, MacArthur to Eaton, 3 March 1948, folder China, S/A (Gray-Pace).

91. House Committee on Foreign Affairs, *United States Foreign Policy for a Post-War Recovery Program*, 2066–76.

92. House Committee on International Relations, *Selected Executive Session Hearings*, 7:241–68.

93. House Report 1585, 20 March 1948, in House Committee on International Relations, *Selected Executive Session Hearings*, 3:216–18; "Legislative History of the China Aid Program," encl. to memorandum, Butterworth to Moore, 20 April 1948, 893.50 Recovery/4-2048, State.

94. Senate Committee on Foreign Relations, *Foreign Relief Assistance Act of 1948*, 341–67, 420–23, 433–87, (quotations from 422, 423, 464, 469); Pach, "Military Assistance and American Foreign Policy," 139–40.

95. Senate Committee on Foreign Relations, *Foreign Relief Assistance Act of 1948*, 439, 442–43, 447, 459, 469–87; Fetzer, "Senator Vandenberg and the American Commitment to China," 292–97.

96. 62 Stat. 158.

97. Vandenberg, *The Private Papers of Senator Vandenberg*, 524.

98. House Subcommittee of the Committee on Appropriations, *Foreign Aid Appropriation Bill for 1949*, 2:352–449, esp. 412–15; Senate Committee on Appropriations, *Economic Cooperation Administration*, 470–72; memorandum, Royall to Forrestal, 12 May 1948, file 091 China Top Secret, P&O; memorandum, Royall to Bradley, Wedemeyer, and Draper, 7 June 1948, file 091 China, Projects Files, S/A (Royall); memorandum, Butterworth to Marshall, 14 June 1948, 893.50 Recovery/ 6-1448, State; memorandum of conversation by Marshall, 7 June 1948, *FRUS: 1948*, 8:84–88. The Congress appropriated only $275 million of the $338 million in economic aid that had been authorized.

99. Quoted in Tsou, *America's Failure in China*, 473.

100. Telegram no. 1264, Stuart to Marshall, 12 July 1948, *FRUS: 1948*, 7:348–51.

101. ORE 45-48, 22 July 1948, file 350.05 (FW 354), P&O; letter, Clark to Butterworth, 12 June 1948; despatch no. 273, Stuart to Marshall, 14 June 1948; despatch no. 312, Stuart to Marshall, 17 July 1948; and memorandum, Butterworth to Marshall, 27 July 1948, all in *FRUS: 1948*, 7:294–301, 365–68, 379–81; Melby, *The Mandate of Heaven*, 268–71.

102. Quotation from letter, Clark to Butterworth, 12 June 1948, *FRUS: 1948*, 7:294–98; Liu, *A Military History of Modern China*, 249–57.

103. Telegram no. CYF 317 OAGA, Barr to Wedemeyer, 8 June 1948, file CCS 452 China (4-3-45) sec. 7 pt. 2, JCS.

104. Telegram no. 091101Z, Badger to Denfeld, 9 June 1948, *FRUS: 1948*, 8:254–56.

105. Telegram no. 1044, Stuart to Marshall, 9 June 1948, ibid., 7:282–83.

106. Memorandum of conversation by Marshall, 11 June 1948, ibid., 8:90–99.

107. For information on the establishment of the joint military advisory group, see Condit, *The Joint Chiefs of Staff,* 2:448–54; *FRUS: 1948,* 8:256–69; and file CCS 452 China (4-3-45) secs. 8–10, JCS.

108. Memorandum, Royall to Forrestal, 19 July 1948, file 091 China (7-19-48), Projects Files, S/A (Royall); study by P&O, 28 July 1948, file 091 China Top Secret (6/27), P&O; NSC 22, 26 July 1948; and NSC 22/1, 6 August 1948, both in *FRUS: 1948,* 8:118–22, 131–35.

109. Memorandum, Hillenkoetter to Truman, 20 July 1948, folder Central Intelligence Memoranda, 1945–48, Intelligence File, PSF.

110. Memorandum, Butterworth to Lovett, 15 April 1948, 893.50 Recovery/4-1548, State; memorandum by Sprouse, 11 May 1948; memorandum, Marshall to Truman, 14 May 1948; letter, Truman to Marshall, 2 June 1948; and letter, Marshall to Forrestal, 17 June 1948, all in *FRUS: 1948,* 8:74–76, 79–80, 99.

111. Letter, Bridges to Marshall, 28 June 1948; letter, Bridges and Taber to Truman, 1 July 1948; memorandum of conversation by Lovett, 9 July 1948; memorandum, Sprouse to Butterworth, 16 July 1948; memorandum, Marshall to Truman, 21 July 1948; and letter, Truman to Marshall, 28 July 1948, all in *FRUS: 1948,* 8:102–3, 107–8, 109–11, 113–14, 115–16, 124–25; minutes of meeting by Jenkins, 8 July 1948, 893.24/7-848, State; minutes of meeting by Jenkins, 14 July 1948, 893.50 Recovery/7-1148, State.

112. The pricing policy was the same for all programs of foreign military aid. The source of the items in the army inventories determined their cost to the program. The army charged replacement prices for items below the minimum retention level, procurement (1945) prices for items above the minimum but below the maximum retention level, and 10 percent of procurement prices for items above the maximum retention level (excess). Summary sheet, Wedemeyer to Bradley, 20 October 1948, file 400 (20 October 48), C/S.

113. On priorities, see letter, Royall to Marshall, 24 July 1948; and letter, Marshall to Royall, 9 August 1948, both in *FRUS: 1948,* 8:116–17, 135–36; letter, Royall to Marshall, 6 August 1948; and letter, Marshall to Royall, 23 August 1948, both in ibid., 1: pt. 2, 601–2, 614–15. On the army's involvement in the aid program, see "History of the China Aid Program," [approx. 1 November 1948], file Foreign—China, 1948, PSF; letter, Wedemeyer to Yang Chitseng, 31 August 1948; and memorandum for record by Gilchrist, 1 September 1948, both in file 091 China Top Secret, P&O.

114. Telegram no. 96, Clubb to Marshall, 25 February 1948; despatch no. 287, Stuart to Marshall, 30 June 1948; and telegram no. 1239, Stuart to Marshall, 30 June 1948, all in *FRUS: 1948,* 7:115, 328–30, 344–45; telegram no. 1536, Stuart to Marshall, 19 August 1948, ibid., 8:138; Stueck, *The Road to Confrontation,* 64.

115. Quotations from letter, Clark to Butterworth, 27 August 1948, *FRUS: 1948,* 8:139; and telegram no. 06005Z, Badger to Denfeld, 6 September 1948, ibid., 144–46; telegram no. 030045Z, Badger to Denfeld, 3 May 1948; letter, Marshall to Forrestal, 28 May 1948; letter and encl., Forrestal to Marshall, 17 June 1948, all in ibid., 310–11, 319–21; Condit, *The Joint Chiefs of Staff,* 2:454–58.

116. Letter, Clark to Butterworth, 27 August 1948, *FRUS: 1948,* 8:139–42; Melby Diary, 19 July 1948, Melby Papers, Truman Library.

117. Quotation from letter, Clark to Butterworth, 7 September 1948; tele-

gram no. 1614, Stuart to Marshall, 1 September 1948, both in *FRUS: 1948*, 8:142–43, 165–67; Hawes, *The Marshall Plan for China*, 84; Stuart, *Fifty Years in China*, 206–8.

118. Memorandum, Cleveland to Hoffman, 1 September 1948, 893.50 Recovery/9-148, State.

119. Quotations from memorandum, Butterworth to Lovett, 18 October 1948, FW 893.50 Recovery/10-1848, State; and memorandum, Johnson to Sprouse, 26 October 1948, 893.50 Recovery/10-2648, State; memorandum, Cleveland to Moore, 31 July 1948, 893.50 Recovery/7-3148, State; Hawes, *The Marshall Plan for China*, 84–87; U.S. Department of State, *United States Relations with China*, 319.

120. Telegram no. 1614, Stuart to Marshall, 1 September 1948; telegram no. 060027Z, Badger to Denfeld, 6 September 1948; telegram no. 060005Z, Badger to Denfeld, 6 September 1948; and letter, Clark to Butterworth, 7 September 1948, all in *FRUS: 1948*, 8:142–46, 164–67; memorandum, Timberman to Wedemeyer, 24 September 1948, file 091 China Top Secret, P&O.

121. Letter, Marshall to Forrestal, 13 August 1948, *FRUS: 1948*, 8:137–38.

122. Letter, Kenney to Royall, 21 October 1948, file 091 China Top Secret, P&O; memorandum for record by Gilchrist, 28 September 1948, both in file 091 China Top Secret, P&O.

123. Letter, Marshall to Forrestal, 17 September 1948, *FRUS: 1948*, 8:174; JCS 1721/14, 31 August 1948, file 091 China Top Secret, P&O; "History of the China Aid Program," folder Foreign—China, 1948, PSF; "Requirements under 7 Army and 3 Division Program," n.d., app. 1 to annex 6 of Final Report of the Joint United States Military Advisory Group to the Republic of China, 28 February 1949, file CCS 452 China (4-3-45), BP pt. 1, JCS.

124. Memorandum, Koo to Truman, 28 September 1948; and letter, Truman to Chiang, 16 October 1948, both in *FRUS: 1948*, 8:174–75, 180; letter, Steelman to Wedemeyer, 13 October 1948; memorandum, Wedemeyer to Steelman, 20 October 1948; memorandum, Truman to Royall, 20 October 1948; and memorandum, Royall to Truman, 22 October 1948, all in folder 13, State Department Correspondence, 1948–1949, WHCF; memorandum, Acheson to Truman, 10 March 1949, folder foreign—China, 1949, PSF; memorandum, Freeman to Butterworth, 12 October 1948, 893.50 Recovery/10-1248, State.

125. Memorandum, Schuyler to Wedemeyer, 13 November 1948, file 091 China Top Secret (20), P&O; telegram white no. 28, Lovett to Clifford, 12 November 1948, folder China (2), Clifford Papers, Truman Library; telegram no. 608, Clubb to Marshall, 29 December 1948; and airgram no. A-67, Clubb to Marshall, 31 December 1948, both in *FRUS: 1948*, 7:699–700, 723–25; letter, Lovett to Forrestal, 19 November 1948, ibid., 8:206–7.

126. Quotation from U.S. Department of State, *United States Relations with China*, 358; Chassin, *The Communist Conquest of China*, 183–99; Forrestal Diaries, 22 November 1948, 2665, Naval History Division; memorandum and encl., Butterworth to Marshall, 6 December 1948, *FRUS: 1948*, 8:226–27; telegram no. 2117, Stuart to Marshall, 6 November 1948; telegram no. 1561, Lovett to Stuart, 7 November 1948; and telegram no. 531, Ward to Marshall, 8 November 1948, all in ibid., 7:543, 545–46, 548–49.

127. U.S. Department of State, *United States Relations with China*, 891–94.

128. Telegram no. MARTEL 115, Marshall to Lovett, 8 November 1948, *FRUS: 1948*, 8:195–96.

129. Quotation from notes, meeting of the National Security Council,

3 November 1948, file CCS 452 China (4-3-45) sec. 11, JCS; memorandum of conversation by Marshall, 25 October 1948; telegram no. MARTEL 111, Marshall to Lovett, 6 November 1948; memorandum of conversation by Lovett, 11 November 1948; telegram no. TELMAR 155, Lovett to Marshall, 12 November 1948; and telegram no. 1608, Lovett to Stuart, 12 November 1948, all in *FRUS: 1948*, 8:183–84, 193, 199–200, 201–3; telegram no. TELMAR 174, Lovett to Caffery, 18 November 1948, ibid., 7:588–89; Purifoy, *Harry Truman's China Policy*, 97–102.

130. Quotations from PPS 45, 26 November 1948, *FRUS: 1948*, 8:214–20; and notes on Cabinet meeting, 26 November 1948, folder Cabinet Meetings, Jan. 9–Dec. 31, 1948, set 1, Connelly Files; Forrestal Diaries, 26 November 1948, 2669, Naval History Division; Paterson, "If Europe, Why Not China?," 35–38.

131. For a different point of view, see Stueck, *The Road to Confrontation*, 54–67.

132. Memorandum ORE 27-48, 3 November 1948, file 091 China Top Secret (19/5), P&O; NSC 22/2, 15 December 1948, *FRUS: 1948*, 8:231–32; memorandum for record by Folk, 20 December 1948, file 092 Top Secret, P&O.

133. Quotation from Melby, *The Mandate of Heaven*, 274; telegram no. 2575, Stuart to Marshall, 18 December 1948, *FRUS: 1948*, 8:235–36.

134. Telegram no. 871 OAGA, Barr to Maddocks, 18 December 1948, file CCS 452 China (4-3-45) sec. 7 pt. 3, JCS.

135. Memorandum, Butterworth to Lovett, 16 December 1948, *FRUS: 1948*, 8:233–34; memorandum and encl., Souers to NSC, 17 December 1948, folder NSC meeting no. 29, 12/16/48, PSF; memorandum on China Aid Program, n.d., folder Foreign—China, 1949, Subject File—Foreign Affairs, PSF.

136. Quotation from JCS 1721/18, 4 January 1949, file 091 China Top Secret, G-3; and memorandum, "China Aid Program," n.d., folder Foreign—China, 1949, Subject File—Foreign Affairs, PSF; memorandum, Royall to Forrestal, 26 January 1949, file 091 China Top Secret, G-3; notes on Cabinet meeting, 31 December 1948, folder Cabinet Meetings, Jan. 9–Dec. 31, 1948, set 1, Connelly Files.

137. Quotation from telegram no. C67574, Royall to Forrestal, 3 February 1949, file 091 China (12-1-47), Projects File, S/A (Royall); memorandum, Maddocks to Royall, 2 February 1949, file 091 China Top Secret (7/1), G-3; memorandum by Acheson, 4 February 1949, folder Memos of Conversation, Jan.–Feb. 1949, Acheson Papers, Truman Library; notes on Cabinet Meeting, 4 February 1949, folder Cabinet Meetings, Jan. 3–Dec. 30, 1949, set 1, Connelly Files; NSC 22/3, 2 February 1949; and editorial note, both in *FRUS: 1949*, 9:479–83.

138. Vandenberg, *The Private Papers of Senator Vandenberg*, 530–31.

139. Memorandum by Acheson, 7 February 1949; and memorandum by Souers, 8 February 1949, both in *FRUS: 1949*, 9:486–87.

140. Letter, Truman to Durant, 7 November 1951, folder "D", General File, PSF.

141. Lilienthal, *Journals*, 2:525.

142. Borg and Heinrichs, *Uncertain Years*, 61–77. See also Dingman, "Strategic Planning and the Policy Process," 6–21.

143. Lilienthal, *Journals*, 2:525; Levine, "A New Look at American Mediation in the Chinese Civil War," 375.

144. For a defense of the opposite conclusion, see Stueck, *The Road to Confrontation*, 54–58.

CHAPTER 7

1. "Statement on the United States Military Assistance Program," by the Department of State, 22 May 1949, *FRUS: 1949,* 4:299.

2. Transcript, Military Assistance Discussions, State Department, 20 April 1949, file N7-1 vol. 1, Asst. SecDef FMA.

3. Quotations from NSC 14/1, 1 July 1948, *FRUS: 1948,* 1: pt. 2, 587; and memorandum, Aurand to Wedemeyer, [October 1948], file 092 Top Secret (118/72), P&O; memorandum, Royall to Forrestal, 6 August 1948, file 474 (8-6-48), S/A (Royall); memorandum, Wedemeyer to Royall and Bradley, 9 August 1948; and memorandum, Royall to Forrestal, 15 September 1948; memorandum, Forrestal to Royall, 26 September 1948; memorandum, Aurand to Wedemeyer, 24 September 1948; memorandum, Wedemeyer to Aurand, 7 October 1948; and memorandum, Wedemeyer to Aurand, 2 November 1948, all in file 092 Top Secret, P&O; memorandum, Royall to Forrestal, 13 October 1948, file 400 (10-13-48), S/A (Royall); memorandum, Aurand to Royall and Forrestal, 28 October 1948, file 400 (3-26-48), S/A (Royall); memorandum, Wedemeyer to Royall and Bradley, 29 October 1948, file 011, P&O; memorandum for Struble, Norstad, and Gruenther, 15 September 1948, file CCS 092 Western Europe (3-12-48) sec. 6, JCS.

4. Quotations from JCS 1868/6, 17 May 1948, file 092 Top Secret (118), P&O; JCS 1868/1, 17 April 1948, file CCS 092 Western Europe (3-12-48) sec. 1, JCS; NSC 14/1, 1 July 1948; *FRUS: 1948,* 1, pt. 2, 585–88. For the strategic concept in the event of a war during fiscal year 1949, see JCS 1844/4, 19 May 1948, file CCS 381 USSR (3-2-46) sec. 13, JCS.

5. Quotations from JCS 1868/20, 17 September 1948, file CCS 092 Western Europe (3-12-48) sec. 6, JCS; JCS 1868/13, 12 July 1948, ibid., sec. 4; JCS 1868/16, 5 August 1948, ibid., sec. 5; JCS 1868/18, 3 September 1948, ibid., sec. 6; JCS 1868/29, 12 November 1948, ibid., sec. 10; JCS 1868/42, 31 December 1948, ibid., sec. 13; memorandum by Bradley, n.d., ibid., sec. 14A, JCS; memorandum, Wedemeyer to Bradley, 20 August 1948; and memorandum, Wedemeyer to Bradley, 10 September 1948; both in file 092 Top Secret, P&O; memorandum SM-79-49, 14 January 1949, file CCS 092 (8-22-46) sec. 16, JCS.

6. Quotation from JCS 1925/1, 2 September 1948, file CCS 092 (8-22-46) sec. 14, JCS; SANACC 360/11, 18 August 1948, file SANACC 360/4-SANACC 360/11, Part 3, SWNCC.

7. Quotations from memorandum, Shaub and Sheppard to Webb, 6 August 1948; and letter, Webb to Lovett, 10 August 1948, both in folder S6-7, series 47.3, Budget; letter, Lovett to Webb, 28 July 1948, ibid.; memorandum, "Highlights of National Defense Ceilings," 12 July 1948, file Organization and Administration—White House, folder The President, Webb Papers, Truman Library; *DSB* 19 (15 August 1948): 211; memorandum, Aurand to Webb, 3 June 1948, file 091 Iran (6/3/48), Projects File, S/A (Royall); memorandum for record, 30 August 1948, file 091 Iran Top Secret, P&O; memorandum, Schwarzwalder to Miles, 6 August 1948, folder International Programs—General—GAROIA, MAP, MSP, series 47.8a, Budget.

8. Quotations from unnumbered telegram, Harriman to Marshall, 14 July 1948, *FRUS: 1948,* 3:183–84; memorandum of conversation by Draper, 19 July 1948, folder Secretary of the Army, Subject File, PSF; memorandum, Hillenkoetter to Lovett and Forrestal, n.d., Forrestal Diaries, 2603, Naval History Division.

9. Letter, Harriman to Lovett, 12 November 1948, file N7-1(3)-A vol. 1, Asst. SecDef FMA; memoranda of conversation by Gruenther, 10 and 11 November 1948, folder Secretary of Defense—Report Data, Subject File, PSF; notes on Cabinet meeting, 26 November 1948, folder Cabinet Meetings, Jan. 9–Dec. 31, 1948, set 1, Connelly Files.

10. Forrestal Diaries, 10 October 1948, 2556–57, Naval History Division.

11. Memorandum of conversation by Gruenther, 10 November 1948, folder Secretary of Defense—Report Data, Subject File, PSF; Forrestal Diaries, 11 November 1948, 2637, Naval History Division.

12. Quotation from memorandum, Hickerson to Labouisse, 12 October 1948; telegram no. 3781, Caffery to Marshall, 20 July 1948; telegram no. Toeca 358, Bruce to Hoffman, 14 September 1948; policy statement of the Department of State, 20 September 1948; telegram no. 5173, Caffery to Marshall, 20 October 1948; and telegram no. 5590, Marshall to Lovett, 28 October 1948, all in *FRUS: 1948*, 3:639–42, 649–59, 661–62, 666–68, 673–74; ORE 53-48, 2 August 1948, folder Central Intelligence Reports—ORE 1948, No. 48-57, Intelligence File, PSF; Leffler, "The United States and the Strategic Dimensions of the Marshall Plan," 291–92.

13. Quotations from memorandum, Hickerson to Labouisse, 12 October 1948; telegram no. 5220, Caffery to Marshall, 5 October 1948, both in *FRUS: 1948*, 3:662–64, 666–67.

14. Quotations from memorandum, Hickerson to Labouisse, 12 October 1948; and letter, Labouisse to Nitze, 27 October 1948; memorandum, Labouisse to Moore, 16 October 1948, all in ibid., 666–67, 668–72.

15. Quotations from policy statement of the Department of State, 20 September 1948; and telegram no. 5220, Caffery to Marshall, 5 October 1948, both in ibid., 651–59, 662–64; Leffler, "The United States and the Strategic Dimensions of the Marshall Plan," 291–94.

16. Letter, Lovett to Harriman, 3 December 1948, *FRUS: 1948*, 3:306.

17. Minutes of the third meeting of the Washington Exploratory Talks on Security, 7 July 1948; minutes of the fourth meeting of the Washington Talks, 8 July 1948; memorandum of the third meeting of the Working Group participating in the Washington Talks, 15 July 1948; memorandum of conversation by Lovett, 20 August 1948; memorandum, "Washington Exploratory Conversations on Security," 9 September 1948, all in ibid., 155–60, 163–69, 186, 214–21, 239–40.

18. Quotation from letter, Hickerson to Caffery, 24 August 1948, 840.20/8-2448, State; letter, Hickerson to Caffery, 17 November 1948, 851.24/11-1048, State; aide-memoire from the French government, 31 August 1948, FW 851.20/8-3148, State; memorandum of conversation by Achilles, 30 September 1948, 851.24/9-3048, State; JCS 1868/23, 8 October 1948, file CCS 092 Western Europe (3-12-48) sec. 9, JCS; JCS 1868/30, 13 November 1948, ibid., sec. 10.

19. Quotation from JCS 1868/58, 9 February 1949, file 092 Top Secret, G-3; telegram no. DELWU 80, Kibler to P&O, 21 October 1948; and telegram no. WAR 91426, Wedemeyer to Kibler, 25 October 1948, both in file CCS 092 Western Europe (3-12-48) sec. 9, JCS.

20. Quotation from memorandum, Jernegan to Satterthwaite, 16 November 1948, 868.00/11-1648, State; State Department memorandum, 18 November 1948, folder Policy Committee on Arms and Armaments #3, ISA; memorandum and encl., Forrestal to JCS, 17 November 1948, file CCS 092 (8-22-46), sec. 15, JCS; JCS 1868/47, 7 January 1949, file 092 Top Secret (5/3), G-3; memoran-

dum, "Foreign Aid Council," n.d., file N7-1(4)-A, Asst. SecDef FMA; letter, Forrestal to Marshall, 16 December 1948, 811.20/12-1648, State; memorandum SM-74-79, 14 January 1949, file CCS 092 (8-22-46) sec. 16, JCS; memorandum for Ohly, 21 September 1948, CD 6-2-46 folder 1, S/D; *DSB* 20 (9 January 1949): 59; *FRUS: 1949*, 1:250.

21. Memorandum and encl., Sherman to Royall, 24 January 1949, folder 400 (January 1949), S/A (Royall); SM-74-79, 14 January 1949, file CCS 092 (8-22-46) sec. 16, JCS; memorandum, Marcy to Peurifoy, 2 December 1948, 840.20/12-248.

22. "Balancing the Budget," 6 November 1948, folder Budget, National, FY 1950, Lawton Papers, Truman Library; memorandum, Peurifoy to Lovett, 8 December 1948, 840.20/12-848, State; FACC M-2, 5 February 1949, folder FACC Agenda, Minutes, Summary of Actions, FACC-MAP; memorandum by Lemnitzer, 10 February 1949, file N7-1(1)-B, Asst. SecDef FMA; memorandum of telephone conversation by Carter, 7 February 1949, folder Memos of Conversation, Jan.–Feb. 1949, Acheson Papers, Truman Library; transcript, Princeton Seminars, 10 October 1953, reel 1, track 1, pp. 5–6, ibid.

23. JCS 1868/24, 14 October 1948, file 092 Top Secret, P&O; FACC D-8, 11 February 1949; and FACC D-8/2, 14 April 1949, both in file FACC Documents, vol. 2, FACC-MAP; JCS 1868/58, 9 February 1949, file 092 Top Secret, G-3.

24. Quotation from JCS 1868/62, 7 March 1949, file CCS 092 (8-22-46) sec. 20, JCS; JCS 1868/57, 9 February 1949; and JCS 1868/58, 9 February 1949, both in file 092 Top Secret, G-3; Condit, *The Joint Chiefs of Staff*, 2:422–27.

25. JCS 1868/62, 7 March 1949, file CCS 092 (8-22-46) sec. 20, JCS.

26. JCS 1844/4, 19 May 1948, file CCS 381 USSR (3-2-46) sec. 13, JCS; JSPC 877/59, 26 May 1949, ibid., sec. 32; memorandum, Timberman to Wedemeyer, 5 August 1948; and report by Plans and Policy Group, 27 September 1948, both in file 381 Top Secret, P&O; JCS 1868/62, 7 March 1949, file CCS 092 (8-22-46) sec. 20, JCS.

27. Report by Department of the Army Coordinating Committee, 9 February 1949, file 381 Top Secret (52), G-3; memorandum, Maddocks to Bradley, 26 January 1949; and JCS 1769/16, 1 March 1949, both in file 092 Top Secret (1), G-3; Princeton Seminars, 10 October 1953, reel 1, track 1, pp. 6–8, Acheson Papers, Truman Library.

28. Quotation from NSC 28/1, 3 September 1948, folder NSC Meeting No. 19, NSC File, PSF; transcript, meeting between Acheson, Lange et al., 11 February 1949, 840.20/2-1149, State; memorandum by Acheson, 10 February 1949, folder Memos of Conversation Jan.–Feb. 1949, Acheson Papers, Truman Library; JCS 1929/4, 28 January 1949, file 091 Norway Top Secret (7/9), G-3; JCS 1868/62, 7 March 1949, file CCS 092 (8-22-46) sec. 20, JCS; Lundestad, *America, Scandinavia, and the Cold War*, 309–19. The Joint Chiefs recommended that Norway receive only a "token" amount should it not join the North Atlantic Treaty.

29. NSC 2/1, 25 November 1947, encl. to JCS 570/102, 28 August 1948, file CCS 360 (12-9-42) sec. 32, JCS; JCS 1868/62, 7 March 1949, file CCS 092(8-22-46) sec. 20, JCS.

30. "Military Assistance Program for FY 1950," 1 February 1949, file N7-1(1)-E.3 Army vol. 1, Asst. SecDef FMA.

31. Quotations from memorandum by Kennan, 24 November 1948, *FRUS: 1948*, 3:286; memorandum by Acheson, 2 March 1949, *FRUS: 1949*, 4:141–45; memorandum of conversation by Anschuetz, 14 January 1949; and Army

Department Study, 26 January 1949, both in Compilation Book; JCS 1868/62, 7 March 1949, file CCS 092 (8-22-46) sec. 20, JCS; E. Smith, "The Fear of Subversion," 150–55.

32. Quotations from Department of State Policy Statement on Austria, 20 September 1948, *FRUS: 1948*, 2:1349; and MAP D-G/42, Draft No. 1, 25 July 1949, MAP Documents vol. 6, FACC-MAP; telegram no. 771, Reber to Marshall, 27 February 1948; and telegram no. 884, Marshall to Reber, 10 March 1948, both in *FRUS: 1948*, 2:1468–69, 1474–75; memorandum by P&O, "Military Aid for Austria," 26 January 1949, Compilation Book.

33. Quotation from memorandum by Thielen to Bolté, 17 May 1949, file 092 Europe Top Secret, (35/3), G-3; letter, Lovett to Forrestal, 7 December 1948; memorandum, Draper to Forrestal, 31 December 1948; memorandum, Collins to Royall, 13 January 1949, all in file 400, Jan.–Dec. 48, S/A (Royall); JCS 1868/62, 7 March 1949, file CCS 092 (8-22-46) sec. 20, JCS.

34. PPS 44, 24 November 1948, *FRUS: 1948*, 4:202.

35. Quotations from ORE 28-48, 17 November 1948, folder Intelligence Reports-ORE 1948, No. 21-24, Intelligence File, PSF; telegram no. Amag 1652, Grady to Marshall, 22 November 1948, *FRUS: 1948*, 4:187–91; and JCS 1826/12, 7 October 1948, file 091 Greece Top Secret (13), P&O; telegram no. Gama 1336, Marshall to Grady, 26 November 1948, *FRUS: 1948*, 4:205; letter, Roundtree to McGhee, 14 January 1949, folder Greece—Correspondence, 1946–51, Grady Papers, Truman Library; transcript, discussion between Royall and Forrestal, 4 January 1949, file 020 Secy of Army, S/A (Royall); Gardner, "Civil War in Greece"; Wittner, *American Intervention in Greece*, 242–53.

36. SANACC 358/8, 24 November 1948, *FRUS: 1948*, 4:191–92, memorandum, Jernegan to Thurston, 11 October 1948, *FRUS: 1949*, 6:1–8; memorandum, McBride to Department of the Army, 14 December 1948, file 091 Turkey Top Secret, P&O; Leffler, "Strategy, Diplomacy, and the Cold War," 818–23.

37. State Department study, "Military Assistance for Iran," 12 January 1949; memorandum of conversation, "Armament Program—Iran," 18 January 1949; and Department of Army Study, "Iran—Foreign Aid," 27 January 1949, all in Compilation Book.

38. Quotations from memorandum, "Military Assistance to Korea," n.d.; memorandum of conversation by Anschuetz, 14 January 1949; and memorandum by International Group, P&O, "Korea," 25 January 1949, all in Compilation Book; memorandum, Swett to Saltzman, 23 February 1949, folder Policy Committee on Arms and Armaments #4, ISA; JCS 1868/62, 7 March 1949, file CCS 092 (8-22-46) sec. 20, JCS; Gaddis, "Korea in American Politics, Strategy, and Diplomacy," 277–98; Cumings, *The Origins of the Korean War*, 169–78.

39. Quotation from memorandum by P&O, "Military Assistance to the Republic of the Philippines," 26 January 1949; memorandum, "Military Assistance Program for the Far East," 12 January 1949; memorandum of conversation by Anschuetz, 17 January 1949, all in Compilation Book; JCS 1868/62, 7 March 1949, file CCS 092 (8-22-46) sec. 20, JCS; Hess, *The United States' Emergence as a Southeast Asian Power*, 342. On the importance of American prestige and credibility in East Asia, see Stueck, *The Road to Confrontation*.

40. Quotations from memorandum, Dreier to Cumming, n.d.; memorandum of conversation by the Department of State, 18 January 1949; memorandum, Freeman to Daniels, 19 January 1949, all in Compilation Book; memorandum, Skidmore to Schuyler, 1 February 1949, file 092 Top Secret (1/8), G-3; JCS 1868/62, 7 March 1949, file CCS 092 (8-22-46) sec. 20, JCS.

41. Quotations from memorandum, "Military Assistance for the Far East," 12 January 1949; and memorandum of conversation by Anschuetz, 17 January 1949, both in Compilation Book; table, "Proposed Military Assistance Program," April 1949, file N7-1(1)-B.1 vol. 1, Asst. SecDef FMA; memorandum of conversation by Hickerson, 27 August 1948, *FRUS: 1948,* 3:223–24; memorandum of conversation, "Armament Program—Norway, Sweden, and Denmark," Compilation Book; UM D-20, [approx. 1 April 1949], ExecSecretariat; memorandum, Daniels to Webb, 2 March 1949, 810.24/3-249, State.

42. Table, "Proposed Military Assistance Program," April 1949, file N7-1(1)-B.1 vol. 1, Asst. SecDef FMA; FACC D-10, 17 February 1949, file N7-1(1)-B.1, Asst. SecDef FMA; telegram no. 627, Acheson to Douglas, 24 February 1949, 840.20/2-2449, State.

43. FACC D-3, Draft No. 8, 7 February 1949, *FRUS: 1949,* 1:254–55.

44. Quotation from report by the Office of the Special Representative for ECA in Europe, [approx. 30 March 1949], file N7-1(4)-B ECA, Asst. SecDef FMA; telegram no. 170, Nitze to Lovett and Gross, 13 January 1949, file N7-1 Foreign Military Assistance vol. 1, Asst. SecDef FMA; memorandum, Tannenwald to Lemnitzer, 13 January 1949, file N7-1(2), Asst. SecDef FMA; telegram no. 346, Holmes to Acheson, 29 January 1949, file N7-1(3)-A Western Union vol. 1, Asst. SecDef FMA; telegram no. 1214, Douglas to Acheson, 26 March 1949, file N7-1(7), Asst. SecDef FMA; MAP D-D/6, Revision No. 3, 28 July 1949, file MAP Documents vol. 3, FACC-MAP; memorandum, Nitze to Foreign Assistance Steering Committee, 31 January 1949, *FRUS: 1949,* 4:54–60; telegram no. TOECA 1174, Siegbert to Hoffman, 20 June 1949, file N7-1(3)-A.5, Asst. SecDef FMA.

45. Quotation from speech by Nourse, "The Impact of Military Preparedness on the Civilian Economy," 5 April 1949, file N7-1(1)-F.4, Asst. SecDef FMA; memorandum, Council of Economic Advisers to the President, 7 December 1948, file Daily Diary, 1948–34, Nourse Papers, Truman Library; memorandum, Pace to Truman, 28 March 1949, folder Mutual Defense (1), WHCF.

46. Quotations from memorandum for Lemnitzer, 19 April 1949, file CCS 092 (8-22-46) sec. 23A, JCS; and notes for use by Johnson, 6 April 1949, ibid., sec. 23; letter, Nourse to Truman, 2 April 1949, file Daily Diary, 1949–40, Nourse Papers, Truman Library; letter, Truman to Nourse, 5 April 1949, file Daily Diary, 1949–41, ibid.; note, McNeil to Gruenther, n.d., file CCS 092 (8-22-46) sec. 26, JCS; memorandum, Goodrich to McNeil and Leva, 13 April 1949, file CD 6-2-46, folder 3, S/D.

47. "Proposed Military Assistance Program," April 1949, file N7-1(1)-B.1 vol. 1, Asst. SecDef FMA; memorandum for Maddocks, 8 April 1949, file 092 Top Secret (1/30), P&O; memorandum, Lemnitzer to Johnson, 8 April 1949, file N7-1, Asst. SecDef FMA; memorandum, Lemnitzer to Gruenther and others, 27 April 1949, file N7-1(1)-B.1, Asst. SecDef FMA; memorandum for the FACC, 3 May 1949, file MAP Documents vol. 1, FACC-MAP; memorandum, "Brief of Budget Comments," n.d., file N7-1(1)-B.1, Asst. SecDef FMA; memorandum, Pace to Truman, 20 April 1949; and memorandum, Acheson to Truman, 20 April 1949, both in folder Military—Department of Defense, Subject File, PSF; "Suggested Remarks for Mr. Pace," 7 April 1949, FW 840.20/4-749, State; Kaplan, *A Community of Interests,* 39–40.

48. FACC D-3, Draft No. 8, 7 February 1949, *FRUS: 1949,* 1:250–57; memorandum, FACC to Foreign Assistance Steering Committee, 25 March 1949, file N7-1(1)-F.2, Asst. SecDef FMA; MAP D-D/14, Draft No. 4, 22 June 1949, folder Military Assistance, 25 July 1949, Lloyd Files.

49. MAP D-G/7, 1 July 1949, *FRUS: 1949*, 1:347; Senate Committee on Foreign Relations, *The Vandenberg Resolution*, 213–16; ORE 41-49, 24 February 1949, file N7-1(1)-E.8, Asst. SecDef FMA.

50. Quotation from ORE 48-49, 10 May 1949, file 350.05 Top Secret (16), G-3; memorandum, Nitze to Foreign Assistance Steering Committee, 31 January 1949, *FRUS: 1949*, 4:56; McLellan, *Dean Acheson*, 157–64; Senate Committee on Foreign Relations, *Reviews of the World Situation*, 21–22.

51. Quotations from FACC D-12/4 Revision No. 1, 11 July 1949, file FACC Documents vol. 3, FACC-MAP; and U.S. Department of State, *The Military Assistance Program*, 40; MAP D-G/27, Draft No. 1, 23 July 1949, file MAP Documents, vol. 5, FACC-MAP.

52. Quotation from telegram no. 2187, Douglas to Acheson, 5 June 1949, *FRUS: 1949*, 4:302; telegram no. 2619, Bruce to Acheson, 23 June 1949, file N7-1(3)-A.2, Asst. SecDef FMA; telegram no. 532, Baruch to Acheson, 22 June 1949, file N7-1(3)-1.3, ibid.; telegram no. 466, Bay to Acheson, file N7-1(3)-B.7, ibid.; telegram no. 480, Sparks to Acheson, file N7-1(3)-B.8, ibid.

53. Senate Committee on Foreign Relations, *The Vandenberg Resolution*, 211–49 (quotations from 233, 237); transcript, "Military Assistance Discussions," 20 April 1949, file N7-1 Foreign Military Assistance vol. 1, Asst. SecDef FMA; "Record of Discussions at the Meeting of the Senate Foreign Relations Committee, Washington, April 21, 1949," *FRUS: 1949*, 1:288–91; Kaplan, *A Community of Interests*, 42.

54. Quotation from memorandum of conversation by Acheson, 24 June 1949, folder Memos of Conversation, June 1949, Acheson Papers, Truman Library; memorandum of conversation by Acheson, 13 April 1949, folder Memos of Conversation, April 1949, ibid.; memorandum of meeting with the president by Acheson, 12 May 1949; memorandum of meeting with the president by Acheson, 27 June 1949; and memorandum of meeting with the president by Acheson, 30 June 1949, all in folder Memos of Conversation, May–June 1949, ibid.; memorandum of conversation by Berkner, 1 July 1949, folder Memos of Conversation, July 1949, ibid.; note by Lloyd, 30 June 1949, folder Military Assistance, July 25, 1949, Lloyd Files; memorandum, Gross to Acheson, 3 May 1949, 840.20/5-349, State; memorandum, March to Gross, 27 May 1949, 840.20/5-2749, State; telegram no. TELAC 56, Webb to Acheson, 3 June 1949, 840.20/6-349, State; "Present Time Schedule," 1 April 1949, folder 16, State Department Correspondence, 1948–1949, WHCF; memorandum, Acheson to Truman, 12 May 1949, *FRUS: 1949*, 4:298–99.

55. Truman had previously requested an interim appropriation of $50 million to prevent any interruption in aid to Greece and Turkey.

56. Quotation from S. 2341, 27 July 1949, copy in Senate Committee on Foreign Relations, *Military Assistance Program*, 633; FACC D-14, Draft No. 1, 9 March 1949, file N7-1(1)-B.3, Asst. SecDef FMA; *PP: 1949*, 395–400. In his message to Congress transmitting the arms bill, Truman mentioned every nation to which he planned to furnish military assistance except Austria.

57. Quotations from Vandenberg, *The Private Papers of Senator Vandenberg*, 503–4; Senate Committee on Foreign Relations, *Military Assistance Program*, 1–18; and summary of daily meeting with the secretary, 3 August 1949, folder Minutes of Secretary's Daily Meetings—1949, ExecSecretariat; memorandum of conversation by Acheson, 26 July 1949, *FRUS: 1949*, 1:361–64; speech by Dulles, 21 September 1949, folder Military Assistance Program, Dulles Papers, Mudd Library; *New York Times*, 29 September 1949, 14; Kaplan, *A Community of*

Interests, 46–47; R. Blum, *Drawing the Line*, 129–30. This section on congressional consideration of the MAP appeared in condensed form in Pach, "Military Assistance and American Foreign Policy," 140–42.

58. Quotation from Vandenberg, *The Private Papers of Senator Vandenberg*, 508; S. 2388, 5 August 1949, copy in Senate Foreign Relations Committee, *Military Assistance Program*, 648–63; notes of telephone conversation by Battle, 3 August 1949, folder Memos of Conversation, August–September 1949, Acheson Papers, Truman Library; memorandum to Senator Smith, 1 August 1949, unmarked folder, Box 99, Smith Papers, Mudd Library.

59. Memorandum of conversation by Gross, 19 July 1949, file N7-1(7), Asst. SecDef FMA; letter, Acheson to Bruce, 26 July 1949, folder Memos of Conversation, July 1949, Acheson Papers, Truman Library; memorandum of conversation by Acheson, 26 July 1949, *FRUS: 1949*, 1:361–64; Vandenberg, *The Private Papers of Senator Vandenberg*, 509–12; Senate Committee on Foreign Relations, *Military Assistance Program*, 19–125; Kaplan, *A Community of Interests*, 45–46.

60. H.R. 5895, 19 August 1949, Senate Foreign Relations Committee, *Military Assistance Program*, 681–82.

61. "Explanation of Amendments . . . to the Military Assistance Bill," n.d., folder Military Assistance Program, Dulles Papers, Mudd Library; memorandum of telephone conversation by Acheson, 22 August 1949, folder Memos of Conversation, August–September 1949, Acheson Papers, Truman Library; Vandenberg, *The Private Papers of Senator Vandenberg*, 513 14.

62. Quotations from U.S. Department of State, *United States Relations with China*, xvi; and Smith Diary, 8 August 1949, 256, Smith Papers, Mudd Library; G. Smith, *Dean Acheson*, 112–21.

63. Quotation from House Committee of International Relations, *Selected Executive Session Hearings*, 5:187–207, 225–42, 452–60; Senate Committee on Foreign Relations, *Military Assistance Program*, 515–50; memorandum of conversation by Acheson, 18 August 1949, folder Memos of Conversation, August–September 1949, Acheson Papers, Truman Library; Stebbins, *The United States in World Affairs, 1949*, 82–83; Cohen, *Dean Rusk*, 39–44; JCS 1721/43, 16 January 1950, file CCS 452 China (4-3-45) sec. 7, pt. 7, JCS; memorandum by Ohly, 1 June 1950; and memorandum, Webb to Truman, 21 June 1950, both in *FRUS: 1950*, 6:98–100, 103–5; R. Blum, *Drawing the Line*, 129–42.

64. House Committee on International Relations, *Selected Executive Session Hearings*, 5:438–49, 575–80; *PP: 1949*, 485; 63 Stat. 714.

65. Kaplan, *A Community of Interests*, 48–49; transcript, Princeton Seminars, 10 October 1953, reel 1, track 1, pp. 9–10, Acheson Papers, Truman Library.

EPILOGUE

1. Memorandum, "Budget Review (Agency Ceilings) 1951," 23 June 1949, folder Bureau of the Budget—Budget Recommendations, FY 51, Book 1, WHCF.

2. Quotations from NSC 52, 5 July 1949; and NSC 52/3, 29 September 1949, both in *FRUS: 1949*, 1:350, 389; NSC 52/1, 8 July 1949, folder NSC Meeting No. 46, NSC File, PSF; JCS 2032/3, 6 August 1949, file JCS Papers, G-3; JCS 2032/5, 22 August 1949, file 092 Top Secret (36), G-3; ORE 74-49, 22 September 1949, folder Central Intelligence Reports, ORE—1949, Intelligence File, PSF.

3. Quotation from JMAC 73/2, 18 August 1949, file 092 Top Secret, G-3; JCS 1920/1, 6 May 1949, file CCS 381 USSR (3-2-46) sec. 28, JCS; minutes, meeting of Operations Deputies, 9 September 1949; and SM 1802-49, 9 September 1949, both in file 092 (8-22-46) sec. 28, JCS; Condit, *The Joint Chiefs of Staff,* 2:303.

4. Quotations from NSC 68, 14 April 1950, *FRUS: 1950,* 1:238, 240, 264, 282, 284; Pollard, *Economic Security and the Origins of the Cold War,* 237–40; Kaplan, *A Community of Interests,* 79–83.

5. Quotation from letter, Acheson to Johnson, 24 March 1950, file CD 6-2-46, S/D; memoranda, Gray to Johnson, 3 March 1950 and 11 April 1950, ibid.; memorandum, Acheson to Truman, 3 January 1949 [1950]; and memorandum, Pace to Truman, 26 January 1950, both in folder Mutual Defense (2), WHCF; "Relationship of Economic Recovery to Defense Effort," [approx. April 1950]; and letter, Bonesteel to Ohly, 29 March 1950, both in folder 5th Meeting, 5/6/50, of the European Coordinating Committee, Harriman Papers, Harriman Residence; JCS 2099/6, 11 May 1950, file JCS Papers, G-3; D.C. 6/1, 1 December 1949, *FRUS: 1949,* 4:352–56; memorandum by Bell, 17 November 1949, ibid., 1:407–9; Pach, "Arming the Free World, 1945–1950"; Ireland, *Creating the Entangling Alliance,* 158–68; Kaplan, *A Community of Interests,* 71–79, 85–90.

6. Transcript, Princeton Seminars, 10 October 1953, reel 1, track 1, pp. 9–10.

7. Wherry quoted in Kaplan, *A Community of Interests,* 48; FMACC M-42, 3 December 1949, file FACC Agendas, Minutes, Summaries of Action, FACC-MAP.

8. Equipment valued at only 5 percent of the fiscal year 1951 MAP appropriation for NATO countries had been delivered to the recipients by late 1951. Memorandum and encl., Lawton to Truman, 15 November 1951, folder Budget—Military, 1945–1953, Subject File—Agencies, PSF.

9. Memorandum, Lemnitzer to Burns, 17 July 1950, folder Defense, Secretary of, Subject File—Foreign Affairs, PSF; memorandum of conversation by Acheson, 31 July 1950, folder Memos of Conversation, July 1950, Acheson Papers, Truman Library; memorandum, Webb to Truman, 21 September 1950, folder State, Secy of (2), Subject File—Agencies, PSF; NSC 68/2, 30 September 1950, *FRUS: 1950,* 1:400; Kaplan, *A Community of Interests,* 104–7.

10. Transcript, "Military Assistance Discussions," 20 April 1949, file N7-1, vol. 1, Asst. SecDef FMA; minutes, meeting of the Foreign Military Assistance Coordinating Committee, 3 December 1949, file OMA 337 (3 Dec 49), FMACC vol. 1, FACC-MAP.

Bibliography

PRIMARY SOURCES

United States Government Records

Department of State, Washington, D.C.
  Policy Committee on Arms and Armaments, Lot 58D133, Department of
    State Disarmament File, 1943–60
National Archives, Washington, D.C.
  Adjutant General's Office, 1947– , Record Group 407
  Assistant Chief of Staff of the United States Army, G-4, Logistics, Record
    Group 319
  Assistant Secretary of the Army, Member of the SWNCC/SANACC,
    December 1944–January 1949, Record Group 335
  Assistant to the Secretary of Defense for Foreign Military Assistance,
    Record Group 330
  Bureau of the Budget, Record Group 51
  Department of State, Decimal File, Record Group 59
  Deputy Chief of Staff of the United States Army, G-3, Plans and Combat
    Operations, Record Group 319
  FACC and MAP Documents, Assistant Secretary of Defense (International
    Security Affairs), Office of Military Assistance, Record Group 330
  Forrestal Papers, General Records of the Department of the Navy,
    1798–1947, Record Group 80
  Marshall Mission, 1944–48, Lot 54D270, Record Group 59
  NNFD Reference File, Minutes of the Meetings of the Committee of Three,
    1944–47, Transcripts Prepared by Milton O. Gustafson, Chief, Diplo-
    matic Branch
  Office of European Affairs, 1934–47, Department of State, Record Group 59
  Office of the Chief of Staff, War Department General and Special Staffs,
    Record Group 165
  Office of the Secretary of Defense, Record Group 330
  Operations Division, War Department General and Special Staffs, Record
    Group 165
  Plans and Operations Division, United States Army, Record Group 319
  Policy Planning Staff, Department of State, 1947–53, Lot 64D563, Record
    Group 59
  Secretary of the Army, Gordon Gray and Frank Pace, Jr., 1949–51, Record
    Group 335

Secretary of the Army, Kenneth C. Royall, 1947–49, Record Group 335
Secretary's Daily Meetings, Lot 58D609, Executive Secretariat, Record Group 59
State-Army-Navy-Air Force Coordinating Committee, Interdepartmental and Intradepartmental Committees (State Department), Record Group 353
United States Joint Chiefs of Staff, Record Group 218
Wedemeyer Mission to China, Lot 55D150, Record Group 59
Washington National Records Center, Suitland, Maryland
Assistant Secretary of State for International Security Affairs, Lot No. 52-24, Record Group 59

Personal Papers

Bentley Historical Library, Ann Arbor, Michigan
Arthur H. Vandenberg Papers
Center of Military History, Washington, D.C.
Byron Fairchild Working Papers
W. Averell Harriman Residence, Washington, D.C.
W. Averell Harriman Papers
Seeley G. Mudd Library, Princeton, New Jersey
John Foster Dulles Papers
James V. Forrestal Papers
George F. Kennan Papers
H. Alexander Smith Papers
Naval History Division, Washington, D.C.
James V. Forrestal Diaries
Harry S. Truman Library, Independence, Missouri
Dean Acheson Papers
George V. Allen Papers
Eben A. Ayers Papers
Clark M. Clifford Files
Clark M. Clifford Papers
Matthew J. Connelly Files
George M. Elsey Papers
Henry F. Grady Papers
Joseph M. Jones Papers
Frederick J. Lawton Papers
David O. Lloyd Files
John F. Melby Papers
Edwin G. Nourse Papers
Paul A. Porter Papers
Sidney W. Souers Papers
Harry S. Truman Papers
President's Secretary's File
Confidential File, White House Central Files
James E. Webb Papers
Yale University Library, New Haven, Connecticut
Henry Lewis Stimson Diaries (microfilm edition)

Oral Histories

Seeley G. Mudd Library, Princeton, New Jersey
John Foster Dulles Oral History Project
    Theodore C. Achilles
    Hugh S. Cumming, Jr.
    John D. Hickerson
    Walter H. Judd
Harry S. Truman Library, Independence, Missouri
    Theodore C. Achilles
    Clark M. Clifford
    Kenner F. Hertford
    John D. Hickerson
    Loy W. Henderson
    Walter H. Judd
    Marx Leva
    Edwin A. Locke, Jr.
    H. Freeman Matthews
    Arthur R. Ringwalt
    Philip D. Sprouse

Unpublished Government Studies

"Bi-Lateral Staff Conversations with Latin American Republics." Manuscript history prepared by Historical Section, Caribbean Defense Command, 1947, Center of Military History, Washington, D.C.

Coakley, Robert W. "Roosevelt and Lend-Lease." Manuscript history, n.d., Center of Military History, Washington, D.C.

Coakley, Robert W., et al. "Resumé of Army Roll-Up Following World War II." Paper, 1968, Center of Military History, Washington, D.C.

Fairchild, Byron. "The US Army and the Military Assistance Program." Uncompleted manuscript history, n.d., Center of Military History, Washington, D.C.

Gardner, H. M. "Civil War in Greece, 1945–1949." Manuscript history, n.d., Center of Military History, Washington, D.C.

Hermes, Walter G. "Survey of the Development of the Role of the U.S. Army Military Advisor." Manuscript study, n.d., Center of Military History, Washington, D.C.

"History of the China Theater." Manuscript history, 1946, Center of Military History, Washington, D.C.

"Lend-Lease as of September 30, 1945." Manuscript prepared by International Division, Army Service Forces, n.d., Center of Military History, Washington, D.C.

Pilgert, Henry P., et al. "The History of Foreign Surplus Property Disposal, 1945–1949." Unpublished manuscript, 1949, copy in Records, Office of the Foreign Liquidation Commissioner, Record Group 59, National Archives, Washington, D.C.

Sparrow, John C. "Demobilization of the United States Army after World War II." Paper, 1951, Center of Military History, Washington, D.C.

Published Documents

Carlyle, Margaret, ed. *Documents on International Relations, 1947–1948*. New York: Oxford University Press, 1952.

Congressional Record. 1946–49. Washington, D.C.

Public Papers of the Presidents of the United States: Harry S. Truman, 1946–1949. 4 vols. Washington, D.C.: Government Printing Office, 1962–64.

Report of the Secretary of Defense Frank C. Carlucci to the Congress on the Amended FY1988/FY1989 Biennial Budget. Washington, D.C.: Government Printing Office, 1988.

U.K. Parliament. *Parliamentary Debates* (Commons), 5th ser., vol. 446 (1947–48).

U.S. Congress. House. Committee on Foreign Affairs. *Assistance to Greece and Turkey*. 80th Cong., 1st sess., 1947.

———. *Emergency Foreign Aid*. 80th Cong., 1st sess., 1947.

———. *Inter-American Military Cooperation Act*. 79th Cong., 2d sess., 1946.

———. *Inter-American Military Cooperation Act*. 80th Cong., 1st sess., 1947.

———. *United States Foreign Policy for a Post-War Recovery Program*. 80th Cong., 1st and 2d sess., 1947–48.

U.S. Congress. House. Committee on International Relations. *Selected Executive Session Hearings of the Committee, 1943–1950*. Vol. 3, *Foreign Economic Assistance Programs*, Part 1. Washington, D.C.: Government Printing Office, 1976.

———. *Selected Executive Session Hearings of the Committee, 1943–1950*. Vol. 5, *Military Assistance Programs*, Part 1. Washington, D.C.: Government Printing Office, 1976.

———. *Selected Executive Session Hearings of the Committee, 1943–1950*. Vol. 6, *Military Assistance Programs*, Part 2. Washington, D.C.: Government Printing Office, 1976.

———. *Selected Executive Session Hearings of the Committee, 1943–1950*. Vol. 7, *United States Policy in the Far East*, Part 1. Washington, D.C.: Government Printing Office, 1976.

U.S. Congress. House. Subcommittee of the Committee on Appropriations. *Foreign Aid Appropriations Bill for 1949*. 2 parts. 80th Cong., 1948.

———. *Supplemental Appropriation Bill for 1948*. 80th Cong., 1947.

U.S. Congress. Senate. Armed Services Committee. *Nomination of General of the Army George C. Marshall to be Secretary of Defense*. 81st Cong., 2d sess., 1951.

U.S. Congress. Senate. Committee on Appropriations. *Economic Cooperation Administration*. 80th Cong., 2d sess., 1948.

———. *Third Supplemental Appropriations Bill for 1948*. 80th Cong., 1st sess., 1947.

U.S. Congress. Senate. Committee on Foreign Relations. *Assistance to Greece and Turkey*. 80th Cong., 1st sess., 1947.

———. *Executive Sessions of the Senate Foreign Relations Committee (Historical Series)*. Vol. 1, 80th Cong., 1st and 2d sess., 1947–48. Washington, D.C.: Government Printing Office, 1976.

———. *Foreign Relief Assistance Act of 1948 (Historical Series)*. Washington, D.C.: Government Printing Office, 1973.

———. *Interim Aid for Europe*. 80th Cong., 1st sess., 1947.

———. *Legislative Origins of the Truman Doctrine (Historical Series)*. Washington, D.C.: Government Printing Office, 1973.

————. *Military Assistance Program: 1949 (Historical Series)*. Washington, D.C.: Government Printing Office, 1974.

————. *Reviews of the World Situation: 1949–1950 (Historical Series)*. Washington, D.C.: Government Printing Office, 1974.

————. *The Vandenberg Resolution and the North Atlantic Treaty (Historical Series)*. Washington, D.C.: Government Printing Office, 1973.

U.S. Department of Commerce. Office of Business Economics. *Foreign Aid by the United States Government, 1940–1951*. Washington, D.C.: Government Printing Office, 1952.

U.S. Department of State. *Foreign Relations of the United States*. Annual volumes, 1942–1950. Washington, D.C.: Government Printing Office, 1963–1977.

————. *Foreign Relations of the United States: 1943, China*. Washington, D.C.: Government Printing Office, 1957.

————. *Foreign Relations of the United States: The Conference of Berlin, 1945*. 2 vols. Washington, D.C.: Government Printing Office, 1960.

————. *The Military Assistance Program*. General Foreign Policy Series 13. July 1949.

————. *Register of the Department of State: December 1, 1946*. Washington, D.C.: Government Printing Office, 1947.

————. *Register of the Department of State: April 1, 1948*. Washington, D. C.: Government Printing Office, 1948.

————. *United States Relations with China: With Special Reference to the Period 1944–1949*. Washington, D.C.: Government Printing Office, 1949.

U.S. Department of State. Agency for International Development. *U.S. Overseas Loans and Grants and Assistance from International Organizations, July 1, 1945–September 30, 1987*. Washington, D.C.: Government Printing Office, 1987.

U.S. Department of State. International Cooperation Administration. *U.S. Foreign Assistance and Assistance from International Organizations, July 1, 1945–June 30, 1960*. Washington, D.C.: Government Printing Office, 1960.

Newspapers and Periodicals

Congressional Quarterly Almanac
Department of State Bulletin
New York Times
Washington Post

Autobiographies, Memoirs, and Published Papers

Acheson, Dean. *Present at the Creation: My Years in the State Department*. New York: W. W. Norton, 1969.

Arnold, H. H. *Global Mission*. New York: Harper & Brothers, 1949.

Berle, Beatrice Bishop, and Travis Beal Jacobs, eds. *Navigating the Rapids, 1918–1971: From the Papers of Adolf A. Berle*. New York: Harcourt Brace Jovanovich, 1973.

Blum, John Morton, ed. *The Price of Vision: The Diary of Henry A. Wallace, 1942–1946*. Boston: Houghton Mifflin, 1973.

Bohlen, Charles E. *Witness to History: 1929–1969.* New York: W. W. Norton, 1973.

Braden, Spruille. *Diplomats and Demagogues: The Memoirs of Spruille Braden.* New Rochelle, N.Y.: Arlington House, 1971.

Byrnes, James F. *All in One Lifetime.* New York: Harper & Brothers, 1958.

————. *Speaking Frankly.* New York: Harper & Brothers, 1947.

Campbell, Thomas M., and George C. Herring, eds. *The Diaries of Edward R. Stettinius, Jr., 1943–1946.* New York: New Viewpoints, 1975.

Chennault, Claire Lee. *Way of a Fighter.* New York: G. P. Putnam's Sons, 1949.

Complete Presidential Press Conferences of Franklin D. Roosevelt. 25 vols. New York: Da Capo Press, 1972.

Connally, Tom, with Alfred Steinberg. *My Name is Tom Connally.* New York: Thomas Y. Crowell, 1954.

Dalton, Hugh. *High Tide and After: Memoirs, 1945–1960.* London: Frederick Muller, 1962.

Davies, John Paton, Jr. *Dragon by the Tail: American, British, Japanese, and Russian Encounters with China and One Another.* New York: W. W. Norton, 1972.

Djilas, Milovan. *Conversations with Stalin.* New York: Harcourt, Brace & World, 1962.

Ferrell, Robert H., ed. *Off the Record: The Private Papers of Harry S. Truman.* New York: Harper & Row, 1980.

Galambos, Louis, ed. *The Papers of Dwight D. Eisenhower.* Vols. 7–9, *The Chief of Staff.* Baltimore: Johns Hopkins University Press, 1978.

Gladwyn, Lord. *The Memoirs of Lord Gladwyn.* London: Weidenfeld and Nicolson, 1972.

Hull, Cordell. *The Memoirs of Cordell Hull.* 2 vols. New York: Macmillan, 1948.

Iatrides, John O., ed. *Ambassador MacVeagh Reports: Greece, 1933–1947.* Princeton: Princeton University Press, 1980.

Kennan, George F. *Memoirs: 1925–1950.* Boston: Little, Brown, 1967.

Khrushchev, Nikita S. *Khrushchev Remembers: The Last Testament.* Boston: Little, Brown, 1974.

Krock, Arthur. *Memoirs: Sixty Years on the Firing Line.* New York: Funk & Wagnalls, 1968.

Leahy, William D. *I Was There: The Personal Story of the Chief of Staff to Presidents Roosevelt and Truman Based on His Notes and Diaries Made at the Time.* New York: Whittlesey House, 1950.

Lilienthal, David E. *Journals.* Vol. 2, *The Atomic Energy Years, 1945–1950.* New York: Harper & Row, 1964.

Marshall, George C. *Marshall's Mission to China.* 2 vols. Arlington, Va.: University Publications of America, 1976.

Melby, John F. *The Mandate of Heaven: Record of a Civil War, China, 1945–1949.* Toronto: University of Toronto Press, 1968.

Millis, Walter, ed. *The Forrestal Diaries.* New York: Viking, 1951.

Munro, John A., and Alex I. Inglis, eds. *Mike: The Memoirs of the Right Honourable Lester B. Pearson.* 3 vols. Toronto: University of Toronto Press, 1972–75.

Rosenman, Samuel I., ed. *The Public Papers and Addresses of Franklin D. Roosevelt.* 13 vols. New York: Random House, Macmillan, and Harper & Brothers, 1938–50.

Smith, Jean Edward, ed. *The Papers of Lucius D. Clay: Germany, 1945–1949.* 2 vols. Bloomington: Indiana University Press, 1974.

Stuart, John Leighton. *Fifty Years in China*. New York: Random House, 1954.
Truman, Harry S. *Memoirs*. 2 vols. Garden City, N.Y.: Doubleday, 1955–56.
Vandenberg, Arthur H., Jr. *The Private Papers of Senator Vandenberg*. Boston: Houghton Mifflin, 1952.
Wedemeyer, Albert C. *Wedemeyer Reports!* New York: Henry Holt, 1958.

SECONDARY WORKS

Books

Albion, Robert Greenhalgh, and Robert Howe Connery. *Forrestal and the Navy*. New York: Columbia University Press, 1962.
Alexander, G. M. *The Prelude to the Truman Doctrine: British Policy in Greece, 1944–1947*. Oxford: Clarendon Press, 1982.
Alvarez, David J. *Bureaucracy and Cold War Diplomacy: The United States and Turkey, 1943–1946*. Thessaloniki: Institute for Balkan Studies, 1980.
Amen, Michael Mark. *American Foreign Policy in Greece 1944/1949: Economic, Military, and Institutional Aspects*. Frankfurt am Main: Peter Lang, 1978.
Arkes, Hadley. *Bureaucracy, the Marshall Plan, and the National Interest*. Princeton: Princeton University Press, 1972.
Atwater, Elton. *American Regulation of Arms Exports*. Washington, D.C.: Carnegie Endowment for International Peace, 1941.
Baram, Philip J. *The Department of State in the Middle East, 1919–1945*. Philadelphia: University of Pennsylvania Press, 1978.
Barnet, Richard J. *Roots of War: The Men and Institutions Behind U.S. Foreign Policy*. Baltimore: Penguin Books, 1972.
Betts, Richard K. *Soldiers, Statesmen, and Cold War Crises*. Cambridge: Harvard University Press, 1977.
Blum, Robert M. *Drawing the Line: The Origin of the American Containment Policy in East Asia*. New York: W. W. Norton, 1982.
Borg, Dorothy, and Waldo Heinrichs, eds. *Uncertain Years: Chinese-American Relations, 1947–1950*. New York: Columbia University Press, 1980.
Braun, Herbert. *The Assassination of Gaitán: Public Life and Urban Violence in Columbia*. Madison: University of Wisconsin Press, 1985.
Brown, William Adams, and Redvers Opie. *American Foreign Assistance*. Washington, D.C.: Brookings Institution, 1953.
Buhite, Russell D. *Patrick J. Hurley and American Foreign Policy*. Ithaca: Cornell University Press, 1973.
Campbell, John C. *The United States in World Affairs, 1945–1947*. New York: Harper & Brothers, 1947.
———. *The United States in World Affairs, 1947–1948*. New York: Harper & Brothers, 1948.
Chassin, Lionel Max. *The Communist Conquest of China: A History of the Civil War, 1945–1949*. Cambridge: Harvard University Press, 1965.
Chern, Kenneth S. *Dilemma in China: America's Policy Debate, 1945*. Hamden, Conn.: Archon Books, 1980.
Child, John. *Unequal Alliance: The Inter-American Military System, 1938–1979*. Boulder, Colo.: Westview Press, 1980.
Coakley, Robert W., and Richard M. Leighton. *Global Logistics and Strategy:*

1943–1945. U.S. Army in World War II. Washington, D.C.: Office of the Chief of Military History, 1955.

Cohen, Warren I. *America's Response to China: An Interpretive History of Sino-American Relations.* New York: John Wiley and Sons, 1971.

———. *Dean Rusk.* Vol. 19 of *The American Secretaries of State and Their Diplomacy.* Totowa, N.J.: Cooper Square Publishers, 1980.

Condit, Kenneth W. *The Joint Chiefs of Staff and National Policy.* Vol. 2, *1947–1949.* The History of the Joint Chiefs of Staff. Wilmington, Del.: Michael Glazier, 1979.

Conn, Stetson, and Byron Fairchild. *The Framework of Hemisphere Defense.* U.S. Army in World War II. Washington, D.C.: Office of the Chief of Military History, 1960.

Connell-Smith, Gordon. *The Inter-American System.* New York: Oxford University Press, 1966.

Craven, Wesley Frank, and James Lea Cate, eds. *The Army Air Forces in World War II.* Vol. 4, *The Pacific: Guadalcanal to Saipan, August 1942 to July 1944.* Chicago: University of Chicago Press, 1950.

Cumings, Bruce. *The Origins of the Korean War: Liberation and the Emergence of Separate Regimes, 1945–1947.* Princeton: Princeton University Press, 1981.

Dallek, Robert. *Franklin D. Roosevelt and American Foreign Policy, 1932–1945.* New York: Oxford University Press, 1979.

Davis, Harold Eugene, John J. Finan, and F. Taylor Peck. *Latin American Diplomatic History: An Introduction.* Baton Rouge: Louisiana State University Press, 1977.

Davis, Vincent. *Postwar Defense and the U.S. Navy, 1943–1946.* Chapel Hill: University of North Carolina Press, 1966.

DeConde, Alexander. *Herbert Hoover's Latin American Policy.* Stanford: Stanford University Press, 1951.

———, ed. *Encyclopedia of American Foreign Policy: Studies of the Principal Movements and Ideas.* 3 vols. New York: Charles Scribner's Sons, 1978.

DeSantis, Hugh. *The Diplomacy of Silence: The American Foreign Service, the Soviet Union, and the Cold War, 1933–1947.* Chicago: University of Chicago Press, 1980.

Divine, Robert A. *The Reluctant Belligerent: American Entry into World War II.* 2d ed. New York: John Wiley and Sons, 1979.

Donovan, Robert J. *Conflict and Crisis: The Presidency of Harry S Truman, 1945–1948.* New York: W. W. Norton, 1977.

———. *Tumultuous Years: The Presidency of Harry S Truman, 1949–1953.* New York: W. W. Norton, 1982.

Duggan, Laurence. *The Americas: The Search for Hemisphere Security.* New York: Henry Holt, 1949.

Elsey, George M. *Roosevelt and China: The White House Story.* Wilmington, Del.: Michael Glazier, 1979.

Estep, Raymond. *United States Military Aid to Latin America.* Maxwell Air Force Base: The Air University, 1966.

Etzold, Thomas H., ed. *Aspects of Sino-American Relations Since 1784.* New York: New Viewpoints, 1978.

Fagg, John Edwin. *Latin America: A General History.* 3d ed. New York: Macmillan, 1977.

Farley, Philip J., Stephen S. Kaplan, and William H. Lewis. *Arms Across the Sea.* Washington, D.C.: Brookings Institution, 1978.

Feis, Herbert. *The China Tangle: The American Effort in China from Pearl Harbor to the Marshall Mission.* Princeton: Princeton University Press, 1953.

——. *Seen From E.A.: Three International Episodes.* New York: Alfred A. Knopf, 1947.

Ferrell, Robert H. *George C. Marshall.* Vol. 15 of *The American Secretaries of State and Their Diplomacy.* New York: Cooper Square Publishers, 1966.

Field, James A., Jr. *America and the Mediterranean World, 1776–1882.* Princeton: Princeton University Press, 1969.

Freeland, Richard M. *The Truman Doctrine and the Origins of McCarthyism: Foreign Policy, Domestic Politics and Internal Security, 1946–1948.* New York: Alfred A. Knopf, 1972.

Friedlander, Saul. *Prelude to Downfall: Hitler and the United States, 1939–1941.* Translated by Aline B. and Alexander Werth. New York: Alfred A. Knopf, 1967.

Frye, Alton. *Nazi Germany and the American Hemisphere, 1933–1941.* New Haven: Yale University Press, 1967.

Fulbright, J. William. *The Crippled Giant: American Foreign Policy and Its Domestic Consequences.* New York: Random House, 1972.

Gaddis, John Lewis. *The Long Peace: Inquiries into the History of the Cold War.* New York: Oxford University Press, 1987.

——. *Russia, the Soviet Union and the United States: An Interpretive History.* New York: John Wiley and Sons, 1978.

——. *The United States and the Origins of the Cold War, 1941–1947.* New York: Columbia University Press, 1972.

Gallicchio, Marc S. *The Cold War Begins in Asia: American East Asian Policy and the Fall of the Japanese Empire.* New York: Columbia University Press, 1988.

Gellman, Irwin F. *Good Neighbor Diplomacy: United States Policies in Latin America, 1933–1945.* Baltimore: Johns Hopkins University Press, 1979.

——. *Roosevelt and Batista: Good Neighbor Diplomacy in Cuba, 1933–1945.* Albuquerque: University of New Mexico Press, 1973.

Gimbel, John. *The Origins of the Marshall Plan.* Stanford: Stanford University Press, 1976.

Goldberg, Alfred, ed. *A History of the United States Air Force, 1907–1957.* New York: D. Van Nostrand, 1957.

Gormly, James L. *The Collapse of the Grand Alliance, 1945–1948.* Baton Rouge: Louisiana State University Press, 1987.

Green, David. *The Containment of Latin America: A History of the Myths and Realities of the Good Neighbor Policy.* Chicago: Quadrangle Books, 1971.

Grow, Michael. *The Good Neighbor Policy and Authoritarianism in Paraguay: United States Economic Expansion and Great-Power Rivalry in Latin America during World War II.* Lawrence: Regents Press of Kansas, 1981.

Haglund, David G. *Latin America and the Transformation of U.S. Strategic Thought, 1936–1940.* Albuquerque: University of New Mexico Press, 1984.

Harbutt, Fraser J. *The Iron Curtain: Churchill, America, and the Origins of the Cold War.* New York: Oxford University Press, 1986.

Harkavy, Robert E. *The Arms Trade and International Systems.* Cambridge, Mass.: Ballinger, 1975.

Hartmann, Susan M. *Truman and the 80th Congress.* Columbia: University of Missouri Press, 1971.

Hathaway, Robert M. *Ambiguous Partnership: Britain and America, 1944–1947.* New York: Columbia University Press, 1981.

Hawes, Grace M. *The Marshall Plan for China: Economic Cooperation Administration, 1948–1949.* Cambridge, Mass.: Schenkman, 1977.

Heller, Francis H., ed. *The Korean War: A 25-Year Perspective.* Lawrence: Regents Press of Kansas, 1977.

Herken, Gregg. *The Winning Weapon: The Atomic Bomb in the Cold War, 1945–1950.* New York: Vintage Books, 1982.

Herring, George C., Jr. *Aid to Russia, 1941–1946: Strategy, Diplomacy and the Origins of the Cold War.* New York: Columbia University Press, 1973.

Hess, Gary R. *The United States' Emergence as a Southeast Asian Power, 1940–1950.* New York: Columbia University Press, 1987.

Hewes, James E., Jr. *From Root to McNamara: Army Organization and Administration, 1900–1963.* Special Studies Series. Washington, D.C.: Center of Military History, 1975.

Hilton, Stanley E. *Hitler's Secret War in South America, 1939–1945: German Military Espionage and Allied Counterespionage in Brazil.* Baton Rouge: Louisiana State University Press, 1981.

Hogan, Michael J. *The Marshall Plan: America, Britain, and the Reconstruction of Western Europe, 1947–1952.* Cambridge: Cambridge University Press, 1987.

Hovey, Harold A. *United States Military Assistance: A Study of Policies and Practices.* New York: Praeger, 1963.

Howard, Harry N. *Turkey, the Straits and U.S. Policy.* Baltimore: Johns Hopkins University Press, 1974.

Huston, James A. *The Sinews of War: Army Logistics 1775–1953.* U.S. Army Historical Series. Washington, D.C.: Office of the Chief of Military History, 1966.

Iatrides, John O. *Revolt in Athens: The Greek Communist "Second Round," 1944–1945.* Princeton: Princeton University Press, 1972.

Ireland, Timothy P. *Creating the Entangling Alliance: The Origins of the North Atlantic Treaty Organization.* Westport, Conn.: Greenwood Press, 1981.

Iriye, Akira. *The Cold War in Asia: A Historical Introduction.* Englewood Cliffs, N.J.: Prentice-Hall, 1974.

Isaacson, Walter, and Evan Thomas. *The Wise Men: Six Friends and the World They Made.* New York: Simon & Schuster, 1986.

Jones, Howard. *"A New Kind of War:" America's Global Strategy and the Truman Doctrine in Greece.* New York: Oxford University Press, 1989.

Jones, Joseph M. *The Fifteen Weeks: February 21–June 5, 1947.* New York: Viking, 1955.

Kahn, E. J., Jr. *The China Hands: America's Foreign Service Officers and What Befell Them.* New York: Viking, 1975.

Kaplan, Lawrence S. *A Community of Interests: NATO and the Military Assistance Program, 1948–1951.* Washington, D.C.: Office of the Secretary of Defense, Historical Office, 1980.

———. *The United States and NATO: The Formative Years.* Lexington: University Press of Kentucky, 1984.

Kerkvliet, Benedict J. *The Huk Rebellion: A Study of Peasant Revolt in the Philippines.* Berkeley: University of California Press, 1977.

Kimball, Warren F. *The Most Unsordid Act: Lend-Lease, 1939–1941.* Baltimore: Johns Hopkins University Press, 1969.

Kolko, Joyce and Gabriel. *The Limits of Power: The World and United States Foreign Policy, 1945–1954*. New York: Harper & Row, 1972.
Kolodziej, Edward A. *The Uncommon Defense and Congress, 1945–1953*. Columbus: Ohio State University Press, 1966.
Kuniholm, Bruce Robellet. *The Origins of the Cold War in the Near East: Great Power Conflict and Diplomacy in Iran, Turkey, and Greece*. Princeton: Princeton University Press, 1980.
LaFeber, Walter. *America, Russia, and the Cold War, 1945–1984*. 5th ed. New York: Alfred A. Knopf, 1985.
Langer, William L., and S. Everett Gleason. *The Challenge to Isolation, 1937–1940*. New York: Harper & Brothers, 1952.
————. *The Undeclared War, 1940–1941*. New York: Harper & Brothers, 1953.
Leighton, Richard M., and Robert W. Coakley. *Global Logistics and Strategy: 1940–1943*. U.S. Army in World War II. Washington, D.C.: Office of the Chief of Military History, 1955.
Lenczowski, George. *The Middle East in World Affairs*. 4th ed. Ithaca: Cornell University Press, 1980.
————. *Russia and the West in Iran, 1918–1948: A Study in Big-Power Rivalry*. Ithaca: Cornell University Press, 1949.
Lieuwen, Edwin. *Arms and Politics in Latin America*. New York: Praeger, 1960.
Lippmann, Walter. *The Cold War: A Study in U.S. Foreign Policy*. New York: Harper & Row, 1972.
Liu, F. F. *A Military History of Modern China, 1924–1949*. Princeton: Princeton University Press, 1956. Reprint. Port Washington, N.Y.: Kennikat Press, 1972.
Louis, William Roger. *The British Empire in the Middle East: Arab Nationalism, the United States, and Postwar Imperialism*. Oxford: Clarendon Press, 1984.
Lundestad, Geir. *America, Scandinavia, and the Cold War, 1945–1949*. New York: Columbia University Press, 1980.
McCann, Frank D., Jr. *The Brazilian-American Alliance, 1937–1945*. Princeton: Princeton University Press, 1973.
McLellan, David S. *Dean Acheson: The State Department Years*. New York: Dodd, Mead, 1976.
McNeill, William H. *The Metamorphosis of Greece Since World War II*. Chicago: University of Chicago Press, 1978.
Martel, Leon. *Lend-Lease, Loans, and the Coming of the Cold War: A Study of the Implementation of Foreign Policy*. Boulder, Colo.: Westview Press, 1979.
Mason, Herbert Molloy, Jr. *The United States Air Force: A Turbulent History*. New York: Mason Charter, 1976.
Matloff, Maurice. *Strategic Planning for Coalition Warfare: 1943–1944*. U.S. Army in World War II. Washington, D.C.: Office of the Chief of Military History, 1959.
May, Ernest R. *"Lessons" of the Past: The Use and Misuse of History in American Foreign Policy*. New York: Oxford University Press, 1973.
————. *The Truman Administration and China, 1945–1949*. The America's Alternative Series. Philadelphia: J. B. Lippincott, 1975.
May, Gary. *China Scapegoat: The Diplomatic Ordeal of John Carter Vincent*. Washington, D.C.: New Republic Books, 1979.
Mecham, J. Lloyd. *The United States and Inter-American Security, 1889–1960*. Austin: University of Texas Press, 1961.
Merli, Frank J., and Theodore A. Wilson, eds. *Makers of American Diplomacy:*

From Benjamin Franklin to Henry Kissinger. New York: Charles Scribner's Sons, 1974.

Messer, Robert L. *The End of an Alliance: James F. Byrnes, Roosevelt, Truman, and the Origins of the Cold War.* Chapel Hill: University of North Carolina Press, 1982.

Miller, Aaron David. *Search for Security: Saudi Arabian Oil and American Foreign Policy, 1939–1949.* Chapel Hill: University of North Carolina Press, 1980.

Miller, James Edward. *The United States and Italy, 1940–1950: The Politics and Diplomacy of Stabilization.* Chapel Hill: University of North Carolina Press, 1986.

Millett, Allan R. *Semper Fidelis: The History of the United States Marine Corps.* New York: Macmillan, 1980.

Motter, T. H. Vail. *The Persian Corridor and Aid to Russia.* U.S. Army in World War II. Washington, D.C.: Office of the Chief of Military History, 1952.

Munro, Dana G. *The United States and the Caribbean Republics, 1921–1933.* Princeton: Princeton University Press, 1974.

Ninkovich, Frank A. *The Diplomacy of Ideas: U.S. Foreign Policy and Cultural Relations, 1938–1950.* Cambridge: Cambridge University Press, 1981.

Notter, Harley D. *Postwar Foreign Policy Preparation.* Washington, D.C.: Government Printing Office, 1949.

O'Ballance, Edgar. *The Greek Civil War, 1944–1949.* New York: Praeger, 1966.

Painter, David S. *Oil and the American Century: The Political Economy of U.S. Foreign Oil Policy, 1941–1954.* Baltimore: Johns Hopkins University Press, 1986.

Paterson, Thomas G. *On Every Front: The Making of the Cold War.* New York: W. W. Norton, 1979.

———. *Soviet-American Confrontation: Postwar Reconstruction and the Origins of the Cold War.* Baltimore: Johns Hopkins University Press, 1973.

———, ed. *Cold War Critics: Alternatives to American Foreign Policy in the Truman Years.* Chicago: Quadrangle Books, 1971.

———, ed. *Containment and the Cold War: American Foreign Policy Since 1945.* Reading, Mass.: Addison-Wesley, 1973.

Peterson, Harold F. *Argentina and the United States, 1810–1960.* Albany: State University of New York Press, 1964.

Pierre, Andrew J., ed. *Arms Transfers and American Foreign Policy.* New York: New York University Press, 1979.

Pogue, Forrest C. *George C. Marshall: Ordeal and Hope, 1939–1942.* New York: Viking, 1966.

———. *George C. Marshall: Organizer of Victory, 1942–1945.* New York: Viking, 1973.

———. *George C. Marshall: Statesman, 1945–1959.* New York: Viking, 1987.

Pollard, Robert A. *Economic Security and the Origins of the Cold War, 1945–1950.* New York: Columbia University Press, 1985.

Poole, Walter S. *The Joint Chiefs of Staff and National Policy.* Vol. 4, *1950–1952.* The History of the Joint Chiefs of Staff. Wilmington, Del.: Michael Glazier, 1979.

Pranger, Robert J., and Dale R. Tahtinen. *Toward A Realistic Military Assistance Program.* Washington, D.C.: American Enterprise Institute for Public Policy Research, 1974.

Price, Harry Bayard. *The Marshall Plan and Its Meaning.* Ithaca: Cornell University Press, 1955.

Purifoy, Lewis McCarroll. *Harry Truman's China Policy: McCarthyism and the Diplomacy of Hysteria, 1947–1951.* New York: New Viewpoints, 1976.

Rabe, Stephen G. *Eisenhower and Latin America: The Foreign Policy of Anticommunism.* Chapel Hill: University of North Carolina Press, 1988.

Ramazani, Rouhallah K. *Iran's Foreign Policy, 1941–1973: A Study of Foreign Policy in Modernizing Nations.* Charlottesville: University of Virginia Press, 1975.

Rearden, Steven L. *The Formative Years, 1947–1950.* Vol. 1 of *History of the Office of the Secretary of Defense,* edited by Alfred Goldberg. Washington, D.C.: Office of the Secretary of Defense, Historical Office, 1984.

Reid, Escott. *Time of Fear and Hope: The Making of the North Atlantic Treaty, 1947–1949.* Toronto: McClelland and Stewart, 1977.

Reynolds, David. *The Creation of the Anglo-American Alliance, 1937–41: A Study in Competitive Co-operation.* Chapel Hill: University of North Carolina Press, 1982.

Rogow, Arnold A. *James Forrestal: A Study of Personality, Politics, and Policy.* New York: Macmillan, 1963.

Romanus, Charles F., and Riley Sunderland. *Stilwell's Command Problems.* U.S. Army in World War II. Washington, D.C.: Office of the Chief of Military History, 1956.

———. *Stilwell's Mission to China.* U.S. Army in World War II. Washington, D.C.: Office of the Chief of Military History, 1953.

Rose, Lisle A. *Roots of Tragedy: The United States and the Struggle for Asia, 1945–1953.* Westport, Conn.: Greenwood Press, 1976.

Rubin, Barry. *The Great Powers in the Middle East, 1941–1947: The Road to the Cold War.* London: Frank Cass, 1980.

———. *Paved with Good Intentions: The American Experience and Iran.* New York: Oxford University Press, 1980.

Sawyer, Robert K. *Military Advisors in Korea: KMAG in Peace and War.* Washington, D.C.: Office of the Chief of Military History, 1962.

Schaller, Michael. *The United States and China in the Twentieth Century.* New York: Oxford University Press, 1979.

———. *The U.S. Crusade in China, 1938–1945.* New York: Columbia University Press, 1979.

Schirmer, Daniel B., and Stephen Rosskamm Shalom, eds. *The Philippines Reader: A History of Colonialism, Neocolonialism, Dictatorship, and Resistance.* Boston: South End Press, 1987.

Schnabel, James F. *The Joint Chiefs of Staff and National Policy.* Vol. 1, *1945–1947.* The History of the Joint Chiefs of Staff. Wilmington, Del.: Michael Glazier, 1979.

Service, John S. *The Amerasia Papers: Some Problems in the History of US-China Relations.* Berkeley: Center for Chinese Studies, 1971.

Shalom, Stephen Rosskamm. *The United States and the Philippines: A Study of Neocolonialism.* Philadelphia: Institute for the Study of Human Issues, 1981.

Sheridan, James E. *China in Disintegration: The Republican Era in Chinese History, 1912–1949.* New York: Free Press, 1975.

Sherry, Michael S. *Preparing for the Next War: American Plans for Postwar Defense, 1941–45.* New Haven: Yale University Press, 1977.

———. *The Rise of American Air Power: The Creation of Armageddon.* New Haven: Yale University Press, 1987.

Smith, Bradley F. *The Shadow Warriors: O.S.S. and the Origins of the C.I.A.* New York: Basic Books, 1983.

Smith, Gaddis. *Dean Acheson.* Vol. 16 of *The American Secretaries of State and Their Diplomacy.* New York: Cooper Square Publishers, 1972.

Smith, Perry McCoy. *The Air Force Plans for Peace, 1943–1945.* Baltimore: Johns Hopkins University Press, 1970.

Smith, Robert Freeman. *The United States and Revolutionary Nationalism in Mexico, 1916–1932.* Chicago: University of Chicago Press, 1972.

Spector, Ronald H. *Eagle Against the Sun: The American War with Japan.* New York: Free Press, 1984.

Stavrianos, L. S. *Greece: American Dilemma and Opportunity.* Chicago: Henry Regnery, 1952.

Stebbins, Richard P. *The United States in World Affairs, 1949.* New York: Harper & Brothers, 1950.

Steel, Ronald. *Walter Lippmann and the American Century.* Boston: Little, Brown, 1980.

Stettinius, Edward R., Jr. *Lend-Lease: Weapon for Victory.* New York: Macmillan, 1944.

Stiller, Jesse H. *George S. Messersmith: Diplomat of Democracy.* Chapel Hill: University of North Carolina Press, 1987.

Stoff, Michael B. *Oil, War, and American Security: The Search for a National Policy on Foreign Oil, 1941–1947.* New Haven: Yale University Press, 1980.

Stueck, William. *The Road to Confrontation: American Policy Toward China and Korea, 1947–1950.* Chapel Hill: University of North Carolina Press, 1981.

———. *The Wedemeyer Mission: American Politics and Foreign Policy during the Cold War.* Athens: University of Georgia Press, 1984.

Stuhler, Barbara. *Ten Men of Minnesota and American Foreign Policy, 1898–1968.* St. Paul: Minnesota Historical Society, 1973.

Thomas, Hugh. *Armed Truce: The Beginnings of the Cold War, 1945–1946.* New York: Atheneum, 1987.

Thorne, Christopher. *Allies of a Kind: The United States, Britain, and the War Against Japan, 1941–1945.* New York: Oxford University Press, 1978.

Truman, Margaret. *Harry S. Truman.* New York: William Morrow, 1973.

Tsou, Tang. *America's Failure in China, 1941–50.* Chicago: University of Chicago Press, 1963.

Tuchman, Barbara W. *Stilwell and the American Experience in China, 1911–45.* New York: Macmillan, 1971.

Tulchin, Joseph S. *The Aftermath of War: World War I and U.S. Policy Toward Latin America.* New York: New York University Press, 1971.

Ulam, Adam B. *Expansion and Coexistence: Soviet Foreign Policy, 1917–1973.* 2d ed. New York: Praeger, 1974.

Varg, Paul A. *The Closing of the Door: Sino-American Relations, 1936–1946.* East Lansing: Michigan State University Press, 1973.

Vigneras, Marcel. *Rearming the French.* U.S. Army in World War II. Washington, D.C.: Office of the Chief of Military History, 1957.

Ward, Patricia Dawson. *The Threat of Peace: James F. Byrnes and the Council of Foreign Ministers, 1945–1946.* Kent, Ohio: Kent State University Press, 1979.

Welles, Sumner. *Where Are We Heading?* New York: Harper & Brothers, 1946.

Westerfield, H. Bradford. *Foreign Policy and Party Politics: Pearl Harbor to Korea.* New Haven: Yale University Press, 1955.

Wilkins, Mira. *The Maturing of Multinational Enterprise: American Business Abroad from 1914 to 1970.* Cambridge: Harvard University Press, 1974.
Wilson, Theodore A. *The Marshall Plan, 1947–1951.* Headline Series 236. New York: Foreign Policy Association, 1977.
Wittner, Lawrence S. *American Intervention in Greece, 1943–1949.* New York: Columbia University Press, 1982.
Wolk, Herman S. *Planning and Organizing the Postwar Air Force, 1943–1947.* United States Air Force General Histories. Washington, D.C.: Office of Air Force History, 1984.
Wood, Bryce. *The Dismantling of the Good Neighbor Policy.* Austin: University of Texas Press, 1985.
Woodhouse, C. M. *The Struggle for Greece: 1941–1949.* London: Hart-Davis, MacGibbon, 1979.
Woods, Randall Bennett. *The Roosevelt Foreign-Policy Establishment and the "Good Neighbor": The United States and Argentina, 1941–1945.* Lawrence: Regents Press of Kansas, 1979.
Wright, L. C. *United States Policy Toward Egypt, 1830–1914.* New York: Exposition Press, 1969.
Xydis, Stephen G. *Greece and the Great Powers: Prelude to the "Truman Doctrine."* Thessaloniki: Institute for Balkan Studies, 1963.
Yergin, Daniel. *Shattered Peace: The Origins of the Cold War and the National Security State.* Boston: Houghton Mifflin, 1977.

Articles

Adler, Les K., and Thomas G. Paterson. "Red Fascism: The Merger of Nazi Germany and Soviet Russia in the American Image of Totalitarianism, 1930's–1950's." *American Historical Review* 75 (April 1970): 1046–64.
Dingman, Roger. "Strategic Planning and the Policy Process: American Plans for War in East Asia, 1945–1950." *Naval War College Review* 32 (November–December 1979): 4–21.
Etzold, Thomas H. "American Organization for National Security, 1945–1950." In *Containment: Documents on American Policy and Strategy, 1945–1950,* edited by John Lewis Gaddis and Thomas H. Etzold. New York: Columbia University Press, 1978.
Feaver, John H. "The China Aid Bill of 1948: Limited Assistance as a Cold War Strategy." *Diplomatic History* 5 (Spring 1981): 107–20.
Fetzer, James. "Senator Vandenberg and the American Commitment to China, 1945–1950." *The Historian* 36 (February 1974): 283–303.
Folly, Martin H. "Breaking the Vicious Circle: Britain, the United States and the Genesis of the North Atlantic Treaty." *Diplomatic History* 12 (Winter 1988): 59–77.
Furniss, Edgar S., Jr. "American Wartime Objectives in Latin America." In *American Military Policy: Strategic Aspects of World Political Geography.* New York: Rinehart, 1977.
Gaddis, John Lewis. "Containment: A Reassessment." *Foreign Affairs* 55 (July 1977): 873–87.
———. "Korea in American Politics, Strategy, and Diplomacy, 1945–1950." In *The Origins of the Cold War in Asia,* edited by Yōnosuke Nagai and Akira Iriye. New York: Columbia University Press, 1977.

————. "Was the Truman Doctrine a Real Turning Point?" *Foreign Affairs* 52 (January 1974): 386–402.

Gelb, Leslie R. "Arms Sales." *Foreign Policy* 25 (Winter 1976–77): 3–23.

Gormly, James L. "Keeping the Door Open in Saudi Arabia: The United States and the Dhahran Airfield, 1945–46." *Diplomatic History* 4 (Spring 1980): 189–205.

Haines, Gerald K. "Under the Eagle's Wing: The Franklin Roosevelt Administration Forges an American Hemisphere." *Diplomatic History* 1 (Fall 1977): 373–88.

Henrikson, Alan K. "The Creation of the North Atlantic Alliance, 1948–1952." *Naval War College Review* 32 (May–June 1980): 4–39.

Hess, Gary R. "The Iranian Crisis of 1945–46 and the Cold War." *Political Science Quarterly* 89 (March 1974): 117–46.

Hilton, Stanley E. "The United States, Brazil, and the Cold War, 1945–1960: End of a Special Relationship." *Journal of American History* 68 (December 1981): 599–624.

Hogan, Michael J. "American Marshall Planners and the Search for a European Neocapitalism." *American Historical Review* 90 (February 1985): 44–72.

————. "Paths to Plenty: Marshall Planners and the Debate over European Integration, 1947–1948." *Pacific Historical Review* 53 (August 1984): 337–66.

————. "The Search for a Creative Peace: The United States, European Unity, and the Origins of the Marshall Plan." *Diplomatic History* 6 (Summer 1982): 267–85.

Hudson, Daryl J. "Vandenberg Reconsidered: Senate Resolution 239 and American Foreign Policy." *Diplomatic History* 1 (Winter 1977): 46–63.

Kaplan, Stephen S. "U.S. Arms Transfers to Latin America: Rational Strategy, Bureaucratic Politics, and Executive Parameters." *International Studies Quarterly* 19 (December 1975): 399–431.

Kemp, Geoffrey. "Dilemmas of the Arms Traffic." *Foreign Affairs* 48 (January 1970): 274–84.

Kemp, Geoffrey, with Steven Miller. "The Arms Transfer Phenomenon." In *Arms Transfers and American Foreign Policy,* edited by Andrew J. Pierre. New York: New York University Press, 1979.

Leffler, Melvyn P. "The American Conception of National Security and the Beginnings of the Cold War, 1945–48." *American Historical Review* 89 (April 1984): 346–81.

————. "Strategy, Diplomacy, and the Cold War: The United States, Turkey, and NATO, 1945–1952." *Journal of American History* 71 (March 1985): 807–25.

————. "The United States and the Strategic Dimensions of the Marshall Plan." *Diplomatic History* 12 (Summer 1988): 277–306.

Levine, Steven I. "A New Look at American Mediation in the Chinese Civil War: The Marshall Mission and Manchuria." *Diplomatic History* 3 (Fall 1979): 349–75.

McCann, Frank D. "Brazil, the United States, and World War II: A Commentary." *Diplomatic History* 3 (Winter 1979): 59–76.

McLellan, David S. "Who Fathered Containment?" *International Studies Quarterly* 17 (June 1973): 205–26.

Mark, Eduard M. "Allied Relations in Iran, 1941–1947: The Origins of a Cold War Crisis." *Wisconsin Magazine of History* 59 (Autumn 1975): 51–63.

May, Ernest R. "The 'Bureaucratic Politics' Approach: U.S.–Argentine Relations, 1942–47." In *Latin America and the United States: The Changing Political Realities*, edited by Julio Cotler and Richard R. Fagen. Stanford: Stanford University Press, 1974.

Messer, Robert L. "Paths Not Taken: The United States Department of State and Alternatives to Containment, 1945–1946." *Diplomatic History* 1 (Fall 1977): 297–319.

Miller, James E. "Taking Off the Gloves: The United States and the Italian Elections of 1948." *Diplomatic History* 7 (Winter 1983): 35–55.

Pach, Chester J., Jr. "The Containment of U.S. Military Aid to Latin America, 1944–49." *Diplomatic History* 6 (Summer 1982): 225–43.

————. "Military Assistance and American Foreign Policy: The Role of Congress." In *Congress and United States Foreign Policy: Controlling the Use of Force in the Nuclear Age*, edited by Michael Barnhart. Albany: State University of New York Press, 1987.

Paterson, Thomas G. "If Europe, Why Not China?: The Containment Doctrine, 1947–49." *Prologue* 13 (Spring 1981): 19–38.

Pfau, Richard. "Containment in Iran: The Shift to an Active Policy." *Diplomatic History* 1 (Fall 1977): 359–72.

Poole, Walter S. "From Conciliation to Containment: The Joint Chiefs of Staff and the Coming of the Cold War, 1945–1946." *Military Affairs* 42 (February 1978): 12–16.

Powers, Richard J. "Who Fathered Containment?" *International Studies Quarterly* 15 (December 1971): 526–43.

Rabe, Stephen G. "The Elusive Conference: United States Economic Relations with Latin America, 1945–1952." *Diplomatic History* 2 (Summer 1978): 279–94.

————. "Inter-American Military Cooperation, 1944–1951." *World Affairs* 137 (Fall 1974): 132–49.

Rabel, Roberto. "Prologue to Containment: The Truman Administration's Response to the Trieste Crisis of May 1945." *Diplomatic History* 10 (Spring 1986): 141–60.

Riste, Olav. "Was 1949 a Turning Point?: Norway and the Western Powers 1947 1950." In *Western Security: The Formative Years*, edited by Olav Riste. New York: Columbia University Press, 1985.

Rosenberg, David Alan. "The U.S. Navy and the Problem of Oil in a Future War: The Outline of a Strategic Dilemma, 1945–1950." *Naval War College Review* 29 (Summer 1976): 53–64.

Smith, E. Timothy. "The Fear of Subversion: The United States and the Inclusion of Italy in the North Atlantic Treaty." *Diplomatic History* 7 (Spring 1983): 139–55.

Stoler, Mark A. "From Continentalism to Globalism: General Stanley D. Embick, the Joint Strategic Survey Committee, and the Military View of National Planning during the Second World War." *Diplomatic History* 6 (Summer 1982): 303–21.

Stueck, William. "The Marshall and Wedemeyer Missions: A Quadrilateral Perspective." In *Sino-American Relations, 1945–1955*, edited by Harry Harding. Wilmington, Del.: Scholarly Resources, 1989.

Sunderland, Riley. "The Secret Embargo." *Pacific Historical Review* 29 (February 1960): 75–80.

Tillapaugh, J. "Closed Hemisphere and Open World?: The Dispute over

Regional Security at the U.N. Conference, 1945." *Diplomatic History* 2 (Winter 1978): 25–42.

Trask, Roger R. "The Impact of the Cold War on United States–Latin American Relations, 1945–1949." *Diplomatic History* 1 (Summer 1977): 271–84.

———. "Spruille Braden versus George Messersmith: World War II, the Cold War, and Argentine Policy, 1945–1947." *Journal of Inter-American Studies and World Affairs* 26 (February 1984): 69–95.

Watt, David. "Withdrawal from Greece." In *Age of Austerity,* edited by Michael Sissions and Philip French. London: Hodder and Stoughton, 1963.

Wiebes, Cees, and Bert Zeeman. "The Pentagon Negotiations, March 1948: The Launching of the North Atlantic Treaty." *International Affairs* 59 (Summer 1983): 351–63.

Wright, C. Ben. "Mr. 'X' and Containment." *Slavic Review* 35 (March 1976): 1–31.

Unpublished Studies

Bohlin, Thomas G. "United States–Latin American Relations, 1949–1953." Ph.D. dissertation, University of Notre Dame, 1985.

Converse, Elliott Vanveltner, III. "United States Plans for a Postwar Overseas Military Base System, 1942–1948." Ph.D. dissertation, Princeton University, 1984.

Henderson, Cary Smith. "Congressman John Taber of Auburn: Politics and Federal Appropriations, 1923–1962." Ph.D. dissertation, Duke University, 1964.

Hinson, Billy Glen. "Plans of the United States for Postwar Military Assistance to Latin America, 1945–1951." Ph.D. dissertation, University of Mississippi, 1977.

Iselin, John Jay. "The Truman Doctrine: A Study of the Relationship of Crisis and Foreign Policy-Making." Ph.D. dissertation, Harvard University, 1965.

O'Brien, Larry Dean. "National Security and the New Warfare: Defense Policy, War Planning, and Nuclear Weapons, 1945–1950." Ph.D. dissertation, Ohio State University, 1981.

Pach, Chester J., Jr. "Arming the Free World: The Origins of the United States Military Assistance Program, 1945–1949." Ph.D. dissertation, Northwestern University, 1981.

———. "Arming the Free World: The Origins of the United States Military Assistance Program, 1945–1950." Paper presented at the annual meeting of the Organization of American Historians, Minneapolis, April 1985.

———. "Launching the Military Assistance Program." Paper presented at the annual Missouri Valley History Conference, Omaha, March 1985.

———. "The Truman Administration and the Decision for a Global Military Assistance Program." Paper presented at the annual meeting of the Society for Historians of American Foreign Relations, Washington, D.C., August 1984.

Pearce, David Lee. "United States Military Aid and Recipient Defense Expenditures: A Quantitative Analysis." Ph.D. dissertation, Syracuse University, 1975.

Quirós, Marcia K. "United States Reactions to the Costa Rican Counter-Revolution." Seminar paper, University of Kansas, March 1988.

Spector, Stephen David. "United States Attempts at Regional Security and the Extension of the Good Neighbor Policy in Latin America, 1945–1952." Ph.D. dissertation, New York University, 1970.

Stamey, Roderick A., Jr. "The Origin of the United States Military Assistance Program." Ph.D. dissertation, University of North Carolina at Chapel Hill, 1972.

Tillapaugh, James C. "From War to Cold War: United States Policy Toward Latin America, 1943–1948." Ph.D. dissertation, Northwestern University, 1973.

Yeuell, Donovan Paul, Jr. "United States Military Aid as an Instrument of National Policy (1945–1955)." Master's thesis, Georgetown University, 1955.

Index

Acheson, Dean, 47, 103, 117, 121, 221; assesses military aid planning, 6; and Soviet intentions, 21; and surplus armaments sales, 25; and military aid to Latin America, 43–44, 51, 52–53; and U.S. policy toward Argentina, 58; urges coalition government in China, 79; assesses China's role in East Asia, 86; and Turkish straits crisis, 99–100, 257 (n. 42); and military aid to Greece, 104; and U.S. policy toward Turkey, 104–5; and planning of Greek-Turkish Aid Act, 109, 112–14; on U.S. interests in Greece, 112–13; on significance of China Aid Act, 184; supports Italian membership in NATO, 211; concern about European morale, 219; at Council of Foreign Ministers, 219–20; criticizes staff work on MAP legislation, 222; and *China White Paper*, 224; and inclusion of China in MAP, 224–25; on NATO defense plans, 229–30
Achilles, Theodore C., 146
Additional Military Production Fund, 216
Ala, Hussein, 94–95
Allen, George V., 94–95, 103–4
American Republic Affairs, Office of, U.S. State Department, 20, 37; and lend-lease to Peru, 35; and Good Neighbor Policy, 39; opposes Inter-American Military Cooperation Act, 47–53; changes in leadership of, 58–59; and inclusion of Latin America in MAP, 215
Anderson, Clinton P., 80
Appropriations Committee, U.S. House of Representatives, 184
Appropriations Committee, U.S. Senate, 177, 182
Argentina: neutrality during World War II, 53–54; Nazi influences in, 53–57; U.S. policy toward, 53–58; denied U.S.

military aid, 53–58, 239 (n. 9); and lifting of embargo on U.S. arms sales, 58
Army, Department of the, U.S., 139–42, 149, 157
Army Air Forces, U.S.: and mobilization, 15–16; and postwar military aid, 15–16; and military aid to Latin America, 36–38; and military aid to China, 70–71, 73
Arnold, Archibald V., 113
Arnold, Henry H.: urges surplus arms sales to foreign nations, 16; and military aid to Latin America, 36–37, 44; and military aid to China, 70
Arnold, W. H., 27
Aurand, Henry S.: demands reform of military aid policy, 156–57, 199; and aid to China, 188
Austria, 211–13
Azerbaijan. *See* Iran: separatist movement in

Badger, Oscar C., 185–86, 189, 191
Barkley, Alben W., 221
Barr, David G.: named commander of army advisory group in China, 176; favors U.S. operational advice to Nationalist army, 185; and aid to Fu Tso-yi, 190; criticizes Nationalist military leadership, 191–92; and delivery of U.S. aid to Nationalists, 193–94
Barrett, David D., 274 (n. 19)
Bell, John O., 231–32
Berlin blockade, 205–6
Bevin, Ernest K.: and Gentlemen's Agreement on arms transfers to Argentina, 46, 56–57; and aid to Greece, 101–2, 108; and aid to Turkey, 104–5; and Western European security, 144–45; fears Soviet expansion, 148
Black Sea straits, 98–100
Blue Book, 55